THE COMING MILLENNIAL KINGDOM

A Case for Premillennial Interpretation

Donald K. Campbell &
Jeffrey L. Townsend

kregel
PUBLICATIONS

The Coming Millennial Kingdom: A Case for Premillennial Interpretation

Copyright © 1997 by Donald K. Campbell and Jeffrey L. Townsend

Published by Kregel Publications, a division of Kregel, Inc., P.O. Box 2607, Grand Rapids, MI 49501. Kregel Publications provides trusted, biblical publications for Christian growth and service. Your comments and suggestions are valued.

For more information about Kregel Publications, visit our web site at http://www.kregel.com.

Cover design: Alan G. Hartman
Cover photo: Copyright © 1997 Kregel, Inc.

Library of Congress Cataloging-in-Publication Data
[Case for premillenialism]
     The coming millennial kingdom / Donald K. Campbell and Jeffrey L. Townsend [general editors].
        p.   cm.
     Originally published: A case for premillennialism.
Chicago: Moody Press, © 1992.
     Includes indexes.
     1. Millennialism. I. Campbell, Donald K.
II. Townsend, Jeffrey L.
BT891.C37   1997   236'.9—dc21   97-30808
                                                          CIP
ISBN 0-8254-2352-x

Printed in the United States of America

1 2 3 / 03 02 01 00 99 98 97

CONTENTS

FOREWORD

Premillennialism is not a fundamental doctrine of evangelical faith. For example, the Bible certainly does not set it forth in the same unequivocal terms or give it the same central position that the deity of Christ, the vicarious atonement, or the second coming have.

Yet to many evangelicals, premillennialism is not merely what the Bible teaches on some minor point. It has a special significance of its own among the "loci" of Christian faith. This view has increased immensely during the last century—especially on the North American scene and on the mission fields strongly influenced by North American missionaries.

THE SHIFT TOWARD PREMILLENNIALISM

Previous to the last century, premillennialism was widely known but was generally reckoned as characteristic of sectarian groups tending to deviate from traditional orthodoxy—the *schwaermerei*, to use a term of Luther's. Occasionally, scholars of outstanding note opted for premillennialism, but they were reckoned as aberrations. They failed to make any great impact on the world of biblical and evangelical scholarship.

The cause of this relatively sudden shift toward premillennialism has never been adequately explained. Several factors certainly influenced it, such as:

(1) the vastly increased depth of Bible study and the increased tools for Bible study, all of which have been growing since the invention of printing;

(2) the hermeneutical shift in churchly interpretation with its emphasis on the natural meaning of a passage in the context of the history and culture in which it was first given;

(3) the hermeneutical shift led, in turn, to a further shift in "orthodox" amillennial teaching on the part of the great systematizers of the seventeenth, eighteenth, and early nineteenth centuries, who sought to bring all biblical teaching into a coherent, noncontradictory whole. It became apparent that much of what the Old Testament prophets predicted for the "end times" could not legitimately be applied to heaven, e.g., he who dies at a hundred will be thought a mere youth (Isa. 65:20);

(4) the "this worldly" trend in evangelical and Christian thought made biblical students more vividly aware of the "earthiness" of the Old Testament prophecies, which nonetheless could not be fitted into the present course of the church from Calvary to second coming, e.g., such passages as, "No longer will a man teach his neighbor, or a man his brother, saying 'Know the Lord,' because they will all know me, from the least of them to the greatest, declares the Lord" (Jer. 31:34, NIV);

(5) American "optimism" led to a revival of postmillennialism on the part of some (modified by Charles Hodge, for example), but to a more realistic optimism in the case of premillennialism;

(6) modern studies of the early church seemed to show it was not really amillennial but premillennial. In fact, many evangelicals (amillennialists included) are quite willing to concede that the church of the first two and perhaps three centuries was predominantly committed to a premillennial view.

Whatever may be the explanation for this turn to premillennialism in the last century, its spread through the evangelical churches cannot be denied. Today, many of the largest and most flourishing evangelical seminaries are committed to premillennialism. Almost all of the Bible institutes and Bible colleges, including the seminaries that emerged from them, are premillenarian, and many older schools of theology not committed on this issue one way or the other have been significantly penetrated by premillennialism.

The Importance of Premillennialism

What then is the importance of premillennialism to its adherents? No doubt, answers to this question from premillenarian students would vary significantly. Two reasons stand out preeminently when evangelicals state why they consider premillennialism important. These reasons also explain why many evangelicals include it in their statement of faith and require it for ordination of ministers or for appointment of seminary professors.

The first, and by all odds the more important of the two, is the close tie premillenarians see between that doctrine and a valid hermeneutic. The Old Testament promise of the restoration of Israel to the land of Palestine and of a period of perfect peace and universal justice on earth just cannot be excised from the text or applied to the church between Calvary (or Pentecost) and the second coming. Neither can it be referred to heaven and the final estate. In his commentary on Revelation, Theodore Zahn with similar assurance expounds the twentieth chapter in premillennial terms. I have heard many premillennialists say: "If you adopt a hermeneutic that will exclude a millennium from the Bible, you can just as easily drop the bodily resurrection of Jesus Christ out of the Bible."

Similarly, I have heard many premillennialists say, "If you believe only the Old Testament, you could possibly be either a premillenarian or a postmillenarian, but you *could not* possibly be an amillenarian." And they often add, "If you believe the New Testament (except for the book of Revelation), you could possibly be an amillenarian or a premillenarian, but you cannot possibly be a postmillenarian. If you believe the whole Bible, you can only be a premillenarian." Allowing for many "happy inconsistencies" on the part of my brothers and sisters who are amillenarians or postmillenarians, I agree there is some truth in these overgeneralizations. The importance of premillennialism to most of its adherents stems from their desire to protect a valid hermeneutic.

The second reason given by premillenarians for holding this doctrine to be important lies in its close ties with a biblical philosophy of history. According to the Bible, God created the world perfect—perfect, that is, as rightly suited for man. And within it, He prepared a garden appropriate for unfallen humans. He gave our race instructions to organize and cultivate the whole earth, to build it into a garden. Of course, man failed. But God will be vindicated. It is not God's fault nor defects in the earth that are to blame. It is the fault of man who perverted it. Some day, by God's grace, He will vindicate His goodness and justice by displaying to all a gardenlike planet. The mess we human beings live in, and the groanings and misery so evident all around us, are the fault of man, not of God and His creation.

God will redeem the earth too, and one day He will display to all that, under the guidance of the Man from Heaven, the earth is truly good and altogether right for humans. Meanwhile, we are not to despise the earth or disparage it as merely an ephemeral moment in universal history, but treasure it to be protected and used for the good of all. Investments by us humans in planet Earth have an enduring value, for they will one day contribute to the vindication of God's wisdom, love, and universal justice. No premillenarian, therefore, can ever consistently use the resources of earth carelessly or ignore the signs of environmental destruction. The earth is good, and God has a plan for it in the future.

The Responses of Premillennialism

Premillennialism has come under severe attacks in the last decade. It has been labeled a new heresy—a twin with the doctrine of inerrancy. This is nonsense. Inerrancy has been the common doctrine of the orthodox church in all its major branches from the time of Christ and the apostles, as any fair reading of history abundantly proves. Yet it is true that premillennialism is tied to inerrancy, and it has no basis apart from a fully trustworthy Bible (which is what inerrancy means).

Others claim premillennialism poses a wooden view of the Bible and requires every word of it to be literal terminology. Such is not the case. All premillenarians recognize the element of figurative language used in many parts of Scripture, often side-by-side with literal language. What they desire is the exact meaning of the text, fairly interpreted by grammatical, historical, and culturally oriented exegesis. That is the only way to appropriate biblical authority and to refrain from reducing the Bible to a book of mere suggestions and optional opinions. The Bible, as the written word of God, must be understood in the plain, normal sense intended by the authors.

Still others charge premillennialists with disparagement of this world and its values, and with an exclusive commitment to "pie in the sky by and by." Just the opposite is the case. Premillenarians hold a high view of this world and insist this is what the Old Testament prophets teach and the New Testament confirms. Ultimately, of course, a Christian's hope is in God and in His redemption—not in the goodness and power of unredeemed and sinful humans. That this earth is good and has value which God Himself chooses to sustain is precisely the point of premillennialism.

The apparent lack of social consciousness among evangelicals during the first half of the twentieth century is commonly blamed on premillennialism. However, that alleged deficiency was due to quite a different cause. It flowed from the evolutionary optimism of a liberalism that held forth the promises of a man-made utopia on earth. Evangelicals were trying to hold up the short end of the log to compensate for the quite unbiblical pressure from liberalism on the other end. We learned our lesson. Christian teaching must not be warped by forming or even emphasizing doctrines in reaction to the opponents of orthodoxy. To preserve their integrity, evangelicals must form their doctrines on the basis of the teaching of all Scripture.

This book seeks to set forth in just such a comprehensive fashion the biblical basis for premillennialism and its significance for evangelical faith. I am proud to share in the work of the fine scholars who have prepared it.

KENNETH S. KANTZER
Distinguished Professor of Systematic Theology
Trinity Evangelical Divinity School

PREFACE

The editors of this volume were motivated by a felt need for a presentation of exegetical evidence for premillennialism, the view that there will be an earthly reign of Christ preceded by His second coming. This conviction was underscored by Kenneth Kantzer's call for careful exegesis and dialogue by all parties to the millennial debate. He wrote,

> Too often . . . Christians have allowed eschatology to divide them. Rather than attack each other's views, we believe it would be far better to engage in a solid exegesis of the relevant scriptural passages. Honest study of the Word as it relates to each millennial view will help us understand and appreciate our own convictions as well as the beliefs of those who disagree with us. ("Agreement Is Not Required," *Christianity Today*, February 6, 1987; 13-I.)

This project therefore was undertaken to present the best exegetical evidence for premillennialism in a positive way. Our purpose was not to attack amillennialism or postmillennialism so much as to state positively why we, the editors and authors of this volume, are premillennialists.

The editors first set out to make a determination of the key passages that support premillennialism. We then attempted to draw together a broad spectrum of premillennial scholars from a variety of schools and backgrounds. This volume reflects some diversity among the advocates of premillennialism, but, given some subordinate differences, the authors unanimously concur that the biblical evidence clearly supports the premillennial interpretation of the Bible.

All of the authors of this book agree that Jesus Christ will reign on this earth for a thousand years following His second coming and prior to the new heavens and new earth. Each writer has attempted to show from the exegesis of pertinent texts that this is the teaching of the Word of God.

Our deep gratitude is expressed to those who so ably assisted in the editing of this material—Dorian Coover Cox, David Fouts, Duane Lindsey, Ela Macdowell of Dallas Seminary, and Bob Ramey of Moody Press.

May these chapters clarify for many the teaching of Scripture regarding the return and reign of our Lord Jesus Christ.

DONALD K. CAMPBELL
and
JEFFREY L. TOWNSEND

1

PREMILLENNIALISM INTRODUCED: HERMENEUTICS

ELLIOTT E. JOHNSON

Professor of Bible Exposition
Dallas Theological Seminary

A widespread consensus suggests that there are two controlling hermeneutical principles at issue in the interpretation of the millennial kingdom.[1] One is the literal interpretation of the Bible; the other is the analogy of faith. In view of this consensus, our discussion will focus on these principles using the same three questions for each principle: What does this principle mean? Is this principle valid? How does this principle function in the interpretation of a millennial kingdom?

DEFINITIONS OF THE HERMENEUTICAL PRINCIPLES

THE PRINCIPLE OF LITERAL INTERPRETATION

Gaining general agreement on the definition of *literal interpretation* has been difficult. Walvoord views literal interpretation as a consistent, general approach to the interpretation of any portion of Scripture. "Premillenarians ... insist that one general rule of interpretation should be applied to all areas of theology and that prophecy does not require

---

1. Hermeneutics, as the science of interpretation, discusses the principles that give normative direction to the task of determining the meaning intended by the author.

spiritualization any more than other aspects of truth. . . . History is history, not allegory. Facts are facts. Prophesied future events are just what they are prophesied."[2] What Walvoord calls for is a normative approach to the interpretation of the Bible within the perspective of a general hermeneutic. This is to be contrasted to a special hermeneutic like spiritualization or allegorization, which may be appropriate for particular portions of the text.

A narrower conception of the definition focuses on a literal or normal sense. The principle of a literal sense is then clarified to be "literal wherever possible" or "literal unless absurd." In either case, a literal or normal sense of words or clauses is preferred unless that sense does not make sense. Boettner finds this attempt to define a normative approach self-contradictory.

> One does not have to read far in the Bible to discover that not everything can be taken literally. We find no labels in the Scripture itself telling us, "Take this literally," or "Take that figuratively." Evidently the individual reader must use his own judgment, backed by as much experience and common sense as he can muster. And that, of course, will vary endlessly from individual to individual.[3]

Thus, in evaluating this view, a normative principle becomes relative since it relies on the interpreter's common sense to decide what is to be taken in a normal sense and what is not.

To prove his point, Boettner seeks to disprove the normative appropriateness of "literal" as a sense advanced by many premillennialists, that is, that every prophecy pointing to the first advent of Christ was literally fulfilled in the literal sense of the terms of the prophecies. He claims that the principle is disproven by the very first messianic prophecy in Scripture, Genesis 3:15. He argues, "Now that prophecy certainly was not fulfilled literally by a man crushing the head of a snake or by a snake biting the heel of a man."[4] All who take this statement of judgment on the serpent as a prophecy of Messiah concede that the serpent is more than an animal and the conflict is more than what the text describes as a conflict between an animal and a person. Thus Boettner, I believe, has established his point: the principle of literal sense is not a normative principle of interpretation because judgments of common

---

2. John F. Walvoord, *The Millennial Kingdom* (Grand Rapids: Zondervan, 1973), pp. 129-30.

3. Loraine Boettner, "Postmillennialism," *The Meaning of the Millennium: Four Views*, ed. Robert G. Clouse (Downers Grove, Ill.: InterVarsity, 1977), p. 134.

4. Ibid., p. 135.

sense must be introduced to override a normative sense in numerous and unspecified instances.

Recognition of this forces us to redefine "literal." What we have discovered is that a normative principle must be a general principle, but a general principle cannot legislate a particular sense or senses. Rather a general principle can only specify general limits to a textual sense. Thus our definition of literal would be appropriately designated as a *system of limits*. This system specifies the general maxim, as Walvoord argued, that any sort of text is consistently interpreted in its own context. As an example, "serpent" as a word normally means "animal" and only an animal. But this normal usage and sense does not legislate that "serpent" in Genesis 3:15 must mean *merely* an animal.

On the other hand, a literal system begins with recognizing "serpent" as an animal. Then it looks to the immediate or extended contexts for other clues to the meaning. This serpent speaks (3:1-5), and speaks as the enemy of God. Thus in the literal system, this serpent is more than an animal; it is God's enemy. Thus if the text is historical it is interpreted in its historical context, or if it is prophetic it is interpreted in its prophetic context. Furthermore, a text should be interpreted not only in the immediate context of the *passage* but also in the extended context of the *whole book* in which it appears.

The value of this literal system is that it specifies a normative *role* for the textual contexts in interpretation and a normative *practice* of interpretation. It thereby excludes ideas extrinsic to the text from either the world of the modern interpreter or even from the world of the original interpreters. It does not exclude prior canonical revelation which is a component of a broader context of the progress of revelation in the biblical canon. This normative approach places biblical interpretation in the realm of general hermeneutics. As such the Bible is interpreted as a book, albeit a divine book.

THE PRINCIPLE OF THE ANALOGY OF FAITH

The fact that the Bible is a divine book, authored by God and composed by man, does introduce special applications of the normative principles of general hermeneutics. Narrative portions are understood to refer to historical realities as the human author is inspired to compose a divinely revealed interpretation of history. Prophetic portions are understood to speak of future events as the human prophet speaks empowered by divine revelation. It is in the realm of these special applications that the second principle arises.

Some have argued that the principle of *the analogy of faith* is clearly defined since it is derived from Romans 12:6. "And since we have gifts that differ according to the grace given to us, let each exercise them accordingly: if prophecy, according to the proportion of his faith" (*kata tēn analogian tēs pisteōs*). Charles Hodge states that the original and proper meaning of the word "'prophet' is interpreter—one who declares the will of God, who explains His mind to others."[5] However, there are strong reasons to question such an interpretation of "prophet."[6] This raises reasonable doubt about the legitimate application of the passage to textual interpretation.

In addition, opinion is divided about the sense of "faith." Pink follows Hodge's interpretation of "proportion" as "measure, rule, standard" and then understands "faith" in an objective sense of the revealed standard.[7] Fairbairn also takes it in an objective sense and says, *"Analogy* in such a connection can only be understood as denoting the common agreement, the standard *kanōn*, or rule, which results from a comparison of one part of Scripture with another."[8] Thus the revealed standard is either an agreed on doctrinal standard or a part of Scripture that interprets another Scripture.

By contrast, Berkhof says, "Correctly interpreted, however, the whole expression simply means, *according to the measure of your subjective faith.*"[9] Hence the term (analogy of faith), as derived from this passage, can only be based on an unusual understanding of Paul's sense. In view of Berkhof's understanding of Romans 12:6, there is no scripturally authorized principle of interpretation to be found in the passage. And Berkhof's position is certainly supported by the context of Romans 12:6. The passage refers to the use of spiritual gifts and not the interpretation of Scripture. The exercise of the prophetic gift according to the prophet's measure of faith does not specify how believers are to use their Bibles.

However, a legitimate basis for the principle of the analogy of faith is the belief in the *unity of meaning* found expressed in the biblical canon. This belief is based on the basic affirmation that God is the author of Scripture. God is not the author of confusion; His Word cannot contradict itself. Therefore we are assured that for all its human authors and for all the centuries involved in its writing, the Bible has only one uni-

---

5. Charles Hodge, quoted by Arthur W. Pink, *Interpretation of the Scriptures* (Grand Rapids: Baker, 1972), p. 31.
6. Harold W. Hoehner, "The Purpose of Tongues in 1 Corinthians 14:20-25," *Walvoord: A Tribute*, ed. Donald K. Campbell (Chicago: Moody, 1982), pp. 56-57.
7. Pink, *Interpretation*, p. 31.
8. Patrick Fairbairn, *Hermeneutical Manual* (Edinburgh: Clark, 1858), p. 103.
9. Louis Berkhof, *Principles of Biblical Interpretation* (Grand Rapids: Baker, 1950), p. 164.

fied body of meaning. Thus analogies of theological correspondence may well exist between different passages within the biblical canon; one passage may contribute to the interpretation of other passages. These analogies need to be specified more clearly because, even though the correspondence is compatible and harmonious, one passage does not necessarily contribute to the interpretation of another passage. Analogies formed by three kinds of correspondence contribute to interpretation.

Analogy between messages

The correspondence is between two passages that involve essentially the same message expressed in both passages. The interpretation begins in recognizing the topics about which each passage speaks. These topics concern the same content, as in the three accounts of the parable of sowing seed (Matt. 13; Mark 4; Luke 8). In addition, what each passage says about the subject must be related so that the passages are understood to make parallel assertions about the common subject or doctrine. This is what Berkhof calls a positive analogy.[10] As an interpretive tool, it is particularly helpful where the message is more clearly or completely stated in one passage than in another passage. This analogy appears commonly in passages dealing with the same content such as Jeremiah 31:30-34 and Ezekiel 36:24-32, or in parallel passages in the synoptic accounts of Jesus' ministry.

Analogy with an antecedent subject

This correspondence arises in the canonical development of what is said about a subject as two passages appear within the progress of revelation. The content of the antecedent affirmation commonly is incorporated into the subsequent affirmation about the same subject. This happens with the term "kingdom of God" in the NT, as it does with many other subjects introduced in the OT. Subsequent references contribute to the developing revelation in the historical progress of the statement of the doctrine of the kingdom. Other examples occur in the use of "redemption" in Exodus 6:6 and Ephesians 1:7, or "the abomination of desolation" in Daniel 9:27 and Matthew 24:15.

Analogy with a subsequent interpretation

This form of analogy relates exclusively to scriptural interpretations of prior prophecies. This analogy involves a subsequent passage (NT) providing a context for the interpretation of an antecedent passage (OT). This is valid only if the analogy involves an interpretation in the NT

10. Ibid., p. 164.

(or in the OT) of earlier prophesied meanings found in the OT. As an example, if Matthew 1:23 is an interpretation of Isaiah 7:14, then Isaiah must refer to a virgin conception and birth.

The quotations of or allusions to the OT in the NT do not all serve the same purpose. Berkhof distinguishes three different types of quotations involving interpretation: "(1) Some serve the purpose of showing that Old Testament predictions, whether direct or indirect, were fulfilled in the New Testament.... (2) Others are quoted for the establishment of a doctrine.... (3) Still others are cited to refute and rebuke the enemy."[11] In distinction to these cases that are interpretations of meanings, Berkhof lists those cited for rhetorical purposes or for the purpose of illustrating some truth.[12] An interpretive analogy exists only when the NT interprets the OT and thus includes in its interpretation meanings either explicitly or implicitly expressed in the OT.

Thus the principle of analogy of faith is a special application of a general hermeneutic derived from and based on a unity of meanings expressed in the collection of books in the canon. The principle of general hermeneutics is that a passage is interpreted in the immediate context. Since God is the ultimate Author of all canonical passages, then the interpretations in the immediate context of these passages are capable of forming valid analogies between related passages. These analagous contexts thus form a special application of the general principle of interpreting a passage in the immediate context. The compatibility of near and distant contexts is based on God speaking with one voice in both contexts. The principle of analogy of faith is certainly acceptable and comprehensive when used with respect for relevant interpretational contexts.

DEFENSE OF THE HERMENEUTICAL PRINCIPLES

While both of these principles (the literal system and the analogy of faith) can be acknowledged as legitimate when defined in general, their validity has been questioned when used in the interpretation of the millennial kingdom. These questions must be addressed.

THE VALIDITY OF LITERAL INTERPRETATION

Premillennial hermeneutics has rested on a literal system of interpretation whether applied to the OT or to Romans 11 or Revelation 20:4-6. Yet it has also been soundly criticized by both friend and foe. These criticisms need to be faced and evaluated in constructing a premillennial hermeneutic.

11. Ibid., pp. 162-63 (original in italics).
12. Ibid., p. 163.

George Eldon Ladd, a self-proclaimed premillennialist, has been most critical of a literal system of interpreting a text in context. His criticism is simple: "The fact is that the New Testament frequently interprets Old Testament prophecies in a way not suggested by the Old Testament context. . . . This is a principle which runs throughout biblical prophecy. The Old Testament is reinterpreted in light of the Christ event."[13] Ladd's criticism, if valid, challenges the literal system at the core.

An exhaustive response to Ladd's claim about the NT interpretation of OT prophecies would involve consideration of each proposed case. In an article of this scope that is impossible. However, if a large number of cases existed, as Ladd claims, it would entail a view of prophetic revelation that would be unsatisfactory. Therefore, this response will seek to prove that a literal system is necessary because of the nature of Scripture and the need of the interpreter.

The nature of Scripture

The literal system is necessary because of the nature of Scripture. Two maxims concerning the nature of Scripture will be discussed. First, Scripture is *sufficiently clear* in context to express what God promised to do. Second, Scripture is *sufficiently complete* in context to establish valid expectations of the future acts of God. If Ladd's criticism were correct that the NT frequently interprets in a way not suggested by context, then the nature of Scripture would be undermined. In addition, if Christ's life, death, and resurrection introduced unexpected facts so that the apparent OT meanings must be reinterpreted, then the nature of OT prophecy would be either unclear or incomplete. Both of these contentions must be challenged.

First, then, the literal system is necessarily valid because prophetic revelation is clear enough in context to express what God promised to do. In considering the clarity of prophetic revelation, consider the nature of written communication.

Prophecy must not be viewed as a picture portrayal of the future any more than narrative literature presents a photograph of what happened in history. That is not the nature of verbal communication, as Wittgenstein realized.[14] Biblical revelation, whether prophecy or history, is verbal communication that is capable of expressing the truth clearly, albeit in broad outline or in a selected description with well-chosen specifics.

13. George Eldon Ladd, "Historic Premillennialism," *The Meaning of the Millennium: Four Views*, pp. 20-21.

The nature of *sufficient clarity* in biblical prophecy may be considered in the earliest statement of Christ's first advent, Genesis 3:15. Certain aspects of the meaning may be clarified from the text in context. An animal speaks to Eve and Adam, but what the animal says are the very words of God's enemy. It follows that an animal is not the only power involved, but the words introduce the presence and power of the enemy of God and man. Later in the canon he is revealed to be Satan. The words of judgment that God speaks to the serpent (3:14) and to His enemy (3:15) specify future enmity and the outcome of that enmity. It is cryptic but adequate to introduce the anticipated conflict.

There are three stages of enmity. The initial stage features the conflict between Eve and the serpent. The second stage, between the seed of the serpent and the seed of the woman, lasts for an unknown period of time. Seed, being a collective term, admits to ambiguity both in number of offspring in any generation, and in the number of generations of offspring with which the conflict will continue. It will continue until the final stage is reached when the serpent again enters the conflict but this time against a seed of the woman who is victorious. Even though the conflict is described in terms of an animal and humans, yet as the enemy is seen as greater than the animal, so the terms of the battle will be greater than man against animal. The text in context provides an outline that is correct and clear in pattern but not complete in all details. Numerous questions are left unanswered. When Christ died on the cross and rose from the dead, the details of the climax were filled in and specified, but the text does not demand to be reinterpreted. Nor does it demand interpretation in a way not suggested in context.

This example illustrates that an OT prophecy is sufficiently clear to express an accurate account of what will happen, though it may not be sufficient to detail how it will happen. When the event takes place, there is a correspondence with what was said. If the correspondence is distinctive of this one event alone, then the prophecy can be interpreted as finally fulfilled. In the case of Genesis 3:15, the resurrection of Christ deals a death blow to Satan's head, after Satan strikes the heel of Christ on the cross. This is sufficient to identify the fulfillment. But Genesis 3:15 provides no hint of the delay in the time of execution of the death blow to Satan.

The prophecy of Genesis 3:15 introduces the first and a potentially ambiguous prophecy of Christ. Yet it is clear enough in context to provide Eve with expectations alluded to in the text (4:1-2, 25-26). Like-

14. Ludwig Wittgenstein, *Philosophical Investigations*, trans. G. E. M. Anscombe (New York: Macmillan, 1958).

wise it is clear enough to be interpreted through the centuries in the church as the "protevangelium." Genesis 3:15 thus illustrates the clarity of prophecy that necessitates a literal system of interpreting a text in its own context.

The first maxim concerned the clarity of Scripture. Since Scripture is clear enough in context to express what God promises to do, it must be read in context to be understood.

The second maxim concerning the nature of Scripture entails statements in context that are *sufficiently complete* to establish valid expectations of the future acts of God. When Ladd raised the objection that the meaning is "not suggested by the Old Testament context," we must question, suggested *to whom*? Clearly it is not suggested to Ladd, but that does not necessarily mean it is not suggested to NT authors. There were numerous first-century saints who were not surprised by the coming of Messiah but were awaiting His coming—Simeon, Anna, Zechariah and Elizabeth, Mary and Joseph, the shepherds, Andrew and Peter, James and John, as well as many unnamed individuals in the believing remnant of the first century. Their expectations naturally would have arisen from the OT texts.

The failure of the OT context to suggest a messianic message to Ladd is related to his expectations drawn from an OT setting. He writes, "The simple fact is, in its Old Testament setting, Isaiah 53 is not a prophecy of the Messiah. Messiah means 'anointed' and designates the victorious, anointed Davidic King."[15] Such a conclusion about the interpretation of Isaiah 53 in context (OT setting) is misleading. There is no one who understands Isaiah 53 in a messianic sense who would limit the OT messianic expectation to a purely political and triumphant king.

Rather, the text of Isaiah 53 is clear and sufficient to specify a servant of Yahweh who would fully achieve God's will through His substitutionary sacrifice. Yet it is not a complete statement of the full messianic doctrine. The question is whether it is sufficient. Philip the evangelist saw it as sufficient. When asked of whom the prophet Isaiah spoke, Philip preached Jesus to be Messiah, the servant (Acts 8:26-40).

The sufficiency of this text to contribute to the context of messianic doctrine depends on a comprehensive construction of the OT context. Such a construction must investigate the role of servant in Israel's historical revelation. Although the term "servant" does not appear in Exodus 19:5-6, the passage introduces the concept of service, for the people who are called to be "a kingdom of priests" have the responsibility to "obey My voice and keep My covenant." A similar sense is delineated

15. Ladd, "Historic Premillennialism," p. 21.

for the king (Deut. 17:14-20) who would "learn to fear" Yahweh and be careful to observe "all the words of this law . . . that his heart may not be lifted above his countrymen." In the Davidic Covenant, God promises to "be a Father to him and he will be a son to Me" (2 Sam. 7:14). Implicit in that relationship is a son realizing his father's will and desires. In Solomon's prayer of dedication for the Temple, he acknowledges the nation as "servants who walk before Thee with all their heart" and further identifies "Thy servant, my father David" (1 Kings 8:23-24).

This antecedent revelation forms a historical and canonical context for Isaiah's ministry to the "house of David" in which Isaiah treats both Ahaz (chaps. 7-11) and Hezekiah (chaps. 36-39) as responsible kings in the house of David to serve Yahweh. Yet in Ahaz's rejection (7:12) and in Hezekiah's pride (39:2), a context is set in the book to introduce an elect one, a king who will serve Yahweh's interests and establish justice (42:1-4). This servant theme introduced by Isaiah's earlier ministry naturally reaches its climax in 52:13–53:12. It is in this sense of a servant-king that Isaiah 53 contributes to messianic doctrine, and that refutes Ladd's reference to a purely political king. Thus Ladd's rejection of a literal system not only implies unacceptable logical consequences about the nature of Scripture, but the rejection is also shown to be inconsistent with particular data in the prophetic revelation.

The need of an interpreter

The second basic argument for the literal system is that it is necessary because of the basic need of an interpreter for normative direction. This need is demonstrated in the inconsistency and arbitrary practice of Ladd. Ironically, Ladd adopted a literal interpretation of Revelation 20:4-6. He identified his reason: "The passage makes perfectly good sense when interpreted literally."[16] The irony turns on two aspects of his practice. First, after arguing against interpretation of an OT prophecy in its context, he then turns to interpret an apocalyptic prophecy in the context of apocalyptic visions. Apocalyptic genre is acknowledged to be the most difficult context with which to work, yet Ladd unequivocally claims it makes "good sense." This is the second aspect of the irony. While Boettner and Hoekema agree with Ladd on a wide variety of hermeneutical issues, they disagree with what makes "good sense" here. Boettner emphatically contends, "I do differ quite radically with his view of the millennium derived from Revelation 20:1-6."[17] Hoekema adds, "Our basic disagreement concerns the interpretation of Revelation 20:1-6."[18]

---

16. Ibid., p. 37.

Then as if to accentuate Ladd's own inconsistency, Boettner sagely wonders about Ladd's view of the presence of the kingdom. Quoting Ladd, Boettner writes, "This means that Christ 'is now the Lord; he is now reigning at the right hand of God. However his present reign is seen only by the eye of faith.' I think that is correct. In fact those words might well have been written by an amillennialist or a postmillennialist."[19] The inconsistency is clear. If Christ's present reign completes the full conquest of God over evil through man, then what biblical reason remains for a yet future reign? With the surrender of the normative practice of interpreting a text in context, then our choice to interpret one text (Rev. 20:1-6) in context (the book of Revelation) has no greater weight than a personal preference. To avoid such arbitrary practice, the interpreter needs a normative principle (interpreting every text in context) as an expression of a general hermeneutic.

The validity of a literal system of hermeneutics rests on the nature of prophetic revelation and on the need of the interpreter for normative direction. A prophetic text is clear enough in context to promise what God would do and in the same context sufficiently complete to establish valid expectations of what God would do. Therefore an initial understanding of a text must be derived from its own context.

THE VALIDITY OF THE ANALOGY OF FAITH

Ladd's argument for "the analogy of faith" in prophecy rests on the perceived inadequacy of literal interpretation. He concludes, "This clearly establishes the principle that the 'literal hermeneutic' does not work. . . . Old Testament prophecies must be interpreted in the light of the New Testament to find their deeper meaning."[20] Ladd's argument is simple: the analogy of faith is necessary because the NT clarifies the deeper meaning of an OT text. This necessity for NT revelation rests on the inadequacy of OT prophecy. In his definition of analogy of faith, Ladd is not concerned about an analogy with antecedent subjects but rather about an analogy between an OT text and a NT interpretation or allusion to the same text.

This application of the analogy of faith is often called "spiritualization" of an OT text's meaning. The analogy is constructed between a NT reference to the spiritual meanings of a subject and an OT reference

---

17. Loraine Boettner, "A Postmillennial Response" [to 'Historic Premillennialism,' by Ladd], *The Meaning of the Millennium: Four Views*, p. 47.
18. Anthony Hoekema, "An Amillennial Response" [to 'Historic Premillennialism,' by Ladd], *The Meaning of the Millennium: Four Views*, p. 55.
19. Boettner, "A Postmillennial Response," p. 48.
20. Ladd, "Historic Premillennialism," p. 23.

to the subject in seemingly natural terms. It is this spiritual meaning that is the deeper meaning. So Ladd speaks approvingly of such a practice by Warfield: "If he 'spiritualized' the millennium, it was because he felt a total biblical hermeneutic required him to do so."[21]

This basic view of interpreting OT prophecy on the analogy of NT revelation (total biblical hermeneutic) about the kingdom of God has broad support. Boettner, a postmillennialist, writes, "I am favorably impressed with Ladd's discussion of the manner in which Old Testament prophecy is interpreted and applied by the New Testament."[22] Hoekema, an amillennialist, writes, "I agree with him [Ladd] that the Old Testament must be interpreted in the light of the New Testament."[23]

The use of an analogy to uncover deeper meanings later expressed in the NT has been further specified by Bruce Waltke, who writes:

> With the transformation of Christ's body from an earthly physical body to a heavenly spiritual body, and with his ascension from the earthly realism to the heavenly Jerusalem with its heavenly throne and the outpouring of his Holy Spirit, the earthly material symbols were done away and the spiritual reality portrayed by the symbols superseded the shadows. Consequently, [OT] prophecies about Israel's future kingdom that pertain to the church age, which began with Pentecost, find a spiritual fulfillment.[24]

In this model, the literal merely understands the symbol or the shadow, while the analogy of faith adds the meaning to complete the spiritual reality of the symbol.

Many premillennial interpreters criticize these attempts to defend the principle of analogy of faith at the expense of the literal principle. Herman A. Hoyt objects, contending that what is appropriate is to interpret "the New Testament in the light of the Old,"[25] which is a variant application of the analogy of faith that I described as an analogy with an antecedent subject. Walter Kaiser also coins a specific term, "Analogy of Antecedent Scripture where chronologically antecedent canonical theology must be checked to see whether it informed the theology under investigation."[26] Hoyt would further criticize Ladd who "comes to the

21. Ibid., p. 20.
22. Boettner, "A Postmillennial Response," p. 47.
23. Hoekema, "An Amillennial Response," p. 55.
24. Bruce K. Waltke, "Kingdom Promises as Spiritual," *Continuity and Discontinuity*, ed. John S. Feinberg and Paul D. Feinberg (Westchester, Ill.: Crossway, 1988), p. 282.
25. Herman A. Hoyt, "A Dispensational Premillennial Response" [to 'Historic Premillennialism,' by Ladd], *The Meaning of the Millennium: Four Views*, p. 43.

New Testament with a system of interpretation which is not derived from the Old Testament and superimposes this upon the New Testament."[27]

The heart of the criticism focuses on Ladd's contention that the NT is needed "to find the deeper meaning." This view both implies the inadequacy of the OT prophecy in which the deeper meaning is not yet expressed and implies the singular sufficiency of the NT to replace the earthly symbols with the recently revealed spiritual realities in the heavenlies. This view of the use of the analogy of faith must therefore be rejected because it discredits the nature of OT prophecy and because it isolates the NT revelation as sufficient in itself. Neither position is compatible with the historic view of the biblical canon as Scripture.

Our argument that the literal system is necessary rests on the clarity of the OT to express what God promised to do. Such promises entail "spiritual" meanings of what God would do, but not all such actions are expressed in terms of symbols unless the OT context so specifies, as it does with the Tabernacle or as it necessarily implies with the sacrifices.

The analogy of faith in which NT interpretation is used is valid because it may well provide a deeper *understanding* of the OT meaning. A NT writer alluding to a prophetic passage provides a valid context of the working of God in history to accomplish what He had promised. Or a NT interpretation of a prophetic reference provides valid understanding of meanings already expressed in the OT texts. The issue is not whether I or any imagined audience *understood* that meaning of the text in the immediate context of the OT alone, but the issue is whether that meaning, understood in the NT, is part of the meaning that was originally expressed in the prophetic OT context. If it was, then the analogy of faith helps to understand the original text in its immediate prophetic context. So the literal system and this use of the analogy of faith are compatible hermeneutical principles. As they are legitimate principles by definition, so they are valid principles when used in a compatible rather than a competitive fashion.

The compatible relation between the two principles allows each to make a valid and necessary contribution. The literal system interprets the clear promise of *what* God would do as expressed in the text. It is sufficient to gain a valid set of expectations of *what* God would do but not a complete explanation of *how* God would accomplish it or *how* various promised actions of God are to be related in history. The analogy

---

26. Walter C. Kaiser, Jr., *Toward an Old Testament Theology* (Grand Rapids: Baker, 1979), p. 16.
27. Hoyt, "A Dispensational Premillennial Response," p. 43.

of faith contributes to how God does accomplish what He promised. The NT records of what God does in history allude to the OT promises of these events, and NT interpretations of these events and of OT texts help us understand how God fulfilled what He promised. In this way the two principles act in a compatible fashion.

It is such a compatible approach that I would like to propose in the following sketch of the biblical revelation of the kingdom.

DEMONSTRATION OF THE HERMENEUTICAL PRINCIPLES

Since this essay will permit only a sketch of a premillennial interpretation, it will focus on a selective and compatible use of the two hermeneutical principles discussed previously. The other articles of this volume will focus on the necessary exegesis to demonstrate validation of premillennial interpretation in individual passages.

This sketch will examine the biblical concept of "kingdom" in Genesis 1-14, demonstrating the *literal system* in the interpretation of the OT. Then the *analogy of faith* will be demonstrated in the interpretation of "kingdom" in the gospels and Acts. Finally, harmonizing these two parts will demonstrate the compatibility of the two hermeneutical principles.

THE PROVIDENTIAL KINGDOM OF GOD

While the term "kingdom of God" does not appear in the creation account, the concept is certainly introduced. The creation account introduces God as the sovereign and unchallenged Creator of the world, time, and man. This ultimate position of God as Creator and ruler of human history is never questioned in the Bible's account of creation or of history. This position of God is variously designated as His *universal* kingdom or His *providential* rule in history. Although this ultimate position of God is properly described as the "kingdom of God," this is not the millennial sense of the "kingdom of God."

THE MEDIATORIAL KINGDOM OF GOD

The millennial sense of the kingdom refers to the rule of God delegated to man, whom He created in His own image (Gen. 1:27). Here the rule of God over the realm of the earth and its creatures is *mediated* rather than direct. It is this "mediated rule" that is thwarted in man's rebellion against God and His will (Gen. 3:1-6). Through the Fall man forfeited his divinely delegated rule to the serpent and his strategy of rebellion. Thereafter man has been ruled by the creature (the serpent, Gen. 3:5).[28]

---

28. Derek Kidner, *Genesis* (Downers Grove, Ill.: InterVarsity, 1967), p. 70.

Man's mediatorial position is restored in anticipation by God's declaration of judgment against the serpent (3:15). His restored position does not become a fact in history until the prophetic word is fulfilled as the seed of the woman deals a death blow to the serpent. In this confidence, however, we can ask what will be involved in man's mediation of God's rule on earth.

Man's mediation of God's rule

(1) Three aspects of mediation introduced. Genesis 1-14 reveals *three* distinct aspects of mediation to which there is repeated reference in the remainder of the canon. The first, as already developed, occurs in the judgment of the evil serpent (Gen. 3:15); the second is introduced in the Abraham account (Gen 12:1-3, 7); and the final aspect of mediation appears in the Melchizedek account (Gen. 14:17-20).

Man's position of rule on earth is reestablished as the seed of the woman executes *God's judgment* on the evil one, the serpent. Thereby God restores the second Adam as the ultimate ruler in God's stead on earth. In this position as anticipated in God's word of judgment, God further reveals His purpose to mediate His will in history.

In the Abraham account, God purposed to bless Abraham and his seed. Such blessing appears in history after God had called him from his natural resources in family and nation to be separated unto God and what He promised to provide (Gen. 12:1-3). God's ultimate purpose in blessing Abraham and his seed, however, was to mediate *blessing to all nations* (12:3). Unstated in this context, but dependent on the antecedent revelation of the reestablishing of God's rule mediated through man over evil (Gen. 3:15), is the question of God's rule over the nations. Since the blessing would be God's blessing, it must be inferred that God's rule over the nations through Abraham's seed would be established with righteousness and would be exercised as a necessary context for God to bless with integrity.

In the Melchizedek account, an additional and distinct aspect of mediation is introduced. Even while Abraham served as the mediator of God's offered deliverance to Lot and the inhabitants of Sodom and Gomorrah, he himself needed *a priestly mediator* before God. Melchizedek directly blesses Abraham in the name of the Most High God. Furthermore, he blesses God Himself. Such activity implies that Melchizedek holds a position that neither the king of Sodom (a worldly nation) nor Abraham (mediator to the nations) share. Though Abraham offered sacrifices and God spoke directly to him, he was not a priest. In fact, he needed a priest and he worshipped God through Melchizedek.

(2) Three aspects of mediation developed. These three aspects of mediation are. alluded to in the outworking of the history of the seed of the woman. The *mediation of conflict* by the chosen seed of the woman begins with Cain, who becomes the seed of the serpent (Gen. 4:7-8), and with Abel, who is succeeded by Seth (Gen. 4:25-26). The lineage of the chosen seed of the woman in each generation is recorded in the genealogies of Genesis 5 and 11. The narrative of the conflict through Noah is developed as he challenges the evil of his generation and enjoys God's deliverance throughout the flood-judgment of that generation. The narrative of each patriarch includes conflict with evil arising both outside his family and inside as well.

A new focus on the age-long conflict emerges with Moses. In the people's acceptance of the Mosaic law (Ex. 19:8; 24:3), Yahweh claims the people's obedient response. Now the nation as a whole is set in direct conflict with the influence and power of evil. Ironically, the nation called to overcome evil in its covenant relationship would itself be overcome by idolatry and legalism.

Incorporated into the mediation of conquest is Yahweh's choice to mediate blessing through Abraham and his descendents. The law offered the nation the opportunity to *mediate blessing* (Ex. 19:5-6) to the nations. In Israel's history, this role was most effectively accomplished under King David. But even David, and Israel with him, was blighted by evil.

This constant recurrence of evil emphasizes the need for *priestly mediation* which first appeared in Melchizedek (Gen. 14:18-20). This aspect of mediation was dramatized in the ladder linking Yahweh with Jacob (Gen. 28:12-22). Job cried out for such a mediator (Job 9:33). In each case, blessing was mediated from God to those who themselves could offer sacrifices but who needed a link directly with God. Interestingly, King David prophetically recognized such a heavenly mediator seated at Yahweh's right hand (Ps. 110:1) and mediating spiritual blessings as a priest in the order of Melchizedek (Ps. 110:4). David's fall before the power of evil (2 Sam. 12:13-14) only made the need of effectual spiritual mediation more imperative.

Christ's mediation of God's rule

These three aspects of man's mediation of God's rule are further developed in Christ. Yet the interpretations of Christ's mediation have resulted in basic differences in understanding God's present and future rule. These differences result from variant uses of the two hermeneutical principles.

An amillennial reading of Christ's ministry concludes that Christ reached a spiritual fulfillment of OT promises. Based on an analogy of faith, such a reading then warrants a reinterpretation of the OT promises to match the fulfillment.

A postmillennial reading of the same ministry concludes that Christ both reached a spiritual fulfillment and introduced a kingdom that would find fulfillment in the history of the church. This use of the analogy of faith warrants an altering of meaning expressed both in OT and NT texts to match more closely OT promises and NT statements of the kingdom.

On the other hand, a premillennial reading of Christ's ministry attempts to understand the harmony between understanding texts in their immediate context and texts in the context of the whole canon. Neither understanding of texts need be altered. There is a harmony in the use of the literal principle and the analogy of faith that results in a premillennial hope.

The initial issue in the three readings of Christ's ministry is the extent of fulfillment in Christ's first advent. It is the thesis of this demonstration that distinguishing three aspects of mediation in God's rule clarifies our understanding of the extent of fulfillment as posed in these two questions: What degree of fulfillment is found by a *literal* reading of the NT record of Christ's ministry? and What expectation of future fulfillment is warranted based on the *analogy of faith* reading of the OT promises?

In person, Jesus as Son of Man, seed of Abraham, son of David completely fulfilled the expectation of what was promised in the OT. The distinctions involving degree of fulfillment do not deal with Jesus' Person but rather with His ministry.

(1) The historic fulfillment of Christ's mediation. *Mediation of the seed of the woman.* After Jesus was baptized, the enemy tempted the Son of God to rebel against the Father's plan. By Jesus' quotation of Scripture, Satan was rebuffed but not conquered (Matt. 4:1-11). What the temptation of Jesus initiated, the cross brought to a climax. Satan struck Christ as He died on the cross (John 13:1-3)—a blow to His heel that felled Him (Gen. 3:15; Acts 2:23). Then, as Peter adds, "God raised Him up" from the dead. Death and the enemy could not keep its hold on Him, since His guilt was not personal. The resurrection from the dead struck the serpent with a head wound just as Moses had written (Gen. 3:15; cf. Acts 2:24).

Mediation of the ministry in the order of Melchizedek. In John the Baptist's introduction of the baptism of repentance for the forgiveness of sins, Jesus joined the repentant remnant to be baptized. In His baptism "for the sake of righteousness," He committed Himself to assume the guilt of the repentant remnant (Matt. 3:15).

Some of this remnant (Peter and Andrew, James and John—Matt. 4:18-20) responded in faith to follow Christ, and other believers experienced the initial blessings of deliverance from guilt and disease. The national leadership, however, rejected Him as an agent of Satan and rejected the deliverance that He mediated (12:14, 24).

The ministry of a priest in the forgiveness of sin rests on a sufficient sacrifice. So Christ, like the serpent in the wilderness, was lifted up, bearing the guilt of all men and receiving God's judgment for that guilt (John 3:14-16; 2 Cor. 5:21). In addition, God also lifted Him up from the dead (Acts 2:24, 29; Ps. 16:8-11) and lifted Him up to His own right hand (Acts 2:33; Ps. 110:1).

In His ascension, Christ was exalted to join the Father on His throne. In exaltation, He enjoyed the position "Lord" (Ps. 110:1) with prerogatives assigned by the Father. These are entailed in the Father's decree (110:4). Jesus "is not merely king, who as a priest provides for the salvation of His people, He is an eternal Priest by virtue of a sworn promise" (v. 4).[29] These prerogatives, as developed in the NT, are primarily priestly (Heb. 4:14–7:28) but include royalty as indicated in the order of Melchizedek (Gen. 14:18). The nature of this royal authority finds expression in the blessing of the king-priest as He ministered as the heir of Abraham.

Mediation of the seed of Abraham. At Jesus' baptism, the heavenly voice announced the Father's satisfaction with His Son's commitment to John's baptism. So God anointed Him with the Spirit for His ministry as king in the line of David (Matt. 3:16-17).

It was as heir to God's promised blessing and as mediator of blessing to a believing Israel that Jesus introduced Himself (Matt. 5:1-2). It was as mediator of entrance into God's kingdom that He introduced His ministry (Matt. 7:13-27). This announcement of kingdom blessing awaited the nation's response.

In its response the nation was divided. The national leaders rejected Christ and His ministry (Matt. 12:14, 24) in a rejection that swelled into an open and public repudiation of Him as He offered Himself as the Davidic king (21:9-10, 23-27, 33-46). On the other hand, a remnant accepted Him (12:48-50), and it was to this remnant that He introduced the new knowledge of the kingdom (13:11-17). This "word of the kingdom" announced a mediation of God's rule on earth not entailed in a Davidic

---

29. Franz Delitzsch, *Biblical Commentary on the Psalms*, 3 vols. (Grand Rapids: Eerdmans, 1959), 3:187.

reign (13:19). It envisioned a fruitful life, pleasing to God on earth, in which fruit grew in response to God's Word proclaimed (13:23). The power of the Word sown in believers' lives, however, would be actively opposed and challenged by the presence and power of the enemy (13:19, 25, 28).

Thus the fulfillment of the blessing promised to Abraham's seed and to David's son was limited by the national leaders' rejection. God's rule would be mediated on earth in the powerful word of the kingdom, but the rule was not after the order of David. Rather, the present exercise of God's rule on earth is displayed through the presence and power of the Holy Spirit given by the ascended Lord according to the promise of the Father (Acts 2:33, 38).

In addition, the presence of this kingdom following Christ's first advent in no way replaced the previously promised kingdom of David nor altered what had been promised to David for Jerusalem (Luke 19:11-27). A hope of a yet future Davidic kingdom remained (Acts 1:6-7).

(2) The future fulfillment of Christ's mediation. After the first advent of Christ, His mediation of God's rule featured that rule associated with His ministry after the pattern of Melchizedek. That ministry was primarily priestly, based on His own sacrifice on the cross. But it also included His authoritative word, present and implemented in the power of the Holy Spirit. That priestly-royal ministry remains in the subsequent fulfillments of God's mediated rule. Christ is a priest forever after the order of Melchizedek.

Mediation of the seed of the woman. Christ's conquest over Satan on the cross will be completed in Christ's conquest over His enemies on the Day of the Lord (Rev. 6:1–19:21) and in the binding and enslavement of Satan for a millennium (Rev. 20:1-6). This completion of the conquest over the enemy (Gen. 3:15) reestablishes God's rule through man over evil in the history of the created world. This righteous judgment of evil will become the basis for a righteous kingdom of blessing on earth.

Mediation of the seed of Abraham and the son of David. The righteous established in the defeat of Satan on the cross became the basis for the mediation of blessing through the Holy Spirit (Luke 11:13). The righteousness established with the binding of Satan will become the basis for the provision of blessings promised to Abraham (Gen. 12:1-3). In addition, the reestablishment of God's reign will be administered according to the promised Davidic order from Jerusalem over Israel and the nations (2 Sam. 7:8-16).

CONCLUSION

Premillennial hope features two stages in Christ's mediation of God's reign on earth over evil: the present Melchizedekian stage of the kingdom and the future Davidic stage of the kingdom. Such a model avoids two errors of interpretation.

One error involves reinterpreting the OT in view of the NT. In this Ladd erred in his conclusion: "God has fulfilled the promise of Psalm 110. Peter, under inspiration, has transferred the throne of David from Jerusalem—Zion (Ps. 110:2)—to heaven."[30] This leads to a reinterpretation of clear, contextual OT meanings and alters them to a reduced, spiritual meaning. This is the error of amillennialism.

The other error fails to accept equally clear texts in the NT that limit Christ's royal authority after His first advent. This is the interpretive error of postmillennialism. Whereas Jesus is heir to David's throne, yet He joins His Father who is already enthroned. Whereas He exercises limited dimensions of the Father's authority and power on earth in the midst of enemies (Ps. 110), the pattern of His present rule matches the pattern of Melchizedek rather than David. These two patterns, although they are related spiritually, are distinct politically and socially.

The model of premillennial faith demonstrated in this chapter preserves the integrity of a literal contextual interpretation as well as the unity of revelation inherent in the analogy of faith. As such, it provides a hermeneutical consistency in definition and application.

30. Ladd, "Historic Premillennialism," p. 31.

2

EVIDENCE FROM GENESIS

ROBERT B. CHISHOLM, JR.
Professor of Old Testament Studies
Dallas Theological Seminary

Those debating the millennial question disagree over the nature and eschatological implications of the Abrahamic Covenant. On the one hand, many premillennialists, regarding the Abrahamic Covenant as foundational to their system, have argued that God's promises to Abraham are unconditional and will be fulfilled literally through the nation Israel.[1] On the other hand, amillennialists and postmillennialists have generally denied the unconditionality of the Abrahamic Covenant and/or argued that its promises are fully realized only through the church, Abraham's spiritual offspring.[2]

It is beyond the scope of this brief study to deal with all the biblical passages referring or alluding to God's promises to Abraham. This essay will focus on the relevant passages in the Abraham narrative

---

1. See, for example, Charles C. Ryrie, *The Basis of the Premillennial Faith* (Neptune, N.J.: Loizeaux, 1953), pp. 48-75; J. Dwight Pentecost, *Things to Come* (Grand Rapids: Zondervan, 1958), pp. 71-94; and John F. Walvoord, *The Millennial Kingdom*, rev. ed. (Findlay, Ohio: Dunham, 1963), pp. 139-93.

2. See, for example, Oswald T. Allis, *Prophecy and the Church* (Philadelphia: Presbyterian & Reformed, 1945), pp. 31-36, 56-58; Louis Berkhof, *Systematic Theology*, rev. ed. (Grand Rapids: Eerdmans, 1953), pp. 295-97; and Loraine Boettner, *The Millennium* (Philadelphia: Presbyterian & Reformed, 1957), p. 318 (favorably quoting Albertus Pieters at this point).

(Gen. 11:27–25:11). I will argue: (1) that all of God's promises to Abraham were conditional at the time they were originally stated, (2) that by solemn oath God progressively ratified all of these promises during Abraham's lifetime, making their eventual fulfillment certain, and (3) that all conditions associated with the promises either were met by Abraham or refer to the fulfillment, not ratification, of the promises.[3]

After surveying the Abraham narrative, I will deal summarily with several important references to the Abrahamic promises elsewhere in Genesis and the OT. Furthermore, I will attempt to show that these later passages assume the unconditionality of the promises and anticipate their literal fulfillment through the nation Israel. In the final analysis, of course, the NT references to the Abrahamic Covenant must be determinative in solving the millennial question. Though other essays in this volume will deal more thoroughly with the pertinent NT passages, I will include a brief summary of my own position with respect to the fulfillment of the Abrahamic promises.

The Genesis Narrative References to the Abrahamic Covenant

When reading through this narrative (Gen. 11:27–25:11), one discovers that God made a series of promises to Abraham over the course of several years.[4] Some of these have conditions specifically attached (cf. 12:1-3; 17:1-8), while others appear in isolation (cf. 12:7; 13:14-17; 15:4-5) or constitute a divine oath (cf. 15:18-21; 22:16-18). The following survey of key passages in the Abraham narrative traces the development of the promises and attempts to show how they were progressively ratified by

---

3. From this point on I will use the following terms and phrases in the senses indicated: (1) "promise": a statement of God's intention to do something on Abraham's behalf, the ratification and fulfillment of which may be subject to certain conditions being met; (2) "oath": a formal statement of God's intention which unconditionally commits Him to a certain course of action; (3) "ratification": the transformation of a conditional promise to an oath by a solemn divine declaration; (4) "realization" or "fulfillment": the actual materialization of God's oath in history (whether partially or completely); (5) "Abrahamic Covenant": God's oath to Abraham, comprising the various promises ratified in the course of the Abraham narrative.

    The proposed distinction between a "promise" and an "oath" may be validated and illustrated from two passages in Genesis involving agreements between men. In Gen. 25:32-33 Jacob, when tricking Esau out of his birthright, makes his brother swear an oath, rather than relying on Esau's word of promise (implied in the rhetorical question, "What good is my birthright to me?"). In Gen. 47:28-30 Jacob, now on his deathbed in Egypt, expresses concern that his body be buried in Canaan. Though Joseph affirms, "I will do as you say" (v. 30), Jacob forces him to swear an oath, formally ratifying and guaranteeing the fulfillment of the promise (v. 31, cf. 50:5-6).

4. Though the Abraham narrative refers to the patriarch by two names (*Abram* in 11:27–17:5 and *Abraham* in 17:5–25:11), this essay will employ "Abraham" throughout.

solemn divine oath in response to Abraham's faith and obedience. By the end of the narrative, the promises possess an unconditional character and may be viewed collectively as God's oath to or covenant with Abraham. Though conditions must still be met for the promises to be completely realized, the certainty of their eventual fulfillment is no longer in question. (In other words, the question is not if the promises will be fulfilled, but when.)

GENESIS 12:1-6

This call narrative records God's commission and initial promises to Abraham (vv. 1-3), as well as the patriarch's obedient response (vv. 4-6). The call proper includes an exhortation (v. 1) motivated by a series of promises (vv. 2-3). The grammatical structure indicates that the realization of the promises is contingent upon a positive response to the exhortation.[5] The following paraphrase (which uses the NIV as its basis) reflects and highlights the logical relationships within the speech:

> Leave your country, your people and your father's household and go to the land I will show you, *so that*[6]
>> I might make you into a great nation,
>> and bless you,
>> and make your name great, *so that*[7]
>>> you *in turn* may be a blessing.
>>> I will bless those who bless you,
>>> but whoever curses you I will curse;
>>> and all the peoples on earth will be blessed through you.

5. Some seem hesitant to acknowledge the presence of a condition in 12:1 (cf. Ryrie, *The Basis of the Premillennial Faith*, p. 54, and Cleon L. Rogers, "The Covenant with Abraham and Its Historical Setting," *Bibliotheca Sacra* 127 [1970]:252). Rogers states that "it cannot be denied that a certain conditional element is present," but he then points out that the structure places emphasis on the cohortatives, not the imperative. For support he appeals to Hans W. Wolff, who understands the imperative as being more like a summons to receive a gift than a condition. See his "The Kerygma of the Yahwist," *Interpretation* 20 (1966):138.

6. The introductory imperative *lek* (v. 1) is followed by three cohortatives introduced with simple *waw* (v. 2). In this sequence the cohortatives express purpose or result. For the grammatical point and examples (cf. Gen. 19:5; 23:4; 24:56; 27:4, 25; 30:25-26; 42:34; 49:1), see E. Kautzsch and A. E. Cowley, eds., *Gesenius' Hebrew Grammar*, 2d Eng. ed. (Oxford: Clarendon, 1910), p. 320, 108*d*. (Gen. 12:2 is not listed among examples cited.)

7. The cohortatives are followed by an imperative (*wehyēh*) with simple *waw*, the latter construction indicating purpose or result in the indirect volitive sequence. For the grammatical point and examples (cf. Gen. 20:7; 45:18), see Kautzsch and Cowley, p. 325, 110i. (Gen. 12:2 is listed among examples cited.)

Abraham's response immediately follows (vv. 4-6), with emphasis being placed on his obedience to the Lord's command (cf. "as the Lord had told him," v. 4). Since Abraham obeyed the only specified condition of fulfillment by moving from Haran to Canaan, one might reasonably conclude that the promises of verses 2-3 became unconditional once he arrived in Canaan.[8] However, one should not reach this conclusion too hastily. In 22:16-18, which records the ratification by divine oath of at least two of these promises (viz., the promises of personal blessing and universal influence), Abraham's obedience in offering up Isaac, not his departure from Haran, is the basis for the oath. In 26:3-5 the certainty of the oath's fulfillment (note the references to personal blessing and universal influence in vv. 3-4) is based on Abraham's obedience in general (note the three plural forms in v. 5: *miṣwōtay ḥuqqôtay wetôrōtāy,* "my commands, my decrees and my laws"). This implies that the journey to Canaan was only the first in a series of obedient responses leading up to the eventual ratification of the promises made in Haran.[9]

GENESIS 12:7

When Abraham arrived in Canaan, the Lord appeared to him and expanded His earlier promise, "To your offspring I will give this land." Though possession of a land was perhaps implied in the earlier exhortation (cf. "go to the land I will show you," v. 1) and in the promise that Abraham would become a great nation, here the Lord specifically identified Canaan as the land of promise He intended to give to Abraham's offspring.[10]

Since no conditions are directly attached to the statement, and Abraham later referred to it as an "oath" (cf. 24:7),[11] this promise could be understood as unconditional from the outset. However, if this were

---

8. Walvoord reasons this way in *The Millennial Kingdom,* p. 149.

9. Of course, in response to Abraham's initial act of obedience God began to fulfill the promises prior to their being ratified. The following context records how God began to bless Abraham personally in accordance with His earlier promise. Despite Abraham's dishonest dealings with Pharaoh, God punished Pharaoh for his inappropriate, though inadvertent, treatment of Sarai and allowed Abraham to leave Egypt a rich man. Because of Abraham's numerous livestock, the land was unable to accommodate his and Lot's herds. Lot moved to the Sodom region where, separated from Abraham, he encountered nothing but trouble. However, despite this initial and partial fulfillment of God's promise to Abraham, there is no guarantee at this point in the narrative of continued blessing, let alone complete fulfillment of the promises.

10. Note, however, that nothing is stated at this point about the land being an eternal possession. This aspect of the promise does not appear until 13:15.

11. In 24:7 Abraham recalls that the Lord promised on oath, "To your offspring I will give this land." The wording here (*leẕarʿākā ʾettēn ʾet hāʾāreṣ hazzʾōt*) is identical to that of 12:7, but differs from other statements pertaining to the gift of the land (cf. 13:15, 17; 15:18).

the case, why did Abraham subsequently express great uncertainty over its fulfillment (cf. 15:7-8),[12] and why was it necessary for God to conduct an elaborate ritual and formally grant the land to Abraham's descendants (cf. 15:9-21)? It is likely that Abraham later referred to the promise of 12:7 as an oath because he viewed it retrospectively through the lens of the formal divine declaration recorded in 15:18-21, not because he regarded the promise as unconditional from the outset.

GENESIS 13:14-17

Following Lot's departure for Sodom, the Lord reiterated and expanded His earlier promises. He repeated the promise of the land (cf. 12:7), but now assured Abraham of personal possession (the earlier promise mentioned only his offspring). He also described the land in more all-encompassing terms[13] and promised that it would be an eternal possession. Building on the promise that Abraham would become a "great nation" (12:2), the Lord declared His intention to make Abraham's offspring as numerous as "the dust of the earth" (13:16). No stated conditions are placed on these promises, though the concluding exhortation to "walk through the length and breadth of the land" (v. 17) was certainly a challenge to respond in faith.

Though the promises of 13:14-17 might appear to be unconditional, the subsequent narrative shows this is not the case. In chapter 17 the promises of numerous offspring and eternal possession of the land are made conditional on Abraham's faithfulness (cf. 17:1-8). Also, as previously noted, the promise of numerous offspring was not ratified until after Abraham offered up Isaac (cf. 22:16-18) and the certainty of its fulfillment is later based on Abraham's obedience to God's requirements in general (cf. 26:3-5).

GENESIS 15:1-21

Despite God's promise of numerous offspring, Abraham remained childless. He asked, "O Sovereign Lord, what can you give me

---

12. It is possible to circumvent this difficulty by proposing that Abraham's question in 15:8 pertains only to his personal possession of the land (note "you" in v. 7 and "I" in v. 8, as well as the absence of any references to his descendants). However, in this case such a distinction is probably overly subtle, especially in light of God's response, in which He grants the land to Abraham's descendants (cf. 15:18). A distinction between Abraham and his descendants would only have been meaningful prior to the promise of 13:15, where the patriarch and his offspring are inextricably linked as recipients of the land promise. This interpretation is consistent with later references to the grant, which speak of it as being made with Abraham (cf. 28:4; 35:12).

13. The exhortation to look in all directions (13:14) and the reference to "all the land that you see" (v. 15) make a significant advance, at least rhetorically, on the simple phrase "this land" used in 12:7.

since I remain childless and the one who will inherit my estate is Eliezer of Damascus?" (v. 2). In response the Lord assured Abraham that he would have a son (v. 4) and repeated His earlier promise to give the patriarch numerous offspring (v. 5; cf. 13:16). When Abraham responded in faith to this latest statement of the promise,[14] the Lord regarded it as "righteousness," that is, as a demonstration of Abraham's faithful character worthy of reward (v. 6).[15] Though the Lord did not yet ratify the promise of numerous offspring, He did reiterate His intention to give Abraham the land of Canaan (v. 7). When Abraham expressed a desire for certainty in this matter (v. 8), the Lord formally granted the promised land to his offspring (vv. 18-21). This land grant was accompanied by a ritual whereby God made it clear that the gift of the land was unconditional (vv. 9-17).[16]

14. The significance of the rare grammatical construction at the beginning of 15:6 (cf. $w^e he'\check{e}min$) remains unclear. In a narrative sequence of this type one expects a *waw* consecutive with *yiqtōl* form, rather than the *qātal* with simple *waw*. Elsewhere in Genesis *qātal* with simple *waw* introduces a new scene (21:25) or simply carries on the narrative sequence (28:6; 34:5). Either function would fit in 15:6. (In 38:5 the construction introduces a parenthetical clause; however, one should probably read a pronoun [$w^e hiw' = w^e hî'$] for MT's $w^e h\bar{a}y\hat{a}$ [cf. LXX].) Gordon Wenham, following Kautzsch and Cowley (p. 339, 112*ss*), states that the construction "probably indicates repeated or continuing action" (*Genesis 1-15*, Word Biblical Commentary [Waco, Tex.: Word, 1987], p. 329). John Ha offers this same explanation (*Genesis 15: A Theological Compendium of Pentateuchal History*, BZAW, 181 [Berlin: Walter de Gruyter, 1989], p. 23).

15. *Ḥāšab* appears with $s^e d\bar{a}q\hat{a}$ in Ps. 106:31 as well. Referring to the events recorded in Num. 25, the psalmist observed that Phinehas's actions on that occasion (specified in Ps. 106:30, cf. "stood up and intervened") were "credited to him as righteousness for endless generations to come." Allusion is made to the unconditional, eternal "covenant of peace" with which God rewarded Phinehas (Num. 25:12-13). Thus $s^e d\bar{a}q\hat{a}$ appears to have here the nuance of "loyal, rewardable behavior." This same nuance fits nicely in Gen. 15, where Abraham's response is followed by a formal ceremony in which God rewards his faith.

16. As many have recognized, God's passing through the animal pieces was a unilateral, self-imprecatory act that unconditionally committed Him to ensure the land grant that follows (cf. v. 18). See, for example, Delbert R. Hillers, *Covenant: The History of a Biblical Idea* (Baltimore: Johns Hopkins, 1969), p. 103; Moshe Weinfeld, "The Covenant of Grant in the Old Testament and in the Ancient Near East," *Journal of the American Oriental Society* 90 (1970):196; Claus Westermann, *Genesis 12-36: A Commentary*, trans. J. J. Scullion (Minneapolis: Augsburg, 1985), p. 228; Bruce K. Waltke, "The Phenomenon of Conditionality Within Unconditional Covenants," *Israel's Apostasy and Restoration*, ed. Avraham Gileadi (Grand Rapids: Baker, 1988), p. 127; and Nahum M. Sarna, *Genesis*, The JPS Torah Commentary (Philadelphia: Jewish Publication Society, 1989), pp. 114-15. Wenham offers a different explanation of the ritual, which he sees as foreshadowing God's protective presence with Israel (*Genesis 1-15*, pp. 332-33). Even if one follows Wenham's interpretation of the ritual, God's unilateral commitment is still apparent. William J. Dumbrell, after summarizing Wenham's position, writes: "In any event the details present a daring anthropomorphism whereby God involves himself in an obligation whose nature is dramatized by an acted oath of self-commitment (cf. Heb. 6:13). In any case, no undertaking is exacted from Abram; God alone is bound" (*Covenant and Creation: A Theology of Old Testament Covenants* [Nashville: Thomas Nelson, 1984], p. 49).

The grant itself appears in verses 18-21, where the Lord solemnly declares, "To your descendants I give this land." Several observations are in order. First, the Hebrew verb translated "I give" (*nātattî*) is a *qātal* form, whereas in earlier statements of the land promise a *yiqtōl* form appears (cf. *'ettēn* in 12:7 and *'ettᵉnennâ* in 13:15, 17). It is likely that this shift marks the actual transfer of the land to Abraham's offspring, whereas before it was merely promised.[17] Though Abraham's offspring would not actually take possession of the land for many years (cf. 15:13-16), the deed to it was now held in trust by Abraham and the land was theirs by lawful right.[18] In light of this, it is best in this context to understand the introductory idiomatic expression "cut a covenant" (v. 18*a*; cf. NIV "made a covenant") in the sense of "concluded an agreement" (in this case a unilateral one), or better, "swore an oath/made a binding declaration."[19]

Second, by granting Abraham's offspring possession of the land, the oath of verse 18 essentially ratified the promise of an heir (cf. 15:4) as well. However, it is important to note that the grant only guarantees possession of the land by Abraham's offspring (cf. 12:7). The related

17. In this case the *qātal* form is best taken as instantaneous (cf. *nātattî* in Gen. 1:29; 9:3; 20:16; 23:11, 13; and 48:22) and translated with the English present tense. Another option is to understand the form as expressing the assurance that the promise (of the actual delivery of the land to Abraham's offspring) would be accomplished. Cf. Kautzsch and Cowley, p. 312, 106*m*; Westermann, *Genesis 12-36*, p. 214; and Wenham, *Genesis 1-15*, pp. 324-25. Classifying the verb as a prophetic perfect, Wenham translates, "I have given," and explains that "the gift, though future, is guaranteed." Even if one understands the verb in this sense, the shift to the *qātal* indicates a more emphatic statement of the promise in the form of an unconditional oath. See also Westermann, p. 229.

18. This land grant has parallels with royal grants from the ancient Near East in which a king rewards a faithful servant. See Weinfeld, "Covenant of Grant," pp. 196-200. More generally, Weinfeld argues that the Abrahamic and Davidic Covenants are modeled after these secular grants. Paul Kalluveettil, offers five objections to Weinfeld's position, the first two of which are particularly relevant to 15:18 (*Declaration and Covenant*, Analecta Biblica, 88 [Rome: Biblical Institute, 1982], p. 180, n. 234). First, Kalluveettil observes that "loyalty is not cited in the [biblical] texts as a motive for the 'gift' of land or dynasty." Second, he argues that the biblical land promise and secular grants "do not belong to the same genre." He explains that the former is "a mere promise," while the latter involve "actual granting of land" and "a decree of land transfer." In the case of 15:18, these objections appear to be invalid. First, though Abraham's loyalty is not specifically cited in v. 18 as a basis for the gift, the oath appears to be a divine response to Abraham's faith and a reward for his "righteousness" (cf. v. 6). Also, 26:5 (which Kalluveettil dismisses as "a deuteronomistic addition," p. 181, n. 236) directly relates the gift of the land to Abraham's obedience. Second, 15:18 is not "a mere promise," but rather "a decree of land transfer" involving the "actual granting of land."

19. See Westermann, *Genesis 12-36*, p. 229. This understanding of the phrase finds support in Ps. 105:8-9, where the promise (*bᵉrît*)/word (*dābār*) that God ratified (cf. *kārat*) with Abraham is equated with the "oath" (*šᵉbûᶜâ*) given to Isaac. On the nuance of "oath" for *bᵉrît*, see note 23 below.

promises of eternal possession of the land and numerous offspring are not mentioned in verses 18-21 because they were not yet ratified by oath, as the subsequent narrative makes clear (cf. 17:1-8; 22:16-18; and 26:3-5).

Third, the geographical description of the land (vv. 18b-21) supersedes earlier descriptions. The pattern of escalation seen in earlier expressions of the land promise (cf. 12:7 with 13:14-15) reaches its climax here as the deed to the promised land is actually handed over. Not only would Abraham's offspring receive "this land" or even "all the land" that he could see with his eyes, but they would possess the entire region from the Euphrates to the river of Egypt.

In summary, chapter 15 records the legal transfer of the land to Abraham's descendants in fulfillment of the promise stated in 12:7. Since this land grant presupposed the eventual existence of offspring, it essentially ratified the promise of an heir as well (cf. 15:4). However, the promises of Genesis 12:2 (great nation, personal blessing, great name); 13:15 (eternal possession of the land); and 13:16/15:5 (numerous offspring) remained unratified and conditional at this point, as the subsequent narrative indicates.

GENESIS 17:1-27

When Abraham reached the age of 99, God appeared to him once more, this time in the role of *El Shaddai* ("God Almighty"), the one who grants fertility and life.[20] As *El Shaddai*, God reiterated His promise to give Abraham numerous offspring (cf. 13:16; 15:5). However, a condition was attached to the promise, as the grammatical structure of verses 1b-2 makes clear. The following paraphrase (which uses NIV as its basis) reflects and highlights the logical relationships within verses 1b-2:

> I am God Almighty;
> walk before me *so that*[21]
> you *in turn* might be blameless/acceptable *so that*[22]

---

20. Each time the name appears in Genesis, it is associated with God's power to grant numerous offspring (17:1-2; 28:3; 35:11; 48:3-4; 49:25) or to preserve life (43:14).
21. When two imperatives are joined by simple *waw*, the second can indicate purpose or result. For the grammatical point and examples, see Kautzsch and Cowley, p. 325, 110g. (Gen. 17:1 is listed as an example, cf. 42:18.)
22. Following an imperative, the cohortative with simple *waw* can indicate purpose or result (cf. note 6).

I *in turn* might make my oath/ratify my promise[23]
between me and you
and greatly multiply your offspring.

For the promises (outlined in more detail in vv. 4-8) to be ratified and thus made certain of fulfillment, Abraham must "walk before" the Lord. This idiomatic expression (*hithpael* of *hālak*) refers here to an intimate relationship with God that is characterized by faithful, obedient behavior.[24] The phrase is used in this positive ethical sense of (1) Enoch (Gen. 5:22, 24), whose "walking with" God was directly related to his being "taken away" by God (in contrast to the other antediluvians listed with him in the genealogy, all of whom experienced physical death), (2) righteous and blameless Noah (6:9), and (3) Abraham and Isaac (24:40; 48:15). The accompanying expression (*weḥyēh tāmîm*) refers to being blameless and acceptable in God's sight as a result of one's loyalty.[25] *Tāmîm* is used of Noah (6:9), whose righteousness contrasted sharply with the sinful men of the antediluvian world and made him acceptable before God and the special recipient of divine favor (cf. 6:5-9).[26]

---

23. No single English word can adequately reflect the range of meaning of *berît*. While the word may refer at times to a treaty or formal agreement, it also refers frequently to promises/oaths or obligations associated with such agreements. In 17:2 God's *berît* includes His promises of numerous offspring and eternal possession of the land (cf. vv. 2b, 4-8). The phrase *nātan berît* either means "to ratify a (heretofore conditional) promise" or "make an oath" (for the latter nuance, see Gen. 9:12 and Num. 25:12).

    Several major studies of *berît* have appeared in recent years, including among others, Ernst Kutsch, *Verheissung und Gesetz*, BZAW, 131 (Berlin: Walter de Gruyter, 1973); Moshe Weinfeld, "*berît*," *Theological Dictionary of the Old Testament*, rev. ed., ed. G. J. Botterweck and Helmer Ringgren, trans. John T. Willis (Grand Rapids: Eerdmans, 1977), 2:253-79; and James Barr, "Some Semantic Notes on the Covenant," *Beiträge zur Alttestamentlichen Theologie*, ed. H. Donner, R. Hanhart, and R. Smend (Gottingen: Vandenhoeck & Ruprecht, 1977), pp. 23-38. For a convenient survey of these and other studies, see Ernest W. Nicholson, *God and His People: Covenant and Theology in the Old Testament* (Oxford: Clarendon, 1986), pp. 83-117. The conclusions of Kutsch, with which Weinfeld is in basic agreement, have been particularly influential. Rejecting the notion that *berît* has the sense of "agreement" (*Bund*), Kutsch proposes that it refers instead to an obligation (*Verpflichtung*) or obligations, whether taken upon oneself (thus equivalent to a pledge or oath), imposed upon another, bilaterally accepted, or imposed by a third party (cf. pp. 1-27 and Nicholson's summary, pp. 89-93).

24. Sarna compares the expression to an Akkadian phrase that refers to loyalty and appears in Assyrian land grants rewarding faithful subjects. He adds, "In the Bible, to 'walk before God' takes on an added dimension. Allegiance to Him means to condition the entire range of human experience by the awareness of His presence and in response to His demands" (*Genesis*, p. 123).

25. Weinfeld understands the phrase as a reference to "perfect or loyal service" and compares it to a semantically equivalent expression in Assyrian royal grants ("Covenant of Grant," p. 186).

26. *Tāmîm* has the nuance of "blameless and therefore acceptable" in Ps. 15:1-2. The lexical nuance of the word is similar when it is used of physically sound and therefore acceptable sacrificial animals (cf. Ex. 12:5).

In verses 4-8 God elaborates on the content of the promise/anticipated oath referred to in verse 2. Expanding on the promise of numerous offspring (cf. v. 2*b*), He declared that Abraham would become the "father of many nations" and that his offspring would include kings (vv. 4, 6). As an outward reminder of the promise, God even changed the patriarch's name from Abram (meaning "exalted father") to Abraham (which, by popular etymology, suggests the meaning "father of many," v. 5).[27] The Lord also announced that He would make His oath eternal (v. 7),[28] grant Abraham and his offspring eternal possession of the land (v. 8*a*),[29] and be the personal God of Abraham and his descendants (vv. 7*b*, 8*b*).[30]

Following this detailed outline of the promises, the Lord placed the obligation of circumcision upon Abraham and his offspring (vv. 9-14). In this section the wide lexical range of *b*ᵉ*rît* is especially apparent. To reflect the precise nuance of this word in each instance, we offer the following paraphrase of verses 9-11, 13-14:

> ⁹Then God said to Abraham, "As for you, you must carry out the obligation [*b*ᵉ*rît*[31]] I am about to impose on you and your descendants after you for generations to come. ¹⁰This is the obligation [*b*ᵉ*rît*] I impose upon you and your descendants after you, the obligation [*b*ᵉ*rît*] you are to carry out: Every male among you shall be circumcised. ¹¹You are to

---

27. See Allen P. Ross, *Creation and Blessing* (Grand Rapids: Baker, 1988), pp. 331-32. For alternative explanations see Sarna, *Genesis*, p. 124.

28. The statement *waḥăqimōtî 'et bᵉrîtî . . . librît 'ôlām* should be translated, "and I will ratify my promise/establish my oath . . . as an eternal oath." The phrase *hēqîm bᵉrît* has this same nuance in 6:18 and 9:9, 11.

29. The NIV translates Heb. *wᵉnātattî* (a *qātal* form with *waw* consecutive) "I will give." The text speaks of possession of the land as future once more (cf. 12:7; 13:15, and contrast 15:18) because *eternal* possession, something not included in the oath of 15:18, is now in view.

30. Technically speaking, the *bᵉrît* made in 15:18 is distinct from the *bᵉrît* referred to in 17:1-8. The former was ratified and pertained to possession of the land and the certainty of future offspring. The latter was not yet ratified (cf. the condition attached in v. 1) and pertained to numerous offspring, eternal possession of the land, and a more personal relationship with God. However, because of the close thematic connection between 15:18 and 17:1-8 (after all, the motifs of land and offspring are central to both passages), one may view the promises of 17:1-8, once they are ratified, as an expansion and intensification of the earlier oath.

31. As already noted (cf. n. 23), *bᵉrît* often carries the idea of an "obligation." In 17:1-8 the obligation was self-imposed by God (i.e., a promise, pledge, oath); in vv. 9-14 the obligation is imposed by God upon Abraham and his offspring (cf. Kutsch, *Verheissung und Gesetz*, pp. 102-15, 142-43, and Nicholson, *God and His People*, p. 106), so that one might even translate *bᵉrît* here as "command, stipulation." For other examples of this sense of *bᵉrît*, see Pss. 78:10; 103:18; 132:12; and Weinfeld, "*bᵉrît*," pp. 257-58.

undergo circumcision, and it will be a reminder of the promise [$b^e r \hat{\imath} t$] which binds us[32]... [13]Whether born in your household or bought with your money, they must be circumcised. The reminder of my promise [$b^e r \hat{\imath} t$] shall be in your flesh as a permanent reminder [$b^e r \hat{\imath} t$[33]]. [14]Any uncircumcised male, who has not been circumcised in the flesh, will be cut off from his people; he has failed to carry out the obligation [$b^e r \hat{\imath} t$] I impose upon you."

The obligation of circumcision imposed upon Abraham should be viewed as another condition necessary for the ratification of the promises mentioned earlier in the chapter. This particular obligation demanded from him the same kind of faith exhibited in his departure from Haran (cf. 12:1-6) and in his response to the promise of numerous offspring (cf. 15:4-6). It may be viewed as the initial step in "walking before" the Lord (cf. 17:1).

However, once Abraham personally satisfied this (cf. 17:23-27; 21:4) and other (cf. 17:1; 22:1-2) conditions, God confirmed the promises by oath (cf. 22:16-18). Though future generations were obligated to observe the rite (cf. 17:11-13), their failure in this regard would jeopardize only their personal participation in the promised blessings, not the oath itself. The language of 17:14 indicates this by warning that the disobedient descendant would "be cut off from his people," that is, be excommunicated from the covenant community. While the violator is punished, the continuing existence of the community is assumed because the fulfillment of the promises would be certain by that time. After imposing the rite of circumcision, the Lord emphasized that the promise of numerous offspring would be realized through a child born to Sarah, not through Ishmael (vv. 15-21). Though God would greatly bless Ishmael (v. 20), Sarah's son, Isaac, would inherit as an eternal oath the promises outlined earlier in the chapter (vv. 19, 21).

GENESIS 18:17-19

Because of His special relationship to Abraham, the Lord decided to reveal to the patriarch His plan to destroy Sodom. In verse 18 the Lord anticipates the fulfillment of the promises He made to Abraham in Haran, stating that "Abraham will surely become a great and powerful nation, and all nations on earth will be blessed through him." The first part of this statement reiterates the promise of 12:2 ("I will make you

---

32. The precise nuance of $b^e r \hat{\imath} t$ in v. 11 is not clear. Following 'ôt, "sign, reminder," it may refer to the promises/anticipated oath of verses 1-8 (cf. our paraphrase), the obligation of circumcision itself, or the agreement in general (with its mutual obligations).

33. In v. 13 $b^e r \hat{\imath} t$ appears to refer, by metonymy, to circumcision as the sign/reminder (cf. v. 11) of the promise?/obligation?/agreement? (cf. n. 32).

into a great nation"), only more emphatically (note the infinitive absolute *hāyō* [NIV "surely"] and the addition of *'āṣûm*, "powerful"), while the second part essentially repeats the promise of 12:3*b* (with some changes in wording). This statement anticipates the oath of 22:16-18, where these promises are ratified and their fulfillment made certain.

In verse 19 the Lord reveals His purpose in choosing Abraham. He states: "For I have chosen him, so that he will direct his children and his household after him to keep the way of the Lord by doing what is right and just, so that the Lord will bring about for Abraham what he has promised him."[34] This verse indicates that obedience by Abraham's descendants was, as Sarna states, "the indispensable precondition for the fulfillment of the divine promises."[35] However, this does not put the promises themselves in jeopardy. It speaks of their fulfillment or realization, not their ratification. Though the promises would not actually materialize in history until the specified conditions were realized, their status as solemnly ratified divine oaths remained certain, thus guaranteeing that God Himself, if necessary, would eventually cause the specified conditions to be met.[36]

GENESIS 22:15-18

The Abraham narrative reaches its climax in chapter 22, which tells of the ultimate test of Abraham's faith. Having finally given Abraham

---

34. On the nuance of *hābî'* here, cf. Horst Dietrich Preuss, "*bô'*," in *Theological Dictionary of the Old Testament*, 2:33.

35. Sarna, *Genesis*, p. 131.

36. The terms "fulfillment," "realization," and "ratification," as used here, are defined in n. 3 above. Making the realization of the soon-to-be ratified promises conditional upon the obedience of Abraham's offspring (v. 19) creates a tension with historical developments, the resolution of which comes through progressive revelation. Israel never kept the way of the Lord by doing what is right and just and therefore never experienced the full realization of God's oath to Abraham. However, as foreseen in part by Moses (Deut. 30:6), God promised to reconcile His people to Himself and transform their inner character through a new covenant mediated by a righteous servant portrayed as an ideal Israel (cf. Isaiah's "servant songs" and Jeremiah's prophecy of the New Covenant [Jer. 31:31-34]). Once accomplished, this reconciliation and transformation would provide the basis for the complete realization of His oath to Abraham. For an insightful discussion of the relationship of the Abrahamic and New Covenants, see Waltke, "The Phenomenon of Conditionality," pp. 128-30, 135-37. On the basis of Gen. 18:18-19, Waltke correctly argues (p. 129) that God's oath, while unconditional, is only extended "to those within Abraham's household who behave ethically" (whom Waltke later labels "Abraham's spiritual progeny" [p. 130]). He is also correct in seeing the New Covenant as the divine solution to the dilemma posed by 18:18-19 when viewed in the light of Israelite history. The fundamental questions then become: What is the precise identity of "Abraham's spiritual progeny," through whom the promises are fully realized? Does this group include a future transformed national Israel or is it limited to the church? Will the New Covenant be fulfilled with national Israel or are its promises fulfilled only in the church? I briefly address these questions later in this essay.

the long-awaited son of promise, the Lord commanded him to sacrifice Isaac (vv. 1-2). Abraham unflinchingly carried out the Lord's orders, as the "staccato" style of verses 3, 9-10 emphasizes.[37] As Abraham prepared to plunge his knife into Isaac, the Lord's messenger finally intervened and declared: "Do not do anything to him. Now I know that you fear God, because you have not withheld from me your son, your only son" (v. 12). The messenger then specifically ratified by divine oath several of the promises made earlier in the narrative, stating that God's commitment to Abraham was in direct response to Abraham's obedience to the command to offer up his only son (vv. 16, 18b).

Several observations are in order. First, Abraham's willingness to offer up Isaac is his supreme act of obedience and brings to culmination the pattern of faith established by his journey to Canaan (12:4-6) and carried along by his positive response to the promise of numerous offspring (15:6) and by his submission to the rite of circumcision (17:23-27; 21:4). At this point in the narrative, the condition laid down in 17:1 is fully satisfied. Abraham has passed the test, as it were (cf. 22:1), and demonstrated his genuine "fear" of God (v. 12). In 24:40, as he reflects on his life, he affirms that he has indeed "walked before the Lord" (note the *hithpael qātal* form of *hālak*), an assessment with which Jacob later agreed (Gen. 48:15).

Second, though the word *berît* does not appear in 22:15-18, the reference to the divine oath (cf. *nišba'tî*, v. 16) indicates that the Lord here ratified the promises included in the *berît* of 17:1-8. Several passages illustrate the close relationship between *berît* and an oath (cf. Gen. 21:31-32; 26:28; 31:44, 53), while others refer to God's *berît* with Abraham and his offspring in terms of an oath (cf. among others Gen. 26:3; Ex. 6:4, 8; Ps. 105:8-9).

Third, four specific promises are ratified by the oath: (1) personal blessing (cf. 12:2),[38] (2) numerous offspring (cf. 13:16; 15:5; 17:2b, 4-6), (3) possession of enemies' cities,[39] and (4) universal influence (cf.

<hr>

37. See Thomas M. Mann, *The Book of the Torah: The Narrative Integrity of the Pentateuch* (Atlanta: Knox, 1988), p. 46.

38. This promise is stated more emphatically here in 22:17 than in 12:2 (note the addition of the infinitive absolute *bārēk*; cf. John I. Lawlor, "The Test of Abraham: Genesis 22:1-19," *Grace Theological Journal* 1 [1980]:24-25).

39. Though the wording of this divine promise is unique to this passage (see, however, Gen. 24:60), it appears to relate to the promise of 12:3: "whoever curses you I will curse" (cf. Gary A. Rendsburg, *The Redaction of Genesis* [Winona Lake, Ind.: Eisenbrauns, 1986], p. 32). It may also relate to the land promise ratified in Gen. 15:18 (cf. Thomas Edward McComiskey, *The Covenants of Promise: A Theology of the Old Testament Covenants* [Grand Rapids: Baker, 1985], p. 53, and David J. A. Clines, *The Theme of the Pentateuch*, JSOT Supplement Series, 10 [Sheffield: JSOT, 1978], p. 36).

12:3; 18:18).⁴⁰ The confirmation of the promises made way back in Haran rounds out and provides closure for the central part of the narrative (in which ratification of the promises in response to Abraham's continuing obedience is the major theme).⁴¹

Fourth, five earlier unratified promises are omitted here: (1) great nation (12:2), (2) great name (12:2), (3) eternal possession of the land (13:15; 17:8), (4) ratification of oath as eternal (17:7, 19), and (5) personal relationship (17:7-8). However, it is likely that the oath uses a part for whole style and that these omitted promises are ratified by implication. The first two (the promises that Abraham would become a great nation and achieve great fame) are easily subsumed under the related promises of numerous offspring and personal blessing, respectively. The ratification of the promise of eternal possession of the land, which is not given in isolation, but is linked in both of its appearances with the promise of numerous offspring (cf. 13:14-17; 17:4-8), may be implicit in 22:17. Psalm 105:8-11 (cf. 1 Chron. 16:15-18) certainly supports this interpretation. The psalmist refers to the land promise to Abraham, Isaac, and Israel as "an everlasting covenant" and "oath" that God observes "forever." The final two promises (ratification of oath as eternal; personal relationship) are inextricably linked with the promise of numerous offspring and eternal possession of the land in 17:4-8 and thus may be viewed as implicitly ratified in 22:17 as well.⁴²

SUMMARY

A close reading of the relevant sections of the Abraham narrative reveals the following: (1) the various promises made by God were originally conditional upon Abraham's faith and obedience (cf. esp. 12:1; 17:1; 22:1, 16-18; 26:3-5); (2) Abraham's faithful and obedient response to God's promises and commands (cf. 12:4-6; 15:6; 17:23-27; 21:4; 22:1-14) satisfied this condition (cf. 22:12, 16-18; 24:40; 26:3-5); (3) all of God's promises to Abraham were ratified by divine oath (cf. 15:8-21; 22:16-18)

---

40. The precise wording here (cf. *wᵉhitbārăkû bᵉzarᵉ'ăkā*) differs from the form of the promise in 12:3 and 18:18: *wᵉnibrᵉkû bᵉkā/bô*. For other statements of this promise, see Gen. 26:4 and 28:14. The significance of the differences is debated (cf. Walter Vogels, *God's Universal Covenant*, 2d ed. [Ottawa: U. of Ottawa, 1986], pp. 42-45).

41. On the close relationship between 12:1-9 and 22:1-19 in the structure of the Abraham narrative, see Rendsburg, *The Redaction of Genesis*, pp. 30-35.

42. The statement "I will establish" (17:7*a*) is linked to the preceding promise of numerous offspring (note the *waw* consecutive with *qātal* form *wahăqimōtî*), while the declaration "I will give" (17:8) is linked to the promise of an eternal covenant (note again the *waw* consecutive with *qātal* form *wᵉnātattî*). The statements "to be your God and the God of your descendants after you" (17:7*b*) and "I will be their God" (17:8*b*) form a bracket around the promise of eternal possession of the land (17:8*a*).

so that by the conclusion of the narrative their complete fulfillment is certain; (4) obligations and conditions relating to Abraham's offspring pertain to participation in (cf. 17:14) or the timing of the fulfillment of (cf. 18:19) God's unconditional promises, but affect in no way the ratification of the promises or the certainty of their realization.[43]

The following outline (NIV quoted) categorizes and traces the development of the various promises:

I. The Promise of Numerous Offspring

    A. Basic form:
        1. Promised in 15:4: "A son coming from your own body will be your heir"
        2. Ratified by implication in 15:18: "To your descendants"
    B. Expanded form (numerous offspring):
        1. Implied in 12:2: "I will make you into a great nation"
        2. Promised in 13:16: "I will make your offspring like the dust of the earth"
        3. Reiterated in 15:5: "So shall your offspring be"
        4. Reiterated in 17:2, 4-6 as part of anticipated oath: "I . . . will greatly increase your numbers," "You will be the father of many nations," "I will make you very fruitful; I will make nations of you, and kings will come from you"
        5. Referred to in 18:18: "Abraham will surely become a great and powerful nation" (cf. 12:2)
        6. Ratified in 22:17: "I will . . . make your descendants as numerous as the stars in the sky"

II. The Promise of Personal Blessing

    A. Promised in 12:2: "I will bless you," "I will make your name great"
    B. Ratified in 22:17: "I will surely bless you"

---

43. With respect to the development of the promises, there appears to be a two-paneled structure within the narrative. Each panel begins with a conditional statement of divine promises and concludes with an oath ratifying various promises. The structure may be outlined as follows:

12:1-3	Promises with condition	17:1-2
12:4	Response of faith	17:23-27
12:10-20	Failure	20:1-18
13:14-17; 15:4-5	Promise/fulfillment of divine intention to give offspring	21:1-7
15:6	Response of faith	22:1-14
15:7-21	Ratification of divine promises	22:15-18

III. The Promise of Universal Influence

    A. Promised in 12:2-3: "You will be a blessing. I will bless those who bless you, and whoever curses you I will curse; and all peoples on earth will be blessed through you"

    B. Referred to in 18:18: "All nations on earth will be blessed through him"

    C. Ratified in 22:17-18: "Your descendants will take possession of the cities of their enemies," and "Through your offspring all nations on earth will be blessed"

IV. The Promise of Possessed Land

    A. Basic Form:
        1. Promised to offspring in 12:7: "To your offspring I will give this land"
        2. Ratified/Granted in 15:18: "To your descendants I give this land"
        3. Ratified in expanded form in 22:17: "Your descendants will take possession of the cities of their enemies"

    B. Expanded form (as eternal possession—never appears in isolation, but in connection with promise of numerous offspring):
        1. Promised to Abraham and offspring in 13:15: "All the land that you see I will give to you and your offspring forever"
        2. Reiterated as part of anticipated oath in 17:8: "The whole land . . . I will give as an everlasting possession to you and your descendants"
        3. Ratified by implication in 22:16-18 in conjunction with ratification of promise of numerous offspring (cf. Ps. 105:8-11)

V. The Promise of Personal Relationship (linked with promise of numerous offspring/eternal possession of land)

    A. Promised in 17:7-8: "To be your God and the God of your descendants," "I will be their God"

    B. Ratified by implication in 22:16-18 in conjunction with ratification of promise of numerous offspring

VI. The Promise of Eternal Oath (linked with promise of numerous off-spring/eternal possession of land)

    A. Promised in 17:7: " I will establish my covenant as an everlasting covenant" (cf. also vv. 19, 21)

    B. Fulfilled in 22:16-18 in conjunction with ratification of promise of numerous offspring (cf. Ps. 105:8-11)

Other Old Testament References to the Abrahamic Covenant

Several OT references to the Abrahamic promises assume their unconditionality and/or anticipate their realization through the nation Israel. The following discussion briefly surveys some of the most important of these.

GENESIS 26:3-5

During a famine that had forced Isaac to move to Philistine territory, the Lord appeared to Isaac and made it clear he was heir to the
Abrahamic promises. The Lord urged Isaac to remain in the promised
land so that he might enjoy the divine presence and blessing (v. 3a).[44] As
further motivation for Isaac to respond positively, the Lord extended to
him several of the Abrahamic promises (vv. 3b-4). He promised to give
Isaac's descendants actual possession of all the lands previously specified (cf. 15:18-21) and to "confirm [i.e., fulfill/bring to realization[45]] the
oath" (26:3) sworn to Abraham by giving Isaac numerous offspring and
granting them universal influence (cf. 22:16-18).[46] The sole basis for the
fulfillment of these promises is Abraham's obedience (cf. *ʿēqeb ʾăšer
šāmaʿ ʾabrāhām bᵉqōlî* in 26:5 with the words of 22:18b: *ʿēqeb ʾăšer šā-
maʿtā bᵉqōlî*) to God's requirements in general (26:5; cf. v. 24).

GENESIS 28:3-4, 13-15; 35:9-13

These passages tell how Jacob became the heir to God's promises to Abraham and Isaac. As Jacob prepared to flee to Haran to escape
Esau's anger, Isaac pronounced a blessing over him. He asked that God
might make Jacob fruitful and give to him and his descendants "the
blessing of Abraham," which is defined as possession of the land He
"gave to Abraham" (28:3-4). By using the *qātal* form (*nātan*) here, Isaac
alluded to the oath by which God formally granted the land to Abraham
and his offspring (cf. 15:18). Isaac assumed that the land already belonged by divine grant to Abraham; the only question in his mind was
whether or not Jacob and his descendants would be the channel of
fulfillment.

As Jacob traveled toward Haran, the Lord appeared to him and
identified Himself as the "God of your father Abraham and the God of
Isaac" (28:13a). Without specifying any conditions, He extended to Jacob

---

44. The grammatical structure of 26:3 (imperative *gûr* followed by two *yiqṭōl* forms with
simple *waw* [possibly cohortatives] stating purpose/result) indicates that God's personal presence with and blessing of Isaac is conditioned upon his staying in the land.
As vv. 3b-5 demonstrate, the condition pertains only to Isaac's experiencing the blessings inherited from Abraham, not to the ratification or ultimate realization of the
promises made on oath to the patriarch.

45. For this nuance of *hēqîm* see among others Lev. 26:9 (with *bᵉrît*); Num. 23:19; Deut.
8:18 (with *bᵉrît*); 9:5 (with *haddābār ʾăšer nišbaʿ yhwh laʾăbōtêkā*, "the word which
He swore to your fathers"); 1 Sam. 1:23; 1 Kings 6:12 (both with *dābār*); and Jer. 11:5
(with *šᵉbûʿâ*).

46. Note the close verbal parallels between 22:17-18 and 26:3-4, especially the comparison of the numerous offspring to the "stars of the heavens" and the precise wording
of the promise of universal influence.

the promises of possession of the land, numerous offspring, and universal influence, and assured him of His continuing presence (28:14-15). When Jacob returned to the land years later, the Lord, in the role of El Shaddai, again appeared to him, changed his name to Israel, and promised him numerous offspring, as well as possession of the land He had earlier granted to Abraham and Isaac (35:9-12). As in 28:4 the use of the *qātal* form (*nātattî*, 35:12) assumes that the land already belonged to Abraham and Isaac.[47]

MOSES AND THE PROPHETS

Moses and the prophets made clear that Israel's sin and eventual exile did not invalidate God's oath to Abraham, further emphasizing its unconditional nature. These passages also imply that ancient Israel did not regard the promises as fully or adequately realized in the preexilic era.

In the conclusion to the covenant curse list of Leviticus 26, Moses promised that God's exiled but repentant people would be restored on the basis of His oath to Abraham and the fathers regarding the land (v. 42). Similarly in Deuteronomy 4:31 Moses, anticipating the eventual exile and repentance of Israel (cf. vv. 25-30), promised the nation: "For the Lord your God is a merciful God; he will not abandon or destroy you or forget the covenant with your forefathers, which he confirmed to them by oath."

Hosea, although warning that God was about to reject His people and send them into exile (cf. 8:13; 9:3; 11:5-6), promised that a day of restoration would come. At that time, in fulfillment of His promise to Abraham, God would make "the Israelites . . . like the sand on the seashore, which cannot be measured or counted" (1:10; cf. Gen. 22:17).

Micah concluded his prophetic message with this statement of praise: "You will be true to Jacob, and show mercy to Abraham, as you pledged on oath to our fathers in days long ago" (7:20). In the preceding verses he pointed out that God's faithfulness to the Abrahamic oath meant the restoration of downtrodden Jerusalem (v. 11), the deliverance of the exiles through a grand new exodus (vv. 14-15), and forgiveness of the nation's sins (vv. 18-19).

Zechariah also anticipated the complete restoration of Jerusalem and through literary allusion related the future fertility of the restored exiles to the Abrahamic promise of offspring (8:4-8). Just as God over-

---

47. The parallels between 17:1-8 and 35:9-12 are striking. They include: (1) *wayyērā'*, "appeared" (17:1; 35:9); (2) the changing of the patriarch's name (17:5; 35:10); (3) *'ănî 'ēl šadday*, "I am God Almighty" (17:1; 35:11); (4) references to numerous offspring, including nations and kings, springing from the patriarch (17:2, 6; 35:11); and (5) references to the land promise (17:8; 35:12).

came the obstacle of Sarah's barrenness and gave Abraham a son in fulfillment of His promise, so He would overcome all obstacles, even the desolation of exile (cf. Zech. 7:14), in fulfilling His promises to Abraham's descendants. Just as Sarah laughed with joy over Isaac, so the streets of Jerusalem would once again be filled with the sound of laughing children, the offspring of Abraham.[48]

1 CHRONICLES 16:15-18 (PSALM 105:8-11)

The author of this Psalm (David, according to 1 Chron. 16:7) viewed God's promise of the land as eternal and irrevocable. As Raymond Dillard points out (in his comments on 1 Chron. 16:8-36) the "use of the lengthy historical portion from Ps 105 emphasizing the promises to Abraham would be particularly relevant to the Chronicler's postexilic audience, for whom the faithfulness of God was a fresh reality in their return to the land."[49] Certainly the appearance of the affirmation in verses 15-18 in this postexilic book attests to that community's faith in the eternal character of God's oath to Abraham, an oath that could not be invalidated even by the nation's rebellion and exile.

New Testament References
to the Abrahamic Covenant

The NT teaches that mere physical descent does not make one a true descendant of Abraham (Matt. 3:9; Luke 19:9; John 8:37-41; Rom. 4:12; 9:6-9). Rather, all who follow Abraham's example of faith, including Gentiles, are his spiritual offspring and recipients of at least some of the Abrahamic promises (Rom. 4:11, 13-16; Gal. 3:6-9, 14, 29). However, these statements hardly entail that the national entity Israel has no future place in God's program. According to Paul, the nation Israel still possesses the ancient covenants and promises (Rom. 9:4). In accordance with the pattern of forgiveness established in Moses and the prophets and in fulfillment of Jeremiah's New Covenant promises, the Lord will someday take away the nation's sins (11:25-27). In so doing He will once more demonstrate that His merciful elective love, based on His unconditional promises to the patriarchs (v. 28), cannot be thwarted, even by His people's rebellion (vv. 28-32).

One can divorce this promise of Israel's salvation from possession of the literal land[50] only by overlooking the contextual demands of

---

48. For a fuller discussion of the literary relationship between Gen. 18:12-15/21:6 and Zech. 8:4-8, see Robert B. Chisholm, Jr., *Interpreting the Minor Prophets* (Grand Rapids: Zondervan, 1990), p. 257.
49. Raymond Dillard, "1 Chronicles," *The NIV Study Bible*, ed. Kenneth Barker (Grand Rapids: Zondervan, 1985), p. 606.

the OT passages from which Paul draws his language in verses 26-27 (Isa. 27:9; 59:20-21; Jer. 31:33-34). The immediate context of each of these passages associates Israel's future salvation with a return to the land and/or the rebuilding of Jerusalem (cf. Isa. 27:1-13; 60:1-22; Jer. 31:23-25, 35-40). By drawing on these passages and specifically relating their fulfillment to the promises to the fathers, Paul reveals his belief that the Abrahamic Covenant will be fully and literally realized in conjunction with the future restoration of national Israel.

CONCLUSION

One must make a careful distinction between statements of divine intention and divine oaths formally ratifying those statements and assuring their eventual realization. I have argued that the statements of divine intention recorded throughout the Abraham narrative are assumed to be conditional until they are ratified by divine oath. This ratification comes in two stages (Gen. 15:9-21; 22:16-18). Thus by the conclusion of the Abraham narrative God's covenant promises to Abraham achieve the level of an oath and are therefore unconditional in nature and certain of fulfillment. Subsequent OT references to the oath assume its unconditionality.

Establishing the unconditional nature of God's oath to Abraham does not necessarily entail a literal fulfillment of its promises through ethnic Israel living in an eschatological kingdom centered in the land of Canaan. For example, some amillennialists, while agreeing that the promises are unconditional, find their fulfillment exclusively in the church. While the church, as Abraham's spiritual offspring, does inherit God's promises to the patriarch and participate to some degree in their fulfillment, this does not preclude a literal eschatological realization of the promises through ethnic Israel. The writers of the OT, including those living in the postexilic period, and the apostle Paul anticipated such a literal fulfillment.

---

50. See, for example, Hans K. LaRondelle, *The Israel of God in Prophecy: Principles of Prophetic Interpretation*, Andrews University Monographs, Studies in Religion, 13 (Berrien Springs, Mich.: Andrews U., 1983), pp. 131-32.

3

EVIDENCE FROM PSALM 89

RONALD B. ALLEN
Professor of Hebrew Scripture
Western Conservative Baptist Seminary

The aftermath of war may be as critical as the outcome of the war itself. This is true of the battle of Solferino, a particularly brutal event in the Austro-Sardinian War (1859). A Swiss philanthropist who was touring Italy at the time saw the battlefield on the day after 40,000 casualties were sustained. Jean Henri Dunant was horrified not only at the numbers of the dead, but especially by the intense suffering of the wounded, the paucity of medical care, and the dying of the untended. In 1862 he published a pamphlet titled *Un Souvenir de Solferino* (A Recollection of Solferino). He concluded his graphic description of the suffering he had witnessed by appealing for all civilized countries to found permanent societies of volunteers who would give help to the wounded in times of war and disaster. Dunant's plea led directly to the establishment of the International Red Cross Movement and indirectly to the subsequent beginnings of the Red Crescent Societies (in Islamic cultures) and Red Star Society (in Israel).

Unexpected results sometimes followed battles in ancient times as well. The aftermath of an especially difficult defeat of the armies of Israel led to a stunning new reality. This defeat (in a battle whose cause, combatants, and time frame have long since been forgotten) led a poet who was also prophet and sage to reassert, under the leading of the Spirit, one of God's greatest promises to His people, God's everlasting covenant with David.

In the nineteenth century, Jean Henri Dunant wrote his booklet and founded societies that function for the good of mankind throughout the world. In biblical times, Ethan the Ezrahite wrote a song that has continuing, climactic ramifications for the good of mankind for the rest of world history. Ethan's song, written after a terrible battle in ancient Israel's history, is now known as Psalm 89. This psalm and its basic theology form the subject of this essay.

An Examination of Psalm 89

AUTHOR AND SETTING

The superscription to Psalm 89 reads, "A Maskil of Ethan the Ezrahite." Each of these words calls for attention; each presents some uncertainty. The word "Maskil" is merely a transliteration of the Hebrew term, a sign of the uncertainty of modern translators concerning the meaning of this somewhat obscure term. The principal suggestions as to its meaning are "contemplative," "didactic," or "skillful" (all noted in the NASB margin). The presumed root for this term is the Hebrew verb *śā-kal* in a Hiphil participial form meaning, "giving attention to" or "pondering."[1] This word is used once in the text of a psalm: "For God is the King of all the earth; sing praises with a skillful psalm" (Ps. 47:7 [v. 8, Heb.]). Elsewhere it is used in the superscriptions of thirteen psalms.[2]

The name Ethan (perhaps meaning "perennial," "ever-flowing" —as in Amos 5:24, of an ever-flowing wadi) is found in 1 Kings 4:31 (5:11, Heb.), along with Heman (of Psalm 88) and other wise men, whose wisdom was surpassed by Solomon's. An Ethan is also associated with a Heman and with Asaph as royal appointees at the time of David the great king (1 Chron. 15:19). This Ethan was a Levite, the son of Kushaiah (v. 17), a singer, who with Heman and Asaph was granted the privilege of sounding bronze cymbals in the festive worship that attended bringing the holy ark to Jerusalem.[3]

1. See Francis Brown, S. R. Driver, and Charles A. Briggs, eds., *A Hebrew and English Lexicon of the Old Testament* (Oxford: Clarendon, 1907), p. 968*d*.
2. In addition to Ps.89, this word is found in the superscription to six psalms attributed to David (Pss. 32, 52, 53, 54, 55, 142), three attributed to the sons of Korah (Pss. 42, 44, 45), two attributed to Asaph (Pss. 74, 78), and one to the sons of Korah and to Heman the Ezrahite (Ps. 88).
3. This Ethan is best identified as the son of Kishi of the family of Merari (1 Chron. 6:44 [v. 29, Heb.]). He should be distinguished, then, from the Ethan (and Heman) son of Zerah, from Judah (2:6), and from the Ethan son of Zimmah of the family of Asaph (6:42 [v. 27, Heb.]).

It appears that Ethan's name was later changed to Jeduthun (perhaps meaning, "the confessor"; see 1 Chron. 25:1, 3, 6), as this is the name associated with Asaph and Heman in the list of the principal families of musicians David appointed for musical leadership in the worship of God. Since an aptitude for music may be transmitted along family lines (witness the celebrated Bach family), it is of interest that Ethan (Jeduthun), Asaph, and Heman were not only great musicians in their own right; they were founders of musical families who ministered to the Lord (1 Chron. 25). Moreover, these were not just singers and players. They used their music in prophesying the word of God (1 Chron. 25:1).

Asaph, Ethan-Jeduthun, and Heman became proverbial in Israel. They tied together music, wisdom, and prophecy. Ethan-Jeduthun also established a distinct musical style. "After the manner of Jeduthun" appears in the titles to three psalms (39, 62, 77). He also founded a perpetual choir, "the sons of Jeduthun" (1 Chron. 16:42; 25:1, 3).

The third term in the superscription that is problematic is the descriptive "the Ezrahite." Ordinarily we would understand a word such as this as a gentilic, a family name, or a place of origin. Some would associate this term with the family of Zerah. Indeed, there is an Ethan (and a Heman) listed in the family of Zerah in 1 Chronicles 2:6. But this is part of the family history of Judah (see v. 3); our Ethan was a Levite, as we have already noted. It is likely that the term "Ezrahite" is to be associated with a word meaning "native born," that is, one who is a true Hebrew musician rather than one from foreign soil.[4]

But having said all this, we still have very little knowledge about when this psalm was written or under what specific circumstance. It seems likely that the ancient tradition in the superscription indicates that the author of the poem is the Ethan-Jeduthun who was David's contemporary.[5] The nature of the conflict that underlies the poem is not known. All we know is that the poet was not only a great musician, he was also a sage and a prophet. The poem is a device, not an artifice, for the proclamation of the word of God in a time of great stress. It also allows for complaint to God and for resolution and renewal of hope based upon

---

4. Contra BDB, p. 280c, but so Mitchell Dahood, *Psalms II: 51-100*, The Anchor Bible (Garden City, N.Y.: Doubleday, 1968), p. 308.

5. Many scholars do not believe there is material of historical or practical interest in the superscriptions. But even though the superscriptions were not part of the psalms as written, they are a part of the psalms as transmitted from ancient times. We may regard them as (reliable) indicators from a primitive period in the transmission of the poems as to their author, setting, and, sometimes, their interpretation.

the great covenant of love that Yahweh had established with His servant David.[6]

AN ANALYTIC OVERVIEW

Psalm 89 is a remarkable poetic work of considerable length in the Hebrew psalter. It has a number of discrete sections, which we may call strophes or movements. Here is an overview of the poem:

Superscription (in the title; v. 1 in Hebrew text).

I. An introductory statement of praise to the Lord for His everlasting covenant with David the great king (vv. 1-4).

II. A celebration of the Lord who has established His gracious covenant with David (vv. 5-18).

6. Perhaps the present psalm is a composite of two parts. The tone of this psalm through v. 37 is one of constant affirmation of the *ḥesed* (loyal love) of Yahweh to His covenant with David. Until v. 38 there is no hint of trouble. It could well be that this part of the poem was written by a contemporary of David (Ethan the Ezrahite) who celebrated with him the Lord's goodness (see David's prayer, 2 Sam. 7:18-29). Psalm 89:38 (v. 39, Heb.) is as abrupt a change as is possible in literature. And the text concludes in verse 51 with no resolution to the disaster alluded to within this grim unit. Kidner notes that the wording is similar to that of Lamentations and would be an appropriate response for one devastated by the destruction of Jerusalem by the Babylonians in 586 B.C. (Derek Kidner, *Psalms 73-150* [Downers Grove, Ill.: InterVarsity, 1975], pp. 324-25).

We already know that there is one addition to the poem (v. 52, the blessing addendum). We have examples of other poems that are composites. Psalm 108, for example, is a composite of sections of Ps. 57 (Ps. 108:1-5 = 57:7-11) and Ps. 60 (Ps. 108:6-13 = 60:5-12). If this is the case, then the last part of Ps. 89 would have been written by a poet hundreds of years after the first section was written, a poet who was devastated by the disaster of his lifetime. Yet, the fact that he penned his dour words on the poem that speaks so ebulliently of faith in the covenant suggests that he hoped against hope that the reality of the covenant would finally be accomplished. Such likely was the thought of the editor who included the psalm in the collection and appended the words of v. 52. One only blesses God when there is continuing faith in Him to do what He said He will do.

Another approach, of course, is to posit the entire psalm as a near-exilic or a post-exilic composition. This is done not only by some critical scholars, but even by more conservative writers, e.g., J. J. Stewart Perowne, *The Book of Psalms*, 2 vols. (reprint, Grand Rapids: Zondervan, 1966), 2:146: "There can be little doubt that this Psalm was written in the latter days of the Jewish monarchy, when the throne of David had fallen or was already tottering to its fall, and when the prospect for the future was so dark that it seemed as if God had forgotten His covenant and His promise."

But we should not move too quickly to assume diverse authorship, composite structure, or a near-exilic/post-exilic origin. Weiser, for example, sees no compelling reason to pinpoint the disaster of this poem at the Babylonian captivity. He believes that it could have been used at any time of national disaster, just as Ps. 18, along with Pss. 2, 110, and 132. See Artur Weiser, *The Psalms: A Commentary*, trans. by Herbert Hartwell (Philadelphia: Westminster, 1962), p. 591. This view is also suggested by Leopold Sabourin, *The Psalms: Their Origin and Meaning* (New York: Alba, 1973), p. 353.

A. In praise of His incomparability (vv. 5-8).
B. In praise of His wonders (vv. 9-14).
C. In praise of His blessings (vv. 15-18).

III. A recital of the content of the Lord's gracious covenant with David (vv. 19-37).

A. The promise detailed (vv. 19-29).
B. The provisions described (vv. 30-34).
C. The permanence defined (vv. 35-37).

IV. An expression of consternation to the Lord at a time of distress, when it seemed that the covenant was no longer in force (vv. 38-45).

V. A double complaint to the Lord to provoke Him to remember His covenant and to restore the fortunes of His people (vv. 46-51).

A. A complaint based on the brevity of life (vv. 46-48).
B. A complaint based on the nature of the enemies (vv. 49-51).

VI. An appendix of blessing (v. 52).

AN ANGRY ACCUSATION (89:38-45)

We begin our study of the psalm at the end, or near the end. As Bruce K. Waltke once described in a chapel message at Dallas Theological Seminary,[7] the study of some psalms is akin to putting on an overcoat. They have to be approached from the inside out in order for the reader to have a sense of direction, a handle as to their meaning.

Psalm 89, which begins with celebration, actually is built upon considerable consternation. Verse 38 sets the mood:

> But Thou hast cast off and rejected,
> Thou hast been full of wrath against Thine anointed.

These words present an accusation against God that forms part of the "You" aspect of the lament psalms.[8] The psalmist says that the very thing God swore not to do is precisely what He has done. What God has done, it seems, is to forget His own promise, it is to cast away His people, to trash His own covenant. The language of the verse is striking. A more forceful rendering is:

7. This was about Ps. 90, delivered, to the best of my memory, during the 1966-67 school year.
8. These psalms feature three pronouns: "I" (am hurting), "You" (do not care, God), and "they" (are winning). See Ronald B. Allen, *Lord of Song: The Messiah Revealed in the Psalms* (Portland, Ore.: Multnomah, 1985), pp. 103-18.

> But as for You, You have thoroughly rejected,
> You are infuriated with Your anointed one.

The first half of the verse is marked by *hendiadys:*[9] "You have spurned and You have rejected" = "You have thoroughly rejected." The object of the verbs is not expressed; the delay for the second colon is dramatic. The word "your anointed" (*mĕšîḥekā*, "your messiah") is stunning, particularly following the harsh verb, "to be infuriated with" (for other uses, see Deut. 3:26; Ps. 78:21, 59, 62).

The language here is invigorated, a paroxysm of pain, a riot of passion. The pronoun "You" is emphasized by the so-called redundant, independent pronoun,[10] marked off by the *waw* disjunctive, followed by two verbs describing rejection and a rare, strong verb for fury. The word "anointed" is further marked by the pronoun suffix "your."

These are words of incredulity. Of what is God thinking? How could He forget? What has happened? Where is God's *ḥesed,* His "loyal love"? What has become of His oath which was to outlast the sun, moon, and stars? And so through time it seems the same. Who today—even among those who claim to be people of faith—really believes in the coming rule of the great son of David? Is it not only a minority of the confessing church who still have this hope?

Israel today is a puny state, contentious and factional, sometimes seeming bent on destroying itself. Its great victories of 1948 and 1967 are old. More prominent are the near disasters of the 1973 Yom Kippur War, the awful period of Lebanese occupation in the 80s, the long wars of attrition against terrorists, the *intefadah* of the late 80s and early 90s, loss of esteem among the nations, a sense at times of not caring about world opinion. Who today dares dream of the revived Davidic kingdom? On the occasion of the 40th anniversary of the state of Israel in 1988, writers on prophetic themes found difficulty even in getting Christian book publishers interested in the idea of Israel and prophecy. Indeed, before the Gulf War of 1991, it appeared that interest in biblical prophecy was at an all-time low in the twentieth century.

The rest of the verses in Psalm 89:38-45 hammer away in the attack on the actions of God. He is addressed directly with words of fury and anger. He is charged with abhorring His covenant, defiling the crown of His servant (vv. 38-39). God has done what God would not do. He has done this in an unexpected military defeat, where walls and

---

9. A Greek word meaning "one-through-two," *hendiadys* speaks of two words or phrases used to express one idea more forcibly.

10. Indeed, there is even a MS tradition that adds a second "but you" before the second verb: "But as for you, you have cast off, and as for you, you have rejected."

strongholds are destroyed (v. 40), where the people suffer greatly in battle (v. 43), where the enemies rejoice over this event (vv. 41-42), and where the anointed of God suffers loss of glory and youth, and grim gain of shame (vv. 44-45).

The language throughout is that of hyperbole. The point is clear, however. The nation and its king have been made defenseless. Anyone is able to pluck at them at will. Their neighbors laugh at them and at their God who should stand in their defense. God has turned back the edge of the sword of His anointed (v. 43a), an idiom that may mean, He has dulled his blade. As a ball player may be said to lose his edge, so the swordsman finds his blade ineffective. It is as though God has deliberately acted in degrading His king, despite His royal promise for the line of David. The humiliation is complete, the pain insufferable.

THE DOUBLE COMPLAINT (89:46-51)

The energy of the section of consternation (vv. 38-45) is marked and dramatic. The attack on God's turning on His anointed is sustained, direct, and impassioned. God has done what God will not do. This is the recurring image. Two brief sections follow; these form a double complaint. The first (vv. 46-48) views the brevity of life. The second (vv. 49-51) focuses on the infamy of the enemies.

The first complaint begins with classic language of lament, "How long, O Lord?" (see Pss. 13, 35). The underlying idea is posited on the notion of the eternality of God. If God is angry, will His anger last forever? If God is forgetful, will He never remember? If God has turned away, will He never return? In verse 47 it is possible that the king himself is given the words to speak. The language is hurtful, ironic, barbed. Here is a more dramatic rendering:

> Remember!
> As for me, how transient is my life!
> For what vanity—
> have You created all mankind?

Here is a desperate verse from a desperate person. Alone and helpless, he considers his end, his death, and the gaping jaws of Sheol (v. 48). Unless God Himself intervenes soon, there will be nothing left of him—and nothing left of the promise of God to him.

The second complaint (vv. 49-51) centers on the response of the enemies at the fall of God's servant. As in other psalms of lament, the psalmist is aware of the effects on others of his fall (see Ps. 13:4). His fall is more than just the loss of one individual. His fall will affect the way others think of God Himself. The enemies of God will find the fall of

God's man to be just another excuse to reproach the Lord, to scorn His Word, to reject His promise. The wording of verse 51 is climactic, ending in the words "Thine anointed." The reproach of the enemies will be boundless when the one anointed by God Himself is found to be in utter ruin.

And so the psalm ends. The poem ends in weary despair, in a resignation of disaster. But there is another verse, which turns the psalm to hope.

THE CLOSING BLESSING (89:52)

An unsophisticated reader of the Psalms might come to verse 52 and simply conclude that this is the natural last verse of the poem. Actually, this verse is the conclusion of a set of psalms (Pss. 73-89) that forms Book 3 in the pentateuch of praise. As the books of Moses are grouped in a set of five books (a "pentateuch"), so the hymns of Israel are divided into five sets to form a fivefold response of praise. Each of the books ends in a coda of blessing to the Lord:

Book 1	Psalms 1-41	ends in the blessing of 41:13.
Book 2	Psalms 42-72	ends in the blessing of 72:18-19.
Book 3	Psalms 73-89	ends in the blessing of 89:52.
Book 4	Psalms 90-106	ends in the blessing of 106:48.
Book 5	Psalms 107-150	ends in the celebrative Psalm 150.[11]

As the superscriptions were added to the psalms after the time of composition, so the poetic addenda to Psalms 41, 72, 89, and 106 were also later additions of editors who shaped the Psalter for Temple worship. The fact that this particular psalm ends in a sense of helplessness in verse 51 but in blessing of God in verse 52 is a fitting, prophetic shift of mood. The very fact that the poem became part of the singing of Israel suggests that finally hope was restored, faith was renewed.

We conclude that the addition of verse 52 is Spirit-directed. The natural reading of the poem by the "unsophisticated" reader proves to be correct. This verse is the new conclusion to the poem—its refined, "natural" ending.

Now, with a sense of the original ending of pain and the new ending of blessing, we may turn to the beginning of the poem. We lift the overcoat of this psalm upon our shoulders, insert arms in sleeves, and take on the meaning of the psalm as it envelops our being.

---

11. See Ronald Barclay Allen, *Praise! A Matter of Life and Breath* (Nashville: Thomas Nelson, 1980), pp. 98-108.

THE INTRODUCTORY PRAISE (89:1-4)

Without question, the key word of this psalm is *ḥesed*, rendered "loving-kindness" in the NASB (and "great love" in the NIV).[12] Many people have learned to sing the words of verse 1 of this psalm in the setting of a modern chorus, based upon the wording of the King James Version:

> I will sing of the mercies of the Lord forever:
> With my mouth will I make known thy faithfulness
> to all generations.

I suspect that few of the tens of thousands who sing this chorus on a given day of public worship have any real idea of its setting in the context of this psalm. Do not most people who sing of the "mercies" of the Lord have in mind His kindness in their lives ranging from eternal salvation to daily protection, from a sense of His nearness to an idea of His love? But while all of these ideas are worthy and appropriate, they are not the intent of this verse in the context of this psalm.

The issue of this psalm is the loyalty of Yahweh to the covenant He made with His servant David, an issue seen clearly by reading verses 1-4 as a unit. The loyal love of Yahweh is not only established forever, it is fixed in the very heavens (v. 2)—the dwelling place of God Himself.

The term "mercies" or "loving-kindness" of God in Psalm 89 is specific, not general: the word refers to God's everlasting promise to David to establish his throne forever in Jerusalem with his seed as the enduring king (vv. 3-4). The sure mercies of Yahweh in Psalm 89 center on the Davidic Covenant of 2 Samuel 7. The term *ḥesed*, which has been

---

12. The term *ḥesed* is paired with the word *'ĕmûnâ*, "faithfulness," a common linking in the poetry of the Bible. Further, the word *'ôlām*, "forever," is linked to the two in verse 1. Interestingly, each of these three key words found in the first verse of the poem are found seven times in the psalm. Here is a listing (English verse numbers, with suffixes as noted):

ḥesed	*'ĕmûnâ*	*'ôlām*
v. 1 (pl)	v. 1 (plus 2ms)	v. 1
v. 2	v. 2 (plus 2ms)	v. 2
v. 14	v. 5 (plus 2ms)	v. 4
v. 24 (plus 1cs)	v. 8 (plus 2ms)	v. 28
v. 28 (plus 1cs)	v. 24 (plus 1cs)	v. 36
v. 33 (plus 1cs)	v. 33 (plus 1cs)	v. 37
v. 49 (pl; plus 2ms)	v. 49 (plus 2ms)	v. 52

Other words used with significant frequency include *bᵉrît*, "covenant" (four times: vv. 3, 28, 34, 39); *kisē'*, "throne" (five times: vv. 4 [plus 2ms], 14 [plus 2ms, of God], 29 [plus 3ms], 36 [plus 3ms], 44 [plus 3ms]); "David (my/thy) servant" (six times: vv. 3, 20, 35 ["David"], 39 ["thy servant"], 49 ["David"], 50 ["thy servants"]).

translated in a wide variety of ways, ties together the notions of love or mercy with loyalty or faithfulness. In general, one splendid way to tie these two ideas together is to translate *ḥesed* by "loyal love." The alliteration is attractive; the pairing is significant. Whom God loves, He loves in loyalty. He is faithful to the one whom He loves. In Psalm 89:1 the word *ḥesed* is in the plural, likely an intensification of the meaning of the word. Perhaps in this verse the rendering might be "abundant love" to draw out the significance of this plural. Hence, we may render the first verse in this manner:

> I am determined to sing praises forever
> > concerning the abundant love of Yahweh.
> To one generation after another
> > I will make known with my mouth Your faithfulness.

There are several features in this translation that are significant: (1) the cohortative of the first verb speaks of the firm determination of the psalmist;[13] (2) the phrase "with my mouth" emphasizes the vocal nature of biblical praise;[14] (3) the word "forever" is an exuberant promise of the psalmist to keep on singing throughout all of life—and beyond; (4) the focus, as noted, is on the *ḥesed*, the loyal love, or abundant love, and on the faithfulness of God—as found in His covenant with David (v. 3).

It is in verses 3 and 4 that the heart of the matter is stated. The poet expresses the words of God:

> "I have made a covenant with My chosen;
> I have sworn to David My servant,
> I will establish your seed forever,
> And build up your throne to all generations."

The words of these verses are deliberate, emphatic, precise. They are words of covenant, explicitly and formally. They recall the wording of God's covenant with Abram (Abraham) in Genesis 12, 15, and 22. They are every bit as strong as anything from Mt. Sinai in God's language to Moses. They are as remarkable as the wording of the (re)-new(ed) covenant in Jeremiah 30-33. Here are the effective words of Yahweh's oath to make of the seed of David a king forever. The poet who

---

13. The cohortative in Hebrew is the volitional form (appeal to the will) for the first person. In general, it may have one of three basic ideas: (1) an expression of wistful desire ("O that I might"), (2) a request for permission ("May I?"), and (3) a statement of determination ("I am determined to do this"). In this poem, surely the last is the proper choice.

14. Allen, *Praise!*, pp. 57-72.

is a seer, a royal prophet as well as a Temple musician, declares the oracles of God, a musical rendition of the prophecy of Nathan to David in 2 Samuel 7.

The subject matter of the psalm could not be clearer. Yet, we repeat, countless thousands sing the chorus of the "mercies of the Lord" with little idea of what those mercies are in this text.

THE COVENANT MAKER (89:5-18)

After the introductory setting of the praise of God for His establishment of covenant promise with David (vv. 1-4), the poet then provides a rhapsody of praise to God who is covenant maker. He is praised for three excellencies: (1) His incomparability (vv. 5-8); (2) His wonders (vv. 9-14); and (3) His blessing (vv. 15-18). For purposes of this essay, (reluctantly) we move quickly through this section. Yet these are significant issues, major foci for the praise of God.

That God is incomparable is a major feature of the prophetic theology of the Hebrew Bible. In a world filled with (imaginary) deities, the prophets shouted that Yahweh alone is God. They picked up the words of the great *Shema*, which climax in the shout "Yahweh alone."[15] They cut through the folly of their age—and ours—and said that there is no other god, only the Lord (Isa. 40). In a world of shabby god-substitutes, the poets spoke of God as greater (Ps. 96:4); but then they shouted that He who is greater than other gods is the only God there is (Ps. 96:5).

The point in Psalm 89 with reference to the incomparability of God is that only He would make such a covenant; only He would be faithful to it. There is none in the universe to be compared to the Lord (v. 6); His faithfulness surrounds Him like an awesome robe (v. 8).

Not only is He incomparable, but also the Lord of covenant is God of wonders. This is the thrust of verses 9-14. The sea, a symbol of malevolent, raging power is no match for Him (v. 9). And Rahab, the dragon of the deep, is but an impotent plaything, bobbing in the seas before Him (v. 10).[16] All things are impotent before Him, and all take joy in Him, for He alone is Creator (vv. 11, 12). Still He is strong; unlike the

---

15. Deuteronomy 6:4 is best rendered: "Hear, O Israel: Yahweh, our God! Yahweh alone!" See Ronald B. Allen, "Trinitarianism: How the God of Scripture Differs from the God of the Rabbis," *To the Jew First*, ed. J. I. Packer, Donald Hagner, and Vernon Grounds (London: Paternoster, forthcoming).

16. See Ronald B. Allen, *Rediscovering Prophecy: A New Song for a New Kingdom* (Portland, Ore.: Multnomah, 1986), pp. 55-68, for a development of the themes of water and dragon gods borrowed from Canaanite mythology, used by the poets of the Bible to speak of the incomparable power and wonder of Yahweh, Lord of creation. See also Elmer B. Smick, "Mythopoetic Language in the Psalms," *Westminster Theological Journal* 49 (1982):88-98.

gods of imagination who mirror the weaknesses and selfishnesses of man, the God of Scripture is powerful (v. 13) and ever-righteous (v. 14).

Again, all these excellencies are to be seen in the context of the covenant God made with David. The one who made this covenant is unique; only He is holy. The one who made this covenant is powerful; only He is Creator. The one who made this covenant is reliable; only He holds out His strong arm. The one who made this covenant is true; His loyal love and faithfulness exude from His presence.

The poet then rhapsodizes on the blessing of Yahweh (vv. 15-18), affirming that there is no people on earth so blessed as that people whose God is the Lord. When one walks in the light of God, there is joy, victory, and sublime comfort. The battle cry of the King is in their midst (see Num. 23:21). This is more than the "joyful sound" (Ps. 89:15, NASB). It is the triumphal blast of the trumpet of God (Ex. 19:19; cf. 1 Thess. 4:16). By verse 18 the point is made clear. Here is a personal translation:

> Surely, our shield belongs to Yahweh,
>   Even our King to the Holy One of Israel.

The king of Israel is unlike the kings of the nations. They may have come to power by acts of virtue or violence; they may be usurpers or of royal blood. But their right to reign is conditional on whims of fortune and populace and machinations of good and evil men.

But the king of Israel, alone of earthly monarchs, truly rules by divine right. Later in world history, European kings would assert the same of themselves. Such is fiction. Only the king of Israel, David the anointed of Yahweh, is the ruler who is God's special possession, chosen vessel, anointed ruler. Other kings and potentates rule by His leave, are used for His purposes, even accomplish His will. But none other is in covenant with Him as was Israel's king. He alone, the people's shield, was the Lord's regent on earth.

With these words of exuberant praise to Yahweh, King of Israel, whose covenant king rules by His grace, the setting is now established to recite the content of the covenant announced in the opening of the psalm.

THE DAVIDIC COVENANT (89:19-37)

The heart of the psalm is in verses 19-37. Here we find an artistic rephrasing of the elements of the covenant Yahweh made with David as recorded in 2 Samuel 7. The song has three movements in this larger section: (1) the promise of the covenant (vv. 19-29); (2) the provision of the covenant (vv. 30-34); and (3) the permanence of the covenant (vv. 35-37).

The first movement, focusing on the nature of the promise, begins in a dramatic manner. Here is a personal translation:

> Then You spoke in a vision to Your faithful one,[17]
> and You said,
> "I have set power[18] on a hero,[19]
> I have exalted one chosen[20] from among the people."

The sovereign choice of David, through prophetic sanction, was followed by anointing with olive oil (1 Sam. 16:13), a point of song in Psalm 89:20. While it was through the agency of Samuel, it was the work of God.

As God promised that He would bless all those who would bless Abram, and would curse one who treated him in a trifling manner (Gen. 12:3), so God speaks of His blessing on David and His cursing on any who would rise against David (Ps. 89:21, 23). There is the power of God on his life; the hand and arm of God, so active in redemption from Egypt (Ex. 15:6), now are powerful over David. There is a sense that to strike at David is to strike at God Himself, so closely does God identify Himself with His servant David. As the king is shield to his people (v. 18), so God is shield to His king.

17. The text of the NASB reads this word as a plural ("Thy godly ones"); the singular, found in many Hebrew manuscripts, is likely preferable here because Nathan seems to be intended. This view is held, with reservations (based on tradition-criticism), by Hans-Joachim Kraus, *Psalms 60-150: A Commentary*, trans. Hilton C. Oswald (Minneapolis: Augsburg, 1989), pp. 200, 208. However, one may grant that the plural is less expected and perhaps the harder reading that scribes might have wished to smooth to a singular. If so, then the "godly ones" or "faithful ones" would include other persons who had oracles from God concerning the coming one (including Abram, who heard a promise concerning the seed [Gen. 12:1-3; 22:18], and the words of Jacob concerning the one who will come to reign [Gen. 49:10]). With respect to David's lifetime, the prophets Samuel (1 Sam. 16:6-13) and Nathan (2 Sam. 7) would both be included.

18. The NASB reads "help," the traditional rendering for the Hebrew noun *'ēzer*. It is now believed that there are two roots with this spelling that have been confused in our dictionaries. One root begins with the Hebrew letter *'ayin*. The other begins with the stronger laryngeal not found in biblical Hebrew, but in Arabic and Ugaritic (*'gayin*). The former word means "help," and the latter means "power." In this passage it is "power" that is demanded (so NIV). See Walter C. Kaiser, Jr., *Hard Sayings of the Old Testament* (Downers Grove, Ill.: InterVarsity, 1988), pp. 22-26.

19. The Hebrew term *gibbôr* means "hero," and is particularly apt for David (recall the stunning story of his victory over Goliath when he was too young to be conscripted into Israel's army, and too small of stature to wear the armor of the king, 1 Sam. 17). One day there will be another, greater hero. This one is *'ēl gibbôr*, "heroic deity" (Isa. 9:6 [v. 5, Heb.]).

20. The term "chosen" was used earlier in verse 3, a splendid parallel with the phrase "David My servant." Here the divine election of David is recounted; he is one selected by God for his own sovereign reasons (1 Sam. 16:6-13). Because the Lord looks on the heart, not on the outward appearance (v. 7), His choice is not the expected one—but it is the correct one.

The "star of David" (with six points) is a well-known symbol of the Hebrew people. The flag of the modern state of Israel shows this star embedded on a prayer shawl (*tallit*). It is now believed that this star is anachronistic to the time of David. But nonetheless, it is a suitable symbol for us to think rightly about the Davidic ideal. Properly, the star is called *magen david*, the "shield of David." It may be regarded as a dual symbol of interlocking triangles. As the Lord is shield to His king, so the king is shield to his people.

The real power of the Davidic reign is seen in verse 24. David's power comes from the Lord. It is the Lord's *ḥesed*, loyal love, that establishes his throne. It is His *'ĕmûnâ*, faithfulness, that gives direction to David's power. For David is stand-in for the King above, concerning whom *ḥesed* and *'ĕmûnâ* are characteristic excellencies (see Ps. 100:5). David is also prototype of the coming King, whose rule will be established in justice and righteousness (see Pss. 96:13; 98:9; Isa. 9:7). Hence, it "is in My name" (Ps. 89:24*b*; cf. v. 16*a*) that the horn (i.e., power, see Num. 24:8) of David will be exalted (see Ps. 89:18). These are threads that are intricately interwoven through the fabric of this psalm.

When the psalmist says that David's hand will be on the sea and the rivers (Ps. 89:25), we discover a link with the ongoing theology of deliverance that reaches from one testament to the other. The first reference in this language is likely to the extent of his reign, that is, from sea to rivers, which means from the Mediterranean to the land of the two rivers (Mesopotamia).[21] By this expansive use of language, we sense something of the divine intention for the extent of the rule of David and his posterity, in fulfillment of earlier promises made to Abram in Genesis 15.

But the language of having one's hands on the sea and the rivers is also a metaphor of power over nature, of control over the elements of hapless rage in the mythopoetic language of the ancient world. This is a piece of the *Heilsgeschichte* (holy, salvation history) that marks the continuity of Scripture leading to the Person of the Savior Jesus.[22]

---

21. Magne Saebø, "Vom Grossreich zum Weltreich," *Vetus Testamentum* 28 (1978), 83-91. The description of a world empire is not so much territorial, he argues, as "theological."

22. Ronald B. Allen, "Is There *Heil* for *Heilsgeschichte*?" paper presented to the Evangelical Theological Society, Jackson, Miss., 1976. The term *Heilsgeschichte* speaks of the forward-directedness of Scripture that culminates in Jesus Christ, the goal of saving history. As described by J. C. K. von Hofmann, *Heilsgeschichte* is not a meaning in Scripture that is "above" history (or separate from history), but the meaning of Scripture that is *in* history. All history has its meaning in Jesus Christ, the "original world-goal" (*das ürbildliche Weltzeil*) to which *Heilsgeschichte* aims and from which it obtains its sense. See Hans-Joachim Kraus, *Die Biblische Theologie: Ihre Geschichte und Problematic* (Neukirchen-Vluyn, Germany: Neukirchener Verlag, 1970), pp. 247-53.

At the beginning, all was wrapped in a murky, watery abyss (Gen. 1:2). But God separated the dry land from the waters as a part of His work in the emerging cosmos (v. 6). In the great saving event of the OT, God's hand was on the sea in the deliverance of Israel from Egypt (Ex. 15). The Creator's hand is on the "sea" in the continual control He exerts over His creation (Ps. 93). Jesus' hand is on the sea as He calms the storms of Galilee (Luke 8:22-25). David is a part of that continuity, pointing ever to the coming one who is his greater son. David is given divine unction to be as god on earth for God who is in heaven. One day God Himself will be on earth—in the Person of Jesus Christ, the goal of all saving history. One day—can this be?—the sea no longer will exist (Rev. 21:1).

It is in Psalm 89:26-27 that we confront the central words of God's covenant with David:

> "He will cry to Me, 'Thou art my Father,
>   My God, and the rock of my salvation.'
> I also shall make him My first-born,
>   the highest of the kings of the earth."

As is generally well-known, there is a paucity of the use of father-son language of God and His people in the pages of the Hebrew Scriptures. This is not to say that the notion was unknown, only that it was seldom stated explicitly that God is the Father of His people.[23] On some occasions we read of God as the Father of Israel (see Ex. 4:22-23; Isa. 63:16; 64:8; Jer. 31:9; Hos. 11:1). The background for this language is probably the ancient Near Eastern suzerain-vassal treaty, where the terms "father" and "son" were used to designate the suzerain and vassal, respectively.[24] For example, in the Amarna letters the vassal often affirms his loyalty to his suzerain with the words: "You are my father and over-lord and I am your son."[25] Second Kings 16:7 supplies a biblical example. Here Ahaz calls himself the "son" of Tiglath-pileser, his suzerain.

When father-son language is used of God's relationship to the Davidic king, the background appears to be the ancient Near Eastern royal grant in which a faithful vassal was rewarded for his loyalty and service. In such cases the lord would sometimes elevate his subject to the status of "sonship" in conjunction with giving the vassal an "eternal"

---

23. See Willem A. VanGemeran, "'*Abbā*' in the Old Testament?" *Journal of the Evangelical Theological Society* 31 (December 1988):385-98.

24. See E. Lipinski, *Le poème royal du Ps. 89:1-5, 20-38*, pp. 57-66, and F. Charles Fensham, "Father and Son as Terminology for Treaty and Covenant," *Near Eastern Studies in Honor of W. F. Albright,* pp. 121-35, ed. Hans Goedicke (Baltimore: Johns Hopkins, 1971).

25. Fensham, "Father and Son," pp. 126-28, 130.

gift involving land or dynastic succession.[26] This relationship was established in the formidable passage of covenant making, 2 Samuel 7, to
which we now turn.

A Coordinate to Psalm 89

Second Samuel 7 is replete with paronomasia, verbal plays that
serve to enliven the ear and the eye, and paradoxically by these puns, to
call attention to the seriousness of the theology of the text. The first
word that arrests attention in this text is the common term "house"
(*bayit*). David observed that he lived in a lovely house of cedar (vv. 1-2),
a sumptuous palace of solid stone and decorative wood (see 5:11). Concerning his palace David must have had considerable pride, given his
many years living as a soldier, fugitive, and vagabond. Magnanimously,
David decided to build a "house" for the Lord, more specifically for the
Ark of the Covenant. Nathan was supportive of this endeavor.

That night, the Lord spoke to Nathan and redirected him. Now
the word "house" is used in a very restrictive sense; how is it possible,
the Lord asked, that He the eternal one might live in a "house"? When,
He asked, did I ask for a "house"? (7:7). At this point, the Lord was
playing with His prophet, reminding him that there was ever the danger
of substituting God's symbols for God Himself. The Ark was merely a
box; God is Lord of eternity.

But God was going to build a "house" for David (v. 11), that is, a
line of posterity, a family. By this time in his life, David already had plenty of children (see 5:13). God was speaking of more than children when
He said "house." He spoke of a divinely sanctioned line of descent that
ultimately would eventuate in the "seed" of the original promise, the
proto-gospel (Gen. 3:15).[27] This is made clear in 2 Samuel 7:12 in the
term "seed" ("descendant," NASB).

Yet another turn on the term "house" comes in verse 13, where
God says that the seed of David will build a "house for My name." This
multileveled pun on the word "house" is exquisite. David's son will
build a "house" for God (the Temple). But God will build a "house" for
David (the proper, royal line). And God will "establish the throne of his
kingdom forever" (v. 13). The "throne" refers to more than a piece of
furniture. It speaks of the seat of power, the right to rule. Thus, even

---

26. See Moshe Weinfeld, "The Covenant of Grant in the Old Testament and in the Ancient Near East," *Journal of the American Oriental Society* 90 (1970):184-203. Note
   esp. pp. 189 and 191, where he cites parallels to Ps. 2:7.
27. See Walter C. Kaiser, Jr., *Toward an Old Testament Theology* (Grand Rapids: Zondervan, 1978), pp. 77-79.

when there is not a king "on the throne," there continues the right to rule for a proper time when the right king will be established by God.

At this point, we read the central words of the covenant: "I will be a father to him and he will be a son to Me" (v. 14). In these words we hear for the first time the notion of divine adoption of kings in the line of David.[28] As each Davidic successor would be crowned, there would come words from prophets or priests that would enunciate this declaration: "You are My son, and I am your Father." This is what Psalm 2 describes; indeed the words of Psalm 2:7 were likely the very words of declaration used in the coronation ceremony:

> "I will surely tell of the decree
> of the Lord:
> He said to Me, 'Thou art My Son,
> Today I have begotten Thee.'"[29]

The new king would be the genetic descendant of David, but the adopted Son of God. He would be declared to be the regent of heavenly majesty among the people of God. Through him, the people as a whole were the community of God, the family of God. He was their royal symbol, the personification of God's care for His people. Needless to say, for this to work, the king would have to be an extraordinary man of faith and principle. And sad to say, only on rare occasions was the ideal even approximated.

But troubles were anticipated; God is never caught by surprise by sinful mankind. The provision was stated from the beginning: "When he commits iniquity, I will correct him with the rod of men and the strokes of the sons of men" (2 Sam. 7:14b). Clearly, God anticipated rebellious kings, even as a parent may be saddened, but not totally taken by surprise, to discover a rebellious child. The correction of the king would come by the rod of men, that is, by military defeat.

But throughout, there would be no loss of ḥesed: "but My lovingkindness [loyal love] shall not depart from him, as I took it away from Saul, whom I removed from before you" (v. 15). It is this citation of ḥesed that Ethan the Ezrahite built upon in his poem of the king. The covenant is based on the loyal love of Yahweh. Ethan rightly seized upon this word, magnified it, made it the subject of song and the focus of joy.

28. Hans-Joachim Kraus speaks of certain relationships between the language of adoption and declarations of adoption in the Code of Hammurabi (Law 170): "You are my children," a legally valid incorporation into the family group. However, he finds the wording of the Davidic Covenant to be more in line with the language of God's covenant with Israel, particularly as the focus is on the elective choice of God. See *Theology of the Psalms*, trans. Keith Crim (Minneapolis: Augsburg, 1986), p. 114.
29. See Allen, *Rediscovering Prophecy*, pp. 155-72.

The climactic verse in the covenant rings the final changes on the term "house": "And your house and your kingdom shall endure before Me forever; your throne shall be established forever" (v. 16). The "house" of David is his seed, his royal line. The throne of David is the symbol of his right, and the right of his seed, to rule. These continue. These never cease.

We are well aware of the ragged nature of the line of faith in the Davidic line. There were a few godly kings, men such as Asa and Josiah, Uzziah and Hezekiah, and others. But there were more who were wicked than who were faithful. And even the good kings had their flaws, their lapses, their outright rebellions.

So finally, the kingdom came to an end under Babylonian conquest. But even with the defeat of Judah and the destruction of Jerusalem, the line of David was not extinguished, nor was the throne of David (the right to rule) abrogated. The line was devoid of power and the throne was empty, but the "house" continued. That line continued all the way to the turn of time, to the birth of Jesus of Nazareth in the ancestral home of the family of David, Bethlehem, Ephrathah, in fulfillment of prophetic words of Micah, contemporary of Isaiah (Mic. 5:2; Matt. 2:1-6).

Once we know that Jesus of Nazareth is *the* Son of God (see Mark 1:11), then all others who were alive at the time who were also descended from David were akin to the brothers of Solomon. They had the same genetic line, but they were not the chosen seed; they were not the "house," only part of the family; they were not to be kings.

This takes us to the death of Jesus. Remarkably, from a human vantage point, He was declared to be the son, the seed, the fulfillment of the house of David, but on His death He Himself had no son. That is, the line came to an end in Jesus.

But on His resurrection, Jesus succeeds Himself. Even though the thousand-year line from David to Himself ends in Him, He has no need of sons. He is the "original world goal" toward which all the salvation-history of the Hebrew Bible points and culminates. It is in His resurrection that the words of 2 Samuel 7:14 and Psalm 2:7 are quoted to be realized in Him (Acts 13:33; Heb. 1:5; 5:5). He who is the eternal Son of God (as the second member of the Holy Trinity), is the adopted royal Son of God (in fulfillment of the Davidic Covenant).[30]

30. Kraus writes, "Psalm 2:7 is quoted in Acts 13:33 in reference to the resurrection of Jesus Christ. The quotation involves the entire divine saying, following the wording of the Septuagint. Thus the temporal designation *sēmeron* ('today') is used. The 'today' is a reference to the miracle of Easter. Jesus became the 'Son of God' through his resurrection" (*Theology of the Psalms*, p. 183).

As Robert P. Gordon observes, the oracle of Nathan is "the matrix of biblical messianism."[31] Indeed, one verse has a clause that is notoriously difficult to translate that may make this point even more certain. In David's exquisite prayer of gratitude to God for the covenant he had received (2 Sam. 7:18-29), he said at one point, "And this is the custom of man, O Lord God" (v. 19*b*). The Hebrew word rendered "custom" in the NASB is the familiar word *tôrâ*, often translated "law," but better rendered "instruction." In this environment, the phrasing is monumental: "This is the charter for humanity, O Lord Yahweh."[32]

It is difficult to overplay the significance of the Davidic Covenant. Eugene H. Merrill writes, "Beyond any question David knew that God had sovereignly chosen him as an instrument through whom He would bring both temporal and eternal blessing to the world."[33]

Presently we know that Jesus is declared to be the one to fulfill the covenant of David; there is the present anticipation of His return to the earth to assume the throne of the royal house. Presently He is stationed at the right hand of His Father (Ps. 110:1). But one day there will come the command of the Father, "Rule in the midst of Thine enemies" (v. 2). At that time the final battle will begin (Rev. 19:11-21), the King will come in His glory, and the kingdom will be established (20:1-6).[34]

THE HEART OF PSALM 89

And so we return to the psalm of Ethan the Ezrahite, to the heart of his poem, verses 26-29. Here the poet marvelously set to music the covenantal language of 2 Samuel 7:

31. Robert P. Gordon, *I & II Samuel: A Commentary* (Grand Rapids: Zondervan, 1988), p. 236.
32. This is a point argued eloquently by Kaiser, *Toward an Old Testament Theology*, pp. 154-55. How notably weak is the translation "and this too after the manner of great men, O Lord God," the rendering of S. Goldman, *Samuel, The Soncino Books of the Bible* (London: Soncino, 1951), p. 229.
33. *Kingdom of Priests: A History of Israel* (Grand Rapids: Baker, 1987), p. 276.
34. Some, of course, see in the Incarnation the fulfillment of the Davidic Covenant. One author, for example, says that "'fulfilment' comes when the Word of the Son of David, who is the 'Son of God,' makes His dwelling and 'tabernacles' among us (John 1.14)" (Hans Wilhelm Hertzberg, *I & II Samuel: A Commentary*, trans. J. S. Bowden, The Old Testament Library [Philadelphia: Westminster, 1964], p. 287). Certainly some form of fulfillment comes in the Incarnation, the dwelling of the Word with man. But Hertzberg's quotation marks around the word "fulfilment" suggest his own temerity at using that word about Christ's first coming when the details of the covenant are examined. Surely the text cannot be *fulfilled* until the scion of David rules on Mt. Zion.

> "He will cry to Me, 'Thou art my Father,
> My God, and the rock of my salvation.'
> I also shall make him My first-born,
> The highest of the kings of the earth.
> My loving-kindness [ḥesed] I will keep for him forever,
> And My covenant shall be confirmed to him.
> So I will establish his descendants forever,
> And his throne as the days of heaven."

These words have their first fulfillment in the life of David. They were then to be fulfilled in his successor and in the descendants who followed from his son. But ultimately, these words take us to the Savior-King, Y'shua of Nazareth. As Kidner notes, the words here become overwhelming, heaped as they are on one individual.[35]

Similarly, the words of covenant provisions (vv. 30-34) and covenant permanence (vv. 35-37) are developed from the words of the covenant in 2 Samuel 7. The emphasis throughout is on God's faithfulness to His promise, His loyal love to His covenant. The covenant is made by God Himself. He is unable to lie (see Num. 23:19[36]); God must do what He promises to do (1 Sam. 15:29). Even more personally, God avers through the poem, "I will not lie to David" (Ps. 89:35). Not only may God not deny Himself, and not only is God unable to lie—how could one even think that God might lie to David, one whom He delights to call beloved?

In fact, the covenant that Yahweh established with David is as secure as moon and stars (Ps. 89:37), heavenly witnesses to the faithfulness of the Lord. As a navigator sets his sextant by the faithful witness of a guiding star, so may the person of faith set his or her guidance system on the sure promise of God to His servant David.[37]

So as we come to the end of the center of Ethan's poem, we distinctly sense the heart of God regarding the Davidic Covenant. This is not simply a proposition. This is not simply a factor of life. Here we

35. Kidner, *Psalms 73-150*, p. 323.
36. Ronald B. Allen, "Numbers," in *The Expositor's Bible Commentary*, 5 vols., ed. Frank E. Gaebelein (Grand Rapids: Zondervan, 1990), 2:901.
37. Some scholars see in the references to the moon and a heavenly witness (star or sun) a connection with the "summoning of witnesses" aspect of the old suzerain-vassal treaty patterns known from the Hittite texts. So E. Theodore Mullen, Jr., "The Divine Witness and the Davidic Royal Grant: Ps 89:37-38," *Journal of Biblical Literature* 102 (1983):207-18. A rejoinder is made by Timo Veijola that the "witness" is the Lord Himself; He is both covenant partner and witness to the covenant ("The Witness in the Clouds: Ps 89:38," *JBL* 107 [1988]:413-17). So also Timo Veijola, "Davidverheissung und Staatsvertrag: Beobachtungen zum Einfluss altorientalischer Staatsverträge aud die biblische Sprache am Beispiel von Psalm 89," *Zeitschrift für die alttestamentliche Wissenschaft* 95 (1983):9-31.

sense the nearness of God, His pulsing presence, His beating heart. For ultimately, the covenant Yahweh made with David leads to the Savior-King. The tracks from this poem to the crown of the Lamb are as clear as any tracks in Scripture.

THE AFTERMATH OF PSALM 89

The covenant that God established with David did not die in the disappointment of the experience of the poet who wrote the words of verses 38-51 (see n. 6) as he battled with faith and fear for his generation at a time of overwhelming military defeat.[38] Nor did the covenant die even when more disasters came upon the people of Israel because of their recurring sin. Indeed, God ever held out His promise. Through the great prophet Isaiah (55:3), the covenant words are renewed to a new generation who would respond in faithfulness to God:

Incline your ear and come to Me.
Listen, that you may live;
And I will make an everlasting covenant with you,
According to the faithful [ḥanneʾĕmānîm] mercies
[ḥasdê[39]] shown to David.

Indeed, it is in this context of renewed mercy on His redeemed people that God promises that His word will be effective (Isa. 55:10-11):

For as the rain and the snow come down from heaven,
And do not return there without watering the earth,
And making it bear and sprout,
And furnishing seed to the sower and bread to the eater;
So shall My word be which goes forth from My mouth;
It shall not return to Me empty,
Without accomplishing what I desire,
And without succeeding in the matter for which I sent it.

These lovely words are true of the Word of God in general, of course (as in Ps. 147:15-18). But contextually, this great promise of the effectiveness of the Word of God relates specifically to the promise that was made to David through the prophet Nathan in 2 Samuel 7 and rhap-

---

38. R. J. Clifford argues that Ps. 89 was written as a coherent psalm of communal lament. When the king was powerless, this seemed to negate the power of Yahweh's victory. Most troubling is the defeat of Yahweh's lieutenant, bringing into question the validity of the promise God had made to him. However, the people had faith enough in Yahweh's commission to David to hold God to His promise. Ultimately, the poem is one of hope in realization of the promise ("Psalm 89: A Lament over the Davidic Ruler's Continued Failure," *Harvard Theological Review* 73 [1980]:35-47).
39. Here, of course, is another linking of loyal love (*ḥesed*) and faithfulness.

sodized in song thorough the prophet, sage, and singer Ethan in Psalm 89. God's determination to establish His king on the throne of David is so sure that He repeats His oath with a compelling reference to His own zeal (Isa. 9:7 [italics added]):

> There will be no end to the increase of His government or of
>   peace,
> On the throne of David and over his kingdom,
> To establish it and to uphold it with justice and righteousness
> From then on and forevermore.
> *The zeal of the Lord of hosts will accomplish this.*

Long after the time of Isaiah, the post-exilic writer of the Chronicles still hearkened back to the Davidic Covenant as his source of hope for God's future with His people. When the chronicler rewrote the story of the kings of Judah, he might, because of post-fall Jerusalem, simply have omitted the promise of the Davidic Covenant. But he seized upon it. He cited the promise in the story of Solomon (1 Chron. 22:9-10). Indeed, the organizing principle of the books of Chronicles may well be the promise of God to David. With each king, each royal successor to David, the hope is presented anew, the flame is passed along. At the end of Chronicles (2 Chron. 36:23), there is mention of the edict of Cyrus king of Persia allowing Hebrew peoples to return to the land of promise to rebuild a "house" in Jerusalem for Yahweh, God of heaven. Is it not possible that the Chronicler had the multi-leveled puns on the word "house" in 2 Samuel 7 in mind when he wrote these words? For in re-building a "house" for the Lord, surely there is hope that God will keep His word in rebuilding a "house" for David His servant.

J. Carl Laney presents five prophetic implications of the promise of God to David in the covenant of 2 Samuel 7, as amplified in the song of Psalm 89:

Israel must be preserved as a nation (cf. Jer. 31:35-36);

Israel must be brought back to their land (cf. Deut. 30:1-5);

David's Son, Jesus the Messiah, must return to rule over the covenanted kingdom (cf. Rev. 19:11-16);

A literal, earthly kingdom for Israel must be instituted, over which Christ will reign (cf. Rev. 20:1-4); and

The kingdom must become an eternal kingdom (cf. 1 Cor. 15:24).

Then Laney concludes, "Since God's promise to David was unconditional, the future fulfillment of those events is certain."[40]

---

40. J. Carl Laney, *First and Second Samuel* (Chicago: Moody, 1982), p. 99.

With these words we may simply concur in joy. For in the apostolic preaching of the cross and the resurrection, there is also the promise of the coming crown: "And as for the fact that He raised Him up from the dead, no more to return to decay, He has spoken in this way: 'I will give you the holy and sure blessings of David'" (Acts 13:34; quotation from Isa. 55:3). The "holy and sure blessings of David" concern his throne, his crown, and his rule over planet Earth. One day, the Savior-King will fill these words to a fullness that will stun Nathan, David, Ethan—and each of us.

Even so, come, King Jesus.

4

EVIDENCE FROM ISAIAH 2

JOHN H. SAILHAMER

Associate Professor of Old Testament
Trinity Evangelical Divinity School

THE INTERPRETIVE APPROACHES TO ISAIAH 2:1-5

Interpretive problems in the prophecies of Isaiah are not new in biblical scholarship, particularly problems relating to the question of the Millennium. The central question in understanding Isaiah's prophecies in relation to the Millennium is that of the reference or subject matter of his visions. What the prophet said in describing his visions is usually clear enough. In his view of things there was to be a future time of peace and prosperity for Israel and the nations when God would fulfill His promises to David.[1] Little debate has been raised on those points. The difficulty lies rather in the prophet's intended reference—when and how are Isaiah's visions to be fulfilled? Did he look for a fulfillment in the immediate historical situation in which he lived? Did he look further in the future, within history, of his people or the church? Or, even beyond that, did he have in mind an event that lies outside of, or at the very conclusion of, human history? Before addressing this question specifically for Isaiah's prophecies, it will be helpful to survey some representative approaches to the problem.

---

1. The basis of Isaiah's vision, as with other prophets, is the divine promise to David in 2 Sam. 7.

HISTORICISM

An approach to Isaiah's prophecies that is current today and has deep roots in the history of interpretation is historicism. This approach seeks to explain Isaiah's visions within the horizons of the political and historical aspirations of Israel at the time the visions were given. Though the approach was already known within medieval Judaism,[2] it was not widely held by Christian Bible scholars until the time of Hugo Grotius (1583-1645). Grotius, whose approach to these prophecies of Isaiah has had a far-reaching effect, attempted to explain the prophetic vision within the context of the prophet's own immediate circumstances and without the aid of the NT.[3] Hence for Grotius, all the prophecies in Isaiah 1-36 had their focus and reference in the events of the reign of King Hezekiah.[4] The elevation of the Temple mount in Isaiah 2:2, for example, "looked to a time in which the city of Jerusalem was liberated from the siege of Rezin and Pekah."[5] Grotius did not dispute the contention that the NT writers understood the prophet to be speaking of Christ and His kingdom, but, he explained, that was because they had read Isaiah's words typologically and not in a historical or literal sense. The prophets had not meant their words to be taken typologically, even though that is the way the NT writers understood them. In Grotius's own day such an interpretation of the prophet's words was virtually unthinkable within the bounds of Christian interpretation.[6] In time, however, Grotius's approach gained wide acceptance.[7]

2. Hans-Joachim Kraus, *Geschichte der historisch-kritischen Erforschung des Alten Testaments* (Neukirchen-Vluyn, Germany: Neukirchener Verlag, 1969), pp. 12f.
3. Ibid., pp. 50f; Ludwig Diestel, *Geschichte des Alten Testamentes in der christliche Kirche* (Jena, Germany: Mauke's Verlag, 1869), p. 431.
4. Ibid., p. 433. At times Grotius added to his interpretation the proviso that the words of the prophets may also be read in *sublimiore sensu* as referring to the Christ—though he usually did so indirectly, as with Isa. 2:2, by crediting such views to the Jews.
5. "*Spectat id tempus quo Urbs ab obsidione Rasinis et Phaceae liberata est*" (Hugo Grotius, *Critici Sacri: sive Annotata Doctissimorum Virorum in Vetus ac Novum Testamentum*, ed. John Pearson, Anthony Scattergood, Francis Gouldman, and Richard Pearson [Amsterdam, 1698], 5:46).
6. Gottlob Wilhelm Meyer, *Geschichte der Schrifterklärung seit der Wiederherstellung der Wissenschaften*, Dritter Band (Göttingen, Germany: Johann Friedrich Römer, 1804), p. 436.
7. A characteristic response to Grotius's method among later orthodox and Enlightenment biblical scholars was the approach of "Double Fulfillment." Granted the prophets spoke of events in their own day, their words were not exhausted in those events but continued to have reference points in the ongoing work of God among His people. "Thus, there was more than a *word* for the future; there often were *events* that served as earnests, place-holders, and elements of the predicted Messiah realized in the historical and temporal scene. They acted as encouragements for OT saints to

AMILLENNIALISM

Since the time of Augustine (d. 430) many have interpreted Isaiah's prophecies as referring to the first coming of Christ and the establishment of His church. Such approaches have commonly followed a spiritual[8] reading of the text, that is, either an allegorical or a typological interpretation of Isaiah's visions. On the other hand some have held this view by attempting to see Christ and the church as the literal sense of Isaiah's prophecies. The view of Johannes Coccejus (1603-1669) seeks both the spiritual sense and the *sensus literalis.*[9] His approach is also important because of the formative influence he had on both covenant theology and pietism as well as later millennialism.[10]

According to Coccejus, Isaiah's visions had their point of reference in the establishment of the invisible church[11] in the NT. For Coccejus, the vision in Isaiah 2:2-4 refers to or has its fulfillment in (1) the incarnation of Christ when the glory of the Lord was manifested among men and (2) the coming of the Holy Spirit at Pentecost initiating the

believe that the total prediction would be realized in space and time in a climactic, total, and final way" (Walter C. Kaiser, Jr., *Toward Rediscovering the Old Testament* [Grand Rapids: Zondervan, 1987], pp. 104f). The first full statement of this view is usually attributed to Thomas Sherlock, *The Use and Intent of Prophecy in the Several Ages of the World* (London: J. Pemberton, 1725). A classic statement is that of Willis Judson Beecher, *The Prophets and the Promise* (Grand Rapids: Baker, 1963).

8. For example Sebastian Munster (1489-1552) began his exposition of Isa. 2 by identifying the message of the prophet with the kingdom of Christ *(Critici Sacri: sive Annotata Doctissimorum Virorum in Vetus ac Novum Testamentum*, 4:33).

9. The view frequently taken of Coccejus's approach is that his overriding consideration in determining the intended reference was that given by the NT writers, namely that he read the NT events back into the words of the prophets (Richard M. Davidson, *Typology in Scripture: A Study of Hermeneutical* typos *Structures* [Berrien Springs, Mich.: Andrews U., 1981], p. 33; Patrick Fairbairn, *The Typology of Scripture* [reprint, Grand Rapids: Zondervan, 1963], pp. 9-14). This is, however, an unfair characterization of Coccejus's method. In actual fact, Coccejus's goal was the literal sense of Scripture. Though in the last analysis the intended reference of the OT was understood to be the history of Christ and His church, Coccejus went to great lengths to show that such a reference was the literal meaning of the text. For example, while it is true that Coccejus said of Isa. 2:2-4, "All those who desire to call themselves Christians acknowledge that this prophecy is about Christ," it should be noted that he said this only after considerable textual and historical argumentation that this was the literal sense of the passage. For Coccejus, the simple fact was that the intended reference of Isaiah's prophecies was Christ and His church. Such a reading of these prophecies is different from a strictly typological or spiritual reading of the prophet's words in light of NT truth.

10. Gottlob Schrenk, *Gottesreich und Bund im Älteren Protestantismus Vornehmlich bei Johannes Coccejus* (Darmstadt, Germany: Wissenschaftliche Buchgesellschaft, 1967), pp. 300ff.

11. This is to be distinguished from the position of Augustine, who saw in these visions a reference to the visible church since Constantine.

mission of the church to spread the gospel among all nations.[12] It is important to note that Coccejus, unlike Grotius and many today, did not see an immediate reference for Isaiah's vision. The only meaning of the vision for Coccejus, was its reference to Christ and the church. It is not that Coccejus had no appreciation for the historical dimensions of Isaiah's words. On the contrary, he argued from just such historical considerations that Isaiah's words could not have had an immediate reference but rather had to refer to the distant future. Moreover, he did not feel constrained to interpret Isaiah's reference to Jerusalem as a type of Christ and the church that could be understood only by reading the NT back into the Old.[13] Rather, he understood the reference to Jerusalem as the prophecy's literal meaning. Throughout his discussion of this passage, Coccejus insisted on the importance of the literal fulfillment of the vision in Jerusalem. He in fact took pains to emphasize that the vision was about the literal city of Jerusalem so that it would not be identified with the city of Rome[14] and hence the visible Roman Catholic Church.[15]

At the same time, however, Coccejus recognized that certain elements of the vision were not to be taken, or rather, could not be taken in their literal sense. Though he saw a literal sense in the reference to Jerusalem, Coccejus interpreted the reference to the Temple mountain spiritually. The reasons he gave for this distinction are first, the fact that the prophet himself in this same verse had provided it with a spiritual interpretation by adding the phrase "the Law shall go out of Zion" (Isa. 2:3). Coccejus argued that this suggested the prophet saw the image of Temple worship as a picture of the spread of God's Word throughout all the nations.[16] Secondly, Coccejus argued that it was simply impossible that "all the nations" could come up to the Temple mount at one time to worship.[17] Such passages prove too enigmatic in their literal sense and thus must be understood spiritually, that is, in light of their NT fulfill-

---

12. *Curae Majores in Prophetiam Esaiae, Opera Omnia* (Amsterdam, 1701), 3:64.
13. This is not to say that Coccejus did not have an appreciation for the value of what he believed to be the NT fulfillment in interpreting a prophetic vision: "In every occasion, however, one may quite simply determine the subject of a prophecy if the method of the works of God in the New Testament recounted here in chapter 1 and at the beginning of 2 is observed, always comparing the latter with the former" (*Curae Majores in Prophetiam Esaiae, Opera Omnia*, 3:68).
14. Ibid., p. 65.
15. Ibid., p. 67.
16. Ibid., p. 65.
17. "Quod in litera impleri non potest" (ibid.).

ment.[18] The key to Coccejus's interpretation of the vision is his understanding of the role of the prophet as one who spoke forth the vision as a promise (*promissio*), clearly speaking of Christ in his words but not clearly understanding the things of which he spoke.[19]

In the history of the interpretation of Isaiah's prophecies, the view of Campegius Vitringa represents, in his terms at least, a middle way between the extremes (*"mediam inter haec extrema viam"*) of Grotius and Coccejus. Though firmly committed to Coccejus's system of covenant theology, Vitringa, like Grotius, strove vigorously for the *sensus literalis* of the historical prophet and thus rejected what he felt was Coccejus's excessive spiritualizing of the OT prophets. In order not to appear arbitrary, Vitringa laid down this basic rule: the vision of the prophet is to be taken in its literal, historical sense (*"a sensu primo, proprio et Grammatico"*) unless it proved improbable or against all common sense to do so (*"secundum primum et proprium sensum iis non conveniunt"*).[20] In his own commentary on Isaiah, Vitringa followed his rule rigorously and with much profit, leading him in many cases to side with those who saw a millennium within the scope of Isaiah's vision.[21]

MILLENNIALISM

Since the time of the early church there have been Christians who have held that the prophecies of Isaiah were to have a literal, historical fulfillment in a thousand-year reign of Christ on the earth. Justin Martyr and Irenaeus, for example, both taught that Christ would return to this earth and rule in Jerusalem for a period of one thousand years.[22] Such views were often stressed in the early church to counter the Hellenistic tendency to spiritualize Scripture, that is, to read it in such a way that only man's soul was seen as eternal.[23]

Since the Reformation many have continued to hold to a literal, millennial interpretation of Isaiah's vision, though the details of their

---

18. Ibid. This is quite different from Fairbairn's assessment of Coccejus: "He evidently conceived that *every* event in Old Testament history, which had a formal resemblance to something under the New, was to be regarded as typical" (Patrick Fairbairn, *The Typology of Scripture* [Grand Rapids: Zondervan, 1963], p. 10).

19. *Curae Majores in Prophetiam Esaiae, Opera Omnia*, 3:61.

20. *Commentarius in Librum Prophetiarum Iesaiae* (Leovardia: Henricus Halma, 1724), 1:16.

21. Ibid., 2:919.

22. George Gunter Blum, "Chiliasmus II," *Theologische Realenzyklopädia* (Berlin: Walter de Gruyter, 1976), p. 729.

23. Ibid.

systems have varied to a great extent.[24] By the middle of the last century Franz Delitzsch could remark that in his day there could hardly be found a believing Christian who did not hold to the idea of a millennium.[25] According to Delitzsch, the prophecies of Isaiah were to be understood with a strict literalism. If Isaiah said that the Temple mount was to be lifted higher than all the high mountains, then for Delitzsch this could only mean that Jerusalem "would one day tower in actual height above all the high places of the earth."[26]

In light of these various approaches to interpreting Isaiah, we propose to address the question by looking at a specific text. Certainly the most challenging for all sides is the passage already alluded to several times, Isaiah 2:2-5.

There is a long-standing debate regarding the reference and nature of the fulfillment of the vision in this passage. Before entering a discussion of whether the vision is to be taken literally or spiritually, it is important to get a clear picture of the vision itself. In what follows we will first attempt to clarify the sense of the vision in its context, as well as its literary and theological function within the overall purpose of the book of Isaiah. We will then discuss the broader and more immediate question of the intended reference of the vision.

THE COMPOSITE IMAGERY OF ISAIAH 2:1-5 [27]

Precisely what picture does Isaiah present to the reader in this vision? Wolfgang Werner is no doubt correct in saying that the image depicted in 2:2-4 is a composite one, drawn from a number of other

24. The most extreme distinction is, of course, between postmillennialism and premillennialism (Richard Bauckham, "Chiliasmus II," *Theologische Realenzyklopädia*, pp. 737-45).

25. Franz Delitzsch, *Die biblisch-prophetische Theologie, ihre Forthildung durch Chr. A. Crusius und ihre neueste Entwickelung seit der Christologie Hengstenbergs* (Leipzig: Gebauersche Buchhandlung, 1845), p. 7.

26. *Biblical Commentary on the Prophecies of Isaiah* (Grand Rapids: Eerdmans, 1969), p. 113. J. Ch. K. Hofmann wrote of Isa. 2:2ff (translated from German), "Hengstenberg is incorrect to say that anyone is simple minded who understands this prophecy in a physical sense rather than a moral one. The clear statement of the text itself speaks for a literal interpretation and passages such as Ezek. 40:2 and Zech. 14:10 also support a literal reading" (*Weissagung und Erfüllung im alten und im neuen Testamente* [Nördlingen: C. H. Beck'schen, 1841], 1:217).

27. The vision recorded in Isa. 2:2-4 is found again in Micah 4:1-3. The two oracles are virtually identical. Micah does not have the formal introduction of Isa. 2:1, but rather the oracle follows immediately on the description of the destruction of the Jerusalem Temple in Micah 3:12. Also, both oracles have different conclusions. Isaiah's closes with a call of exhortation to the house of Jacob to follow the Torah like the nations in

biblical texts.[28] The composite nature of the imagery is evident already in 2:2, where the image of nations flowing into Zion is linked to that of Zion's exaltation above the highest mountains. If read as one image the improbable sense of the passage would be that the nations were to "flow" up to the exalted Jerusalem.[29] According to Werner, the key elements of the imagery are: (a) the preeminence of Mount Zion, (b) Gentile pilgrimage to Zion, (c) Yahweh's judging the nations, and (d) the final destruction of armaments.

ZION'S PREEMINENCE ABOVE ALL

> 2:2a In the last days the mountain of the house of the Lord will be established as the chief of the mountains and will be raised above the hills;

While many in the past have erred by reading too much into the phrase "in the last days,"[30] just as often not enough has been read out of it. Already, Grotius, following Rashi,[31] read here simply "hereafter" (*posthac*). The discovery of the phrase *ana achrat umi* in the Assyrian texts[32] has shown that Rashi's suggestion is possible. As Wildberger, however, has argued, the term in Isaiah is used in conjunction with and corresponding to other terms such as *'aḥărê-kēn* in 1:26 that clearly point to "a future affected by God's breaking in on the course of history."[33] If one's understanding of the term "eschatological" does not exceed this,

the last days, while Micah's ends with a contrast between the nations who follow their own gods and Israel who worships only the Lord. Micah also contains an additional line describing the time of peace, Micah 4:4. (Hans Wildberger, *Biblischer Kommentar Altes Testament, Jesaja* [Neukirchen-Vluyn, Germany: Neukirchener Verlag, 1972], 1:76).

28. *Eschatologische Texte in Jesaja 1-39, Messias, Heiliger Rest, Volker* (Würzburg, Germany: Echter Verlag, 1982), pp. 154, 159.

29. On the basis of such a reading of the imagery, for example, Watts suggested God's "attraction for nations and peoples is so great that they 'flow' uphill to the summit of the mountains" (John D. W. Watts, *Word Biblical Commentary* [Waco, Tex.; Word, 1985], 24:29).

30. Most biblical scholars in the past have followed the lead of the LXX, "in the last days," the Targum, "in the end of the days," and the early Jewish commentaries, e.g., Kimchi, "Every place where it says 'in the last days' it refers to the days of the Messiah" (*The Commentary of David Kimhi on Isaiah*, ed. Louis Finkelstein [New York: Columbia U., 1926], p. 11). Rashi, however, does not give an eschatological meaning to the phrase.

31. Rashi's comment, *l'hr šyklw hpoš'ym*, "After the sinners are gone," ties the passage to the conclusion of the book of Isaiah, *wᵉyāṣᵉ'û wᵉrā'û bᵉpigrê hā'ănāšîm happōšᵉîm bî* (Isa. 66:24a).

32. Eberhard Schrader, *The Cuneiform Inscriptions and the Old Testament* (London: Williams and Norgate, 1885), 1:141.

33. Wildberger, *Biblischer Kommentar Altes Testament, Jesaja,* 1:82.

then, says Wildberger, the phrase "in the last days" can be viewed as an introduction to an eschatological prophecy.[34] As is clear from the next verse, as well as usage elsewhere in Scripture,[35] "the mountain of the house of the Lord" is Mount Zion, the hill upon which Jerusalem is situated. The "house of the Lord" is the Temple.[36] So the sense of the vision is that "in the last days" the mountain where the Temple sits will be established and lifted high above the mountains and hills around it.

The fact that in Isaiah's day, as in our own, the Temple mount did not tower over other mountains and hills, raises the question of the precise sense of Isaiah's words. The lexical meaning of the terms "established"[37] (*nākôn*) and "lifted up"[38] (*wᵉniśśā'*) is clear enough, though their use within the syntax of the verse has been the object of considerable debate. Does this passage envisage Mount Zion being established and lifted up high in the "last days" as it had never before been situated, or does it foresee merely that this is the way Mount Zion has always been characterized and will continue to be when the "last days" arrive? In other words, are the conditions described here to be understood as a physical change in the geography of Mount Zion or are they conditions that have prevailed throughout the history of Israel? Young is correct in saying of this verse, "It is essential for a right understanding of the passage that the force of these words be clearly seen."[39] For Young, the argument rests on the syntactical sense of the Niphal participle with the verb *hyh*. Citing the work of Green, he argues that the passive participle with *hyh* expresses "a condition as existing rather than an act as performed at the time referred to."[40] According to Young,

> the word "established" expresses the idea of permanent duration, which idea is strengthened by the auxiliary "shall be," ... the words are not to be translated as a future passive, "will be established." Thus, this

---

34. Ibid. Jenni, who argued that the phrase "in the last days" is not used in a technical sense in the OT, saw Isa. 2:2 as the closest example of a technical, eschatological use of the phrase (*Theologisches Handwörterbuch zum Alten Testament* [Munich: Chr. Kaiser Verlag, 1971], 1:118).

35. 2 Chron. 33:15.

36. Isa. 37:1, 14; 38:20, 22; 66:20.

37. Francis Brown, S. R. Driver, and Charles A. Briggs, *A Hebrew and English Lexicon of the Old Testament* (Oxford: Clarendon, 1907), p. 465.

38. Ibid., p. 669.

39. Edward J. Young, *The Book of Isaiah: The English Text, with Introduction, Exposition and Notes* (Grand Rapids: Eerdmans, 1965), 1:100.

40. Young, p. 100, cites William H. Green, *A Grammar of the Hebrew Language* (New York: John Wiley & Sons, 1889), 278:4a.

passage does not describe something that will take place or materialize during the latter days. It describes rather a condition that will already be in existence when the latter days begin to run their course.[41]

Young's purpose was to show that it is not the establishment and exaltation of Mount Zion in the last days that is in view in this vision but rather the fact that when the last days begin, the mountain of the house of God will already have been established.[42] In reading the text in such a way, Young has provided an explanation that avoids any major changes at the time of the "last days." Thus the reference of the passage could be to Christ and the church without having to spiritualize the notion of an elevated Temple mount. Furthermore, Young carries his analysis over to the next predicate, w^eniśśā', by arguing that "the prophet does not use the future passive, 'it will be lifted up,' but simply expresses the condition of Zion with respect to the hills, namely, that it is 'lifted up.'"[43]

Young's position, however, is not tenable.[44] In syntactical constructions such as these, the verb hyh does not merely serve to "strengthen" the idea of duration, but also to locate it in time giving it a future sense.[45] Passive participles with hyh are used both for future durative actions that begin at a point in the future[46] and for simple future actions that express the obtainment of a condition.[47] It is this use of the verb as a simple future that corresponds with the traditional rendering of Isaiah 2:2 as future: "The mountain of the house of the Lord will be established . . . and will be raised." More importantly, elsewhere in the book of Isaiah, when a passive participle is used with hyh, the clear sense of the

41. Young, *The Book of Isaiah*, p. 100.
42. Ibid. Young translated 2:2a, "And it shall come to pass in the last days that established shall be the mountain of the house of the Lord at the top of the mountains" (p. 94).
43. Ibid., p. 101.
44. In the same paragraph cited in Green's grammar (278:4), the passive participle with hyh is said "to indicate the time to which [the participles] are to be referred or the aspect under which they are to be conceived" (p. 337). The example Green gives is significant in that it is nearly identical to that of Isa. 2:2, nākôn yihyeh (1 Chron. 17:14). In speaking of the seed of David whom God was to raise up, it is said that his throne will be established forever. Since David is referred to in this passage with the second person pronoun (e.g., 1 Chron. 17:11) and the future seed of David by the third person, the description of the establishment of "his" throne can only refer to the future throne of the seed of David.
45. Paul Joüon, *Grammaire de l'hebreu biblique* (Rome: Institut Biblique Pontifical, 1923), par. 121e; E. Kautzsch and A. E. Cowley, eds., *Gesenius' Hebrew Grammar*, 2d Eng. ed. (Oxford: Clarendon, 1910), par. 116r. The future appears to be the only sense for Jer. 36:30, "his dead body shall be cast out [passive participle with hyh] to the heat of the day and the frost of the night."
46. Deut. 28:29, "but you shall [hyh] only be oppressed [passive participle] and robbed [passive participle] continually."
47. Ex. 34:2, "So be ready [hyh with nākôn] by morning."

construction is that of a simple future event, for example, Isaiah 19:10, "And the pillars of Egypt will be crushed [*hyh* with passive participle]." Young implies in his discussion of this verse that if the simple future were intended in 2:2, the verb would have been imperfect. However, in Hebrew syntax, the passive of simple imperfects can have the same range of meaning as the passive participle with *hyh*, for example, Psalm 89:38. All the more important is the fact that the sentence in Isaiah 2:2*a* is continued in 2:2*b* by a perfect with the *waw* consecutive, which expresses a simple future action, "and all the nations will stream [*wᵉnā-hārû*] to it."

Not only do these syntactical considerations argue against Young's interpretation of this passage, but also his interpretation finds little support in the history of exegesis, in either the translations[48] or commentaries.[49] In summary, according to the traditional view, Isaiah envisioned a time yet future when the Temple mount would be lifted up and exalted over all the other mountains. This was not to be a continuation of the past glory of the Temple, but a new status or stature for Jerusalem that would come in the "last days."

What, then, did the prophet mean when he said the mount was to be "established" and "lifted up"? The Niphal of *kôn* is found only here in the book of Isaiah. It is used widely throughout the Psalms and wisdom literature,[50] particularly in contexts dealing with creation themes.[51]

---

48. LXX: *hoti estai en tais hēmerous emphanes to oros kyriou . . . kai hypsōthēsetai*; Vulgate: *et erit in novissimus diebus praeparatus mons domus Domini in vertice montium et elevabitur super colles*; RSV: It shall come to pass in the latter days that the mountain of the house of the Lord shall be established as the highest of the mountains, and shall be raised above the hills; Geneva Bible: It shall be in the last dayes, that the mountaine of the House of the Lord shall be prepared in the top of the mountaines, and shall be exalted above the hilles.

49. Calvin: And it shall come to pass in the last days, that the mountain of the Lord's house shall be established (*ut statuatur*) in the top of the mountains, and shall be exalted (*et erigatur*) above the hills; Vatablus: *et elevabitur supra colles*; Grotius: *et erit in novissimis diebus praeparatus mons domus Domini in vertice montium*; Coccejus: *exaptatus erit mons domus Jehovae in capite montium, et sublatus prae collibus*; Vitringa: *ut mons Domus Jehovae constabiliatur in vertice montium, et extolatur supra colles*; Delitzsch: *feststehen wird da der Berg des Hauses Jahve's an der Spitze der Berge und erhaben über Hügel*; Duhm: *Festgegründet wird sein der Berg Jahves, und das Haus unsers Gottes auf dem Haupt der Berge*; Wildberger: *Da wird fest gegründet sein der Berg des hauses Jahwes und erhaben sein über alle Hügel*.

50. E. Gerstenberger, *Theologisches Handwörterbuch zum Alten Testament* (Munich: Chr. Kaiser Verlag, 1971), 1:813.

51. Werner, *Eschatologische Texte in Jesaja 1-39*, p. 155.

The earth "stands fast (*tikkôn*), it will not be moved."[52] *Nāśā'* ("lifted up") is used elsewhere in Isaiah to describe high mountains and hills.[53] Its parallel terms are *rûm* ("rise up") and *gābah* ("be high"). At the beginning of this passage, then, after the introductory formula has directed the reader to the "last days," the Temple mountain, Zion, is described as steadfast and lifted higher than the mountains around about.[54]

It is customary to read the description of the height of the mountain as a reference to its majesty and splendor.[55] Such a reading, however, overlooks the importance of these references in Isaiah and the general sense of the terms *nāśā'*, *rûm*, and *gābah*. They suggest that physical height is in view and not merely glory and majesty.[56] It is, of course, possible to draw an inference from physical height and elevation to the sense of glory and majesty, but only after it is made clear that the sense of the words is first of all physical height.

The image of Zion's elevation is known also from other biblical texts.[57] Gressmann has argued that the notion of a "Mountain of God" (*der Gottesberg*) exalted over all other mountains was part of a larger complex of biblical images that served to link Israel's eschatology with the biblical doctrine of creation.[58] Also, according to Otto Kaiser, "there is a reminiscence of the conception of paradise located upon the mountain of God, cf. Ps. 48:2, Isa. 14:13f.... Just as at the beginning of world history, God founded the earth above the seas of the primeval ocean, so that from henceforth it could no longer be shaken (cf. Pss. 24:2; 93:1; 96:10; 1 Chron. 16:3), he will one day create for the temple in Jerusalem a place which shall not be shaken for all time to come."[59] Hence, as it is put in Isaiah 51:3, God will make Zion's wilderness "like Eden, and her desert like the garden of the Lord."

52. Pss. 93:1; 96:10; 1 Chron. 16:30.
53. Isa. 2:14; 30:25; 57:7.
54. Werner, *Eschatologische Texte in Jesaja 1-39*, p. 155.
55. Calvin: "At length this hill was actually raised above all the mountains, because from it was heard the voice of God, and sounded through the whole world, that it might lift us up to heaven; because from it the heavenly majesty of God shone brightly; and lastly, because, being the sanctuary of God, it surpassed the whole world in lofty excellence" (*Commentary on the Book of the Prophet Isaiah*, trans. William Pringle [Grand Rapids: Baker, 1979], 1:92).
56. Karl Marti, *Kurzer Hand-Commentar zum Alten Testament, Das Buch Jesaja* (Tübingen: J. C. B. Mohr, 1990), p. 25.
57. Ezek. 40:2; Zech. 14:10; Ps. 48:2; Isa. 40:3-5.
58. Hugo Gressmann, *Der Messias* (Göttingen: Vandenhoeck & Ruprecht, 1929), p. 181.
59. Otto Kaiser, *Isaiah 1-12: A Commentary* (Philadelphia: Westminster, 1972), p. 26.

GENTILE PILGRIMAGE TO ZION

> 2:2b-3 And all the nations will stream to it, and many peoples will come and say, "Come, let us go up to the mountain of the Lord, to the house of the God of Jacob; that He may teach us concerning His ways, and that we may walk in His paths." For the law will go forth from Zion, and the word of the Lord from Jerusalem.

Integral to the imagery of the eschatological return to paradise (*der Gottesgarten*) is the picture of the rivers that flow (*nāhar*) out from the mountain of God.[60] In the present context Isaiah appears to have artfully pressed that image into a description of the flow (*nāhar*) of the Gentile nations into Zion to hear God's Torah.[61] Another factor behind this imagery may be the notion of a "river" (*nāhār*) in the midst of God's city from which His people are refreshed.[62]

The pilgrimage of Gentiles into Jerusalem, where they receive God's law, recalls Israel's own historical experiences, including their initial pilgrimage to Mount Sinai to receive God's Torah[63] and their yearly journeys to Jerusalem.[64] What had been Israel's experience in the past would one day be that of all the nations.[65] Similar expressions of this hope can be found elsewhere in Isaiah (18:7; 19:16-25).[66]

The textual differences between Isaiah 2:3b and Micah 4:1b point out the emphasis the Isaiah passage puts on Gentile participation. "Peoples" (*'ammîm*—without the article) in Micah 4:1b is read[67] in Isaiah as "the nations" (*haggôyim*—with the article) and is extended in Isaiah by

---

60. See Ps. 46:5; Zech. 13:1; 14:8; Ezek. 47:1-12. Gressmann, *Der Messias*, p. 179. Cf. Gen. 2:10, *u°nāhār yōṣē' mē'ēden l°hašqôt 'et-haggān*.

61. Wildberger, *Biblischer Kommentar Altes Testament, Jesaja*, 1:83.

62. Ibid.

63. "Just as Israel once travelled in the desert to the mountain of God in order to receive the law there (cf. Ex. 19ff), the nations now travel on pilgrimage to the sanctuary of the people of the twelve tribes, to the house of the God of Jacob" (Otto Kaiser, *Isaiah 1-12*, p. 27). Also Werner, *Eschatologische Texte in Jesaja 1-39*, p. 159.

64. Hans-Joachim Kraus, *Gottesdienst in Israel, Grundriss einer Geschichte des alttestamentlichen Gottesdienstes* (Munich: Chr. Kaiser Verlag, 1962), p. 230.

65. "At the present time there was only one people, viz. Israel, which made pilgrimages to Zion on the great festivals, but it would be very different then" (Franz Delitzsch, *Biblical Commentary on the Prophecies of Isaiah*, trans. James Martin [Grand Rapids: Eerdmans, 1969], p. 114).

66. Gressmann, *Der Messias*, pp. 181ff.

67. The precise textual relationship between Isa. 2:2-4 and Micah 1:1-4 is not clear.

the word "all."[68] Wildberger is no doubt correct in seeing the stress on "all the nations" over against "(some) peoples" as a theological emphasis of Isaiah's eschatology.[69] The focus is on every nation, not just some.

It is important to note that the "law" (*tôrâ*) that comes out of Zion is identified in Isaiah 2:3 with "His ways" (*midderākāyw*) and "His paths" (*be'ōrhōtāyw*), two terms that, when used together, are prominent in wisdom literature.[70] The term *tôrâ* is used already in Isaiah 1:10 to describe the prophet's own message.[71] In these early instances in Isaiah the "Law" that came forth is interpreted along the same lines as in Deuteronomy 4:6—God's statutes and judgments are "wisdom" (*hokmâ*) and "understanding" (*bînâ*). God's wisdom was given to Israel so that they might become a "wise and understanding people" (Deut. 4:6). Hence in Isaiah, that which was once the sole possession of Israel (in Deuteronomy) was to become the way of life for all nations. A similar view of the conversion of the Gentile nations can be seen in Jonah 1:16 and 3:5ff, where the Gentiles are portrayed as rank and file (*regelmässigen*) Israelites after their conversion. An important point to be made is that the imagery found here does not imply that in the "last days" the Law given at Sinai would again be kept as of old. Rather, as already was the case in the book of Deuteronomy, the "law" was conceived as a revelation of divine wisdom, the means for becoming a wise and understanding people. The translation "law" in Isaiah 2:3 in the NASB rather than "Law," then, accurately reflects the emphasis of this passage away from the Sinai Law per se. The "law" as used here in Isaiah is the internalized law of passages such as Jeremiah 31:33 and Ezekiel 36:27.

YAHWEH'S JUDGING OF NATIONS

2:4*a* And He will judge between the nations, and will render decisions for many peoples.

In sharp contrast with the themes of chapter 1, where Yahweh is pictured as the Judge of His people Israel and His city Jerusalem,[72] here our attention is turned to "Yahweh as Judge of the nations," a leading

---

68. That this is not merely an exchange of the term in Micah 4:1*b* (*'ammîm*) with that in Micah 4:2*a* (*gōyim rabbîm*) is shown from the fact that in Isaiah the article is consistently added to "nations" (*haggôyim*) in the first line (2:2*b*, 4*a*) and omitted from "peoples" (*'ammîm*).

69. Wildberger, *Biblischer Kommentar Altes Testament, Jesaja*, 1:83.

70. Prov. 2:8, 13, 20; 3:6; 8:20; 12:28. "Die beiden Termini meinen an allen Stellen den weisen und klugen Lebenweg" (Werner, *Eschatologische Texte in Jesaja 1-39*), p. 157.

71. *Tôrat 'ĕlōhênû* ("The Torah of our God").

72. See Isa. 1:17-18.

motif in Israel's eschatology.[73] Throughout the prophetic literature it is presupposed that God's judgment of the nations will serve as a necessary prelude to the establishment of universal peace.[74] The same terminology is found elsewhere in Isaiah for both God's universal judgment (51:5; 66:16) and that of the new Davidic king (11:3f; 16:5).[75] The idea is prevalent in the theology of the Psalms as well.[76] Again, as in the first half of the verse, the textual differences between Isaiah 2:4*a* and Micah 4:3*a* point to the theological emphasis of Isaiah on the universal scope of his vision. Thus Micah's "many peoples" (*'ammîm rabbîm*), indefinite without the article, is rendered in Isaiah simply as "the nations" (*haggōyim*).

FINAL DESTRUCTION OF ARMAMENTS

> 2:4*b* And they will hammer their swords into plowshares, and their spears into pruning hooks. Nation will not lift up sword against nation, and never again will they learn war.

The last image in the passage is drawn from the broader theme of the "Return to Paradise,"[77] that is, harmony among the nations (*Völkerfriede*). Just as the early chapters of Genesis take pains to show that war and death are a result of man's rebellion, so the description of the end is one where the instruments of war will no longer be necessary.[78] It is of importance to note that only in this passage (with Micah 4) is there a link between the notion of *Völkerfriede*[79] and the pilgrimage to Zion. Form critically the motif of the Zion pilgrimage characteristically ends with the arrival of the people and the presentation of their tribute.[80] Thus the scene in Isaiah 2:4 changes in a somewhat unpredictable way at the close of the vision. The people, having accepted Zion and God's ways as the basis of their living, are again at home going about the peaceful task

---

73. G. Liedke, *Theologisches Handwörterbuch zum Alten Testament*, Band II, ed. Ernst Jenni and Claus Westermann (Munich: Chr. Kaiser Verlag, 1976), p. 1008.

74. A. Jepsen, "Eschatologie II. im AT," *Die Religion in Geschichte und Gegenwart*, 3. Auflage, ed. Kurt Galling (Tübingen: J. C. B. Mohr, 1957), 2:658.

75. Liedke, *Theologisches Handwörterbuch zum Alten Testament*, p. 1008.

76. See Hans-Joachim Kraus, *Psalmen, I. Teilband* (Neukirchen-Vluyn: Neukirchener Verlag, 1966), p. 200.

77. Gressmann, *Der Messias*, p. 153.

78. "For every boot of the booted warrior in the battle tumult and cloak rolled in blood, will be for burning, fuel for the fire" (Isa. 9:4 [5 Eng.]); "And the bow of war will be cut off. And He will speak peace to the nations" (Zech. 9:10); "He makes wars to cease to the end of the earth; He breaks the bow and cuts the spear in two; He burns the chariots with fire" (Ps. 46:10 [9 Eng.]). See Gressmann, *Der Messias*, p. 153.

79. Werner, *Eschatologische Texte in Jesaja 1-39*, pp. 161ff.

80. R. Bach, "Der Bogen zerbricht, Spiesse zerschlägt und Wagen mit Feuer verbrennt," *Probleme biblisher Theologie*, ed. H. W. Wolff (Munich, 1971), pp. 13-26, quoted in Werner, *Eschatologische Texte in Jesaja 1-39*, p. 161.

of converting their instruments of war into plows and pruning shears. This innovation at the conclusion of the vision is apparently intended to stress that the peace here described is to be lasting.

The Literary Strategy of Isaiah 2:1-5

Recent trends in redaction criticism[81] and compositional criticism[82] in the prophetic literature have rekindled scholarly interest in the role each prophetic oracle plays in relation to the message of the whole of the book of Isaiah. Such an interest has long been the particular focus of earlier and more conservative approaches to the prophets. It is important, then, to describe the meaning of Isaiah 2:2-4 within the broader context of its role in developing the message of the book.

The immediate context of Isaiah 2:2-4 consists of an introductory phrase (v. 1) and at its conclusion a transition (v. 5)[83] to the next literary unit (vv. 6ff). The discussion of 2:1 has more often than not been entangled in the question of sources and authorship of the book.[84] As important as those questions are, our focus here is on the compositional purpose of 2:1. Why was it put here? How does it contribute to our understanding of 2:2-4 and the remainder of the section?[85] The most notable feature of this opening phrase is its similarity with Isaiah 1:1, usually taken to be a title for a large part of the book, if not the whole of the book. A comparison of the two headings shows that they differ in two significant respects. (1) Instead of "vision" (*ḥāzōn*), 2:1 has simply "the word" (*haddābār*). Watts is probably correct in saying that the use of *haddābār*, "the word," here should be "understood to refer to one-speech or oracle, not a collection."[86] Thus 2:1 directs the reader's attention to the specific vision that follows.[87] (2) 2:1 omits the chronological

81. George Fohrer, *Exegese des Alten Testaments Einführung in die Methodik* (Heidelberg: Quelle & Meyer, 1983), pp. 139ff.

82. Ibid.

83. A comparison of Isa. 2:2-4 with Micah 4:1-3 shows that Isa. 2:1 and 2:5 do not belong to the original vision but are part of the literary context joining it to the book of Isaiah.

84. See John N. Oswalt, *The Book of Isaiah, Chapters 1-39* (Grand Rapids: Eerdmans, 1986), pp. 113ff, for a brief discussion of the issue.

85. The conclusion of the section is most likely chap. 5, since chap. 6 begins with a new heading. Wildberger sees the new section beginning in chap. 13 and thus takes the whole of 2:1–12:6 as a unit. Also see Rolf Rendtorff, *Das Alte Testament Eine Einführung* (Neukirchener-Vluyn, Germany: Neukirchener Verlag, 1983), p. 202.

86. Watts, *Word Biblical Commentary*, p. 28.

87. Watts, following Peter Ackroyd, "A Note on Isaiah 2:1," *Zeitschrift für die alttestamentliche Wissenschaft* 75 (1963):320, suggests that the heading "may be intended to counter the claim that these words belong to Micah (Micah 4:1-3)." And, more

references to the kings. The fact that these chronological limits are omitted in 2:1 may have been to emphasize that the intended reference was not an event in the immediate historical context of Isaiah, but as 2:2*a* goes on to say, an event that had its reference "in the last days."[88]

The transitional verse, Isaiah 2:5, shows clearly the particular meaning 2:2-4 was to have within this larger section of the book of Isaiah. In this verse the prophet has addressed Israel, the "house of Jacob," and admonished them to walk "in the light of the Lord." Just as in the last days the nations were going to say, "Come, let us . . . walk in His paths" (Isa. 2:2-4), so now the house of Jacob is encouraged to anticipate them and live in God's light. As Young has said, "What the foreign nations will do in the latter days thus forms an occasion for the prophet to incite his own people, to whom the promises of future blessing had been made, to imitate the practice of these nations."[89] The importance of this observation lies in the fact that it shows that the author of the book of Isaiah understood this passage to be about the work of God in the future. The focus of this passage was not on the present. Its vision was about a future that stands in stark contrast to the present.

Within the larger context of the book of Isaiah, the role of 2:2-5 is clear. It is one of the recurring notes of salvation in the midst of the prophet's proclamation of judgment.[90] As such it contributes to the overall message of the book, which is, generally speaking, that in the midst of the darkest hour of God's judgment upon unrighteousness, God's people need only trust in Him and look in faith[91] to His promised redemption.

What each of these perspectives on 2:2-4 have shown is that the sense and intention of this small text focuses on God's plan for the future. Thus the content and sense of these verses as discussed above is commensurate with the meaning given them in the final composition of the book. From the very beginning the passage appears to have been

importantly, it attempted to ensure that the vision was read as an authentic oracle of Isaiah. Such an explanation finds little support within the text itself, and what support it finds outside the text, namely the similarity of Isa. 2:1-4 and Micah 4:1-3, is surely more a concern of the modern biblical scholar than of an ancient writer.

88. A similar view of 2:1 was apparently held by the Greek translators of Isaiah, as can be seen in the different way they have rendered the preposition '*l.* In 1:1 '*l* is rendered by *katà*, showing that they saw it in reference to the judgments of God against (*katà*) Judah and Jerusalem, whereas in 2:1 '*al* is rendered by *perì*, suggesting that they had 2:2-4 specifically in mind.

89. Young, *The Book of Isaiah*, p. 114.

90. See Rendtorff, *Das Alte Testament Eine Einführung*, p. 212. Claus Westermann, *Grundformen prophetischer Rede* (Munich: Chr. Kaiser Verlag, 1960), p. 68.

91. Hans-Christoph Schmitt, "Redaktion des Pentateuch im Geiste der Prophetie," *Vetus Testamentum* 32 (1982):176; R. Smend, "Zur Geschichte von *h'myn*," *Hebräische Wortforschung,* Vetus Testamentum Supplement 16 (1967):284-90.

understood as a picture of a future age when Jerusalem would be restored and would become the center of the worship of God among all nations.

The question that now remains is that of the reference of the vision.

THE LITERAL REFERENCE OF ISAIAH 2:1-5

As Wildberger has noted, it has long been debated whether the images presented in this passage are to be taken "spiritually" or "physically."[92] Will the Temple mountain, Zion, be physically raised up one day higher than the other mountains around about and also higher than all the high mountains of the earth? Will the Temple again be built upon the mountain? Will the nations of the world flow into Jerusalem and begin to worship God at the Temple?

There is little doubt that this is the image presented in Isaiah's vision. The question is, however, should we understand the vision and its reference in such a literal and physical sense? There are several features of the passage that suggest the vision was meant to be taken literally and physically, that is, that Isaiah is here looking forward to the physical restoration of Jerusalem and reign of the Messiah on earth in the "last days."

INDICATED BY THE LITERARY GENRE

Biblical prophetic books generally consist of both narrative and poetic texts. While both narrative and poetic texts can be used to describe real events and persons, narratives, as a rule, describe events "realistically," whereas poetic texts describe such events figuratively.[93] For the most part, Isaiah 2:2-4 is a poetic text. Leaving aside the finer points of the nature of the meter and parallelism in 2:2-4, there is enough balance and restatement in these verses to suggest that the passage is, at least in origin, poetic.[94] From the point of view of genre, however, this is not the last word that can be said about the passage. A comparison with its duplicate in Micah 4:1-3, for example, shows that the form of Isaiah is at points less poetic than Micah.[95] It is clear that the parallel line in Micah

---

92. Wildberger, *Biblischer Kommentar Altes Testament, Jesaja,* 1:83.
93. Otto Eissfeldt, *Einleitung in Das Alte Testament* (Tübingen: J. C. B. Mohr, 1964), p. 63.
94. Wildberger, *Biblischer Kommentar Altes Testament, Jesaja,* p. 78. According to Young, the vision in Isaiah is not "poetry" but rather "elevated poetic prose" (*The Book of Isaiah,* p. 101).
95. Wildberger, *Biblischer Kommentar Altes Testament, Jesaja,* p. 78.

4:1*a* ("established at the top of the mountains, raised up above the hills")[96] displays a form of parallelism and has a recognizable meter. It is thus a poetic line. However, as the line appears in Isaiah, the variation in word order and arrangement of Isaiah 2:2*a* have blurred both the parallelism and the meter. In other words, it is no longer formally a poetic line; it is, rather, a piece of narration.

Furthermore, the use of the nouns "peoples" and "many nations" in Micah shows that the terms are meant as poetic word pairs and hence virtually synonymous. In Isaiah, however, there has been a conscious attempt to distinguish between the "all peoples" and the "many nations," showing that the terms are not taken as synonymous descriptions of the same groups but rather have reference to distinct groups of peoples. Note also that the article is not used with these terms in the Micah passage, but that it is used in Isaiah with "nations" in both occurrences. Such variations between Micah and Isaiah show that in its present form in Isaiah, the ostensible poetic features of the vision have become narration. The implication of this observation is that the passage within its context in Isaiah is intended to be taken more as narrative than as poetry and hence, one would conclude from the standpoint of genre, more "realistically" than "figuratively." Thus the genre of the Isaianic vision suggests we should not hurry to apply a figurative interpretation to it, as if it were pure poetry, but rather we should attempt to read it as referring literally to a time of the physical restoration of Jerusalem in the last days.

INDICATED BY THE LITERARY CONTEXT

The comparison with the parallel passage in Micah 4 offers further support for understanding a literal reference in Isaiah 2. The original reference of the Micah text can be seen, within the context of the book of Micah, in the description of the destruction of the Jerusalem Temple that immediately precedes this passage in 3:12, "Zion will be planted as a field, Jerusalem will become a heap of ruins." There is little doubt that this description was to be understood as a reference to the actual Temple in Jerusalem. This is already the sense of the passage at the time of Jeremiah's prophecies regarding the fall of Jerusalem (Jer. 26:18-19). The elders in Jeremiah's day recalled these words of Micah as prophesying the literal destruction of Jerusalem that was averted because King Hezekiah repented. If the prophecy regarding the destruction of Jerusalem was understood literally, even though it was poetic in form, it is natural to take the vision of its restoration literally as well.

96. *Nākôn bᵉrōʾš behārîm uᵉniśśāʾ hûʾ miggᵉbāʿôt.*

Thus it follows that even in the more poetic version of the vision, Micah 4:1-3, the reference was understood literally as the reestablishment of the Temple in Jerusalem.

A similar context is found for the Isaiah vision. The judgment oracle in Isaiah 1:2ff is clearly to be taken with a literal reference to the sins of the nation of Israel. The "faithful city" had become a "harlot" full of murderers (Isa. 1:21). But as the chapter comes to a conclusion, the promise is given that it will again "be called the city of righteousness, a faithful city" (Isa. 1:26). Just as in the book of Micah, the visions of destruction in Isaiah 1 have their reference in the literal city of Jerusalem. By the same token it seems reasonable to conclude that the visions of the restoration of that desolate city are also to be understood within the framework of a literal reference to Jerusalem. There is no reason to suppose that the prophets' description of Israel's future restoration was any less concrete than their description of Israel's destruction.

INDICATED BY THE LITERARY TYPE

Even though the form of these visions is poetic, the above observations show that the visions refer literally to historical entities. Micah's words "Zion will be plowed as a field" (3:12) are poetic speech[97] and no doubt use figurative language, but the quotation of these words in Jeremiah 26:18-19 and their application show that they referred literally to the city of Jerusalem. This should serve as a warning against ruling out a literal historical reference on the basis of a text's poetic genre.[98]

We cannot, of course, draw from these examples an absolute conclusion that every detail of even the poetic description of the prophets' vision must or can be taken literally. If we read the vision in Isaiah 2:2-5 as referring to a future restoration of Jerusalem and the worship of God in the days of the Messiah, there still remains the further question of the extent of the literal reference. The fact that the vision has poetic as well as narrative features cautions against overlooking any figurative language in its description. We need not, for example, take the swords to refer to actual swords at the time of the fulfillment, but rather the images are to be taken as references to actual implements of war. The same can be said of plowshares as implements of peace. We have already seen that the sense of the word "law" in this vision need not and should not be taken as a reference to the Mosaic Law and the priestly cultus. By the same token, the literal fulfillment of the Zion pilgrimage (Isa. 2:3) need

97. *Wîrûšālaim 'îyyîn tihyeh wehar habbayit lebāmôt yā'ar.*
98. See Theodor Zahn, *Das Evangelium des Matthäus* (Leipzig: A. Deichertsche Verlagsbuchhandlung, 1922), pp. 192-94; George E. Ladd, *Crucial Questions about the Kingdom of God* (Grand Rapids: Eerdmans, 1954), p. 148.

not imply the actual rebuilding of the Temple in Jerusalem. Indeed, Vitringa is correct in pointing out that the focus on the Temple in this vision is not in the interest of the cultus as much as the academia. The nations come to Jerusalem not so much for worship as for instruction.

Finally, the expectation of a literal, physical elevation of the Temple mountain is no more necessary in this passage than is the expectation that the nations will actually "flow" as a river into the city. Even the *Scofield Bible* (both editions), known for its literal interpretation of these passages, takes the mountain in this verse to be symbolic.[99] The poetic features of the vision argue against our insisting on an unrealistic literal sense of the text. They do not, however, warrant a wholesale spiritualization of the vision. It is, in fact, passages such as this that have kept alive the Christian's hope for the future on this earth and the current events of history. It is a passage that has forced Christians of every age to focus their hope on the God of history and the God of creation.

It should be obvious by now that what has been said regarding the interpretation of Isaiah's vision in 2:2-5 applies to the whole of his vision of the future throughout the remainder of the book, specifically, Isaiah 11:1-16; 60; 61:3–62:12; 66. For example, 11:1-16 represents the classic depiction of the future reign of Christ. Again the center of the vision is the reign of the Davidic king in Jerusalem (vv. 1, 10). The extent of the kingdom is worldwide: "For the earth shall be full of the knowledge of the Lord as the waters cover the sea" (v. 9). The nature of the kingdom suggests that at the time of the reign of the Davidic Messiah the whole world will be in submission to Him and at peace with each other: "And the wolf will dwell with the lamb . . . for the earth shall be full of the knowledge of the Lord" (vv. 6-9). At that time, as well, God will again gather together the remnant of Israel and Judah (vv. 11-13) and they will again dwell in their land (vv. 14-16).

It hardly needs saying that the vision here described makes abundant use of figurative language. The king is described as a "branch," the lion eats straw; knowledge is like the waters of the sea. As we have attempted to show in regards to Isaiah 2:2-5, however, the use of figurative language does not permit us to give a figurative explanation to the vision and apply it to the church in this age.[100] Young recognizes this

---

99. C. I. Scofield, *The Scofield Reference Bible* (New York: Oxford University, 1917), p. 714; and *The New Scofield Reference Bible* (Oxford: Oxford University, 1967), p. 714.

100. As Calvin did: "Though Isaiah says that the wild and the tame beasts will live in harmony, that the blessing of God may be clearly and fully manifested, yet he chiefly means what I have said, that the people of Christ will have no disposition to do injury, no fierceness or cruelty. They were formerly like lions or leopards, but will

point and argues that both the scope (all creation) and extent of the vision (complete change of man's nature) implies a reversal of the account of the Fall in Genesis 3, and thus its fulfillment lies ultimately in the "new creation."[101] Though he has rightly appreciated the literal reference of this text, Young's appeal to the "new heavens and new earth" as the time of fulfillment of this vision overlooks the "this worldly" dimensions of Isaiah's words. If we are to take the vision's reference literally, then it is important to note that the remnant are to be gathered from among those historical and geographical nations where they have been dispersed (e.g. Assyria, Egypt, and Cush). In the same way that the reference to these historical, political nations makes a figurative interpretation unlikely, the references to these nations also rules out the totally "new" creation of Isaiah 65:17. It is hardly possible that Isaiah would have envisioned these nations, so much a part of the old fallen creation, as a part of the new heavens and new earth. If at that time the "former things" will be forgotten (65:17), it is unlikely that Isaiah would have spoken of Assyria and Egypt as yet a part of that new world. There is a "this-worldliness" (*Diesseitlichkeit*)[102] to this vision that persistently resists our association of it with the final eternal state of the new heavens and new earth. Hoekema, who holds the same view as Young on this passage, argues that this part of the vision had a historical fulfillment already in the return of the people from Babylonian captivity in the 6th century B.C.[103] Hoekema is correct in recognizing the implications of this aspect of the vision, but ultimately he must appeal to "multiple fulfillments of prophecy"[104] to retain an eschatological focus for Isaiah's vision.

An appeal such as Young's to the "new creation" as the literal reference of Isaiah's visions is frequently met in amillennial discussions.[105] Hoekema, for example, recognizes that these OT passages suffer

now be like sheep or lambs; for they will have laid aside every cruel and brutish disposition. By these modes of expression he means nothing else than that those who formerly were like savage beasts will be mild and gentle" (*Commentary on the Book of the Prophet Isaiah*, 1:384).

101. *The Book of Isaiah*, p. 391.
102. Paul Volz, *Jüdische Eschatologie von Daniel bis Akiba* (Tübingen: J. C. B. Mohr, 1903), p. 67.
103. Anthony A. Hoekema, *The Bible and the Future* (Grand Rapids: Eerdmans, 1979), p. 206.
104. Ibid.
105. Willem A. VanGemeren, "Israel as the Hermeneutical Crux in the Interpretation of Prophecy (II)," *Westminster Theological Journal* 46 (1984):254-97; O. Palmer Robertson, "Hermeneutics of Continuity," *Continuity and Discontinuity: Perspectives on the Relationship between the Old and New Testaments*, ed. John S. Feinberg (Westchester, Ill.: Crossway, 1988), pp. 89-108; Anthony A. Hoekema, *The Bible and the Future* (Grand Rapids: Eerdmans, 1979).

"impoverishment"[106] when applied to the church or to an eternal state in heaven, makes them the center point of his view of a final eternal state here in heaven. The visions of Isaiah, argues Hoekema, are not to be spiritualized and applied (only) to the church and heaven, nor are they to suffer further "impoverishment" Hoekema contends by applying them to a thousand-year period here on earth (the Millennium of Rev. 20). They are rather to be literally applied to the new earth that will constitute the eternal dwelling place of all God's redeemed.[107]

While such a literal application of Isaiah's visions is preferable to the traditional spiritualizing of these texts, it is clear that these texts as we now have them do not fit easily into the scope of the eternal state described in Isaiah 65:17 and Revelation 21. In the first place, the "this-worldly" or "present worldly" scope of Isaiah's visions comports poorly with the view that Isaiah had in mind for the eternal state. As was noted above, Hoekema must argue that much in the visions has an immediate historical reference, for example, the return from Babylonian captivity, in order to explain those elements that are not suited to an eternal state (e.g., the focus on Assyria and Egypt). Furthermore, Hoekema is compelled again to resort to a figurative interpretation of Isaiah's words in order to apply them to the eternal state. Thus when Isaiah speaks of the death of an infant during this time or of a youth who dies at one hundred years (Isa. 65:20), Hoekema must conclude that this is merely "picturing in figurative terms the fact that the inhabitants of the new earth will live incalculably long lives."[108] Hoekema is certainly within the bounds of a literal approach to see Isaiah's words as a figurative picture of the nature of life on earth during this time. However, one must ask just how appropriate to the eternal state is his understanding of the imagery of 65:20. It is hard not to see in Isaiah's words an assumption that at this time death and misfortune will still be factors in man's earthly life. Even as figurative language there is a crucial difference between "eternal life" and "dying at a ripe old age."

Finally, the attempt to make the prophecies of Isaiah apply to both the present age and the "new heavens and new earth" is based on an ambiguous notion of reference. As VanGemeren has acknowledged, "Fulfillment is then not a state of perfection. Fulfillment is a process which takes us through the OT, NT, and the history of the church."[109]

---

106. *The Bible and the Future*, p. 206.
107. "Passages commonly interpreted as describing the millennium actually describe the new earth which is the culmination of God's redemptive work" (ibid., p. 201).
108. Ibid., p. 202.
109. Willem A. VanGemeren, "Israel as the Hermeneutical Crux in the Interpretation of Prophecy (II)," p. 279.

Robertson calls this notion of reference a "multi-staged fulfillment,"[110] which is apparently the same as Beecher's "manifold fulfillment."[111] Whatever may be said about the merits of this view of the prophet's reference, there is little basis from such a position to rule out the traditional millennial interpretation of the prophecies of Isaiah. If, in the process of multiple fulfillments, Isaiah's visions could find their fulfillment spiritually in the church and also physically in the "new creation," there is hardly a basis for ruling out a millennial fulfillment such as is described in Revelation 20.

THE INTERPRETIVE SUMMARY OF ISAIAH 2:1-5

Humility and openness should characterize any reading of the prophecies of the book of Isaiah. Formidable arguments can be marshaled on either side of the question of a millennial fulfillment of his visions. In the past the issues that separated an amillennial interpretation from a millennial one revolved around whether the prophet's words were to be taken literally, that is, as he originally intended them, or spiritually, in light of the establishment of the church in the NT. In recent discussions there has been a noticeable shift in focus. Few today seem willing to take the exegetical stance that the content of the NT should be read back into Isaiah's words. The starting point, at least, should be the original intention of the prophet as expressed in the book of Isaiah itself.

Taking such a starting point, we have attempted to show that Isaiah's visions of the future looked to a time when the Davidic kingship would be restored in Jerusalem and the Messiah would reign over that kingdom and rule all the nations of the world. In other words, they look to a time that fits remarkably well with John's vision of the earthly reign of Christ in Revelation 20. Taken at face value Isaiah's visions appear to speak of a literal fulfillment in Jerusalem itself and thus are not easily pressed into a reference to the establishment of the church. To do so would involve a strategy of "multiple fulfillments" that has little exegetical basis in the text of Isaiah.

Moreover, the attempt of amillennial scholars such as Hoekema to find a literal fulfillment of Isaiah's visions in an earthly eternal state does not do full justice to the content of the visions themselves. Though commendable for its focus on the physical dimensions of Isaiah's visions, the interpretation of the visions as a description of the eternal state overlooks the manifest "this-worldly" scope of the prophecies themselves.

---

110. Quoted in VanGemeren, ibid., p. 281.
111. Beecher, *The Prophets and the Promise*, p. 129.

It is readily acknowledged today that a nascent eschatological hope can be found throughout the textual and literary strategies of the composition of the prophetic books. We have attempted to describe a part of this hope as it relates to the book of Isaiah. To suppose, as many do, that such expectations could not have been the intention of the prophets themselves who spoke these words puts undue weight on the assumption that the prophets were not influential in the process of composing their books. Certainly the examples we have (such as Jer. 36) show that the prophets and their message are not to be separated from the work of writing their books.

Historically, it is hard to understand Israel's prophets any other way than that they longed for a physical, that is, earthly, reestablishment of the Davidic monarchy. The fact that prophetic books such as Isaiah continued as Scripture long after the postexilic period shows that their reference looked far beyond any temporal fulfillment within Israel's own immediate history. If our goal is to describe the reference of Isaiah's visions as he would have understood them, we can only hope to do so by paying close attention to the sense of those visions as they are given us in the book of Isaiah. That sense, as we have suggested in this chapter, fits best in the context of an earthy reign of Christ in Jerusalem as a precursor to the eternal state.

5

EVIDENCE FROM JEREMIAH

WALTER C. KAISER, JR.
Professor of Old Testament
Trinity Evangelical Divinity School

In the marvelous words known as the New Covenant, Jeremiah transcends all previous predictions of the glories of God's promises to Eve, Shem, Abraham, Isaac, Jacob, David, and his prophetic companions. Even though Jeremiah has frequently been called the weeping prophet and the prophet of sorrows, few will scale the heights of joy that Jeremiah depicts of God's final day of victory. God's kingdom, His coming Davidic king, and His redemption and restoration of His people Israel are set forth in some of the most memorable texts in the OT.

More than any other prophet, except perhaps Ezekiel, Jeremiah has posed the problem of the ultimate unification of Northern and Southern Kingdoms in the land of the ancient promise. It is this issue that raises the interpretive problem. Will the readers of Jeremiah's prophecies place the time of their fulfillment in the days of God's concluding acts as He wraps up history and prior to His introduction of the eternal state? Will the interpreter also receive these texts as the writer Jeremiah intended them to be taken under the Spirit of God: about a real Israel in a real land?

Answering these questions can serve to highlight the basic features and advantages of premillennialism. Premillennialism has at least three basic features: (1) it is a philosophy of history; (2) it involves a system of interpretation; and (3) it is a theology of salvation-history.

As a philosophy of history[1] premillennialism insists that God is able to complete in space and time what He began in His ancient promises to the patriarchs and David. It is not as if God decided that His promise of the land was somehow no longer valid or that He was now tiring of that promise and had therefore decided to scrap it. No, God will end history with a real, geopolitical Israel in the geographical territory that He announced she would have even back in the book of Genesis. This will demonstrate that the Lord is sovereign over the nations and the events of time.

Many in the Reformed tradition have offered unusually fine theologies of culture, including a believer's biblical, legitimate, and necessary response to the arts, leisure, nature, and learning. The surprising missing ingredient in many of these explanations of the cultural mandate is the divinely revealed symbol of the land of Israel as God's indication that He is in charge of history and that He is going to end it just as He planned to do from the beginning. God's activities do include political and geographical elements. If we Westerners persist in excluding these elements from our view of history, we shall be vulnerable to the charge of dualism, docetism, and spiritualism.[2]

The hermeneutical issue is just as significant. It is not merely a dispute over interpreting the promises given to Israel in a spiritual or literal manner; it is also a question as to whether the Abrahamic-Davidic Covenant[3] will be handled as a bilateral or unilateral covenant, that is, whether it is a conditional or unconditional covenant. The evidence seems overwhelmingly to say that it is unilateral, in that only God obligated Himself to keep the covenant. In no way did He make the provisions of His great promise for salvation, the coming of the Messiah, or the gift of the land rest on any mortal's work or contribution to that marvelous offer.[4]

1. See Ramesh P. Richard, "The Premillennial Interpretation of History," *Bibliotheca Sacra* 138 (1981):203-12; and James Oliver Buswell, *A Systematic Theology of the Christian Religion* (Grand Rapids: Zondervan, 1963), 2:541.
2. See the frank discussion of this point by the Reformed writer Hendrikus Berkhof, *Christ the Meaning of History*, trans. Lambertus Buurman (Richmond: Knox, 1966), pp. 147-53.
3. Here the Abrahamic and Davidic Covenants are viewed as one because of their common elements and their continuity in the prophetic revelation of God.
4. For further development of this argument, see my *Toward an Old Testament Theology* (Grand Rapids: Zondervan, 1978), pp. 92-94, 156-57; also my *Toward Rediscovering the Old Testament* (Grand Rapids: Zondervan, 1987), pp. 46-58. Contrast O. T. Allis, *Prophecy and the Church* (Philadelphia: Presbyterian & Reformed, 1945), pp. 31-48, with Charles Ryrie, *Dispensationalism Today* (Chicago: Moody, 1965), pp. 52-61.

From the previous two considerations flows the third advantage of premillennialism, a theology of salvation-history. God's word of judgment to Israel was not His final verdict. It is followed by His word of grace that takes the form of Israel's return to Canaan. In fact, it is impossible to separate the gift of salvation offered to Abraham and his spiritual descendants from the word concerning the land of Canaan and Israel in the last days. Romans has the theme of Jew and Gentile woven from its theme in the first chapter to the end of the book. It is a shame that many interpreters deal with the Jewish question in Romans 9-11 as if it were an interruption in the discussion of the great salvation our Lord has offered. No, Romans 9-11 is not a parenthesis in the argument; it is at the heart of God's single plan of salvation-history detailed throughout Scripture.

Now all these claims are difficult to handle in the abstract and as generalizing statements that encompass the whole of the Bible. Much more satisfying and convincing is the actual exegesis of individual texts. This chapter proposes to highlight in detail a selection of some of the main teaching blocks of texts found in the book of Jeremiah that favor a literal and unconditional fulfillment of God's promises in our kind of space and time. It will not even be helpful to say that these passages are literally fulfilled, but realized only in the eternal state of the new heavens and the new earth rather than during the thousand-year period when God concludes the historic process prior to introducing the eternal state.[5] Instead, God has obligated Himself to conclude the historic process by doing exactly what He promised He would do so many centuries ago. Especially significant in this discussion will be Jeremiah 3:14-18; 16:14-18; 23:3-8; 29:10-14; 31:35-40; and 33:7-21.

JEREMIAH 3:14-18

God's promise of the final restoration of the separated Northern and Southern Kingdoms of Israel and their blessing "at that time" (Jer. 3:17) and "in those days" (v. 18) became the basis for a call for repentance even in the days of Jeremiah.

There can be little doubt that this passage points to the final period. If the temporal references "in those days" (vv. 16, 18) and "at that time" (v. 17) are insufficient in and of themselves to decide the question, then the unheard of conditions certainly settle the question: "nor shall they walk anymore after the stubbornness of their evil heart" (v. 17) and "the house of Judah will walk with the house of Israel, and they will come together" (v. 18).

5. For a defense of the eternal position, see Anthony Hoekema, *The Bible and the Future* (Grand Rapids: Eerdmans, 1979), pp. 203-11.

Five startling promises made in this passage can be fulfilled only in the historic future and in the ancient land God promised to the patriarchs. The *first* is that even though there be only one Jewish person from every city and two from every clan or family, the living God will not forget even so small a remnant in any foreign nation or city. They will[6] be restored to the city of Jerusalem and its territories. Judah would go into exile, but God's pledge would not be revoked. It must not be interpreted to imply that the number who will be returned is minuscule, for the restoration was for Israel as a nation. Nor should it be inferred that this promise was accomplished only in those who obeyed in that generation, for Jerusalem is referred to as the seat of the king of God over all nations (v. 17).

A *second* feature of the days of restoration will be rulers, or "shepherds," who will rule "after [God's] own heart" (Jer. 3:15), an obvious allusion to the informing theology of 1 Samuel 13:14, where Jehovah had sought in David a man after God's own heart. Some have contended that these shepherds were realized in Zerubbabel, Joshua, Ezra, the apostles, and their successors. They, indeed, may be numbered as the beginnings of the fulfillment,[7] but no shepherd will completely fulfill this promise until that final Good Shepherd (cf. Ezek. 34:23) comes in the future kingdom of God. (This kind of multiple fulfilment is true of much prophecy which exhibits this "now" and "not yet" tension all in the same meaning.) Only with that Shepherd will the people be able to feed on knowledge and wisdom, for He will keep the law of God (Deut. 4:6). The expectation was that the dynasty of David would culminate in the kingship of Messiah.

The *third* promise was about their multiplication and fruitfulness (Jer. 3:16; cf. Jer. 23:3; Ezek. 36:11; Hos. 1:10; Rom. 11:12 *to plērōma autōn*). The ancient word given at Creation (Gen. 1:28) and initially fulfilled as Israel became a nation (Ex. 1:12) would be completed "in those days."

The *fourth* and most unexpected prediction is that the most sacred piece of furniture in all of Israel would lapse into obscurity and not

---

6. The Hebrew verbs in vv. 14*b*-15 are to be taken as future. Normally perfects with the *waw*-conversive are read as imperfect (i.e., future) in meaning when they are preceded by an imperfect tense of the verb. The verb in 3:14*a*, however, is a perfect, *'anōkî bā'altî*, which, incidentally, the LXX translates as a future, following the imperative *šûbû*. This probably represents an early eschatological interpretation. See Elmer A. Martens, "Motivations for the Promise of Israel's Restoration to the Land in Jeremiah and Ezekiel" (diss., Claremont Graduate School, 1972), pp. 39-40.

7. For an explanation of how the meaning can still be single yet have "now" and "not yet" aspects to it, see my *Back Toward the Future: Hints for Interpreting Biblical Prophecy* (Grand Rapids: Baker, 1989), pp. 117-24.

be thought of anymore (Jer. 3:16). The Ark of the Covenant, traditionally the throne of God, would now be replaced by Jerusalem, the new throne of God. In the future Jerusalem itself would be the place of the presence of the living God (v. 17), just as the Ark of the Covenant had been under the Old Covenant (Lev. 16:2; 1 Sam. 4:4; 1 Chron. 13:6; Ps. 80:1). The text reminds us of the description of the new Jerusalem in Revelation 21:22-24.

The picture of the nations gathering in Zion is one of the grand pictures of the prophets (cf. Isa. 2:1-4; Zech. 2:11; Mic. 4:1-4). And with all of this comes the curtailment of evil (cf. Rev. 20:1-3), for now the name of the Lord will be dominant and that name will be the new standard for all that is right, just, and true (the Jeremiah text describes what is generally true of the millennial age, the Satan-led revolt at the end being the exception [cf. Rev. 20:3, 7-9]).

The *fifth* and final promise of this text that fits with a premillennial scheme of interpretation alone is the vision of the kingdom, which was divided in 931 B.C. after Solomon's days, being reunited once again (Jer. 3:18). This has never happened since the tragic schism took place. Nevertheless, verse 18 promises that the two southern tribes of Judah and Benjamin would be joined together with the separated ten northern tribes "in those days." Contrary to the expectation of some commentators, this hope was not accomplished under the return of Zerubbabel (536 B.C.), Ezra (557 B.C.), or Nehemiah (445 B.C.) because: (1) neither the whole of Judah nor the whole of Israel participated in the return; (2) few Judahites, much less Gentile nations, returned spiritually to the Lord; (3) the ten tribes of the north were not reunited with the southern two in any of these three returns (or in the advent of the Christian church, where some attempt to see the fulfillment of this text); and (4) there is no evidence that people no longer walked in sin or the evil of their own hearts.

Even more telling is the specific word that ends verse 18: the land to which they will be restored will be "the land that I gave your fathers as an inheritance." Surely this note limits the fulfillment of the promise to the land with the boundaries described in the promise included in the patriarchal and Davidic covenants. Jeremiah is speaking of a well-defined land on this earth, not a new-earthly fulfillment. The complete fulfillment of this prophecy must be reserved for that final period of history when God brings back the clans of Israel and Judah to their Messiah and the land of promise on this earth. The denial of a millennium (amillennialism) or the projection of it to some form of the eternal state, or even the identification of it with some present success of the church or Israel all fall short of the marvelous specificity found in these five predictions.

JEREMIAH 16:14-18

The restoration of Israel to her land is here compared with the Exodus from Egypt, and verses 14-15 are almost an exact equivalent of Jeremiah 23:7-8. The Lord Himself is the guarantor of the oath that He takes in this promise of a future restoration.

Speaking of the coming days (v. 14), Jeremiah once again announces a definite return to the land (v. 15). The land is defined as the "land which I gave to their fathers." The same promise is repeated in Jeremiah 23:7-8 in a different context. So noteworthy will this future return be that it will overshadow the Exodus from Egypt.

Verses 16-18 continue the message of judgment begun earlier in the chapter. Israel and Judah must "first" (v. 18) be made to pay for their iniquity. Even though the Septuagint version of this verse omits "first," the preferred reading is to retain it (on the basis of retaining the more difficult reading). In that case, the reference of the "first" is to the announced future restoration in verses 14-15. The understanding of repayment is not one of compensating God, but rather it is, as in Deuteronomy 15:18 and Isaiah 40:2, an adequate and ample, though in no sense an equivalent, measure for their sin.

Jeremiah 16 concludes in verses 19-21 with a further reason for assigning the restoration to the land to a future day. In order that the nations may know the power and name of the Lord, He must first deal with the sin of Israel and Judah. Thus the tribulation of Israel's most desperate hour will have as one of its chief benefits the fact that the nations of the world will come from the ends of the earth (v. 19) and recognize that the Lord is the only sovereign and almighty God (v. 21). While Jeremiah does not say specifically how the nations will obtain such knowledge, it may well be that the deliverance of Israel (v. 15) in the final day (cf. Jer. 30:7; Dan. 12:1; Rev. 12:13-14) may serve as the great impetus for the nations coming to know the Lord. Such an action will expose the impotency of the nations, their worthless gods, and the power of the living God.

To sum up, a restoration of the historic land, which overshadows even the Exodus in fame, preceded by a time of unprecedented trouble for Israel, can fit only the premillennial scheme.

JEREMIAH 23:3-8

The announcement of the coming of the final king in the line of David lies at the heart of this great messianic text. The point, however, must not be missed—it will be Messiah's second coming when He will rule and reign righteously over all. It is precisely in this context that

Israel is promised her gathering from all of the countries of the disper-sion (23:7-8 as in 16:14-18).

The doctrine of the "remnant" repeats a theme heard frequently in Jeremiah (see especially chapters 24 and 40-44). The Lord Himself will not only gather His flock of the nation of Israel from every country into which they have gone, but He will also make them increase greatly (v. 3). This is very similar to 3:16.

The "shepherds" of 23:4 are not to be contrasted with the "righ-teous Branch" (= "rightful or legitimate scion") of verse 5. The plural number of shepherds only stresses that there were a number in the Abrahamic-Davidic line of the final messianic person who was to come in the last day, even as we have explained above on 3:15. "Shepherds" is a generic plural having a collective sense resulting in the final one of whom each was only a partial representative (cf. the similar use of "anti-christs" in the line of "the Antichrist" who is to come, 1 John 2:18).

The "righteous Branch" promised by Jeremiah had already ap-peared in Isaiah 4:2 as "the Branch of the Lord," a genitive of source, that is, the messianic scion who had His origins in God (a concept having its inception in 2 Sam. 23:5: "Will not God cause to sprout [= 'branch out'] all my salvation and all my desire?" David said; and again in Ps. 132:17: "I will make a horn sprout [= 'branch out'] for David; I will set up a lamp for My Messiah"—this author's trans.). The name "Branch" for Messiah will also appear later in Zechariah 3:8 and 6:12.

Messiah will be called (notice, not "named") "The Lord our righ-teousness." Some translate the last part of this title as if it were a predi-cate—"is our righteousness." But the Masoretes were careful to indicate that that is precisely what was not meant here. They showed by punctua-tion marks that the Hebrew word we translate as "our righteousness" was to be directly joined to "the Lord." What is more, they also put a dividing line in the text to prevent anyone from understanding that "our righteousness" was the predicate of the Lord. Our Lord alone, then, is the norm for "right-ness" and justice that will be the norm during the Millennium when He reigns in the land.

In the era when Messiah was reigning as king "in the land" (v. 5), Judah and Israel would be led out of all the countries of the earth and allowed to dwell securely and multiply greatly in their own land.[8] Only a

8. Walter Brueggemann, *To Pluck Up, To Tear Down: A Commentary on the Book of Jeremiah 1-25* (Grand Rapids: Eerdmans, 1988), pp. 199-200, places this promise at the first advent: "The promise articulated here is taken up in the 'Common Lectionary C' in the use of Jer. 33:14-16 during Advent. Quite clearly, the Church has handled the text with reference to Jesus. Such a use requires an interpretive posture that recog-nizes that the text 'does and does not' run toward Jesus." Brueggemann also said in

premillennialist can understand how or when such an event could take place. Obviously, Israel has never enjoyed such an existence from 586 B.C. up to the writing of this chapter. The promises of verses 7-8 have already appeared and have been discussed in 16:14-15. Verse 6 will reappear in Jeremiah 33:16.

JEREMIAH 29:10-14

Jeremiah directed a letter to the exiles in Babylon indicating that Babylon's power would last for only seventy years. But there was hope, and that is the part of his letter that interests us here.

In these verses, God's plan for Israel is stated. First, Babylon's power would last for a mere seventy years. While some have suggested that the counting for these seventy years should begin at the fall of Nineveh (611 B.C. to the fall of Babylon in 539 B.C., 72 years), or the year of Nebuchadnezzar's accession in 605 B.C. (= 66 years), or even the first deportation of Daniel and his three companions in 606 B.C., we may in fact be dealing with a round number to match the predicted seventy years of captivity of Israel from the captivity of Daniel and his three friends in 606 until the initial rebuilding of the Temple (Ezra 3:8) in 536 B.C. (= 70 years). It is remarkable that Jeremiah would predict that the power of Babylon would last so briefly, but that is how it also happened under the guiding hand of God.

The second prediction made in this letter to the captives in Babylon was that the nation of Israel would be regathered in her original inheritance (29:10). They would return home. Just as Yahweh had visited (*pāqad*) Israel with judgment, so He would visit (*pāqad*) them with blessing and "fulfill [His] good word." The content of that "good word" is now explained in the infinitive clause which follows: "to bring you back to this place."

God had not acted on the basis of the whims and caprices of most despots history has known; instead, He had never forgotten His publicly announced plan for His people Israel that involved their welfare, future, and solid confidence for a happy ending to all their present trials. There was not one item of evil in His plan for His people. The word translated "future" in verse 11 is literally "end" (*'ăḥarît*). "End" is often used for the expected outcome or the issue of a matter (cf. Prov. 5:4; 16:25; 23:18; Isa. 46:10). Note that the two words "end" and "hope"

the same place that the "exilic anticipations for restoration . . . [are] the very anticipations that the Christian community has found embodied in Jesus of Nazareth." It is clear that Brueggemann has failed to heed the temporal signals and the unique conditions indicated in the text. They point to the end of history, not to the deliverance of the Christian community.

are used synonymously. This again points us to another well-known phrase for the messianic era, "the end of days" (Gen. 49:1; Hos. 3:5; Mic. 4:1). But notice that the messianic promise is here linked inseparably with the ultimate gift of the land to Israel.

The most frequently used expression in Jeremiah in connection with the theme of the restoration begins in 29:14, "I will restore your fortunes" (*wešabtî 'et šebyytkem*). Out of the twenty-six occurrences of this term in the OT, twelve are found in Jeremiah.[9] Despite a large number of monographs written on this expression, there is no precise agreement among scholars as to its meaning. The phrase is most common in Jeremiah 30-33, where it occurs seven times (30:3, 18; 31:23; 32:44; 33:7 [twice], 11, 26 [*qerē*]).

God would "restore [or return] the captivity" as He had promised in the passage where He first used this expression, Deuteronomy 30:3. Not only is the expression in Jeremiah 29:14, "restore your fortunes," rooted in Deuteronomy 30, but this whole pentateuchal chapter must have been on Jeremiah's mind as he wrote his letter. Verse 14 is a brief summary of Deuteronomy 30:3-5 just as verses 12-13 were a brief renewal of the promise in Deuteronomy 4:29-30. If the present generation in captivity in Babylon refused to call on God in prayer, to seek Him with all their heart, then they would not participate in any of the foretastes of the blessings of the end day, just as the generation in the wilderness had failed because of their unbelief to experience the blessing of entering the land.

While the promise of restoration looks, in part, to the days of Cyrus and Zerubbabel, just as the first promise of Israel's entrance into the land did, it would be a mistake to assume that is all the text was talking about. Verse 14 specifically envisions not just a return from Babylon where the present captives were being addressed, but "from all the nations . . . where [God] had driven them." To speak in this manner was to go beyond the horizon of the present disaster and to give God's plan for the distant future. Such wide-ranging sweeps of history are not uncommon in prophetic literature. This was the promise that had been made to the fathers of their country, Abraham, Isaac, and Jacob.

J. A. Thompson commented that "the condition of their occupancy of the land was obedience. There was nothing automatic and nothing permanent for those who rejected Yahweh and his covenant."[10] This is

---

9. Martens, "Motivations for the Promise of Israel's Restoration to the Land in Jeremiah and Ezekiel," pp. 172-96. See his discussion of the bibliography and suggested roots from which this expression may have emerged.
10. J. A. Thompson, *The Book of Jeremiah* (Grand Rapids: Eerdmans, 1980), p. 548.

true, of course, if we refer only to the participation in the promise, but in no way could any generation of Israelites frustrate the certainty of the unconditional promise itself. That rested on God's faithfulness, not Israel's.

Once again Jeremiah leaves us with promises which can only be fulfilled by a worldwide regathering of Israel to the same land from which God sent her into Babylonian captivity (viz. the land of Palestine). The fulfillment must be yet in the future, and it must be upon the present earth. Thus, Jeremiah's promises support the claims of premillennialism.

JEREMIAH 31:35-40

Probably toward the end of his career, Jeremiah issued a little book of comfort in Jeremiah 30-31, very much in the spirit and tone of Isaiah 40-66 or Hosea 1-3. It is a moving piece with unusual beauty. Its theme is the restoration of Israel to her land, the appearance of messianic times, and the establishment of the "New Covenant" (Jer. 31:31-34).

With *six majestic strophes* Jeremiah describes the messianic times.[11] The *first* strophe (Jer. 30:2-11) describes the great distress that will come to Jerusalem in the day of the Lord's wrath. Since one would not ordinarily think there would be two periods of unprecedented tribulation on the earth, it is fair to believe that the one Jeremiah announces is the same one Jesus speaks of in the Olivet Discourse (Matt. 24-25). These passages cannot refer to the destruction of Jerusalem in A.D. 70, for the Davidic monarchy was not restored after that date and the Jews were not saved out of it, but were killed by the thousands and many were carried away.

The *second* strophe (30:12–31:6) says that Israel's wound is incurable and her sin so heinous that she must be severely punished. But Yahweh will heal her, and Jerusalem will be rebuilt. The hillsides of Samaria will be replanted with vineyards, and Zion will become a resort for pilgrims once again with great music and dancing at the festivals.

The *third* strophe (31:7-14) features the weeping and supplication of the returnees in repentance. Great rejoicing follows as Israel assumes the position as head of the nations. The land again becomes fruitful and a great multitude makes its way to Zion.

Rachel weeping for her children begins the *fourth* strophe (31:15-22). Her children have gone into exile, but there is the hope of

11. See Charles Augustus Briggs, *Messianic Prophecy: A Critical Study of the Messianic Passages of the Old Testament in the Order of Their Development* (New York: Scribner's, 1889), pp. 246-57. I am indebted to Briggs for the outline of Jer. 30-31 that follows.

their return from captivity. As Ephraim begins to confess his sin, God turns to him with compassion and the tender love of a father.

The New Covenant is the high point of the *fifth* strophe (31:23-34). God is more than able to counterbalance His judgments with the blessing of writing that same law, only this time on the hearts of His people. In that day there will no longer be a need for Levitical teachers or prophets to instruct any in the ways of God. All will know Him, both small and great.

The *sixth* and final strophe (31:35-40) culminates this first part of the book of comfort. The divine covenant will be as inviolable as the ordinances of heaven, for God has not by any means entirely rejected His people or His ancient promise. It is this section we wish to investigate now.

Jeremiah makes a strong point: as surely as the laws of nature are inviolable, so certainly shall Israel continue as a nation before God. Even though they would suffer national dissolution, they were still destined in the divine program to be a distinct people. Looking beyond national Israel for the fulfillment of this prophecy in the church, as a spiritual Israel, fails to grapple with the certainty of the statements in Jeremiah 31:36-37. God will as easily renege on His promise to the patriarchs as He will renege on His ordinances that He set with the sun, moon, and stars. If the celestial bodies are still abiding by God's appointment (Gen. 1:14-16), then why would we conclude that He has decided to drop His promise to the descendants of Israel? Just as the measuring of the heavens and the searching out of the foundations of the earth are impossible, so God's casting off of Israel is likewise impossible.

The devastated city of Jerusalem will also be rebuilt, but in the end days. The imagery of an eschatological measuring of the city appears in Ezekiel 40-48 and in Zechariah 2. The measuring will be done in that final future restoration of Jerusalem. The reference to well-known points in the city suggests a restoration of Jerusalem on this earth. The extent of the rebuilding begins on the northeast corner at the Tower of Hananel (cf. Neh. 3:1; 12:39; Zech. 14:10). The Corner Gate apparently is on the northwest side of the city where King Uzziah built towers (2 Chron. 26:9; cf. 2 Kings 14:13; Zech. 14:10). By these two points the northern boundaries of the future city are set. The location of Gareb is not known, but as the name implies "scabby, leprous," it may be the hill of the lepers outside the city to the northwest. Some connect Goah with the place of capital punishment. Certainly the valley of dead bodies is the valley of the sons of Hinnom, that defiled place on the south side of the city where the accumulated filth of the city with its ever-present worms and burning fires reeked of defilement. The Horse Gate is probably on the east side.

The point is that the extension of the city of Jerusalem in the final day will include areas previously defiled, but the unholy will be rendered holy by the personal appearance of the Messiah, the Son of God. Furthermore, it shows also that the city will no longer need such places of contamination, since everything will be holy to the Lord. That day will never come without the appearance of the Messiah in righteousness, peace, and justice. That can only take place in connection with the second advent of our Lord.

JEREMIAH 33:7-21

Jeremiah has even more promises concerning Israel's glorious future in the Millennium. Yahweh will bring healing, peace, safety, cleansing, forgiveness, and restoration in that marvelous day of the future.

Despite the destruction of Jerusalem, the Lord God promised healing and peace (v. 6). The exiles would be returned (v. 7) and Israel's sin would also be cleansed and forgiven (v. 8). Jerusalem would become the joy and glory of the nations of the earth (v. 9). The effects of the curse of God, repeated three times in verses 10-13, would be lifted and joy would return to the countryside and Zion once again.

Verses 14-16, at first reading, seem to be just a repetition of Jeremiah 23:5-6. In fact, the whole section of verses 14-26 has been omitted from the Alexandrian text of the Septuagint. Because of this omission and because both the house of David and that of the Levitical priests is said in this section to be of eternal duration, it has not been uncommon for modern commentators to regard 33:14-26 as spurious. Fortunately, others have regarded such a judgment as utterly preposterous. Accordingly, E. W. Hengstenberg[12] has shown that the LXX in Jeremiah often omitted whatever had been stated previously, since the Greek translators were not able to understand the purpose and the meaning for the repetition. Given the fact that verses 15-16 are almost verbatim for what is in 23:5-6, and 33:20-25 in thought and in many of the words is partially represented in 31:35-37, the complete text of 33:14-26 was deleted from the LXX. Scholars like J. D. Michaelis, Jahn, and Movers started a trend of prejudice against this passage, it would appear, mainly because such an increase and duration of the Levites and the house of David were considered unthinkable. But this, comments Hengstenberg in the passage we have already cited, proves little more than the fact that these men understood the text no better than did the ancient Greek translators.

---

12. E. W. Hengstenberg, *Christology of the Old Testament, and a Commentary on the Messianic Predictions*, trans. Theodore Meyer (Edinburgh: Clark, 1872), 2:460-62.

The greatest interpretive battle over this text centers, as with most of these passages depicting a happy day of Israel's return, on whether the church or even a postexilic Israel is being addressed, or as we are contending here, a revived national Israel after the second advent of our Lord but prior to the eternal state. The text seems extremely clear in predicting the climax to that "good word" (Jer. 33:14) offered in Deuteronomy 28:1-14 and 1 Kings 8:56. That "good word" embodied all the blessings God had predicted would come to Israel. Moreover, verse 17 repeats almost verbatim the ancient word given to David in 2 Samuel 7:16, reiterated by David to Solomon in 1 Kings 2:4, acknowledged by Solomon in his dedication of the Temple in 1 Kings 8:25, and renewed by the Lord Himself in His promise to Solomon in 1 Kings 9:5.

Shall we attribute Jeremiah 33:14-26, as Theodore Laetsch[13] does, to the "glory of the New Testament Church" after the first advent of Messiah? Or shall we attribute these verses and ones like them to a restored national Israel after the second advent of our Lord? Laetsch argues that the raising up of the Branch pointed to the unique coming of Christ prior to His establishing the Christian church, through which the Lord now dispenses His judgment and through the gospel announces His righteousness.

But Laetsch ultimately stumbles, as do all who attribute such prophecies as these only to our Lord's first coming, when he inquires why Jerusalem is called "the Lord our righteousness." He correctly answers that Jerusalem is given this high title, which in Jeremiah 23:6 was given to our Lord, simply because Yahweh Himself will be present in that day in Jerusalem. But unhappily, Laetsch goes on to ask, "By what right may the Church be called Jehovah Our Righteousness?"[14] Laetsch replies that the answer to that question belongs to God. He may name the church what He will; in fact, He called His name over the Tabernacle, the Temple, the people of Israel, the Gentiles, and Jerusalem.

But Laetsch has missed the fact that no equivalence is set up in this text or context for making Jerusalem a type, illustration, or allegory of the church. That is precisely what is needed here and it is missing. In addition to this fact is the further problem that when God calls His name over something or someone, it generally indicates ownership. But here we have the attribution of the quality of righteousness which could never be true of the city of Jerusalem prior to the Millennium, when only the actual presence of the King of kings would guarantee such an attribution, nor is it true of the Christian church, which likewise is devoid of

13. Theodore Laetsch, *Bible Commentary: Jeremiah* (St. Louis: Concordia, 1965), pp. 268-73.
14. Ibid., p. 270.

such righteousness as exists absolutely in "Yahweh our Righteousness." Therefore we urge Christian and Jewish interpreters to place the moment of fulfillment of these texts in the days when "justice and righteousness [are executed] on earth" (v. 15) and when Yahweh "restore[s] the fortunes of the land" (v. 11).

The specific millennial promises found in Jeremiah 33:14 and following, where the prophet moves from the general to the particular, are: (1) The Messiah, God's righteous Branch will appear (v. 15). (2) Messiah will execute true justice and righteousness once again in the land (v. 15), a reference to His second coming. (3) From this point on, there will never be a break or an absence of an heir to occupy the Davidic throne (i.e., Christ Himself) or of servants to carry out the worship of God. (4) As long as the fundamental laws of the universe continue, so long will God's promise with the patriarchs, David's seed, and Phinehas continue; God's Servant, Messiah, and His ministers in His courts would not cease to exist (vv. 19-22).

CONCLUSION

These texts are merely representative passages of the great theme of the restoration of the nation Israel in the final day. Of course, major differences in interpreting them result from competing presuppositions. Some will continue to insist that the promises to Israel have been fulfilled in the church or will be fulfilled in the eternal state. But our contention remains that such a view has captured only part of the truth while missing the major emphasis that has been placed by Jeremiah on the indissolubility of the ancient promises made to ethnic-political Israel. If the sun and moon are still shining, then the Abrahamic-Davidic promise is still intact. And there is no way that one can separate the spiritual aspects of that immutable covenant (e.g., the One Seed, the gospel) from the physical or material references to the land of Canaan.

Neither can some of the fulfillment of these predictions be reserved solely for the eternal state, for in that case one must face the fact that evil still rears its ugly head occasionally before the final conquest of Satan and his forces in many of these passages.

We urge Christ's church to take another careful look at these prophetic passages. Nowhere can it be shown that most, all, or even some of the promises made to Abraham, Isaac, Jacob, or David, have been nullified, modified, exchanged, or transformed in value. They are as abiding as the present heaven and earth; in other words, as lasting as the historical process is prior to the introduction of the eternal state. To be sure, many of the features of the reign of God introduced in seminal form during the times of the Gentiles and the church come into full flower during the Millennium and then into God's absolute control during the eternal state. But this affirmation in no way darkens the original future that God had laid out for Israel. One day Israel will return to her land from every country on the face of the earth. They and all Gentile believers will experience the personal presence of the living, resurrected Christ in a real, restored Jerusalem. From there Christ will rule and reign with all His saints with an unqualified justice and righteousness such as this old earth has longed to see since the fall of humanity in the Garden of Eden. Great will be the day of our Lord Jesus Christ.

6

EVIDENCE FROM EZEKIEL

MARK F. ROOKER
Professor of Old Testament and Hebrew
Criswell College

The book of Ezekiel has frequently been the subject of controversy. Some early Jewish rabbis questioned whether the book should even be included in the OT, as it apparently contradicted the law of Moses on a number of points. The contents of the book have continued to foment discussion through the centuries. Among contemporary evangelical Christians the book has been subject to much debate as well, particularly in the area of eschatology. It is the purpose of this essay to examine the contribution of Ezekiel to biblical eschatology by examining an important prophetic text, Ezekiel 36:16-38, and then consider the important issues involved in the Temple worship of Ezekiel 40-48.

GOD'S REPUTATION RESTORED IN THE MILLENNIUM
(EZEKIEL 36:16-38)

The book of Ezekiel can be divided into three sections: (1) prophecy of judgment before the destruction of Jerusalem (chaps. 1-24); (2) prophecy against the nations (chaps. 25-32); and (3) prophecy of comfort after the destruction of Jerusalem (chaps. 33-48).[1] Ezekiel 36:16-38 is a prophecy in the final division of the book after the fall of Jerusalem that offers hope to the nation. The passage is a very important section of the book, as it contains many of the book's major eschatological motifs as well as providing a synopsis of Ezekiel's theology.[2] The passage has two major sections (36:16-21 and 36:22-38). Verses 16-21 present the problem; verses 22-38, the solution. In the second major section, 36:22-38, two additional subsections, verses 33-36 and 37-38, advance issues discussed in verses 22-32.

The pericope begins in verse 16 with the introductory phrase, "Then the word of the Lord came to me saying," and ends with the formulaic statement, "Then they will know that I am the Lord" in verse 38.[3] Thus, at the outset, we are alerted to the goal of the divine communication to Ezekiel—Ezekiel's communication of the revelation from Yahweh is to result in the recognition of Yahweh. The introductory phrase of verse 16 indicates the beginning of the first division, while the rest of the sections are introduced by the phrase "Thus says the Lord God" (vv. 22, 33, 37). The exegetical outline of the passage could be presented as follows:

I. Yahweh's present concern about His reputation (36:16-21).

   A. Yahweh has sent Israel into exile for defiling the land (vv. 16-19).

   B. Israel's exile causes Yahweh to have concern for His reputation (vv. 20-21).

II. Yahweh's future restoration of His reputation (36:22-38).

   A. Yahweh will vindicate His name among the nations by restoring His people to their homeland (vv. 22-32).

   B. Yahweh will renovate the land (vv. 33-36).

   C. Yahweh will increase the inhabitants of the land (vv. 37-38).

---

1. M. H. Segal, *Introduction to the Bible*, 2 vols. (Jerusalem: Kiryat-Sepher, 1977), 2:417 (in Heb.); S. R. Driver, *An Introduction to the Literature of the Old Testament* (Cleveland and New York: Clark, 1956), p. 279. Similarly, Gleason Archer, *A Survey of Old Testament Introduction* (Chicago: Moody, 1964), pp. 368-69. The book could also be divided on the basis of the three great visions of the book: 1:1–3:15; 8:1–11:25; 40:1–48:35. See H. Van Dyke Parunak, "The Literary Architecture of Ezekiel's *Mar'ôt 'Elohîm*," *Journal of Biblical Literature* 99 (1980):61-74.

2. Georg Fohrer and Kurt Galling, *Ezechiel*, Handbuch zum Alten Testament (Tübingen: J. C. B. Mohr, 1955), p. 202.

3. Ezek. 37:1 clearly begins a new pericope describing Ezekiel's transportation in a vision.

YAHWEH'S PRESENT CONCERN ABOUT HIS REPUTATION (36:16-21)

Ezekiel 36:16 begins with the formula: "Then the word of the Lord came to me saying." This phrase, which occurs forty-six times in the book of Ezekiel, alerts the reader that a new section is being introduced.[4] It also indicates that the subsequent information is based on a revelation-experience of the prophet.[5] The content of that revelation begins in verse 17 with a history lesson describing the spiritual condition of the nation prior to their exile. Their deeds have "defiled" (tm') the land, hence jeopardizing their greatest blessing.[6] This defilement is compared to the uncleanness that would result from contact with a woman in her menstruation (Lev. 15:19).[7] The expression should be seen in light of the Mosaic law (Lev. 18:28), where defiling the land was said to result in banishment from the homeland. Thus, God responds in accordance with His Word to Israel's sin, which is specifically designated as murder and idolatry (v. 18),[8] by pouring out his wrath[9] and scattering His people among the nations (v. 19).[10] The land could no longer tolerate the moral defilement.[11]

The banishment of the nation resulted in something far worse, however. In verse 20 we are told that "when" (wayyābô')[12] Israel was in

---

4. See Walter Zimmerli, "The Special Form- and Traditio-Historical Character of Ezekiel's Prophecy," *Vetus Testamentum* 25 (1965):515-16.

5. Moshe Greenberg, *Ezekiel 1-20*, The Anchor Bible (Garden City, N.Y.: Doubleday, 1983), p. 83.

6. Walter Eichrodt, *Ezekiel*, trans. Cosslett Quinn (Philadelphia: Westminster, 1970), p. 494.

7. Comparing defilement with the uncleanness that resulted from menstruation occurs in Ezek 18:6; 22:10; 36:17. The analogy of menstruation might also have been used to indicate the fact that Yahweh has had to physically remove Himself from Israel just as a man was not to approach, i.e., must distance himself from a woman during her menstruation. Thus A. B. Ehrlich, *Ezekiel*, Mikrâ Ki-Peshutô (New York: KTAV, 1969), p. 355 (in Heb.).

8. The phrase "because they have defiled it with their idols" is *ûb⁰gillûlêhem timm⁰'ûbā*. The term *gillûlîm*, "idols," is found in the book of Ezekiel 39 of its 48 occurrences in the OT. The etymology of the term is unclear, but it may be related to the root for "dung," and may thus pejoratively associate idols with dung. See G. Johannes Botterweck and Helmer Ringgren, eds. *Theological Dictionary of the Old Testament* (Grand Rapids: Eerdmans, 1974-86), s.v. "*gillûlîm*," by H. D. Preuss. Ezekiel often associates this term with the root *tm'*, "unclean." See also Ezek. 14:6-7, 11; 20:7, 18, 31; 22:3; 23:7, 13 17, 30, 38-39; 37:23.

9. In the same way that Israel has "poured out" (*špk*) blood so Yahweh "pours out" (*špk*) His wrath (v. 18). The punishment is thus commensurate with the crime.

10. The pairing of *puṣ*, "to scatter," with *zrh*, "to disperse," occurs in Ezek. 12:15; 20:23; 22:15; 29:12; 30:23, 26.

11. Eichrodt, *Ezekiel*, p. 494.

12. The juxtaposition of two *waw* consecutive imperfects may suggest sequence (E. Kautzsch and A. E. Cowley, *Gesenius' Hebrew Grammar* [Oxford: Clarendon, 1910], 164b, p. 501).

exile "they profaned" (*wayḥall^elû*) Yahweh's holy name.[13] The nations of the world would not interpret Israel's exile to be due to her disobedience and consequent discipline. On the contrary, the enemies of Israel would conclude that Yahweh could save neither His people nor His land.[14] God announced His response to this conclusion out of concern for the reputation of His name (v. 21).[15] Verse 21, which stresses the concern Yahweh has for His name, should be taken as the pivotal verse of the entire passage, repeating the fact that Israel had profaned Yahweh's name as well as providing the motivation for the verses that follow.

YAHWEH'S FUTURE RESTORATION OF HIS REPUTATION (36:22-38)

Following the justification for Israel's exile and dispersion, the announcement of Yahweh's response begins in verse 22 with the term *lākēn*, "therefore." This term, which occurs most frequently in prophetic literature, functions as a connecting link between two distinct units, drawing special attention to the response that is about to be made.[16] As a result of the profanation of His reputation, Yahweh announces that He is "about to act."[17] The motive for Yahweh's coming intervention is concern for His reputation, not compassion for the covenant people.[18] Verse

---

13. The atrocity of this event is brought out more forcefully as the Hebrew roots for "profane" (*ḥll*) and "holy" (*qdš*) function as antonyms (e.g., *Theological Dictionary of the Old Testament*, s.v. "*ḥll*," by W. Dommershausen). The reference to "name" should be viewed as synonymous to "honor." See Ernst Jenni and Claus Westermann, eds., *Theologisches Handwörterbuch zum Alten Testament* (Zürich: Chr. Kaiser Verlag München, 1984), s.v. "*šēm*," by A. S. van der Woude. See also George Arthur Buttrick, ed., *Interpreter's Dictionary of the Bible* (Nashville: Abingdon, 1962), s.v. "name," by R. Abbab; and Sheldon H. Blank, "Isaiah 52.5 and the Profanation of the Name," *Hebrew Union College Annual* 25 (1954):8. The two roots also occur in opposition in v. 23.

14. Rashi, *Miqrayôt Gedalôt*, 5 vols. (Jerusalem: Eshkol, 1976), 4:254*a* (in Heb.). See Num. 14:16 and Ex. 32:12 where Yahweh's reputation is linked to the welfare of Israel.

15. Literally, Yahweh "grieved" (*ḥml*) for His name (similarly, see Ezek. 5:11; 7:4, 9; 8:18; 9:5, 10; 16:5). Ezekiel 20 also refers to Yahweh's concern for His name.

16. See W. Eugene March, "Laken: Its Functions and Meanings," *Rhetorical Criticism: Essays in Honor of James Muilenburg*, ed. Jared J. Jackson and Martin Kessler (Pittsburgh: Pickwick, 1974), pp. 256-84. The term is frequently followed, as it is here, by the phrase *kōh 'āmar 'adōnay yhwh*, "Thus says the Lord God." This combination occurs 24 times in the book of Ezekiel, in response to an undesirable circumstance. See Greenberg, *Ezekiel*, p. 111.

17. The participle *'ōśêh* expresses imminency, indicating that something is "about to" happen. For this use of the participle, see Bruce K. Waltke and M. O'Connor, *An Introduction to Biblical Hebrew Syntax* (Winona Lake, Ind.: Eisenbrauns, 1990), 37.6*f*, p. 627.

18. This is expressed in the phrase *lō' l^ema'ankem*, "It is not for your sake" (v. 22).

23 explains the goal of the restoration of Yahweh's reputation: Then the nations "will know that I am the Lord,"[19] declares the Lord God, "when I prove Myself holy among you in their sight."

The phrase "know that I am the Lord" is a characteristic Ezekielian phrase and is referred to as the "statement of recognition." Yahweh's acts of intervention in the book of Ezekiel are always intended for a stated objective—that His people or the nations recognize that "I am Yahweh." The acts of Yahweh thus do not occur for their own sake but are directed toward human groups or all people in general. The statement of the recognition of Yahweh functions as a conclusion, providing the motivation for the action as well as the desired result—that Yahweh be duly acknowledged among the nations. It is the ultimate goal of the action taken by Yahweh.[20] Hence, verses 22-23, taken together, should be viewed as a summary statement for the entire passage. How Yahweh's reputation is vindicated, how He is proven holy in the midst of Israel, is the subject of the following verses.

Verse 24 begins a lengthy section that explains how Yahweh will restore His name, which has been profaned in the eyes of those who have seen His people defeated and exiled. He will begin to vindicate His name by taking the exiled Israelites from other nations and returning them to their own land (v. 24).[21] This verse addresses the central problem of the preceding verses—the desecration of Yahweh's reputation among the nations—and introduces the solution to the prevailing dilemma. After Israel has been returned God will cleanse her[22] from all her "filthiness" (*ṭum'ôtêkem*) and from all her "idols" (*gillûlêkem*) (v. 25).[23]

---

19. The root *yd'*, "to know," occurs in the book of Ezekiel more than in any other book of the OT. The overwhelming majority of these occurrences in the book are in the phrase "know that I am Yahweh" (Walter Zimmerli, *I Am Yahweh*, trans. Douglas W. Scott [Atlanta: Knox, 1982], p. 31).

20. Zimmerli, *I Am Yahweh*, pp. 5, 35-37.

21. The use of the possessive suffix with the noun *ădāmâ*, "land," indicates that the native land is in view (H. H. Schmid, "*ădāmâ*," *Theologisches Handwörterbuch zum Alten Testament*; similarly, J. G. Plöger, "*ădāmâ*," *Theological Dictionary of the Old Testament*). The NASB translation "your own land" nicely reflects this nuance. This qualification is supported by the fact that the "lands" of the nations in this verse are indicated by the other common Hebrew noun for "land" (*hā'ărāṣôt*).

22. The expression "Then I will sprinkle clean water on you" is figurative. Normally the expression refers to cultic cleansing prescribed by the law (Num. 19:17-19; Ps. 51:9). Cassuto maintains that the chronology of the verses is significant, i.e., the regathering in the land must precede the spiritual cleansing (Umberto Cassuto, *Ezekiel*, Law, Prophets, Writings (Tel-Aviv: Yavneh, 1977), p. 116 (in Heb.).

23. Note the repetition in v. 25 of the root *tm'* and the term *gillûlîm*, which were expressed as the basis for the exile in vv. 18-19 above. The repetition of the terms in this section indicates that Yahweh is completely transforming the disposition of the Israelites described in the previous section.

In addition, God will give the nation *lēb ḥādāš uᵉrûaḥ ḥădāšâ*, "a new heart²⁴and a new spirit"²⁵ (v. 26). The key word *ḥādāš*, "new," which Jeremiah 31:31 associates with the New Covenant, is here associated with the heart, which changes as a result of Yahweh's new activity. The new heart indicates the spiritual change that will take place.²⁶ The result of this transformation will be that the nation of Israel, due to the bestowal of God's Spirit, will no longer be disobedient to God's commands as described above (vv. 16-21), but rather will be predisposed to keeping God's laws and statutes (v. 27).²⁷

In verse 28 the established fact that Israel will be dwelling in her land is mentioned again with the added qualification that the specific land that will be given to Israel is indeed the land of the Israelite patriarchs (*la'ăbōtêkem*). This reminds the nation that this is the land that had been promised by Yahweh on the basis of a covenant oath. That the covenant relationship is in the forefront of thought here is reinforced by the final phrase of verse 28, "so you will be my people and I will be your God." This is a formula expressing the special covenant bond brought about by God with the nation of Israel.²⁸ Upon Israel's return the land will become so fertile that the nation will never experience famine or its shame again (vv. 29-30).²⁹ Just as there will be spiritual

---

24. This new heart will replace the old *lēb hā'eben*, "heart of stone." According to the Babylonian Talmud the "stone" is one of the seven names of *yṣr hr'*, "the evil inclination." Ezekiel 36:26 is cited as proof (*b. Sukk.* 52*a*). Similarly, Rashi comments that the "new heart" causes the human inclination to become good (*Miqrayôt Gedalôt*, 4:254*a*).

25. "Spirit" in the OT is never simply an "insight, understanding," but a power or driving force. See Hans Walter Wolff, *Anthropology of the Old Testament* (Philadelphia: Fortress, 1938), p. 38. It might be understood as "disposition" (Eichrodt, *Ezekiel*, p. 499).

26. Cassuto, *Ezekiel*, p. 116.

27. Kimchi suggests that the phrase "My Spirit" refers to Yahweh's "Holy Spirit" (*Miqrayôt Gedalôt,* 4:254*a*). In reference to the believer's spiritual life we see the same interchange of the human spirit and the Holy Spirit as we find in Rom. 8:9-11. See Andrew W. Blackwood, Jr., *Ezekiel: Prophecy of Hope* (Grand Rapids: Baker, 1965), p. 219.

28. See Thomas Edward McComiskey, *The Covenants of Promise* (Grand Rapids: Baker, 1985), p. 57. This phrase contains the only occurrence of the longer independent pronoun *'ānōkî*, "I," in Ezekiel. The use of this form of the pronoun here could be an indication that the phrase constitutes an allusion to an ancient covenant formula. See Mark F. Rooker, *Biblical Hebrew in Transition: The Language of the Book of Ezekiel* (Sheffield: *JSOT*, 1990), pp. 72-74; F. Giesebrecht, "Zur Hexateuchkritik. Der Sprachgebrauch des Hexateuchischen Elohisten," *Zeitschrift für die alttestamentliche Wissenschaft* 1 (1881):251; and A. Kropat, *Die Syntax des Autors der Chronik*, Beiheft zur Zeitschrift für die alttestamentliche Wissenschaft (Giessen: Alfred Töpelmann, 1909), p. 75.

29. The statement in verse 29 that the nation will be delivered from all uncleanness (*mikkōl tum'ôtêkem*) "I will save you from all your uncleanness," should be seen as semantically equivalent to the spiritual renovation described in vv. 26-27 (Cassuto, *Ezekiel*, p. 116). For discussion of the abundance of vegetation in the messianic kingdom in rabbinic literature, see *b. Keth.* 111*b*.

transformation experienced by the individuals within the nation, so the land of Israel itself will be revived.

These blessings are designed to bring the nation to repentance (v. 31).[30] Again Yahweh reminds the nation that it is not for the sake of Israel that this will be accomplished—the motivation for the action is solely the restoration of Yahweh's reputation (v. 32). The repetition of the motive for Yahweh's reputation as well as the repetition of the identical phrase "I am not doing this for your sake" (*lō' l^ema'ankem 'ănî 'ōśeh*) from verse 22 makes a frame for the section, giving it unity as well as setting the parameters for the division of the passage.[31]

The passage is followed by two subordinate passages both introduced by the phrase, "thus says the Lord God" (vv. 33, 37). These sections reiterate the ideas of the main section (vv. 22-32). In the first section (vv. 33-36), after mention is again made of the fact that Israel will be cleansed ("I will cleanse you from all your iniquities"),[32] the prophet begins to provide further details on the blessing of the land in verses 33*b*-36. The land and its cities, though once desolate and ruined, will be be rebuilt, inhabited, and fertile (vv. 33-34).[33] The land will return to Edenlike conditions (v. 35).[34] This section ends on the note that this is to be a testimony to the surrounding nations that remain that this has all been accomplished by Israel's God (v. 36).

---

30. This is conceptually similar to Paul's statement in Rom. 2:4 that the kindness of God leads to repentance.

31. These boundary indicators thus enclose vv. 22-32 and support our suggestion that vv. 22-32 be viewed as the main section of the passage. Verses 16-21 provide the motivation, while vv. 33-38 reiterate themes found in the main section.

32. The phrase is introduced by the infinitive construct with the preposition, which is a primary formula for introducing a temporal clause in Hebrew. Thus the phrase should be viewed as a subordinate clause indicating the time for the subsequent action of restoration of the land but logically subordinate in thought. Note the repetition of the root *ṭhr*, "to cleanse," in this temporal clause. This root occurs three times in v. 25.

33. The *hiphîl* perfect tense *w^ehôšabtî*, "I will cause to be inhabited," in v. 33 has its typical causative nuance here, indicating that it is exclusively due to the agency of the Lord that the nation will occupy the land. Similarly, in verse 29 the *hiphîl* stem is employed in the form *w^ehôša'tî* ("I will save"), in reference to the nation being delivered from all her uncleannesses. These verbs, which accentuate the fact that Yahweh is taking the initiative, have the nation and the land as objects—the two beneficiaries of Yahweh's activity in this passage.

34. The repetition of the important verb *rbh*, "to multiply," in vv. 29-30, 37 from the creation account (Gen. 1:22, 28) might also suggest that Yahweh is alluding to a recreation or transformation of the present earth. Also in v. 29 Yahweh commands (*qr'*) the vegetation to come forth just as He did in Genesis. This verb occurs in Gen. 1:5, 8, 10. Price has also noted the correspondence (John Randall Price, "Theocratic Theodicy: An Exegetical and Theological Study of Ezekiel 36:16-38" [Th.M. thesis, Dallas Theological Seminary, 1981], p. 51).

The blessing on the people is further developed in the second subsection (vv. 37-38), specifically, the increase in population. This is indicated in the phrase "I will increase their men like a flock" (*'arbeh 'ōtām kaṣṣō'n 'ādām*, 36:37).[35] This phrase seems to correspond verbally and semantically to the promise given to Abraham about his posterity *wᵉ'arbeh 'ôtᵉka bim'ōd mᵉ'ōd*, "I will multiply you exceedingly" (Gen. 17:2),[36] providing another link to the covenant made with the forefathers, particularly the promise made to Abraham. The section closes with the statement of recognition "that they may know that I am the Lord." The repetition of this statement emphasizes again the restoration of Yahweh's reputation—the world will know that He is Lord.

We have seen in Ezekiel 36:16-38 that Yahweh will act to restore His reputation by restoring His people to the land of Israel. He will transform His people qualitatively (vv. 25-29*a*), as well as quantitatively (vv. 37-38). The land will be radically altered as well (vv. 29*b*-30, 33*b*-36). The motivation for this restoration is the reputation of Yahweh (vv. 22-23), which structurally and thematically occupies the central position of this pericope.

The question now arises as to the time and/or manner of the fulfillment of this prophecy. The answer to this question is largely based upon one's hermeneutical or interpretive method of reading the Bible. Our approach to the biblical content is to interpret the book in a normal fashion.[37] This method requires us to make a distinction between references to Israel and the church, especially in the reading of biblical prophecy. This is justified on the basis of the fact that Israel and the church are clearly distinguished by the biblical writers.[38]

35. Blackwood believes the promise of offspring should be viewed as the ultimate blessing of this passage (*Ezekiel: Prophecy of Hope*, p. 221). Rashi insists that the comparison made to the sheep which were sacrificed for sins suggests that an allusion is also being made to the forgiveness of iniquities (*Miqrayôt Gedalôt*, 4:254*b*). This figurative way of describing the future increase in population may have had special significance for Ezekiel's audience, as they may have had a vivid memory of the Passover feast during the reign of Josiah when 30,000 sheep were sacrificed (2 Chron. 35:7).
36. The NASB translation unfortunately obscures the fact that the identical verb form is used in both of these passages.
37. This hermeneutical approach is developed at length in the first chapter of this volume.
38. See especially S. Lewis Johnson, Jr., "Paul and 'The Israel of God': An Exegetical and Eschatological Case-Study," *Essays in Honor of J. Dwight Pentecost*, ed. Stanley D. Toussaint and Charles H. Dyer (Chicago: Moody, 1986), pp. 181-96; and C. E. B. Cranfield, *The Epistle to the Romans*, The International Critical Commentary, 2 vols. (Edinburgh: Clark, 1979), 2:448. Moreover, in the book of Ezekiel, "Israel" always refers to the covenant nation as a whole, including all twelve tribes. See Walter Zimmerli, "Israel im Buche Ezechiel," *Vetus Testamentum* 8 (1958):75-90; and *Ezekiel*, 2 vols. (Philadelphia: Fortress, 1983), 2:563-65.

In our survey of Ezekiel 36:16-38 we saw the announcement that the restored nation would be characterized by a new heart and a new spirit. When would this description have been true of the nation of Israel? It would be difficult to maintain that these qualities characterized the nation of Israel upon their return from the Babylonian exile. The books of Nehemiah and Malachi, in particular, point out the many sins of the Israelite community after the return from exile. They are denounced for such sins as intermarriage, nonprescribed offerings, withholding tithes and offerings, immoral priests, and negligence.[39] From the perspective of the postexilic community, the fulfillment of the spiritual transformation described by Ezekiel lay in the future. Its fulfillment was also seen to be future from the vantage point of the NT church (Rom. 11:26-27).

Another prophetic motif dealt with in Ezekiel 36 has to do with the restoration to the land and the blessing of the land of Palestine. The restoration was first raised in 11:7 and is mentioned in many other passages in the book of Ezekiel (e.g., 11:17-21; 20:33-38, 42; 34:11-16, 24, 30-31; 36:28; 37:21-28; 39:28). Restoration to the homeland, a theme mentioned in the Mosaic Covenant (Lev. 26:40-45; Deut. 30:1-10), was based upon the eternal covenant to Abraham (Gen. 12:1-3).[40] The land to which the Israelites return will be a transformed land with increased fertility, never to be subject again to famine.[41] This expectation was the hope of the exiles upon returning from Babylon, and their disappointment in the lack of fulfillment of this promise is clear from the postexilic prophets Haggai and Zechariah.[42]

It should be clear that the realization of these promises did not come to fruition in the postexilic period, nor have they been fulfilled today. Israel as a nation is not regathered and has not experienced spiri-. tual regeneration, and the land of Palestine is not characterized by the supernatural fecundity described in Ezekiel 36:22-38.[43]

---

39. Marcus Dods, *The Post-Exilian Prophets* (Edinburgh: Clark, 1879), p. 129.

40. Greenberg, *Ezekiel*, p. 304; Ralph Alexander, *Ezekiel*, The Expositor's Commentary, ed. Frank E. Gaebelein, 12 vols. (Grand Rapids: Zondervan, 1986), 6:793, 927; H. A. Ironside, *Expository Notes on Ezekiel the Prophet* (New York: Loizeaux, 1949), p. 108; Dwight Pentecost, *Thy Kingdom Come* (Wheaton, Ill.: Victor, 1990), pp. 78, 113. The theme of restoration to the homeland may also be seen in Ezek. 20:40-42; 28:25-26; 34:13.

41. This supernatural fecundity of the land is particularly developed in Ezek. 47:1-12 and may also be observed in such passages as Isa. 35:1-2; 55:13; and Zech. 8:12. See Charles Lee Feinberg, *The Prophecy of Ezekiel* (Chicago: Moody, 1969), p. 210.

42. Zimmerli, *Ezekiel*, 2:246.

43. E.g., see John F. Walvoord, *The Millennial Kingdom* (Grand Rapids: Zondervan, 1959), pp. 212-13. Perhaps another indication that the prophecy has not been fulfilled and that it was intended for a future time is the reference to the phrase "nations that are left round about you" in Ezek. 36:36. It is extremely difficult to

TEMPLE WORSHIP RESTORED IN THE MILLENNIUM
(EZEKIEL 40-48)

We have seen the means by which Yahweh will gain the acknowledgment and respect of the nations. He will restore a transformed people to a transformed land. This transformed nation, which will be predisposed to obedience, will naturally desire to obey God and offer worship. Thus we now logically consider the much debated chapters of Ezekiel 40-48—Temple worship in the Millennium. While chapters 40-48 constitute a new vision of the prophecy, this section should not be seen in isolation from what has occurred earlier in the book. Many of the themes and motifs presented in chapters 1-39 are repeated in the final vision in a more detailed fashion. As Levenson has stated: "The immensely detailed vision of the restored community in Ezekiel 40-48 comes as no shock to the sensitive reader of chaps. 1-39."[44] Many have noted in particular the correspondence between the discussion of the Spirit's entering the new Temple (43:4-5) and the presentation of the Spirit's leaving the Solomonic Temple in chapters 8-11.[45]

THE SANCTUARY WILL BE REBUILT

Chapters 40-48 are an expansion particularly of Ezekiel 37:27-28 where the promise is given that Israel will have a sanctuary forever. Greenberg has noted well the significance of Yahweh's declaring to the nation of Israel: "[I] will set My sanctuary in their midst forever" (37:26):

> The fivefold repetition of "forever" stresses the irreversibility of the new dispensation. Unlike God's past experiment with Israel, the future restoration will have a guarantee of success; its capstone will be God's sanctifying presence dwelling forever in the sanctuary amidst his people. The vision of the restored Temple (and God's return to it) in chapters 40-48 follows as a proleptic corroboration of these promises.[46]

pinpoint what event in Israel's history could have provoked this description. The most plausible circumstance would seem to be the destruction of the nations at the second coming of Christ (Rev. 19).

44. Jon Douglas Levenson, *Theology of the Program of Restoration of Ezekiel 40-48* (Missoula, Mont.: Scholars Press, 1976), p. 112.
45. Zimmerli, *Ezekiel*, 2:326; and Brevard Childs, *Introduction to the Old Testament as Scripture* (Philadelphia: Fortress, 1979), p. 367.
46. Moshe Greenberg, "The Design and Themes of Ezekiel's Program of Restoration," *Interpretation* 38 (April 1984):182. On the significance of "forever" in this passage, see McComiskey, *Covenants*, p. 24. For a complete discussion of the term *'wlm*, "forever," as well as its etymological background, see Ernst Jenni, "Das Wort *'ôlām* im Alten Testament," *Zeitschrift für die alttestamentliche Wissenschaft* 64 (1952):197-248; idem, 65 (1953):1-35.

The purpose or goal of the erection of the Temple is indicated by the statement of recognition in Ezekiel 37:28: "And the nations will know that I am the Lord." Thus the construction of the Temple will be another means whereby Yahweh's name will be vindicated among the nations.

Various views have been put forth regarding the interpretation of the reference to the Temple mentioned Ezekiel 40-48. Broadly speaking, we may list these interpretations under three categories: (1) one of the historic Temples in Israel's past; (2) a symbolic temple; and (3) the future millennial Temple.

It is clear that the Temple described in Ezekiel is not the Jerusalem Temple erected by Solomon. A comparison of the features of the first Temple, which was destroyed in Ezekiel's lifetime, with the one Ezekiel describes quickly indicates that the two are patently distinct. It can easily be shown that Ezekiel's Temple had different dimensions and paraphernalia.[47] Since Ezekiel prophesied shortly after the destruction of the Solomon's Temple, it might be natural to consider the possibility that Ezekiel was prophetically describing the next historical temple that would come upon the scene, the Temple erected under Zerubbabel's leadership in 516 B.C. Yet the Temple described by Ezekiel likewise has different dimensions from this Temple built after the return from the Babylonian exile.[48] Moreover, those who experienced the return from captivity did not try to carry out the worship program described by Ezekiel. This indicates that they believed that the eschatological hope expressed by Ezekiel was not fulfilled in their time.[49] When Zerubbabel's Temple, the repaired but diminished Solomonic Temple, was completed the cultic ritual was carried on just as it had been done before the Babylonian exile, that is, according to the Mosaic legislation (Neh. 8, 10). Furthermore, nothing suggests that the glory of the Lord filled the second Temple in the way described in Ezekiel 43:1-12, which is comparable to the abiding of God's glory in the Tabernacle (Ex. 40:34-35) and the Solomonic Temple (1 Kings 8:10-11; 2 Chron. 5:13-14; 7:1-3).[50] Thus we

---

47. Harold Hoehner, "The Reinstitution of Sacrifices in the Millennium" (Th.M. thesis, Dallas Theological Seminary, 1962), pp. 15-27; Zimmerli, *Ezekiel*, 2:345, 377, 387; Greenberg, "The Design and Themes of Ezekiel's Program of Restoration," p. 193; Menahem Haran, "The Law-Code of Ezekiel XL-XLVIII and Its Relation to the Priestly School," *Hebrew Union College Annual* 50 (1979):61-62; and Gerald Curtis White, "Ezekiel 40-48" (Th.D. diss., Concordia Seminary, 1967), p. 44.

48. R. Kraetzschmar, *Das Buch Ezechiel* (Göttingen: Vandenhoeck & Ruprecht, 1900), p. 263; Eric Sauer, *From Eternity to Eternity* (Grand Rapids: Eerdmans, 1954), pp. 181-82. See also Yehezkel Kaufman, *History of the Religion of Israel*, 4 vols. (Jerusalem: Bialik Institute & The Dvir Co., 1956), 4:525 (in Heb.).

49. Levenson, *Program of Restoration*, p. 162; and Greenberg, "The Design and Themes of Ezekiel's Program of Restoration," p. 208.

50. Alexander, *Ezekiel*, p. 969.

should conclude that Ezekiel was not describing a Temple that has previously existed in Israel's history.

The view that Ezekiel's Temple is merely symbolic, representing something other than a physical temple, should be rejected as well. Those who disapprove of the literal interpretation of the passage and opt for a spiritualized or symbolic meaning are far from speaking with one voice regarding what the new Temple of Ezekiel does signify. It has been argued, for example, that the temple represents heaven, the new heavens and new earth, the church, Christ and His community of believers, or Jesus Himself.[51] This lack of unanimity is an argument against the strength of this position. Indeed, the intricate detail in the description of the temple does not seem to mesh with a spiritualized interpretation.[52] As the Jewish scholar Levenson has noted:

> The highly specific nature of the description of the Temple, its liturgy and community bespeaks a practical program, not a vision of pure grace. For example, when the text says that eight steps led up to the vestibule of the inner court (Ezek. 40:31), can this be other than a demand that the new Temple be constructed just so? . . . what Ezekiel was shown is the divinely constructed model, the *tabnît* like the one David showed Solomon (1 Chron. 28:11-19).[53]

If the vision is to be taken symbolically, it must be asked what is the correspondence between the minute details and the symbolized blessings. Satisfactory answers have not been forthcoming. The details are typologically similar to those given for the Tabernacle in the wilderness as well as Solomon's Temple—both being built after the layout was presented in detailed and descriptive design.[54] Similar references to a

---

51. E.g., see Anthony A. Hoekema, *The Bible and the Future* (Grand Rapids: Eerdmans, 1979), pp. 205-6; I. Howard Marshall, "Church and Temple in the New Testament," *Tyndale Bulletin* 40 (1989):209; Philip Edgcumbe Hughes, *Interpreting Prophecy* (Grand Rapids: Eerdmans, 1976), p. 132; and C. F. Keil, *Ezekiel*, Commentary on the Old Testament (Grand Rapids: Eerdmans, 1973), p. 137. Hoekema is critical of other amillennialists who have understood Ezek. 40-48 and similar passages as referring to the church or heaven.

52. See Charles Feinberg, *Ezekiel*, p. 237. The measurements, to use Levenson's words, are presented in "maddening detail" (*Program of Restoration*, p. 16).

53. Levenson, *Program of Restoration*, p. 45. Moreover, the content of Ezek. 40-48 is similar to the material of Num. 27-36 (ibid., pp. 43-44). Similarly, we should note that the arrangement of the book of Ezekiel is typologically the same as that found in the Pentateuch—both focus on a redemption from exile followed by the giving of legislation. Thus Kaufman, *History*, 4:524, 566-67.

54. Greenberg, "The Design and Themes of Ezekiel's Program of Restoration," pp. 184-85. See also Menahem Haran, "*miqdāš*," *Biblical Encyclopaedia*, 8 vols. (Jerusalem: Bialik Institute, 1950-82), 5 (1968):304-59 (in Heb.).

temple in the messianic kingdom include Isaiah 2:2-4[55] and Haggai 2:9. An expectation of a rebuilt temple in the messianic age was part of later Jewish expectation as witnessed by the Dead Sea Scrolls[56] as well as rabbinic literature.[57] As Levenson has noted concerning the latter: "In Rabbinic eschatology, the goal of Israel's deliverance . . . is the Land of Israel, centered on the rebuilt Temple."[58]

TRUE WORSHIP WILL BE REINSTITUTED

Ezekiel 40-48 not only indicates that there will be a temple in the Millennium, but also seems to indicate that sacrifices will be reinstituted in this temple as well. Premillennialists have characteristically taken these sacrifices to refer to memorials of Christ's sacrifice, ceremonial forgiveness, or representative worship.

The first position argues that the sacrifices be understood as memorials of the death of Christ in the same way the Lord's Supper now has this function (e.g., Luke 22:19).[59] This position has been criticized on the grounds that Ezekiel does not call the sacrifices memorials but states, on the contrary, that these future sacrifices will result in atonement (*kpr*)[60] for the house of Israel (43:20, 26; 45:15, 17, 20).

55. Rashi, *Miqrayôt Gedalôt*, 4:259a.
56. See especially 4QFlor and J. M. Allegro, "Further Messianic References in Qumran Literature," *Journal of Biblical Literature* 75 (1956):174-87. The *Temple Scroll*, which is largely the instruction manual for a new temple, acknowledged a future messianic temple as well (11QTemple 29:8-10). For translation and comments, see Yigael Yadin, *The Temple Scroll* (New York: Random House, 1985), p. 113; and Johann Maier, *The Temple Scroll* (Sheffield: *JSOT*, 1978), pp. 32, 86; and Marshall, "Church and Temple in the New Testament," p. 216.
57. See Cassuto, *Ezekiel*, p. 126. E.g., *Tg. Onq.* Gen. 49:10-11; *Tg. Neb.* Isa. 2:2-4; *Tg. Ket.* Song of Sol. 1:17; 8:1; *Sipre Deut.* sec. 352; *Midr. Ps.* 90; *Midr.* Song of Sol. 4:16. For additional rabbinic material on this subject see Ferdinand Weber, *Jüdische Theologie auf Grund des Talmud und Verwandter Schriften* (Leipzig: Dörffling & Franke, 1897), pp. 374-76. This is also a view prevalent among contemporary Jews (Haim Zer Hirashberg, "'aḥârît ḥayyāmîm," *Biblical Encyclopaedia* [in Heb.]; and Martin Levin, "Time for a New Temple?" *Time* [Oct. 16, 1989], pp. 64-65).
58. Levenson, *Program of Restoration*, p. 33. In addition, those who reject a literal temple in the Millennium often are prone to disallow the existence of a temple in 2 Thess. 2:4 that the man of sin profanes (Hoekema, *The Bible and the Future*, p. 160; Marshall, "Church and Temple in the New Testament," p. 212).
59. Walvoord, *The Millennial Kingdom*, pp. 312-14.
60. Many have argued that this root should be connected with an Arabic cognate with the meaning of "to cover." This rendering would reinforce the view that the sacrifices in question were not efficacious in removing sin but only "covered" sin. This understanding is not likely, however, since the verb refers to "making atonement." See R. Laird Harris, "kāpar," *Theological Wordbook of the Old Testament*, ed. R. Laird Harris, Gleason L. Archer, and Bruce K. Waltke (Chicago: Moody, 1980).

A second interpretation of the sacrificial system in Ezekiel views the sacrifices as referring to ceremonial or temporal forgiveness of sin. Advocates of this position argue their case on the basis of the nature and purpose of OT sacrifices, which were viewed as being efficacious, resulting in the forgiveness of sin (Lev. 1:4; 4:26-31; 5:16; Num. 15:25-26).[61] The OT sacrifices did provide atonement, in the sense of temporal or ceremonial forgiveness.[62] Proponents of this position harmonize the Ezekielian sacrifices with NT teaching such as: "Now where there is forgiveness of these things, there is no longer any offering for sin" (Heb. 10:18), by maintaining that the author of Hebrews was addressing the role of OT sacrifices as types of the sacrifice of Christ. With respect to the OT believer's salvation, the sacrifices were types of the ultimate sacrifice, the atonement made by the Messiah, the sacrifice that would establish the payment for sins once for all.[63] Thus the OT sacrifice could simultaneously provide atonement for forgiveness (Heb. 9:13) while foreshadowing Christ's sacrifice, which would be the ultimate ground for the payment of sin and the removal of guilt. Freeman nicely harmonizes this dual function of the OT sacrifice: "While they truly atoned for the sins of the worshiper, yet the Old Testament sacrifices were validated in the mind of God on the basis of the all-sufficient, truly efficacious sacrifice of the Lamb of God slain from the foundation of the world (1 Pet. 1:20)."[64] The sacrifices in the Millennium, though they should not be viewed as a reinstitution of the Mosaic system, would function in a similar manner for the nation of Israel.[65] This function of the sacrifices as depicted in

61. Similarly, Charles C. Ryrie, *Dispensationalism Today* (Chicago: Moody, 1973), p. 127. This function of the sacrifices may be harmonious with what the writer of Hebrews meant when he said that the Mosaic offerings "cleansed the flesh" (Heb. 9:13-14*a*).

62. In modern theological parlance the offering of sacrifices pertained to the believer's sanctification. This is harmonious with Ryrie's position (*Dispensationalism Today*, p. 128).

63. Allen P. Ross, "The Biblical Method of Salvation: A Case for Discontinuity," *Continuity and Discontinuity: Perspectives on the Relationship between the Old and New Testaments,* ed. John S. Feinberg (Westchester, Ill.: Crossway, 1988), p. 176.

64. Hobart E. Freeman, "The Problem of the Efficacy of Old Testament Sacrifices," *Bulletin of the Evangelical Theological Society* 5 (1962):73. Similarly, John S. Feinberg, "Salvation in the Old Testament," *Continuity and Discontinuity: Perspectives on the Relationship between the Old and New Testaments,* ed. John S. Feinberg (Westchester, Ill.: Crossway, 1988), p. 72.

65. The sacrificial practices in Ezekiel are different in many details from the Mosaic legislation. The program of worship as seen in the book of Ezekiel has a different number of feasts, and different numbers and kinds of animals used in sacrifices. It is also completely devoid of important features of the Mosaic sacrificial system such as the high priest, the ark, and the Day of Atonement. See Eliezer Margolis, "The Laws of the Priests and Sacrifices in Ezekiel," *Tarbiz* 22 (1950-51):21-27 (in Heb.). This variance from the Mosaic code was in fact the reason many Jews resisted including Ezekiel as part of the Hebrew canon. See *b. Menaḥ.* 45*a*.

Ezekiel would resemble their role in the life of the OT believer, being efficacious for ceremonial cleansing.[66] They will thus have the function of temporal cleansing as mentioned in Hebrews 9:13.[67]

A third view does not take the sacrifices in a literal sense but views Ezekiel writing in the 6th century B.C. describing worship from his unique perspective. This position understands the prohibition in the book of Hebrews in a more comprehensive sense than was taken above. This view apparently reflects the position of the editors of *The New Scofield Reference Bible* regarding the sacrificial system described in Ezekiel 40-48: "Since the N.T. clearly teaches that animal sacrifices do not in themselves cleanse away sin (Heb. 10:4) and that the one sacrifice of the Lord Jesus Christ that was made at Calvary completely provides for such expiation (cp. Heb. 9:12, 26, 28; 10:10, 14), how can there be a fulfillment of such a prophecy?"[68] Ezekiel in referring to the literal worship of Yahweh in the Millennium would be forced to use terms and concepts with which the audience was familiar. As H. A. Ironside states: "Prior to the work of the cross there could be no other way of presenting that work prophetically than by directing attention to such offerings as the people understood."[69]

Similar practices occur in other portions of Scripture when, for example, a future eschatological battle is described with the participants using spears, bows, and arrows.[70] The writers were thus describing battle scenes using language familiar to their own times. Similarly, in eschatological passages that describe the restoration of Israel from foreign nations, only nations such as Assyria and Egypt are mentioned (e.g., Zech. 10:10). Are we to conclude that the Jews have been dispersed to these nations only? Surely we are to understand the author writing from the perspective of his own times in predicting the future restoration of the nation of Israel from all the nations of the world.[71] In a similar vein, in describing worship in the millennial age, Ezekiel uses language his audience would understand. One might naturally ask, "How else could worship have been described?" In its favor, this view gives progressive

66. See John C. Whitcomb, "Christ's Atonement and Animal Sacrifices in Israel," *Grace Theological Journal* 6 (1985):210-12.
67. For evidence of the belief in the execution of sacrifices in the days of Messiah from rabbinic literature, see *b. 'Abod. Zar.* 24a and *Num. Rab.* 17.
68. *The New Scofield Reference Bible*, p. 888; H. A. Ironside, *Expository Notes on Ezekiel the Prophet*, p. 289.
69. Ironside, p. 305.
70. Walter C. Kaiser, Jr., *Toward an Old Testament Theology* (Grand Rapids: Zondervan, 1978), p. 244.
71. Robert B. Chisholm, Jr., *Interpreting the Minor Prophets* (Grand Rapids: Zondervan, 1990), pp. 64-65, 264.

revelation its full due. Since the NT has ruled out the future existence of sacrifices after the once-for-all sacrifice of Jesus Christ (Heb. 10:18), we should expect no other and understand Ezekiel to be generally speaking of a future worship practice in the millennial age. The same could not be said of the erection and existence of the Temple, as we are not told in the NT that this promise has been fulfilled.

CONCLUSION

Out of concern for His reputation, Yahweh will act to restore the defiant nation of Israel to a revived Promised Land. The people of Israel will be given a new disposition, which will result in obedience to God and worship in a new Temple. As a result of these events Yahweh will be esteemed among the nations. The reception of spiritual blessings of the New Covenant by the church today (such as the gift of the Holy Spirit and forgiveness of sin [e.g., Ezek. 36:25-27]) certainly does not mean that the church has replaced Israel, nor does it mean that the New Covenant blessings have been exhausted, as Paul makes clear in Romans 11:11-32.[72] Pentecost explains well how the benefits of the New Covenant can apply to both Israel and the church:

> A more acceptable understanding is that while the New Cove-
> nant was made with the house of Israel and Judah, there are benefits
> from the enactment of that covenant of which the church (comprising
> both Jews and Gentiles) partakes.... We can logically and consistently
> conclude, then, that this is Israel's covenant; but on the basis of the
> blood of the covenant, those outside that nation likewise may experi-
> ence the removal of guilt and the forgiveness of sins.[73]

Thus the promises made to Israel in the book of Ezekiel will find their fulfillment in the thousand-year millennial age (Rev. 20:1-6). It will be during the Millennium that Israel will be regathered in her land and given a new heart and a new spirit and thus be predisposed to obeying God. The land will be restored, yielding vegetation in abundance, and will house the Temple as the special place of Yahweh's presence.[74] With this abundant evidence of Yahweh's power, all the nations will know that Yahweh is God. There is a bright hope for the future of the nation of Israel (Rom. 11:29). Yahweh is staking His reputation on it.

---

72. Whitcomb, "Christ's Atonement and Animal Sacrifices," p. 203.
73. Pentecost, *Thy Kingdom Come*, p. 175.
74. The millennial age will constitute the transition period leading into the eternal state. This distinction between the messianic kingdom and the *'wlm hb'*, "the world to come," was often made by the rabbis (A. Cohen, *Everyman's Talmud* [New York: Schocken, 1975], pp. 356, 364; Ralph Lerner, "Moses Maimonides," *History of Political Philosophy*, ed. Leo Straus and Joseph Cropsey [Chicago: U. of Chicago, 1963], p. 196).

7

EVIDENCE FROM DANIEL

KENNETH L. BARKER
Executive Director
NIV Translation Center

The purpose of this volume is to establish the exegetical basis for premillennialism. In the present case, one may ask: What is the exegetical basis for premillennialism within the book of Daniel? Are there key passages within this marvelous portion of Holy Writ that exegetically establish the doctrine of premillennialism so that it can be traced faithfully and consistently throughout the book? Fortunately, an affirmative answer is found early in the pages of Daniel, in the second chapter.

Daniel 2:44 is a key verse under consideration: "In the time of those kings, the God of heaven will set up a kingdom that will never be destroyed, nor will it be left to another people. It will crush all those kingdoms and bring them to an end, but it will itself endure forever."[1] Indeed, "the kingdom of our Lord and of his Christ" (Rev. 11:15; cf. Ps. 2:2, Dan. 4:17, 25, 32; 5:21) is the central focus of biblical theology.[2]

---

1. All Scripture quotations in this chapter, unless otherwise noted, are taken from the *Holy Bible, New International Version* (North American Edition), copyright 1973, 1978, 1984 by the International Bible Society, used by permission of Zondervan Bible Publishers.

2. See Kenneth L. Barker, "The Scope and Center of Old and New Testament Theology and Hope," *Dispensationalism, Israel and the Church*, ed. Craig A. Blaising and Darrell L. Bock (Grand Rapids: Zondervan, 1992).

To relate this theological theme to the presentation of a case for premillennialism in the book of Daniel would require exegesis of at least Daniel 2:31-45; 7; 8:15-26; 9:24-27; 11:36-45; and 12. All we can realistically hope to accomplish within the limited scope of a single chapter is to examine carefully the most significant of these passages, i.e., those that specifically deal with the concept of a yet future "kingdom" (2:31-45 and 7:15-28).[3] Daniel 9:24-27 will also be touched on briefly for its unique contribution to the study.

Obviously, any approach (including mine) is influenced by its hermeneutical system and theological presuppositions. Interpreters will continue to arrive at different conclusions on such passages until they can fully agree at the hermeneutical and presuppositional levels. First, for example, based on internal considerations (Dan. 10:1), I hold that the book of Daniel is a unified entity written about 535-530 B.C. by the man who bore that name. It is not simply a collection of court tales in chapters 1-6 that form the basis of apocalyptic visions in chapters 7-12, both parts written in the Maccabean era, ca. 165 B.C.[4] Second, because of my (I hope consistent) adherence to what I have elsewhere called the grammatical-literary-historical-theological method of exegesis,[5] I have a more literal reading of the text—while allowing for figurative language—than some of my amillennial friends, who have a more allegorical, symbolical, or "spiritual" understanding of the text.

DANIEL 2:31-45

Walvoord introduces his comments on Daniel 2 with these words: "Nowhere else in Scripture, except in Daniel 7, is a more comprehensive picture given of world history as it stretched from the time of Daniel, 600 years before Christ, to the consummation at the second advent of Christ."[6] In Daniel 2:31-45 God, in order to demonstrate that He sovereignly controls history,[7] provides through Daniel (see vv. 26-28) the interpretation of King Nebuchadnezzar's latest dream that centered on

---

3. It will be noted here that these passages are themselves interpretations of the dreams of Nebuchadnezzar and Daniel respectively. As interpretations, they would be expected to make such dreams clearer, not more confusing.

4. For a recent study from this perspective see J. J. Collins, "The Court Tales in Daniel and the Development of Jewish Apocalyptic," *Journal of Biblical Literature* 94 (1975):218-34.

5. Kenneth L. Barker, "Zechariah," in *The Expositor's Bible Commentary*, ed. Frank E. Gaebelein et al. (Grand Rapids: Zondervan, 1985), 7:600.

6. John F. Walvoord, *Daniel the Key to Prophetic Revelation* (Chicago: Moody, 1971), p. 44.

7. John E. Goldingay, "Daniel," in *Word Biblical Commentary*, ed. David A. Hubbard et al. (Dallas: Word, 1989), 30:56. Unfortunately, Goldingay holds to the late (Maccabean) date for the book of Daniel.

a large statue. The statue concerns four temporal human kingdoms and the kingdom established by God, so that there are actually five kingdoms in Daniel 2.[8] It is this fifth kingdom with which we are concerned.

The fifth kingdom is represented in Nebuchadnezzar's dream as a stone that smashes the statue's feet and then becomes a great mountain that fills the whole earth (2:35). Is it meant to be another earthly kingdom? Or is this final kingdom, established by God Himself (v. 44), to be understood rather as the eternal state? Does the passage suggest a literal earthly kingdom within time, or does it demand one in eternity? Is it possible that one kingdom with two stages is in view—the earthly kingdom, to give way to the eternal kingdom? To determine the answer to these questions, it is necessary to examine the meaning of the term "kingdom."

The Aramaic term that Daniel employs consistently for "kingdom" in 2:4b-7:28 is *malkû*.[9] Ezra contains the only biblical Aramaic outside Daniel that employs this term (4:24; 6:15; 7:13, 23), and there it refers to the earthly kingdoms of the Persian rulers Darius I Hystaspes (522-486 B.C.) and Artaxerxes (464-424 B.C.). In Daniel, however, a distinction arises between the kingdoms of this earth, which perish (2:39; 5:7; 6:1; etc.), and that which is to endure forever, which God will establish (4:3; 6:26).[10] There does not seem to be any indication that Daniel's use of *malkû* ("kingdom") demands an earthly provenance to the exclusion of the

---

8. Most evangelical scholars (as well as numerous early church Fathers), representing all eschatological schools of thought, are agreed that the four human kingdoms were Babylonia, Medo-Persia, Greece (and its divisions after the death of Alexander the Great in 323 B.C., with special emphasis on Egypt under the Ptolemies and on Syria under the Seleucids—see 8:22), and Rome. The identifications are rendered virtually certain when one correlates the data of chap. 2 with those of chaps. 7-8, Goldingay (ibid., pp. 50-51) and others to the contrary notwithstanding. Cf. James A. Montgomery, *A Critical and Exegetical Commentary on the Book of Daniel* (reprint, Edinburgh: Clark, 1979), pp. 59-63, 185-92. For a more sympathetic presentation of the evidence, see C. F. Keil, *Biblical Commentary on the Book of Daniel*, Biblical Commentary on the Old Testament, ed. C. F. Keil and F. Delitzsch (Grand Rapids: Eerdmans, 1955), pp. 245-83; Charles Boutflower, *In and Around the Book of Daniel* (reprint, Grand Rapids: Kregel, 1977), pp. 13-34.

9. The appearance of the term will vary morphologically in the articular (or determined or definite), construct, plural, and plural construct forms. The Hebrew portions of Daniel refer to a kingship or dominion (*malkût*) rather than a kingdom (*mamlākâ*). Admittedly, distinguishing between the two Hebrew terms in this way is a generalization, but it seems to hold true in the majority of cases outside Daniel. The former term is employed by the Hebrew portions of Daniel to the exclusion of the latter.

10. There are no doubt some who would regard 4:3 and 6:26 as referring also to the millennial kingdom/eternal state vis-a-vis Rev. 20-22. However, for the sake of argument, I am using these as clear examples of the heavenly provenance of God's kingdom, recognized by Nebuchadnezzar and Darius as a kingdom distinct from their own.

heavenly—nor vice versa, in fact. The term is broad enough to refer to either a perishable earthly kingdom or an imperishable "heavenly" kingdom.

Is the term broad enough, however, to refer to a unique kingdom that has both earthly and "heavenly" provenances? In other words, can the word be used to refer to a kingdom established by God upon the earth in which He reigns, which will later merge or expand into a new heaven and a new earth, where it will endure forever? Or in terms of the present debate, does the term as used in Daniel 2:44 and 7:27 allow for an earthly millennial kingdom followed by the eternal state? Though usage of the word is inconclusive and cannot by itself answer this, other terms within the passage may offer keys to a solution.

What are the particulars concerning the fifth kingdom of Daniel 2? There are *four notable features*. *First*, it is said in 2:34-35 that *hitgᵉzeret 'eben dî-lā' bîdayin* ("a stone was cut out, yet not with hands")[11] that "struck the statue on its feet of iron and clay and smashed them." This stone is interpreted[12] in 2:44 as the God-established kingdom (*malkû*) that will crush and put an end to the final human kingdom represented by the feet of the multi-metallic image. That the kingdom represented by the stone cannot be the church (also juxtaposed with a stone in Matthew 16) has been amply demonstrated by Culver.[13]

Second, this stone "became a huge mountain and filled the whole earth" (2:35).[14] The phrase "filled the whole earth" (*ûmᵉlāt kol-'ar'ā'*) seems to indicate an earthly provenance for this kingdom.[15] Too, the fact that in the context it is replacing earthly kingdoms might likewise suggest an earthly provenance.[16]

11. Author's translation. The translation "yet not" seems preferable to "that not," the translation suggested by BDB, *A Hebrew and English Lexicon of the Old Testament*, p. 1088.

12. One must note that this interpretation is that of the book of Daniel itself.

13. Robert D. Culver, *Daniel and the Latter Days* (Chicago: Moody, 1977), pp. 131-34. Culver points out that (1) the church is not a political entity; (2) the growth of the church has not seen the sudden, cataclysmic destruction of Gentile kingdoms depicted; (3) the church will never overcome all of the Gentile kingdoms; and (4) that the gospel should be used to smite and destroy is inconsistent with the NT. (Culver's entire book is well worth reading.)

14. The phrase "became a huge mountain" is expressed in Aramaic as *hăwāt lᵉtûr rab*, utilizing the verb *hăwâ* plus the following *lᵉ* preposition to express "to become." This pattern is also found with the Hebrew *hāyâ* plus *lᵉ* to express a movement from one state of existence to another. In this context, it could indicate the movement from the point of the inauguration of the kingdom to the point of its universality. As expressed above, it cannot refer to the church.

15. The fact that the context of chaps. 2, 7, and 8 indicates that world-controlling powers are in view here rules out the possibility of hyperbole.

16. Montgomery insists that this must be an earthly kingdom (*A Critical and Exegetical Commentary on the Book of Daniel*, p. 178). Goldingay writes, "Daniel promises a new future, one which is not merely an extension of the present. . . . It is of supernatural origin. But it is located on earth, not in heaven" ("Daniel," p. 59).

Third, this kingdom established by God is described in 2:44 as one "that will never be destroyed" (*dî l*^{e}*'olmîn lā' titḥabbal*) and that "will itself endure forever" (*u*^{e}*hî' t*^{e}*qûm l*^{e}*'olmayyā'*). Incorporated in both phrases is the root *'lm*, a common Semitic word that, though it can refer to an indefinite past time, most frequently refers to an indefinite future of continuous existence.[17] The point to be made here is this: If the kingdom established by God that destroys the earthly kingdoms is itself earthly, yet endures forever, then the term "kingdom" itself must have both earthly and heavenly aspects.

Fourth, 2:44 also states that this "kingdom" established by God "will not be left to another people" (*ûmalkûtâ l*^{e}*'am 'oḥŏrān lā' tiš-t*^{e}*biq*).[18] Coupled with 7:27 (see below), where it is stated that sovereignty over all earthly kingdoms will be given to the people of the saints of the Most High, one may conclude here either that the kingdom will not be given to any people other than those designated in chapter 7, or that the kingdom ultimately will not rest in the hands of earthly people, ostensibly because it has become heavenly in provenance.

It has now been demonstrated that to understand fully the use of "kingdom" (*malkû*) in Daniel 2, information must be drawn both from the vision itself (2:34-35) and from the interpretation of that vision (2:44). In Daniel 2 at least, the term allows for both earthly and heavenly aspects, or provenances. In this passage, the kingdom begins within space-time history on earth and continues into the eternal state on the new earth (cf. Rev. 21:1-3).

DANIEL 7:15-28

If one judges from the volume of material written on it, Daniel 7 is one of the most important chapters in all of Scripture.[19] Chapter 7 presents the first of four dream-visions or revelations God gave to Daniel.

---

17. Cf. BDB, s.v. *'lm*.

18. *Malkûtâ* is understood here as equivalent to *malkûtā'*, in keeping with the frequent orthographical confusion between final *ā'* and final *â*.

19. Studies on Dan. 7 from various theological perspectives include the following: Martin Noth, "Die Heiligen des Höchsten," *Norsk Teologisk Tidsskrift*, 56 (1955):146-61; C. H. W. Brekelmans, "The Saints of the Most High and Their Kingdom," *Oudtestamentliche Studien* 14 (1965):305-29; G. R. Beasley-Murray, "The Interpretation of Daniel 7," *Catholic Biblical Quarterly* 45 (1983):44-58; Gerhard F. Hasel, "The Identity of 'The Saints of the Most High' in Daniel 7," *Biblica* 56 (1975):173-92; V. S. Poythress, "The Holy Ones of the Most High in Daniel VII," *Vetus Testamentum* 26 (1976):208-13; Ziony Zevit, "The Structure and Individual Elements of Daniel 7," *Zeitschrift für die alttestamentliche Wissenschaft* 80 (1968):385-96; and William H. Shea, "The Neo-Babylonian Historical Setting for Daniel 7," *Andrews University Seminary Studies* 24 (1986):31-36.

It is a dream-vision of four beasts,[20] the Ancient of Days, the Son of Man,[21] and His kingdom. The vision is described in verses 1-14, then interpreted in verses 15-27. Is this kingdom of the Son of Man to be understood in the same manner as the kingdom of Daniel 2? In other words, are there both earthly/temporal and heavenly/eternal aspects to this kingdom as there are to the kingdom in 2:31-44? As in chapter 2, one needs to examine the use of the term both in the initial vision (vv. 13-14) and in its interpretation (v. 27) to appreciate fully its use within the context.

The context of 7:14 indicates that the presentation of a kingdom to the Son of Man is the last segment of the vision given to Daniel. It is important to note with Culver that this does not occur until the other earthly kingdoms have been destroyed (compare 7:11-12 with 7:17, 23, 26).[22] In 7:14, the Son of Man is given dominion, glory, and a kingdom[23] ($w^e l\bar{e}h\ y^e h\hat{i}b\ \check{s}olt\bar{a}n\ w\hat{i}q\bar{a}r\ \hat{u}malk\hat{u}$). One immediately notes the use of $y^e q\bar{a}r$ instead of the expected $k\bar{a}b\hat{o}d$ for "glory." Its use here could be significant in that it is most frequently used elsewhere in both biblical Hebrew and biblical Aramaic to refer to earthly preciousness or honor.[24] The purpose of this bequeathal was that all peoples, nations, and tongues might serve Him ($w^e k\bar{o}l\ 'am^e mayy\bar{a}'\ 'umayy\bar{a}'\ w^e li\check{s}\check{s}\bar{a}'nayy\bar{a}'\ l\bar{e}h\ yipl^e$-$h\hat{u}n$).[25] The terms involved apply to everyone.[26] This can take place only after the Son of Man receives the kingdom, since such universal

---

20. The four beasts present a more aggressive picture of the four kingdoms earlier represented as metallic portions in the statue of Nebuchadnezzar's dream in chap. 2. For comparison, see the chart in *The NIV Study Bible*, ed. Kenneth Barker et al. (Grand Rapids: Zondervan, 1985), p. 1311.

21. The issue concerning the identity of the Son of Man in 7:13-14 is important. Conservatives generally agree that the person of the Messiah is in view (the term "Son of Man" was a favorite self-appellation of our Lord), but other scholars identify the Son of Man here as the nation of Israel. The reason for this latter understanding is that the Son of Man of vv. 13-14 is not interpreted per se in 7:27. In his stead, the people of the saints of the Most High receive the kingdom. For more discussion of the issue, see Joyce G. Baldwin, *Daniel: An Introduction and Commentary* (Downers Grove, Ill.: InterVarsity, 1978), pp. 148-54.

22. Culver, *Daniel and the Latter Days*, p. 138.

23. NIV: "authority, glory, and sovereign power."

24. An exception would be Zech. 11:13. The related adjective $y\bar{a}q\bar{a}r$ is likewise most frequently found to describe earthly preciousness. One cannot stretch this point too far, since fewer scenes of heaven are offered in the OT than scenes of earth.

25. This understands the *waw* on $w^e k\bar{o}l$ to be a *waw* of purpose, also called a conjunctive-sequential *waw*. Cf. T. O. Lambdin, *Introduction to Biblical Hebrew* (New York: Scribners, 1971), p. 162.

26. The expression $'amemayy\bar{a}'\ 'umayy\bar{a}'\ w^e li\check{s}\check{s}\bar{a}nayy\bar{a}'$ is used in Dan. 3:4 to refer to everyone under the rule of Nebuchadnezzar; i.e., everyone under the authority of the Neo-Babylonian Empire.

service has not been the case historically.[27] Whether this supports a millennial kingdom again depends on the contextual use of "kingdom."

Verse 14 also affirms that "his dominion is an everlasting dominion that will not pass away" and that "his kingdom is one that will never be destroyed" (*ûmalkûtēh dî-lā' tithabbal*). The phrase is almost identical to that used in 2:44 (see above). This plus the fact that the scene presented takes place in heaven (7:13) may support the view that the dominion, glory, and kingdom presented to the Son of Man are heavenly. However, as in 2:44 above, the context of the chapter as a whole is dealing with earthly kingdoms,[28] and more information is needed to determine whether the use of the term here and in 7:27 allows for a kingdom with both heavenly and earthly aspects.[29]

As was mentioned above, the kingdom is given to the Son of Man following the destruction of the four kingdoms. It is the fourth kingdom that wages war with the saints of the Highest One (7:21, 25). In 7:26 and 27 judgment is made that removes sovereignty from the little horn (the leader of the fourth kingdom) and gives dominion of all the kingdoms of the world (lit., "the kingdoms under all the heavens" [*malkᵉwāt tᵉḥôt kol-šᵉmayyā'*]) "to the saints, the people of the Most High" (*yᵉhîbat lᵉ'am qaddîšê 'elyônîn*). This must then be an earthly kingdom that is given, since dominion of all the kingdoms is placed into their hands.

Who are these people described in verse 27? How are they related to the Son of Man? Many scholars have thought that the use of "Holy Ones" (Heb.: *qᵉdôšîm*; Aram.: *qaddîšîn*) in the OT must refer to angels. Others have thought that righteous, redeemed people are in view. Brekelmans has done an exhaustive study comparing the use of the term "Holy Ones" in biblical, apocryphal, pseudepigraphical, and Qumran literature.[30] He states that in comparison with biblical literature, the term in Daniel 7 may indeed refer to men rather than angels.[31] Continuing in his study of apocryphal and pseudepigraphical literature,[32] Brekelmans

---

27. Three scenarios are possible in this phrase: (1) all on earth serving the Son of Man in heaven; (2) all in heaven serving the Son of Man in heaven; or (3) all on earth serving the Son of Man on earth. These correspond roughly to postmillennial, amillennial, and premillennial positions, respectively.

28. Supporting this contention are vv. 17 and 23, both of which use the term *'ar'ā'* and v. 25, which reveals the attempt of the little horn to make changes in times and in law (*zimnîn wᵉdāt*). The latter word is *dāt*, which normally means human as opposed to divine law, though in the mouth of a Gentile it can refer to God's law. The point to be made here is that time is an earthly concept, as is human law.

29. One may well note here Daniel's words in 7:16 as he sought to know the "exact meaning of all this."

30. These involve both Hebrew and Aramaic usages.

31. "The Saints of the Most High and Their Kingdom," p. 308.

32. He dates Daniel late (cf. p. 325), hence his study in these areas.

mentions that the term is often used of men and may indicate three groups: (1) those who are saved at the final judgment; (2) the souls of the dead who believed in God; and (3) the righteous men on earth.[33] Following the study of Qumran literature, Brekelmans states in his conclusion that since "in the literature shortly before and after Daniel *qdušym* was used of both angels and men . . . only the context in which it occurs can help to reach a decision which sense of the word is used in a particular text."[34] Fortunately, such a study has been done.

Poythress undertakes a study of the term within the context of Daniel 7, especially concentrating on the term "people" (*'am*). He concludes that "the interpretation that 'holy ones' refers to angels is inconsistent with the final state of the Aramaic text. . . . The final text shows that the use of 'holy ones' for eschatological faithful Israel was semantically acceptable."[35] Thus it may be established that in the end times following the demise of the fourth kingdom, dominion of the entire world will be handed over to faithful Israel (cf. 7:18).[36]

At this point one must reconcile 7:18 with 7:27. In 7:18 it is said that "the saints of the Most High will receive the kingdom and will possess it forever—yes, for ever and ever." In 7:27, the saints receive the kingdom, but it is said, "His kingdom will be an everlasting kingdom, and all rulers will worship and obey him." Two points must be made here. First, eternity is ultimately in view (note the emphatic repetition in 7:18—*'ad-'ālmā' we'ad 'ālam 'olmayyā'*). So, even though the kingdom received is earthly, it continues for eternity (and thus into "a new heaven and a new earth"—Rev. 21:1).[37] Second, in some sense, the kingdom

---

33. Ibid., p. 318.

34. Ibid., pp. 325-26. Brekelmans later states: "The above texts attest beyond doubt that the idea of the eschatological kingdom of the righteous was a very common one. If Daniel 7 deals with the dominion of the angels over all the nations, one must say that this chapter stands alone in all the literature of this period. If this result of our inquiry should be right, the opinion that the holy ones of the Most High in Daniel 7 are heavenly beings, must be called a very improbable one."

35. "The Holy Ones of the Most High in Daniel VII," p. 213. The NIV translation is thus correct in rendering the phrase as an appositive: "the saints, the people of the Most High."

36. Hasel apparently broadens the term to include faithful Gentiles when he writes that these saints are "to be identified with God's faithful followers who constitute His remnant people, who are His chosen ones, set apart from the rest of the nations, persecuted by the power opposing God, but keeping the covenant faith and maintaining their trust and confidence in God from whom they finally receive an everlasting kingdom" ("The Identity of 'The Saints of the Most High' in Daniel 7," p. 192).

37. Contra E. J. Young, *The Prophecy of Daniel* (Grand Rapids: Eerdmans, 1949), p. 78, who writes: "The kingdom of God is of divine *origin* and eternal *duration*. For this reason, it cannot be the millennium, which is but 1000 years in length. Since the kingdom is divine, it is therefore eternal" (italics his). One must ask the question, does eternality preclude earthly provenance? If so, in what sense can the kingdom of God exist on earth in the present age?

received by the Son of Man (v. 14) is the same kingdom received by the saints of the Most High.[38] This language at least allows for one kingdom under the authority of the saints who are themselves under the ultimate authority of the Son of Man. Thus this passage contains an eschatological depiction of "one like a son of man" who will come in glory with the clouds of heaven to judge all nations and rule the world.

DANIEL 9:24-27[39]

If Daniel 7 has been the most frequently discussed chapter in Daniel, then Daniel 9:24-27 is undoubtedly Daniel's most frequently discussed pericope.[40] Though the passage is understood in many circles to refer to the first advent of the Messiah and to the Great Tribulation, it may be that the kingdom is inherent in the terms used in 9:24, particularly in the second part of the verse. *Six goals* are stated in this one verse.

38. Montgomery sees the pronominal suffixes in the latter half of the verse as referring to the singular collective *'am*, rather than to the Most High or the Son of Man (*A Critical and Exegetical Commentary on the Book of Daniel*, p. 315). This is also the view of Young (*The Prophecy of Daniel*, p. 162). Though this may occur in Hebrew from time to time (e.g., Deut. 21:10), the more usual case is that of the plural suffix referring to a collective singular (E. Kautzsch and A. E. Cowley, eds., *Gesenius' Hebrew Grammar*, 2d Eng. ed. [Oxford: Clarendon, 1910], p. 135). To my knowledge, there has been no study of this practice in comparative Aramaic literature that might confirm the validity of Montgomery's point here. If Montgomery and Young are correct, there may be implications in the issue of the identity of the Son of Man in 7:13-14. Most versions translate the pronominal suffixes as singular, making the nearest referent the Most High of 7:25, or perhaps the Son of Man of 7:13-14.

This syntactical problem reintroduces the issue broached above in note 21. Is the Son of Man in vv. 13-14 to be identified as the nation Israel in vv. 18 and 27? Though the present forum is perhaps not appropriate for such a discussion, may it not be that Daniel has in view here the ideal representative of Israel, analogous to Isaiah's ideal "Servant of the Lord" whom he addressed as Israel (Isa. 49:3)? In the present context, then, it would be the ideal Israel who would receive the kingdom, depicted in 7:14 as one "like a Son of Man" (Beasley-Murray, "The Interpretation of Daniel 7," p. 55). Keil's words are instructive here: "The delivering of the kingdom to the people of God does not, according to the prophetic mode of contemplation, exclude the Messiah as its king, but much rather includes Him, inasmuch as Daniel, like the other prophets, knows nothing of a kingdom without a head, a Messianic kingdom without the King Messiah" (*Biblical Commentary on the Book of Daniel*, p. 235).

39. It is quickly admitted that these verses are among the most difficult to interpret in Daniel. Montgomery says, "The history of the exegesis of the 70 Weeks is the Dismal Swamp of O.T. Criticism" (*A Critical and Exegetical Commentary on the Book of Daniel*, p. 400). The textual, lexical, and chronological problems demand a more lengthy discussion than space allows.

40. For recent studies, see William H. Shea, "Poetic Relations of the Time Periods in Daniel 9:25," *Andrews University Seminary Studies* 18 (1980):59-63; J. Doukhan, "The Seventy Weeks of Daniel 9: An Exegetical Study," *Andrews University Seminary Studies* 17 (1979):1-22; Thomas Edward McComiskey, "The Seventy Weeks of Daniel against the Background of Ancient Near Eastern Literature," *Westminster Theological Journal* 47 (1985):18-45; Robert C. Newman, "Daniel's Seventy Weeks and the Old

It has long been held among conservatives that the *initial three goals* decreed in 9:24 were fulfilled at least in part by the vicarious, substitutionary, atoning death of our Lord Jesus.[41] Concerning the timing of the *second three goals*, opinions are as varied and numerous as the expositors or commentators offering them, with conclusions falling generally along one's view of eschatology.[42] What indications are there within this verse that an earthly millennial kingdom might be in view?[43]

Before examining this question in detail, it is important to note that in the context, all six of these goals are earthly. The prophecy regards Daniel's people Israel, an earthly nation, and Daniel's holy city Jerusalem. *The third goal* speaks of atoning for wickedness using the legal term *kipper*, concerning which the book of Leviticus speaks so eloquently. The fact that it is the sin of man rather than the sin of fallen angels that can be atoned for also provides an earthly dimension to the context. Visions and prophets are earthly terms (angelic beings having need of neither). Finally, if one accepts the Holy of Holies as it is normally understood in the OT, an earthly temple is in view.[44]

Testament Sabbath-Year Cycle," *Journal of the Evangelical Theological Society* 16 (1973):229-34; Gerhard F. Hasel, "The Seventy Weeks of Daniel 9:24-27," Ministry Insert 5D-21D, *Ministry* 49 (May 1979); Roger T. Beckwith, "Daniel 9 and the Date of Messiah's Coming in Essene, Hellenistic, Pharisaic, Zealot and Early Christian Computation," *Revue de Qumran* 10 (1981):521-42; and Harold W. Hoehner, *Chronological Aspects of the Life of Christ* (Grand Rapids: Zondervan, 1977), pp. 115-39.

41. Depending on how one deals with the textual problems in the first two goals (*lᵉkallēʾ* versus *lᵉkallēḥ*, and Kethib *wᵉlaḥtōm* ["and to seal up"] versus Qere *ûlᵉhātēm* ["and to finish"] supported by a number of Hebrew manuscripts and editions with secondary support from the LXX [and its descendants]), one may conclude that sin is forever banished (most modern versions would suggest this) or that sin is adequately dealt with by the Messiah's coming. The textually uncontested use of the term *kipper* in the third of these goals would seem to support the latter proposition. To accept the former proposition, though a valid textual decision, would seem to project the completion of all six goals to the beginning of the eternal state, something neither amillennialists nor premillennialists would like to do. About the textual option in the first phrase, Baldwin writes, "If this is to be *finished*, we are being told about the final triumph of God's kingdom and the end of human history" (*Daniel: An Introduction and Commentary*, p. 168).

42. Mauro states that all six goals were "fully accomplished" after the ascension, with which statement Young concurs (Philip Mauro, *The Seventy Weeks and the Great Tribulation* [Boston: Hamilton, 1923], p. 53; Young, *The Prophecy of Daniel*, p. 201). Walvoord and Culver see the ultimate fulfillment of all six goals as immediately subsequent to the Tribulation, though obviously based on the work of Christ at His first advent (cf. Walvoord, *Daniel the Key to Prophetic Revelation*, pp. 220-23; Culver, *Daniel and the Latter Days*, pp. 167-68).

43. Such a study remains somewhat tenuous inasmuch as the term "kingdom" is conspicuously absent from the pericope.

44. Lacocque sees this term as referring to the Aaronic priesthood, whereas Young sees it as referring to the Messiah Himself (Andre Lacocque, *The Book of Daniel* [Atlanta: Knox, 1979], p. 194; Young, *The Prophecy of Daniel*, p. 201).

"To bring in everlasting righteousness" (*ûlᵉhābî̂ ṣedeq 'ōlāmîm*) is *the fourth goal*. Regarding the root *'lm*, one may see the preceding discussion on 2:31-45. Concerning righteousness (*ṣedeq*), also a legal term, one must of course acknowledge that the believing Christian today has the very righteousness of God and that, by its nature, that righteousness must be everlasting (cf. 2 Cor. 5:21). In this sense, the work of Christ on the cross made this fourth goal possible for the individual. But the nation of Israel and the city of Jerusalem are in view in Daniel 9.[45] If "everlasting righteousness" based on the atoning work of Christ is to be brought in for Israel as a nation, it must be brought in while Israel is still constituted as a nation, i.e., before the eternal state begins.[46] The only possible point in time when this could occur and remain within the time parameters offered (i.e., within the 490 decreed years) would be at the end of the Great Tribulation and at the inception of an earthly kingdom. This concept of the kingdom seems to be consistent with the book of Daniel (see the earlier discussion) and with Scripture as a whole.

The sixth goal is "to anoint the most holy" (lit., "to anoint a holy of holies," *wᵉlimšōaḥ qōdeš qŏdāšîm*). As was mentioned above, the most frequent use of *qōdeš qŏdāšîm* is in reference to the Holy of Holies, first in the Tabernacle, later in the Temple (cf. Ex. 26:33-34; 2 Kings 7:50). Though *qōdeš qŏdāšîm* can refer to Temple environs (cf. Ezek. 43:12), normally only cultic personnel and utensils are "anointed" (cf. Ex. 29:36; Lev. 8:10-12).

If the anointing of a holy of holies in Daniel 9:24 refers to a temple, its provenance must be earthly, inasmuch as there is no temple in the New Jerusalem (cf. Rev. 21:22).[47] The only possible point in time for the anointing of an earthly temple must be late in the Great Tribulation or early in a millennial kingdom for the following reasons. First, if the terminus a quo for the 490 years is Nisan 444 B.C.,[48] any anointing of the most holy place in 520 B.C. (Zerubbabel's Temple) would have preceded that of 9:24. Second, the reanointing of the altar after the desecration

45. At this point, one of the basic precepts of the dispensationalist, that Israel is at least to some extent distinct from the church, is indispensable to the argument.

46. Admittedly one could argue against this because of the New Jerusalem of Rev. 21.

47. If, on the other hand, the terms here refer to a person, that person is most likely the Messiah of 9:25, one who is "greater than the temple" (Matt. 12:6). Though this is possible and attractive in the context, I tend to see a most holy place here rather than a person, due to the technical nature of the term *qōdeš qŏdāšîm*.

48. Following the date demonstrated by Hoehner (*Chronological Aspects of the Life of Christ*, p. 128), while recognizing that starting in 458-57 B.C. and using solar (instead of lunar or prophetic) years will also work chronologically. Although some have attempted to construe the 70 "sevens" as indicative of something other than 490 years, I have yet to find a truly convincing or compelling reason to abandon the general approach taken by Hoehner and others.

by Antiochus IV Epiphanes in 165 B.C. precedes the atoning work of Christ; the passage sequence suggests that this anointing follows that work. Third, to my knowledge, the most holy place was not anointed from that time until the time of the destruction of Jerusalem in A.D. 70. That leaves only a yet future temple to be anointed. If the Temple of Ezekiel 43 is to be taken as millennial, it becomes a likely candidate for this event.

CONCLUSION

Does the book of Daniel support exegetically an earthly kingdom ruled by the Lord Jesus Christ followed by the continuation of that kingdom in the new heavens and new earth? From the passages considered, the answer seems to be in the affirmative.

Daniel 2:31-45 indicates that the Aramaic word for "kingdom" may include the concept of a kingdom with both earthly/temporal and heavenly/eternal aspects. The context in Daniel 2 allows for one kingdom beginning on earth and continuing into the eternal state. This kingdom is established by God, fills the whole earth after destroying all other earthly kingdoms, and will never be destroyed.

Daniel 7:15-28 adds that this kingdom is presented to "the saints, the people of the Most High," who are themselves under the authority of the Son of Man (cf. 7:13-14 with 7:27). It may be that these people are "eschatological faithful Israel,"[49] or that they also include believing Gentiles.[50] The passage also reaffirms 2:31-45 in that this kingdom is begun on earth following the destruction of the fourth kingdom and continues into eternity.

Daniel 9:24-27 is significant to the discussion in that the terms used in the fourth and sixth goals stated for the people of Israel in 9:24 may suggest that this kingdom will be characterized by everlasting righteousness and will also demand the presence of an earthly temple.

It is just as important to point out that Daniel does not speak to several issues related to millennialism. It does not mention (1) the length of time for the space-time stage of the kingdom; (2) the specific chronological details of the kingdom; and (3) any possible rebellion at a given stage in the kingdom. But Daniel does affirm the nature of the kingdom as having a beginning on earth and continuing into the eternal state, and so being indeed "the kingdom that will never be destroyed."[51]

---

49. Poythress, "The Holy Ones of the Most High in Daniel VII," p. 213.
50. Cf. Hasel, "The Seventy Weeks of Daniel 9:24-27," p. 192.
51. For additional evidence see the argumentation in my forthcoming chapter referred to in n. 2, as well as Robert L. Thomas, *Revelation 1-7: An Exegetical Commentary* (Chicago: Moody, 1992), p. 71 (on the similar use of Greek *basileia*, "kingdom," primarily the messianic rule and kingdom).

8

EVIDENCE FROM JOEL AND AMOS

HOMER HEATER, JR.
Professor of Bible Exposition
Dallas Theological Seminary

T he Minor Prophets come from disparate circumstances extending over some four hundred years. Discussing them in the context of issues pertaining to premillennialism is a daunting task indeed. One possible approach, though tenuous, is to select passages and present them as some kind of a paradigm. Two passages are selected, one from Amos and one from Joel, and are treated in what the author believes is their chronological order. Because this order is different from the canonical order, more will be said further in the chapter about a later date for Joel.

AMOS 9:11-12 AND ITS USE IN ACTS 15

Considerable discussion has been devoted to Amos 9, particularly in the context of the debate over continuity/discontinuity between the Old and New Testaments. Most recently O. Palmer Robertson in a festschrift honoring S. Lewis Johnson[1] used Amos 9:11-12 as a paradigm for the NT interpretation of the OT. He concludes that James's use of the

---

1. O. Palmer Robertson, "Hermeneutics of Continuity," *Continuity and Discontinuity: Perspectives on the Relationship between the Old and New Testaments*, ed. John S. Feinberg (Westchester, Ill.: Crossway, 1988), pp. 89-108.

passage is normative for our understanding of the OT promises to the nation Israel. His conclusions stand between the dispensational/premillennial position and the old amillennial position.[2] While the passage is indeed being fulfilled in this present age, he says, this is only the "first stage" of fulfillment. There will be a future restoration of all things, but it will take place when there is a recreation of heaven and earth in eternity.

Robertson's conclusions[3] are welcome in that they allow for an understanding of the OT prophetic text that takes into consideration the original setting and audience. This is in contrast to the older amillennial hermeneutic that allowed little contextual meaning to prevail. The major problem with Robertson's approach, however, is that it still does not allow a special place for Israel prior to eternity as a fulfillment of the OT prophecies. The language of the prophets was surely understood in its time to refer to people, places, and events known to them. While the passing of time and changing of circumstances require some shift of meaning, that shift should not be so extensive as would be required under a "new earth" fulfillment in eternity.

At the risk of redundancy, I believe another look at the passage is in order with the primary question for hermeneutics being "Does Acts 15 exhaust the meaning of the OT message cited?"

THE CONTEXT OF AMOS 9:11-12

The message of Amos throughout is one of judgment against the people of God, whereas chapter 9 contains clear promises of hope. Consequently, few critical scholars are willing to see the genuineness of Amos 9:11-15.[4] However, Paulo is right in saying, "It is not necessary to conclude that 9:11-15, since they treat the reestablishment, are foreign to the prediction of the prophet. These verses, on the contrary, agree quite

2. E. B. Pusey represents the older position when he says, "Israel was restored in the flesh, that, after the flesh, the Christ might be born of them, where God foretold that He should be born. But the temporal fulfillment ended with that Event in time in which they were to issue, for whose sake they were; His Coming. They were but the vestibule to the spiritual. As shadows, they ceased when the Sun arose. As means, they ended, when the end, whereto they served, came. There was no need of a temporal Zion, when He Who was to send forth His law thence, had come and sent it forth. No need of a Temple when He Who was to be its Glory, had come, illumined it, and was gone. No need of one of royal birth in Bethlehem, when *the Virgin* had *conceived and borne a Son*, and *God* had been *with us*. And so as to other prophecies. All which were bound to the land of Judah, were accomplished" (*The Minor Prophets: A Commentary* [reprint, Grand Rapids: Baker, 1950], 1:340).

3. Developed further in *The Books of Nahum, Habakkuk, and Zephaniah*, New International Commentary on the Old Testament (Grand Rapids: Eerdmans, 1990).

4. H. W. Wolff, *Joel and Amos: A Commentary on the Books of the Prophets Joel and Amos*, trans. W. Janzen, S. D. McBridge, Jr., and C. A. Muenchow, *Hermeneia—A Critical and Historical Commentary on the Bible* (Philadelphia: Fortress, 1977), pp. 351ff.

well with the context of the prophecies on the day of Yahweh."[5] Anderson and Freedman say, "In some places, and quite clearly toward the end of the book, Amos sounds a positive note. Judgment, even when severe, even when total, is not the end. In spite of everything, Yahweh and his people still have a future."[6] We are assuming that words of hope in chapter 9 were given by the eighth-century prophet Amos.

Amos, a Judean, directed his message primarily to and against the Northern Kingdom of Israel. Their prosperity under Jeroboam II had led them to a proud self-sufficiency. Amos had to cut through a smug religiosity by calling down on their heads the judgment of Yahweh. Like a human father who punishes his child with tears of compassion, Yahweh promised to destroy His people. Yet in the midst of dire threats, He promised restoration: "Nevertheless, I will not totally destroy the house of Jacob" (9:8). Though they will go into captivity under the cruel Assyrians in 722 B.C., "I will restore the captivity of My people Israel" (9:14). Though the primary direction of his message was to Israel, Amos also castigated Judah (2:4-5) and Zion (6:1). Further, throughout the prophecies of Amos and Hosea, the Northern Kingdom is referred to and thought of as the people of the covenant of Yahweh. It should not surprise us, therefore, to see this reference in Amos 9 to the restoration of the Davidic dynasty in the last portion of the book, particularly since Amos finished out his life in Judah (1:1). The future of God's people will be as a unified people. The falling hut of the Southern Kingdom will be restored as a part of the blessing of God upon the then errant Northern Kingdom.

The passage beginning with 9:11 says specifically that the "hut" of David is falling or will fall.[7] I would see the participle as referring to present action.[8] Both the Northern and Southern Kingdoms reached new heights in the days of Jeroboam II and Uzziah/Azariah. However, the Northern Kingdom began to feel the pressure of Assyria and declined rapidly after Jeroboam's death. Likewise, Uzziah suffered an incursion of

---

5. A. Paulo, *Le Probleme Ecclesial des Actes a la Lumiere de Deux Propheties d'Amos* (Montreal: Bellarmin, 1985), p. 73. For further defense of the unity of the prophecy, see W. Sanford LaSor, et al., *Old Testament Survey* (Grand Rapids: Eerdmans, 1982).

6. F. I. Anderson and D. N. Freedman, *Amos: A New Translation with Introduction and Commentary* (New York: Doubleday, 1989), pp. 6-7. They argue that with the exception of the phrase "the fallen hut of David," the eschatological passages of chap. 9 could fit into many different periods. Furthermore, if more were known about that obscure phrase, one might not be required to place it after the 6th cent. However, so far as one can now determine, they argue, it must have been written after David's dynasty had fallen—i.e., after 586 B.C. (p. 893).

7. The Davidic Covenant in 2 Sam. 7 is presumed in this passage.

8. Hence, the prediction could have taken place prior to the debacle of 586 B.C.

Tiglath-Pileser III in the latter days of his reign and Judah began to slip.[9] Consequently, Amos could argue, from a historical as well as prophetical view, that the hut of David was falling and would fall.

However, God is not finished with the Davidic dynasty. He promises to raise up, to reestablish David's hut. Then the metaphor shifts from "hut" to a "walled city," which, when it falls, will have breaches and ruins. This reference is to Jerusalem or Zion as a literal city from which David ruled. It will need to be rebuilt as part of God's promised blessing on His people. The prophecy is a reference to the restoration of the Davidic kingdom to the position it had ("as in the days of old") under the first great king with whom Yahweh had made a covenant.

Part of that restoration includes the control of the enemies of the people of God (Amos 9:12; cf. Ps. 2). The archetypical enemy of Israel/Judah was Edom (9:12). The idea of restored Israel possessing Edom in the *eschaton* (the end time) is also addressed in Numbers 24:18, Isaiah 11:14, Ezekiel 25:12-14, and Obadiah 18-20. As Wolff says,

> In any case this witness is dominated by the confident expectation that a Davidic imperium, long since demolished, would be the focal point of the coming global reign of Yahweh. The restored imperium would correspond in splendor to that of the empire "as in days of old" (*kymy 'wlm*) and would embrace the remnant of the arch-enemy Edom, but also of all the other nations.[10]

THE SEPTUAGINT TEXT OF AMOS 9:11-12

The Septuagint text (LXX) has a critical divergence from the Masoretic Text (MT) that also has had an impact on Acts 15 (albeit indirectly). It is found in 9:12*a*.

MT: *l^ema'an yîrešû 'et-š^e'ērît 'ĕdôm* ("That they may possess the remnant of Edom")

LXX: *hopōs ekzētēsōsin hoi kataloipoi tōn anthrōpōn* ("That the rest of mankind might seek")

The inferential particle *l^ema'an* (often "in order that") is translated with *hopōs* and the subjunctive, usually meaning "in order that." *Yîr^ešû* means "to possess" and in the Amos context (MT) represents the promise to Israel that in her revived state, she will possess what is left over of Edom, her traditional enemy and often the paragon of enmity against

---

9. For a thorough defense of the idea that Azariah of Judah headed up an anti-Assyrian coalition, see Hayim Tadmor, "Azarijau of Yaudi," *Scripta Hierosolymitana* 8 (1961):232-71.

10. Wolff, *Joel and Amos*, p. 352. For Edom as the enemy of God's people, see, e.g., Isa. 34; 63; Jer. 49; Ezek. 35; and Obadiah.

God. The LXX has read *yidrᵉšû* (*dāraš* "to seek"). The *y* and the *d* are not usually morphologically confused.[11] There are no variants in the Hebrew manuscripts. The sign of the direct object (*'ēt*) requires that "remnant" (*šᵉ'ērît*) be treated as an accusative, while the LXX turns it into a nominative: "That the rest might seek." *Tōn anthrōpōn* ("of mankind") is reading *'ādām* ("man/mankind") for *'ĕdôm* ("Edom"—presuming a text without *mater lectionis*). Instead of MT: "That they may possess the remnant of Edom," the LXX has "That the rest of mankind might seek." A major issue is whether there was a direct object in the LXX.[12]

It can be seen that the LXX is virtually identical to the MT of Amos 9:11-12 except for 9:12*a*, where the reading in the LXX provides a significantly different meaning for the passage in Amos. The subject in verse 12 in the MT is Israel, the verb means to possess, and the object is Edom and all the nations. In the LXX, the subject is mankind and all the nations/Gentiles, the verb means to seek out, and there is no object. Consequently, the Greek leaves the issue hanging: What will mankind and all the Gentiles seek? Codex Alexandrinus provides an object, as does Acts 15: *ton kurion* ("the Lord").

How is one to explain the LXX text? Its treatment of the Hebrew context is conservative, and therefore a deliberate divergence here would not be expected. Furthermore, the Old Greek leaves a normally transitive verb without an object: "That the rest of mankind and all the nations might seek . . ." One might argue that the *'et* has been read *'ôtî* ("That the rest of mankind might seek *me*")[13] However, the Old Greek (usually represented in manuscripts B, W, V) does not have a direct object expressed. The object *me* ("me") shows up only in Lucian, which, by all accounts, whether proto-Lucian or Lucian, is late. *Ton kurion* ("the Lord," as in Acts) appears in Alexandrinus and dependent minuscules.[14] Most agree that Codex Alexandrinus has a tendency to harmonize OT texts to the NT. The fact that there are two different objects in the Greek

---

11. Except in Wolff's commentary, p. 351.
12. See below for a discussion of the LXX data.
13. H. Alford, *The Greek Testament*, 4 vols. in 2 (Revised. Chicago: Moody, 1958), 2:165-66. J. de Waard, *A Comparative Study of the Old Testament Text in the Dead Sea Scrolls and in the New Testament* (Grand Rapids: Eerdmans, 1966), p. 25. He cites C. Van Gelderen, *Het Boek Amos* (Kampen, Neth.: Kok, 1933), p. 295, in support of someone reading *'yty* ("me") which would have led to a translation in the third person: *ton kurion* ("the Lord"). He rejects the argument on the same grounds presented here, namely, the Old Greek does not support it. Pusey points out that Isa. 11:10 contains a parallel idea in the phrase *'ēlāyw gôyim yidrᵉšû*—"the nations shall seek him" (*The Minor Prophets*, 1:338). This passage may well have influenced the Greek translators and the NT citation.
14. See J. Ziegler, ed., *Duodecim Prophetai*, vol. 12, *Septuaginta V.T. Graecum* (Göttingen: Vandenhoek & Ruprecht, 1943), for the data.

tradition, coupled with the fact that the uncials normally representing Old Greek do not have a direct object and thus have difficult syntax, argues for an original Greek without an object.[15]

JAMES'S STATEMENT INVOLVING AMOS 9:11-12

The Jerusalem Council (Acts 15) was confronting the crucial issue of the requirements for Gentiles to enter salvation. James had the final word (vv. 13-21). The central statement is "God first concerned Himself about taking from among the Gentiles a people for His name" (v. 14). To support his point James said, "And with this the words of the Prophets agree, just as it is written." It is important to note the plurals "words" and "Prophets."

Amos 9:11-12	Acts 15:16-18
In that day I will raise up the fallen booth of David, and wall up its breaches; I will also raise up its ruins, and will rebuild it as in the days of old; *that they may possess the remnant of Edom and all the nations* who are called by My name, declares the Lord who does this.	After these things I will return, and I will rebuild the tabernacle of David which has fallen, and I will rebuild its ruins, and I will restore it, *in order that the rest of mankind may seek the Lord*, and all the Gentiles who are called by My name, says the Lord, who makes these things known from of old.

The theological and hermeneutical issue in this passage lies at the heart of our debate. However, the textual issue is intertwined with it, since the use to which James put these words is better suited by the LXX translation than the MT. While the theological issue is the paramount one for this discussion, the source of James's statement must be discussed as well.

JAMES'S QUOTATION COMPARED WITH AMOS 9:11-12 (LXX)

When Acts 15:16-18 is compared with the LXX of Amos 9:11-12, eight significant differences emerge. The data are as follows:

(1) Acts: *meta tauta ana/epistrepsō* ("After these things I will return"), for LXX: *en tē hēmera ekeinē anastēsō* ("in that day I will raise up"). The source for this phrase is debated. Usually it is assigned to Jere-

---

15. Earl Richard says that there are "several indications that the addition is redactional," but he does not deal with the LXX variations ("The Creative Use of Amos by the Author of Acts," *Novum Testamentum* 24 [1982]:37-53).

miah 12:15. However, the LXX there reads: *meta to ekbalein me autous epistrepsō* ("After I have cast them out, I will return").[16]

(2) Acts: *anoikodomēsō tēn skēnēn*[17] ("I will rebuild the tabernacle"), for LXX: *anastēsō tēn skēnēn* ("I will raise up the tabernacle").

(3) Acts: *kateskammena* ("ruins"), for LXX: *peptōkota* ("fallen [stones]").

(4) Acts: Nothing, for LXX: *kai ta kateskammena autēs anastēsō* ("and I will raise up her ruins").

(5) Acts: *anorthōsō* ("I will restore"), for LXX: *anoikodomēsō* ("I will build again"). *Anorthōsō* ("I will restore") translates *kûn* ("prepare, establish") in the LXX 11 out of 15 times. Seven of those passages refer to the establishment of the throne of David or the house of David (2 Sam. 7:13, 16, 26; 1 Chron. 17:12, 14, 24; 22:10). This has no doubt influenced the reading in Acts.[18]

(6) Acts: Nothing, for LXX: *kathōs hai hēmerai tou aiōnos* ("just as the days of old").

(7) Acts: *ton kurion* ("the Lord"), where LXX has no object.

(8) Acts: *gnōsta ap aiōnos* ("known from of old"). This last phrase has no counterpart in Amos. It is usually assigned to Isaiah 45:21, which contains a diatribe against idols and says, "Declare and set forth your case; indeed, let them consult together. Who has announced this from of old? Who has long since declared it?" The LXX has here *Ei anangelousin engisatōsan, hina gnōsin hama tis akousta epoiēsen tauta ap archēs* ("If they will declare, let them draw near, that they may know together, who has caused these things to be heard from the beginning"). As can be seen, there is no direct correspondence between the text of Acts and Isaiah. A similar sentiment is there: "Yahweh, in contrast to the idols, has known all things from the beginning." Thus in Acts, God's plans for the Gentile inclusion in His program are likewise from the beginning.

---

16. Interestingly, when Peter cites Joel 2:28 (MT, 3:1): *wᵉhāyâ 'aḥărê-kēn* ("And it will come about after this"), he has *kai estai en tais eschatais hēmerais* ("And it shall be in the last days," Acts 2:17) for the LXX: *kai estai meta tauta* ("And it shall be after these things"). Are these two phrases synonymous to the apostles? (See also Earl Richard, "The Creative Use of Amos by the Author of Acts," p. 47, n. 23.)

17. Note Zech. 1:16: *šabtî lîrûšālāim bᵉraḥămîm bêtî yibbāneh bāh* ("I will return to Jerusalem with compassion; My house will be built in it") = *epistrepsō epi Ierousalēm en oiktirmō kai ho oikos mou anoikodomēthēsetai en autē* ("I will return to Jerusalem in mercy and my house shall be rebuilt in it").

18. Earl Richard argues for an internal Lucan use of the word, but the LXX evidence, I believe, is stronger ("The Creative Use of Amos by the Author of Acts," p. 48).

AN AMOS 9:11-12 TESTIMONIUM FOR ACTS 15

From the days of C. H. Dodd, there has been the theory of "testimonia," a body of texts used by the NT writers for the source of their OT support. Certainly the instruction of the Lord to His disciples after the resurrection would lend weight to such a possibility (Luke 24:25-27). However, McCartney argues that the texts chosen were probably liturgically familiar in the diaspora synagogues.[19]

De Waard argues for a common source for the Acts citation and that of Qumran.[20] However, the similarities between the Acts passage and the Qumran texts may be overstated.[21] It should also be noted that Qumran does not have the critical 12th verse of Amos 9, which is the essential part of James's statement. That Amos 9:11 was considered messianic by the Qumran sectaries as well as the apostles should cause little surprise, since it is tied into the Davidic covenant and refers to the restoration of Davidic rule. What is surprising is that Qumran at one place applies the "hut of David" to the restored law of the community (and links it with 2 Sam. 7): "The books of the Law are the hut of the king; as He said, *I will raise up the hut of David which is fallen.* The king is the Assembly."[22] But *4QFlorilegium* I,12 interprets Amos 9:11 messianically,

> [Citing portions of 2 Sam. 7] This is the Branch of David who will arise with the Seeker of the Law and who will sit on the throne of Zion at the end of days; as it is written, *I will raise up the tabernacle of David which is fallen.* This *tabernacle of David which is fallen* [is] he who will arise to save Israel.[23]

19. "This fact becomes more apparent when we ask why the New Testament writers chose the particular texts they did. Was it because it was divinely revealed to them that these texts were special texts which, unlike most Old Testament texts, held a fuller meaning than grammatical-historical exegesis would establish? This answer seems unlikely, because it is probable that many, if not most, of the texts were liturgically familiar in the diaspora synagogues and may have been chosen simply for that very reason" (D. G. McCartney, "The New Testament's Use of the Old Testament," *Inerrancy and Hermeneutic; A Tradition, a Challenge, a Debate,* ed. H. M. Conn, [Grand Rapids: Baker, 1988] p. 102). Earl Richard, on the other hand, disagrees with the testimonium hypothesis ("The Creative Use of Amos by the Author of Acts," p. 46, n. 22).

20. J. de Waard, *A Comparative Study of the Old Testament Text,* p. 25.

21. Earl Richard, "The Old Testament in Acts: Wilcox's Semiticisms in Retrospect," *Catholic Biblical Quarterly* 42 (1980):330-41.

22. See A. Dupont-Sommer, *The Essene Writings from Qumran,* trans. G. Vermes (Gloucester, Mass.: Peter Smith, 1973), p. 134, for a translation and commentary on the Damascus Document.

23. Ibid., p. 313, and de Waard for the text, p. 24. Longenecker, "Acts," *Expositors Bible Commentary,* 12 vols, ed. F. Gaebelein (Grand Rapids: Zondervan, 1981), 9:446, wrongly attributes Acts 15:17 to Qumran.

CONCLUSION

Whether there was such a thing as a formal group of "testimonia," there was certainly a group of accepted ideas in the Jewish community that were derived from their interpretation of the OT.[24] A casual reading of the Acts passage should lead us to the conclusion that we are dealing with no mere citation of an OT passage.[25]

(1) The phrase "to this agree the words of the prophets" indicates immediately that James was taking an *ad sensum* approach to the OT.

(2) The opening phrase "after these things" may be theological in its orientation,[26] but it is more probably a paraphrase of "in that day."[27]

(3) Three words in Acts differ from the LXX of Amos: *anoikodomēsō* ("I will rebuild"), *kateskammena* ("ruins"), and *anorthōsō* ("I will restore"). As shown above, *anorthōsō* ties the unit to 2 Samuel 7. Two phrases in Amos are missing from Acts: *kai ta kateskammena autēs anastēsō* ("And its ruins I will raise up"), and *kathōs hai hēmerai tou aiōnos* ("just as the days of old"). An object (*ton kurion* ["the Lord"]) is supplied for the verb, and an additional phrase is found at the end: *gnōsta ap aiōnos* ("known from of old").

24. Otherwise, how could we understand the scribes' combination of verses regarding such topics as the Messiah (2 Sam. 5:2; Micah 5:2, and perhaps Gen. 49:10 with Matt. 2:5); the argument for the Messiah being greater than David (Ps. 110 with Matt. 22:42-45); the use of judges (*'ĕlōhîm*) to silence criticism about His claims (Ps. 82:6 with John 10:34-35); and the son of man as Messiah (Matt. 26:64-65 with Dan. 7:14).

25. C. K. Barrett says, "The verse however is not a citation; James claims that the words of the prophets are in agreement with it" ("Luke/Acts," *It Is Written: Scripture Citing Scripture*, ed. D. A. Carson and H. G. M. Williamson [Cambridge: Cambridge U., 1988], pp. 243-44, n. 4).

26. See J. E. Rosscup, "The Interpretation of Acts 15:13-18," Th.D. diss., Dallas Theological Seminary, 1966, pp. 130ff. He argues with James M. Stifler (*An Introduction to the Study of Acts of the Apostles* [New York: Revell, 1892], pp. 140-41) that sequence is the intent: *first* the Gentiles will be called out (v. 14) and *afterward* ("after these things") the promises to Israel will be established. (See Rosscup's bibliography on dispensational writers on this point.) E. F. Harrison, on the other hand, says, "No doubt these things [messianic kingdom] are predicted in Scripture at various points, but the introduction of a whole panorama of prophecy at the Jerusalem Council goes far beyond the demands of the situation" (*Acts: The Expanding Church* [Chicago: Moody, 1975], p. 234).

27. Note the Joel 3/Acts 2 interchange pointed out above. Further, the verb *ana/epistrépsō* should not be asked to bear the theological load of the return of Christ (J. F. Walvoord, *The Millennial Kingdom* [Findlay, Ohio: Dunham, 1959], pp. 205-6), because it is probably to be considered *hendiadys*, as is fairly common in Hebrew. The meaning would be "I will raise up again" as in Jer. 12:15 "I will return and show them mercy" = "I will again have mercy," so Thompson, *Jeremiah*, New International Commentary on the Old Testament (Grand Rapids: Eerdmans, 1980), p. 359 and NIV.

(4) The opening phrase ("after these things") and the closing phrase ("known from of old") though usually identified with Jeremiah 12:15 and Isaiah 45:21, respectively, can be only loosely linked with those passages.[28]

These four points lead me to the conclusion that we do not have here a citation of Amos, but of a theological idea derived from the OT concerning a time when Gentiles will be included in God's program for Israel. That inclusion can be seen in the MT of Amos 9 in that Gentiles will be brought under the dominance of a restored Israel.[29] The LXX form of the text, which was probably an inadvertent mistranslation of an MT type text (perhaps without the *'et*) or a Hebrew text form reflecting already the differences (*'ādām/yidrᵉšû* ["mankind/they may seek"]), became part of that theological statement.[30]

Consequently, it would be better to view Acts 15:15-18 as a theological summary of the OT teaching on Gentile inclusion in the eschaton. The teaching contains a phrase found in the LXX of Amos, which had been accepted by the Jewish/Christian community. It is a true statement of OT intent. There is no doubt in my mind that the MT reading is original, but the reading "that all mankind and the Gentiles might seek the Lord" is a valid statement of OT theology. The use of the phrase from the LXX of Amos 9:12 merely illustrates the general truth.

With Longenecker, I would hold that the citation is merely to show that the tenor of OT Scripture[31] supports the idea of Gentiles coming to God *without losing their identity.*[32] James was not ignoring the future restoration of Israel and equating the "hut of David" with the

---

28. Earl Richard says, "Luke's compositional techniques and thematic concerns provide sufficient explanation for this modification" ("The Creative Use of Amos by the Author of Acts," p. 48, n. 27).

29. See C. C. Torrey, who says, "But even our Masoretic Hebrew would have served the present purpose admirably, since it predicted that 'the tabernacle of David,' i.e., the church of the Messiah, would 'gain possession of all the nations which are called by the name [of the God of Israel]'" (*The Composition and Date of Acts* [reprint, Cambridge, Mass.: Harvard U., 1969], p. 39).

30. See Richard Longenecker's discussion in *Biblical Exegesis in the Apostolic Period* (Grand Rapids: Eerdmans, 1975), pp. 85-88. He says, "In the first place, while the quotations of Acts are fairly representative of the LXX in general, the LXX alone is not sufficient to explain all their textual phenomena" (p. 88).

31. McCartney follows Dodd in saying, "A fulfilment [sic] use of Scripture can retain the original context of an Old Testament passage by focusing that whole context on Christ. Thus not just the quoted words but the whole context is being brought into view by the citation and, according to Dodd, even forms the 'theological sub-structure' for the New Testament writers" ("The New Testament Use of the Old Testament," p. 113).

32. See Longenecker, "Acts," *Expositors Bible Commentary*, 9:446-47.

church; he merely said that one element of what will happen in the future was happening in his day.

Thus James did not intend to exhaust the meaning of Amos 9:11-12. Indeed the inclusion of Gentiles in God's redemptive work is in view, but the dynasty of David will rule on the earth, an earth known to Israel in an OT setting. Edom as the archetypical enemy of Israel will be subdued under the feet of a converted and restored Israel. This needs to happen on the earth as the culmination of God's promise to His chosen one, David.

JOEL 2:28-32 AND ITS USE IN ACTS 2

The second passage I would like to address is the *crux interpretum,* Joel 2:28-32 (3:1-5, Heb.) with some consideration of 3:1-21 (4:1-21, Heb.) vis-à-vis Acts 2:14-21.

Many argue for an early date for Joel (based primarily on its position in the canon),[33] but it should probably be dated later because of a more fully developed theology, particularly with reference to the Day of Yahweh.[34] Amos, clearly datable in the eighth century, speaks of the Day of Yahweh as if the people of Israel had a limited understanding of it (5:18). They perceived the Day of Yahweh only in terms of Yahweh taking vengeance on the enemies of Israel.[35] Amos instructs them, however, that the Day of Yahweh is a two-edged sword. God's own people will suffer the pain of His judgment because of their stubborn refusal to yield to Him.

"THE DAY OF YAHWEH" IN JOEL 1-2

The first major hermeneutical issue in Joel is whether chapter 1 and chapter 2 refer to the same event. Generally, chapter 1 is interpreted as a locust plague in Joel's day that in some sense prefigures the eschatological Day of Yahweh in chapter 2.[36] Hans Wolff, for example, in his

33. See, e.g., E. B. Pusey, *The Minor Prophets,* 1:10, and Gleason Archer, *A Survey of Old Testament Introduction* (Chicago: Moody, 1964), pp. 292-94, who presents various other arguments for an early date.

34. For a good discussion of the date of Joel, see C. F. Mariottini, "Joel 3:10 [H4:10]: 'Beat Your Plowshares into Swords,'" *Perspectives in Religious Studies* 14 (1987):125-30. For a discussion of developed theology in Joel, see L. C. Allen, *The Books of Joel, Obadiah, Jonah and Micah,* New International Commentary on the Old Testament (Grand Rapids: Eerdmans, 1976), p. 36.

35. For a good discussion on the history of the study, see M. Weiss, "The Origin of the 'Day of the Lord' Reconsidered," *Hebrew Union College Annual* 37 (1966):29-71.

36. D. Stuart believes the locusts are symbolic in both chapters for the Babylonian armies (*Hosea-Jonah,* Word Biblical Commentary [Waco, Tex.: Word, 1987], p. 242). R. D. Patterson treats chap. 1 as locusts and chap. 2 as Assyria and Babylon as well as an eschatological army ("Joel," in *Expositors Bible Commentary,* ed. Frank E. Gaebelein [Grand Rapids: Zondervan, 1985], 7:245).

insightful analysis of the book, argues that chapter 1 is a historical plague of locusts, but that chapter 2 takes that historical situation and draws from it a warning about the eschatological Day of Yahweh.[37] He believes that 2:1-11 refers to the eschatological Day of Yahweh as does 2:19ff. Consequently, his structure is (1) locusts (1:1-20); (2) eschatological Day of Yahweh (2:1-11); (3) plea for repentance (historical, 2:12-17) to which the people responded and God was merciful; (4) eschatological blessing (2:19b-32) and judgment on nations (3:1-21). Keil holds to a similar position.[38]

I believe the key to relating chapter 2 to chapter 1 is found in the tenses in 2:18-19, and that they argue for a unitary structure in the first two chapters.[39] In the MT, the verbs in 2:18-19 are what used to be called *waw* consecutive imperfects but are now usually referred to as preterites. They are the typical syntactical form for narration in past time. They may be used for future time, but in such cases they are usually anchored to a perfect tense cast in the future with the *waw* consecutive.[40] Some have tried to repoint the forms as jussives, but Wolff cogently argues against the effort. The normally expected translation of these four verbs would thus be, "Then the Lord was zealous for His land, and He had pity on His people. And the Lord answered and said to His people, 'Behold, I am going to send you grain.'" In other words these actions took place in Joel's day in response to the prayers of the people. KJV, NASB, and NIV have translated them future, because they see all of chapter 2 as eschatological.

I would argue therefore: (1) that the same terrible locust plague in Joel's day is in view in both chapters. The prayer of the people in Joel's day was "do not make Thine inheritance a reproach" (2:17). The thing causing the "reproach" was the locust plague. Surrounding peoples would say something like "Yahweh has obviously abandoned His people." Parallel similes and descriptions link both chapters. Even the description of the earth and heavens (2:10) should be understood as

---

37. Hans Wolff, *Joel and Amos*, pp. 41-42.

38. C. F. Keil, *The Twelve Minor Prophets*, Biblical Commentary on the Old Testament (reprint, Grand Rapids: Eerdmans, 1951), 1:179-209.

39. So Allen, *The Books of Joel, Obadiah, Jonah and Micah*, pp. 64-68. Wolff follows my understanding of the tenses, but his literary interpretation is different (*Joel and Amos*, p. 60).

40. See E. Kautzsch and A. E. Cowley, eds., *Gesenius' Hebrew Grammar*, 2d Eng. ed. (Oxford: Clarendon, 1910), sec. 111w. This is the way D. Stuart takes them, but there is no perfect form to act as a prophetic perfect anchor (*Hosea-Jonah*, p. 258). Joüon says, "In the sphere of the future, *wayyiqtōl* (as *qātal* sec. 112g-h) is rare. After a prophetic perfect (sec. 112h): Isa. 9:5; Joel 2:23" (*Grammaire de l'Hébreu Biblique* [Rome: Institut Biblique Pontifical, 1923], p. 326).

coming from the impact of the awful locust invasion. The locusts are called a nation in 1:6 and God's army in 2:11. Thus Joel refers to the plague as a "local" day of Yahweh in which God brought judgment on His people.

(2) In light of the calamity in chapter 1, the people of Israel are to consecrate a fast (obviously for the purpose of intercession). God's plea for repentance occurs in four imperatival units in these chapters: 1:2 "Hear this, O elders, and listen, all inhabitants of the land"; 1:14 "Consecrate a fast, proclaim a solemn assembly; gather the elders and all the inhabitants of the land"; 2:1 "Blow a trumpet in Zion, and sound an alarm on My holy mountain"; 2:15 "Blow a trumpet in Zion, consecrate a fast, proclaim a solemn assembly." They are to pray, "Spare Thy people, O Lord, and do not make Thine inheritance a reproach, a byword among the nations. Why should they among the peoples say, 'Where is their God?'" (2:17).

(3) Though there is no direct statement of the fact, the people apparently responded as God demanded.

(4) He promised to send abundant crops and to remove their reproach (the locusts or "northern army"; 2:19-20). He promised to restore all that the locusts had eaten (2:25) and to bring abundance of rain.[41]

ESCHATOLOGICAL PROMISES IN JOEL 2

However, as God expands on His wonderful promises of restoration, He begins to telescope the historical past with the distant future.[42] I

---

41. An objection might be raised about the statement in 2:19, translated in NASB, "And I will never again make you a reproach among the nations." This phrase is clearly an answer to the "paradigm prayer" God gave them in 2:17: "Spare Thy people, O Lord, and do not make Thine inheritance a reproach, a byword among the nations." The phrase "never again" is *lō'... 'ôd*. This syntactical combination occurs over 100 times. Several times it is translated "never again," because it often occurs in prophetic passages containing future promises. However, it can simply mean "no longer" with no reference to whether the situation could be repeated (e.g., Judg. 2:14; Ezek. 33:22). The context in Joel refers to the historical reproach brought on Israel because of the locust plague. That reproach was removed when God destroyed the locusts and restored the vegetation to the people.

42. The practice in prophetic writing of moving from a historical event to the eschaton we are calling "telescoping," for want of a better term. Perhaps we could illustrate it best from Jesus' instructions to the twelve in Matt. 10. The situation in 10:1-15 occurred during Jesus' three years of ministry. He was preparing the twelve for their ministry of proclamation of the kingdom of Israel to the people of Israel ("lost sheep of the house of Israel"). Suddenly, however, Jesus used language that cannot in any way be localized in time or place to the twelve in Palestine. The description is apocalyptic and full of tribulation. The intense persecution will cause the disciples to flee from city to city (10:23), and this statement culminates in the most astounding comment in the chapter: "For truly I say to you, you shall not finish going through the cities of Israel, until the Son of Man comes." Schweitzer argues that Jesus actually

believe this begins at 2:26*b*: "Then My people will never be put to shame" (*w^{e}lō'-yēbōšû 'ammî l^e'ôlām*). Joel moves from the locust plague in his day to the restoration of God's repentant people in the eschaton. The description of marvelous provision replacing the horrible devastation of the locusts reaches a crescendo with "Then My people will never be put to shame" (v. 27*b*). God's repeated goal in the OT is to come to the place where "He is the Lord God in the midst of Israel and they are His people" (v. 27*a*).[43] That goal will be achieved in the eschaton. The blessing of God in physical plenty includes God's presence among His people. This eschatological promise then leads the prophet Joel to deliver one of the most beautiful and wonderful promises of Israel's restoration in the OT (2:28-32). It begins with the promise "And it will come about after this that I will pour out My Spirit on all mankind" (2:28*a*).

Two things stand out in this wonderful unit: (1) The people of God must turn to God in repentance before the devastating Day of Yahweh can be turned back. Any blessing by God upon Israel must be in response to spiritual repentance. Thus there is a spiritual dimension to all that God does for His people.

(2) On the other hand, the blessings in response to that spiritual activity are connected with the land. The negative ideas are locusts, desolate wilderness, reproach among nations, darkness and gloom, and darkening of the sun and moon. The positive ideas are locusts removed, grain, new wine, oil, reproach among nations removed, fruitful trees, full vines and fig trees, early rain, latter rain, threshing floors full of grain, vats overflowing with new wine and oil, plenty to eat, and satisfaction. In view of the fact that the plague and its devastation are understood by all to refer to literal conditions in Israel in Joel's day, should not one expect the language of blessing to be understood in the same context and in the same way? When we look at the rest of the book of Joel, and when we compare it with the book of Acts, it is important to remember these two principles.

thought He would set up the eschatological kingdom during His lifetime, and that that kingdom would be preceded by tribulation. However, according to Schweitzer, this expectation failed to materialize and required reevaluation (see, e.g., A. Schweitzer, *The Mystery of the Kingdom of God: The Secret of Jesus' Messiahship and Passion*, trans. W. Lowrie [New York: Macmillan, 1950], pp. 48-52; and *The Kingdom of God and Primitive Christianity*, trans. L. A. Garrard [New York: Seabury, 1968], pp. 111-14). Jesus, however, made no mistakes about His mission. What we have in Matt. 10 is a telescoping of events from the time of Jesus and the apostles to the eschatological future. There is no grammatical indication of a shift, but it is unmistakable. The first fifteen verses were enacted with the movement of the twelve through the land of Israel; the remainder of the chapter has yet to be enacted. I suggest that something similar is happening in the book of Joel.

43. E.g., Jer. 24:7; 32:38; Ezek. 11:20; 37:23, 27; and Zech. 8:8.

The chronology of the events of 2:28-32 is important. To what does "after this" (v. 28) refer? The phrase *'aḥărê-kēn* ("after this") occurs some forty-four times. At least thirty of these refer to sequence in time. But it is used in 2 Samuel as a literary device to take up the next topic in cases where it can be shown that time sequence is not involved.[44] VanGemeren has shown that this phrase in Isaiah 1:26 is used topically.[45] Isaiah speaks of a time when Jerusalem will be called a faithful city. It is after (*'aḥărê-kēn*) she has been restored by Yahweh. Sequence, however, is not the emphasis. As a matter of fact the events are really simultaneous. The same thing could be said for Jeremiah 16:16 and 21:7.

The time element of Joel 2:28-32 therefore should not be considered step two in a process in which 2:21-27 is step one. These are concomitant events. Since Joel has telescoped the eschaton (2:26b-27) with the historical (2:19-26a), the next issue he wishes to take up is the Spirit's work in the process. *'Aḥărê-kēn* ("after this") is thus a transitional idea rather than a sequential event.[46]

The work of the Spirit

The essential passage, 2:28-32, must be logically related to the preceding promise of the restoration of the people of Israel. The statement is universalistic in nature: all flesh, male and female, old and young are involved. Even the remote people of society, the male and female servants, will have the Spirit poured out upon them.[47] The chiastic structure begins with "I will pour out my Spirit" (v. 28) and ends with "I will pour out my Spirit" (v. 29).

The implications of the Spirit's ministry

I agree with VanGemeren that 2:28-32 explicates 2:26-27.[48] The center of Yahweh's eschatological work is found in 2:27: "I am the Lord your God and there is no other." This refers to the redemption of the people of Israel in the eschaton when they turn to Him in repentance and receive forgiveness. The work of the Spirit comes simultaneously (2:28-29). The result of the Spirit's work seems to emphasize communi-

---

44. 2 Sam. 8:1 (1 Chron. 18:1); 2 Sam. 10:1 (1 Chron. 19:1); 2 Sam. 13:1; 15:1; 21:18; 2 Kings 6:24.

45. W. A. VanGemeren, "The Spirit of Restoration," *Westminster Theological Journal* 50 (1988):85-86.

46. Contra Wolff, who says, "'Afterward' (*'aḥărê-kēn*) is a seldom [!] encountered conjunctive formula. It forms the transition to all those further oracles in chaps. 3 and 4 [2:28–3:21, Eng.] which bring prophetic promise for a more distant time" (*Joel and Amos*, p. 65).

47. The same four people groups are to observe the Sabbath (Ex. 20:10).

48. W. VanGemeren, "The Spirit of Restoration," p. 88.

cation (prophecy, dreams, visions), but the emphasis may be parallel to the New Covenant promises in Jeremiah 31:33-34, where God's law will be internalized, and they shall know the Lord from the least to the greatest, "for I will forgive their iniquity, and their sin I will remember no more."

The second part of Joel 2:28-32 deals with the phenomena associated with the Day of Yahweh. For this description one needs to compare Isaiah 13:6-10 and Zephaniah 1:14-18. When the Lord returns to set right the wrongs of His creation, these phenomena in nature will occur. The language of Joel 2:10-11 refers to the massive invasion of the locusts and the impact it has on the heavens, sun, moon, and stars. The effect on the sun and earth becomes a type of the eschatological Day of Yahweh. Yahweh's work in nature will, by implication, bring great distress and suffering upon the earth. Obviously, not all will be delivered from it. "Whoever calls on the name of the Lord will be delivered" (Joel 2:32). Those who repent and turn to the God of Israel will escape from the effects of the judgment on the earth.

The victory of God's people over the nations

The Jewish people apparently originally understood that the Day of Yahweh was a time in which they would be avenged of their enemies (Amos 5:18). Joel 3:1-21 turns to that topic. The theme of reversal of fortunes (3:1) is played out when Israel, oppressed by the nations, becomes the ruler of nations (cf. Jer. 32:44 for the phrase "restore the fortunes"). Edom, the archetypical enemy of Judah will be dominated by the Jews (3:19). Amos 9:12 contains the same theme. There is no way to know how God will work this out in the last days, for the Edomites have been subsequently assimilated into the populations now occupying their territory, but there will be some connection with the people of the last days and the Edomites of Joel's day. The reading of these prophecies in an OT context leads to the idea that historical people and places will be on God's stage of history and the stage will be the land on which Joel and the locusts walked. But what a transformation will take place when God redeems those who call on Him, delivers them from their enemies, and places them in a dominant position over the nations who will also turn to Him.

PETER'S USE OF JOEL 2

Elsewhere in this work another author discusses Acts 2 and Joel 2. At this point we need only discuss the tensions between a hermeneutic that allows the language of Joel to apply to Israel in the eschaton and at the same time to believers in the church age.

We will work with the assumption that when Peter says, "But this is what was spoken of through the prophet Joel," he is not speaking of analogy or allusion, but fulfillment (Acts 2:16). If this is the case, how can there be "both . . . and"—both Israel and the church, or the church now and Israel later?

When Peter preached on the Day of Pentecost (Acts 2) and later at the Temple (Acts 3) he was working out of an OT milieu. He refers to the Davidic Covenant as well as to Joel's prophecies in Acts 2. He speaks of the "promises to your fathers." In Acts 3 he makes some of the clearest statements about his assumptions that the OT kingdom promises are about to be fulfilled. Phrases like "times of refreshing" (*kairoi anapsuxeōs*; v. 19) and "period of restoration of all things" (*chronōn apokatastaseōs pantōn*, v. 21) refer to OT promises with earthly significance. It is difficult to see these in any other way.

Peter seems to be saying that the messianic age in some sense has begun since the Messiah has come and is now ascended. The apostles asked a key question in Acts 1:6, "Lord, is it at this time You are restoring the kingdom to Israel?" Jesus did not directly answer their question, but He did not say that their question was unwarranted. Peter was therefore fully justified in seeing the application of the redemptive work of the Messiah (Joel 2:32: "and it will come about that whoever calls on the name of the Lord will be delivered"). The deliverance spoken of in Joel is physical, but the emphasis on remnant in the OT always has spiritual overtones (as Paul uses it in Rom. 10:13).

That the earthly aspects of the Davidic Covenant and of Joel's promises are not yet fulfilled and are in some way conditioned on Israel's national repentance is evidenced by Peter's statements in Acts 3:19-21. The "period of restoration of all things" is the eschatological time when the extensive OT discussion of an ideal time for Israel that partakes of both spiritual and physical conditions will be implemented.

Conclusion

Both Joel and Amos addressed the Jewish people of their day. The promises made by both prophets are set in the context of the people of Israel and the land of Israel.

Amos says that the Davidic dynasty will be established on the earth, prosperity will come to Israel, all nations will be brought under the aegis of Israel, and Israel will "not again be rooted out from their land which I have given them, says the Lord your God" (9:15). While Gentile inclusion is the theme James uses in Acts 15, one should not conclude that the meaning of Amos 9 is exhausted by James. The people of Israel will enjoy the physical blessing of God on the earth prior to eternity.

The messianic age in a sense began in Acts 2 because the Messiah had come. Peter can therefore use Joel 2:28-32*a* to explain the phenomenon of Pentecost. However, the context of Joel indicates a time of restoration and blessing for Israel that is dissimilar both to what is happening in the church and what will happen in eternity. To this agree the words of all the prophets of Israel. What is referred to as the Millennium meets the requirements of the parameters of the OT hope for Israel.

9

EVIDENCE FROM MATTHEW

DAVID K. LOWERY
Professor of New Testament Studies
Dallas Theological Seminary

A number of subjects in Matthew's gospel are currently matters of lively debate, leading one editor to describe the gospel as a "storm center in contemporary scholarship."[1] One of the debated subjects concerns the question of Israel's future. Does Matthew portray Israel as a reprobate people who because of their rejection of Jesus as Messiah have irrevocably forfeited their place as the people of God? More than one interpreter answers that question affirmatively, and as a corollary concludes that Matthew no longer sees Israel as an object of mission.

That Matthew does portray Israel as reprobate is true. That he sees Israel replaced as the representative people of God is also true. But that he regards this state of affairs as final or irrevocable is incorrect. Nor does he see only Gentiles as the object of the church's mission. To Israel as well, the gospel must be preached, with the expectation that ultimately many will hear it gladly. No one passage or line of argument is definitive in this regard, but the cumulative point of several lines of inquiry leads to this conclusion.

---

1. Graham Stanton, "Introduction: Matthew's Gospel, A New Storm Centre," in *The Interpretation of Matthew*, ed. Graham Stanton (Philadelphia: Fortress, 1983), p. 1.

Matthew's Ethnic Background

One line of inquiry concerns the identity of the author and the relationship, if any, that he and his church maintained with Judaism. The supposition related to questions of this sort is that a Gentile author, writing primarily for Gentiles, will have little or no interest in matters concerning the future of Israel. And, if a relationship with Judaism exists at all, it will be for the most part an antagonistic one. There is a division of opinion about this subject, however, and not a little uncertainty on the part of some who have considered the issue. In the preface to a recent study on Matthew by Paul Minear, G. B. Caird wrote: "I have always found Matthew's Gospel the most puzzling book in the New Testament, partly because it is so hard to put a human face to the author."[2] Was, for example, Matthew a Jew, as most believe, or a Gentile?

Kenneth W. Clark wrote an article in 1947 entitled "The Gentile Bias in Matthew," in which he argued that the excoriation of the Jews was so intense that the gospel must have been written by a Gentile.[3] This viewpoint was expanded a few years later in monographs by Nepper-Christensen[4] and Strecker.[5] It was also argued by Van Tilborg[6] and, recently, by Meier.[7]

In addition to the strong denunciation of Israel that pervades the gospel, the proponents of Gentile authorship support their claim by appealing to instances where the author is said to display an ignorance of distinctly Jewish matters. A text like Matthew 16:12 is usually cited as an example of this ignorance, where Matthew refers to the "teaching of the Pharisees and Sadducees." Meier, for example, argued that anyone familiar with the doctrinal differences separating the parties would not link them in this way.[8] He found another example of ignorance at 22:23, where Matthew purportedly displays ambivalence about the denial of the resurrection by the Sadducees. According to Meier, the text might read, "Sadducees, saying there is no resurrection," implying that this was the conviction of some but not necessarily all Sadducees.[9] Lapses of this

---

2. Paul S. Minear, *Matthew: The Teacher's Gospel* (New York: Pilgrim, 1982), p. x.

3. Kenneth W. Clark, "The Gentile Bias in Matthew," *Journal of Biblical Literature* 66 (1947):165-72.

4. Poul Nepper-Christensen, *Das Matthäusevangelium. Ein judenchristliches Evangelium?* (Aarhus: Universitetsforlaget, 1958).

5. Georg Strecker, *Der Weg der Gerechtigkeit*, 3d ed. (Göttingen: Vandenhoeck & Ruprecht, 1971).

6. Sjef van Tilborg, *The Jewish Leaders in Matthew* (Leiden: E. J. Brill, 1972), p. 171.

7. John P. Meier, *The Vision of Matthew* (New York: Paulist, 1978), pp. 17-25.

8. Ibid., p. 20.

9. Ibid., pp. 20-21.

sort are understandable for a Gentile but hardly, so the argument runs, for a Jew.

What may be concluded about the author in view of these observations? First, the fact that joint reference is made to the teaching of the Pharisees and Sadducees at 16:12 does not mean that their teaching was seen as identical. The contrary conclusion may be based on a misunderstanding of a point of grammar formulated by Granville Sharp to the effect that singular nouns of personal description joined by one article and linked by a copula refer to one and the same person.[10] Sharp excluded instances in the plural, however, as well as all proper nouns.

Matthew 16:12 should probably be compared to the similar construction in Luke 14:21, "Go out at once into the streets and lanes of the city." Two plural nouns are joined by one article and a copula. But the streets and lanes remain distinguishable entities. The sentence could be translated, "streets of the city and lanes of the city." Matthew probably groups together Pharisees and Sadducees as parties whose teaching contained aspects inimical to Christian doctrine, but it does not follow that he is unaware of the doctrinal differences that distinguish the two groups. In fact, according to Levine, Matthew's version of the incident about plucking grain on the Sabbath (Matt. 12:1-8; Mark 2:23-28; Luke 6:1-5) shows that "Matthew is expert in the Law and its application."[11]

The second example of Matthew's alleged ignorance of Jewish matters is also problematic. Meier contended that Matthew's text (22:23), as opposed to the similar statements in Mark (12:18) and Luke (20:27), implies that only some and not all of the Sadducees denied the doctrine of the resurrection.[12] But, in fact, the texts all say the same thing. Mark 12:18 may be translated, "And Sadducees came to Him, who say there is no resurrection." The qualifying clause, "who say there is no resurrection," is made up of a relative pronoun (*hoitines*), a finite verb, and an infinitive of indirect discourse with a predicate accusative.

Luke 20:27 may be translated, "When some of the Sadducees came, who say there is no resurrection." Instead of a relative pronoun and finite verb as in Mark, Luke used an articular participle, either adjectival or substantival in simple apposition to the phrase "some of the Sadducees," in which he uses the indefinite pronoun (*tines*). If any text is

---

10. Granville Sharp, *Remarks on the Uses of the Definitive Article in the Greek Text of the New Testament*, 3d ed. (Philadelphia: Hopkins, 1807).

11. Etan Levine, "The Sabbath Controversy According to Matthew," *New Testament Studies* 22 (July 1976):480-83. Cf. also W. Boyd Barrick, "The Rich Man from Arimathea (Matt 27:57-60) and 1QIsaᵃ," *Journal of Biblical Literature* 96 (June 1977):235-39.

12. Meier, *The Vision of Matthew*, pp. 20-21.

open to the charge of ambiguity it is Luke's (or even Mark's *hoitines*) rather than Matthew's.

Matthew 22:23 may be translated, "On that day Sadducees came to him, saying there is no resurrection." The qualifying clause is composed of an anarthrous adjectival participle. It is anarthrous because the word it modifies, "Sadducees," is anarthrous. The predicate is identical to Mark's and Luke's apart from a change in word order. The charge of ambiguity on Matthew's part will not stand.

The same may be said for the suggestion that Matthew's harsh denunciation of Israel and his underscoring of the nation's guilt could not come from a Jew.[13] Consideration of Paul's letter to the Romans gives reason to doubt such a conclusion. On the one hand Paul can express his devotion to Israel in the most poignant terms, wishing himself accursed on their behalf (9:1-5), while on the other hand condemning Israel for their unbelief (11:20), hardness of heart (10:21), and hypocrisy (2:17-24).

In a study focusing on the anti-Jewishness in the gospel, Hare sifted the evidence and concluded that Matthew's strong statements about Israel were more understandable from a Jewish rather than a Gentile Christian who, like Luke, might be inclined to write more dispassionately about the synagogue and Judaism.[14]

Corroboration of this viewpoint may be found in a study of the second-century work *5 Ezra* made by Stanton.[15] He found that the author expressed ánti-Jewish and pro-Gentile views while at the same time displaying a profound anguish for the nation Israel. He concluded that it must have been written by a Jewish Christian.

While only a few arguments against the proposition that Matthew's gospel was written by a Jew have been considered, it would appear that these, at least, are not convincing and provide no good basis for overturning the usual view. Those who have argued that the gospel is written by a Gentile (and, in turn, primarily for Gentiles) often claim as a corollary that hope for Israel's future is rejected by Matthew as well. But this, too, is a contention without foundation as the subsequent discussion of particular texts will show. Before that, however, some attention

---

13. Compare the Jewish sectarians at Qumran, who describe other Israelites as "sons of darkness" (1QS 1:10; 1QM pass.) and "sons of corruption" (1QS 9:16; CD 6:15; 13:14), among other epithets. Cf. Shemaryahu Talmon, *The World of Qumran from Within: Collected Studies* (Jerusalem: Magnes, 1989), pp. 280, 283.

14. Douglas R. A. Hare, *The Theme of Jewish Persecution of Christians in the Gospel According to St. Matthew* (Cambridge: Cambridge U., 1967), p. 165.

15. Graham Stanton, "5 Ezra and Matthean Christianity in the Second Century," *Journal of Theological Studies* 28 (April 1977):67-83.

needs to be given to another aspect of the argument that Matthew entertains no hope for Israel's future, connected with the belief that Matthew and his community have severed all ties with Judaism.

MATTHEW'S RELATIONSHIP WITH JUDAISM

A more complex issue than the question of Matthew's nationality concerns the relationship of Matthew and his community to Judaism. In broad terms the question is whether Matthew's community saw itself as a sect within Judaism or as a group dissociated from the Jews.

It is generally accepted that Jewish Christians maintained connections with Judaism to one degree or another before the revolt and subsequent destruction of Jerusalem and the Temple in A.D. 70. After that date, particularly in the wake of rabbinical consolidation at Jamnia, it became (so it is argued) increasingly difficult to do so. The date of A.D. 85 is usually mentioned in connection with the twelfth benediction of the synagogue prayers, the "Birkath ha-Minim," in which condemnation is invoked for Christians and heretics.[16] Though establishing this date with any certainty poses numerous problems,[17] it may be taken as a rough indication of the time when it was no longer likely, or for that matter possible, for a Jewish Christian to think of himself as a participating member of Judaism.[18]

While many interpreters of the gospel are persuaded that Matthew wrote from the vantage of a community already dissociated from Judaism, a few defer. Schlatter, for example, concluded that the gospel predated the separation of Judaism and Christianity.[19] Subsequently, Bornkamm argued that the Temple tax pericope (17:24-27) showed that

---

16. A version from the Cairo Geniza reads: "For apostates let there be no hope, and the kingdom of insolence mayest thou uproot speedily in our days; and let Christians (*noserim*) and heretics (*minim*) perish in a moment, let them be blotted out of the book of life and let them not be written with the righteous. Blessed art thou, O Lord, who humblest the insolent" (quoted by William Horbury, "The Benediction of the *Minim* and Early Jewish-Christian Controversy," *Journal of Theological Studies* 33 [April 1982]:20).

17. Cf. Reuven Kimelman, "*Birkat Ha-Minim* and the Lack of Evidence for an Anti-Christian Jewish Prayer in Late Antiquity," in *Jewish and Christian Self-Definition*, ed. E. P. Sanders (Philadelphia: Fortress, 1981), 2:226-44.

18. Horbury, "The Benediction of the *Minim* and Early Jewish-Christian Controversy," pp. 19-61. But cf. Steven T. Katz, who argued that the evidence does not support a Jewish ban on Christians and therefore Christians were probably not totally separated from Jews before A.D. 135, if even then ("Issues in the Separation of Judaism and Christianity after 70 C.E.: A Reconsideration," *Journal of Biblical Literature* 103 [March 1984]:43-76).

19. Adolf Schlatter, *Die Kirche des Matthäus* (Gutersloh: Bertelsmann, 1929), pp. 17-19.

the community was "still attached to Judaism."[20] Hummel likewise argued that the gospel reflected a debate within Judaism, carried on after the fall of Jerusalem but before A.D. 85.[21] Davies also seems to have lent support to this position, though he found evidence of a "great gulf . . . between the Christian community and the Synagogue."[22] More recently, it was Goulder's conclusion that Matthew wrote from within the bounds of Judaism, before the introduction of the "Birkath ha-Minim," but that he nonetheless "expects to be persecuted for his heterodoxy."[23]

For most interpreters there is no question about whether or not Matthew and his church saw themselves as dissociated from Judaism. The question is rather to what degree this was so. Trilling, for example, believed that Matthew's community saw itself as the "true Israel" entirely distinct from the nation.[24] Yet he believed that the pericope about the Temple tax showed that the association of some in the church with Israel was still possible.[25] Schweizer likewise thought that the passage about the Temple tax indicated "that dialogue with the Jewish synagogue had not yet been broken off" even though "the Christian community had conclusively split with the Synagogue."[26]

Others, however, see the distance between Israel and the church as much greater. According to Strecker, Matthew's apparent interest in the Pharisees is a historicizing device by means of which he warns the leaders of his own Gentile community. The mission to Israel is a thing of the past, part of an era of salvation-history irretrievably gone.[27] Walker developed a similar thesis in a study of salvation-history in the gospel.[28] Matthew's community, for Walker, concerned itself with Israel only as a "past phenomenon of salvation-history."[29] Others, like Van Tilborg[30] and

20. Günther Bornkamm, "End Expectation and Church in Matthew," *Tradition and Interpretation in Matthew*, ed. Günther Bornkamm et al. (Philadelphia: Westminster, 1963), p. 20.

21. Reinhart Hummel, *Die Auseinandersetzung zwischen Kirche und Judentum im Matthäusevangelium* (Munich: Kaiser, 1963), p. 29.

22. W. D. Davies, *The Setting of the Sermon on the Mount* (Cambridge: Cambridge U., 1964), p. 286; cf. 290, n. 3.

23. M. D. Goulder, *Midrash and Lection in Matthew* (London: SPCK, 1974), p. 152.

24. Wolfgang Trilling, *Das wahre Israel: Studien zur Theologie des Matthäus-Evangeliums*, 3d ed. (Munich: Kosel-Verlag, 1964), p. 47.

25. Ibid., p. 224.

26. Eduard Schweizer, *The Good News According to Matthew* (Atlanta: Knox, 1975), p. 16.

27. Strecker, *Der Weg der Gerechtigkeit*, pp. 139-40; Georg Strecker, "The Concept of History in Matthew," *The Interpretation of Matthew*, ed. Stanton, pp. 67-84.

28. Rolf Walker, *Die Heilsgeschichte im ersten Evangelium* (Göttingen: Vandenhoeck & Ruprecht, 1967).

29. Ibid., p. 145.

30. Tilborg, *The Jewish Leaders in Matthew*, p. 171.

Hare,[31] interpreted the denunciations of Israel as a sign that the break with Judaism was clear and final.

If the gospel is read in a straightforward manner, there seems no denying that it contains a strong polemic against Israel. Gaston, for example, concluded that Matthew bore a hatred for Israel that Christians today cannot accept.[32] But Légasse has examined the anti-Jewish theme in the gospel as a whole and concluded that Matthew addresses hypocritical and unfaithful Christians in equally severe tones.[33]

In sorting out the various positions concerning the relationship of Matthew and his community to Judaism, the chief reasons for believing that the community was dissociated from Judaism may be stated. In the first place, the text of 21:43 ("the kingdom of God will be taken away from you"), without parallel in the other gospels, seems to state the rejection by God of the nation Israel. A statement like that, so it is argued, is likely only in the context of a group who have cut their ties with Judaism. Similarly, in 28:15 the Jews are singled out as those who circulate the story that Jesus' body was stolen by the disciples. That "the Jews" can be designated so suggests that a definite break had taken place between Matthew's community and Israel. In the same way Matthew refers to "their" scribes (7:29) and "their" synagogues (4:23; 9:35; 10:17; 12:9; 13:54), unusual designations if the community thought of itself as a sect of Judaism.

But there are some conceptual and verbal similarities to these statements in the letter of Paul (also a Jew) to the Romans. For example, Paul too can describe Israel as a rejected people (11:15). He also refers to Israel and the Jews as a group with whom he has no part: Israel pursued righteousness but did not attain it (9:31); the Jew relies on the law (2:17). He can refer to "their" adoption (9:4) and "their" patriarchs (9:5). Yet he can also describe Israelites as "my brothers" (9:3).

How did Paul, as a Jewish Christian, think of himself in relation to Judaism? A curious picture emerges from the account in Acts.[34] Near the end of Paul's second missionary journey he cut off his hair in con-

31. Hare, *The Theme of Jewish Persecution of Christians in the Gospel According to St. Matthew*, p. 153.
32. Lloyd Gaston, "The Messiah of Israel as Teacher of the Gentiles: The Setting of Matthew's Christology," in *Interpreting the Gospels*, ed. James Luther Mays (Philadelphia: Fortress, 1981), pp. 78-96. Cf. C. Leslie Mitton, "Matthew's Disservice to Jesus," *Epworth Review* 6 (1979):47-54. Cf. also Francis Wright Beare, whose conclusion on an exposition of Matt. 23 contained this remark: "A Christian expositor is under no obligation to defend such a mass of vituperation" (*The Gospel According to Matthew: Translation, Introduction, and Commentary* [San Francisco: Harper & Row, 1981], p. 461).
33. Simon Légasse, "L'antijudaïsme' dans l'Évangile selon Matthieu," *L'Évangile selon Matthieu*, ed. M. Didier (Gembloux: J. Ducolot, 1972), pp. 417-28.

nection with a vow (18:18). He avoided the province of Asia near the end of his third journey in order to reach Jerusalem by Pentecost (20:16), presumably, among other reasons, to celebrate the feast (24:17). When he arrived in Jerusalem he visited the elders of the church (21:18). At their request he undertook rites of purification along with four other men (21:23-26). When the Jews from Asia incited a riot in the Temple court leading to Paul's rescue by the Romans and the subsequent opportunity to address the crowd, he declared himself a Jew (21:27-39). Before Felix he referred to his ceremonial purity (24:18).

No less curious is the Jews' description of Paul as one who belonged to the Nazarene sect (24:5). Paul responded by describing himself as one who worshiped the God of the fathers according to the Way, "which they call a sect," a designation which he, apparently, wished neither to affirm nor deny (24:14). At the end of the book Paul is pictured as one who can address leaders of the Jews in Rome as "brothers" and declare to them that he had "done nothing against our people or the customs of our fathers" (28:17). He is portrayed on the one hand describing his opponents as "Jews" and on the other hand as bearing no malice against his "nation" (28:19).

Paul could write about becoming like a Jew in order to win the Jews (1 Cor. 9:20) and yet also describe the faithful person as a "spiritual Jew" (Rom. 2:29). It seems that Paul wished to maintain his association with the Jews and to continue some Jewish practices, possibly for evangelistic purposes alone (cf. Rom 1:16; 1 Cor. 9:20), while at the same time remaining the apostle of Christ to the Gentiles. His letter to the Romans illustrates that he could write almost despairingly about the present state of the Jew and his unbelief (Rom. 9:1-5; 10:1-2, 21) while at the same time holding out hope for the conversion of some (11:5). Additionally, the account in Acts suggests that Paul maintained at least some of the customs and practices of Judaism.

Matthew's relationship to Judaism seems no more and no less enigmatic than Paul's. Matthew and his community saw themselves as the church of Christ (16:18; 18:17), but for various reasons, evangelism probably among them, were unwilling to dissociate themselves completely from Judaism and some of its practices (such as the Temple tax). This is a further indication that Matthew does not regard Israel's present plight as irreversible or irredeemable. In part this is related to his conviction that the promises of the OT made to Israel by God have not been rendered

34. On the historical reliability of Acts, see F. F. Bruce, "Is the Paul of Acts the Real Paul?" *Bulletin of the John Rylands Library* 58 (1976):282-305; Martin Hengel, *Acts and the History of Earliest Christianity* (London: SCM, 1979).

(nor will they become) null and void. But this point is related to Matthew's understanding of the OT, which is the substance of the next section.

MATTHEW'S USE OF THE OLD TESTAMENT

Also related to the question of the future of Israel is the use made of the OT in the gospel. While Matthew bears similarity to the rest of the New Testament in the general treatment of the OT, in one respect the gospel is unique. That is in the series of quotations that are introduced by a distinctive phrase employing the verb "fulfill" in the passive voice (*plērōthēnai*). The first example occurs at 1:22, where events leading up to Christ's birth are said to have taken place "that what was spoken by the Lord through the prophet might be fulfilled." Immediately following this Isaiah 7:14 is cited (1:23). Ten or eleven similar citations follow (2:5-6, 15, 17-18, 23; 4:14-16; 8:17; 12:17-21; 13:35; 21:4-5; 26:56; 27:9-10), depending on whether 26:56 is included, since no specific text is cited (Jesus' passion is said to have occurred "that the Scriptures of the prophets may be fulfilled"). It has been suggested that this text, which is similar to Mark 14:49 ("that the Scriptures might be fulfilled"), may have been the stimulus for the other citations.[35] There is general agreement that they are an integral part of the evangelist's gospel.[36]

What significance the distribution of the quotations might have for discovering more about Matthew's theology was considered by Rothfuchs.[37] He noted that the four quotations employed in Matthew's account of the Galilean ministry (4:14-16; 8:17; 12:17-21; 13:35) were all drawn from Isaiah and stressed Jesus' ministry to Israel, a ministry in line with God's promises to His people.[38]

Van Segbroeck reflected on Rothfuch's isolation of the texts from Isaiah and drew an additional implication. Isaiah was outspoken not only about God's willingness to save Israel but also about Israel's lamentable obduracy and rejection of His message. According to Van Segbroeck, this

35. Donald Senior, *The Passion Narrative According to Matthew* (Louvain: Leuven U., 1975), pp. 151-55.
36. Cf. O. Lamar Cope, *Matthew: A Scribe Trained for the Kingdom* (Washington, D.C.: Catholic Biblical Association of America, 1976), pp. 121-22; George M. Soares Prabhu, *The Formula Quotations in the Infancy Narrative of Matthew* (Rome: Biblical Institute, 1976), p. 104.
37. W. Rothfuchs, *Die Erfüllungszitate des Matthaus-Evangeliums* (Stuttgart: Kohlhammer, 1969), p. 78.
38. Ibid., pp. 181-83.

factor too may have figured in Matthew's attraction to this prophet who had spoken so pointedly about Israel's failure.[39]

The church's use of the OT was bound to raise questions about God's promises to Israel, as Ziesler noted with reference to Paul.[40] The problem is no less acute for Matthew. He also begins his gospel by emphasizing Jesus' relationship to Abraham and David (1:1). God's promises to these two may serve to illustrate the nature of the problem.

In Genesis 12:2-3 God promised Abraham that he would make him into a great nation through which all the world would be blessed. This promise was ratified by a covenant (15:1-21) described as "everlasting" (17:7-8). Later, the deliverance of Israel from Egypt is attributed to God's "remembering (His) covenant" (Ex. 6:4-8).

In 2 Samuel 7:8-16 God promised David that his house, throne, and kingdom would endure forever. The perpetuity of this covenant is subsequently mentioned (e.g., Ps. 89:28-37; Jer. 33:14-26; 1 Chron. 22:10). Jeremiah prophesied that David would be raised up to rule over a reunited Israel and Judah (30:9-10). The fortunes of David and the nation are also intertwined in Isaiah, where reference is made to an "everlasting covenant" (55:3).[41]

The problem in Matthew's day was that Israel did not look like a nation enjoying an "everlasting covenant." The people had rejected Christ and His emissaries and in turn had the kingdom taken from them (Matt. 21:43) and their house left a desolation (23:38). The Christian reading the OT may well have wondered: "Has God kept His promises to Israel? If not, how can I be sure He will keep His promises to me?" This question is particularly acute for Matthew because he alone among the gospel writers records the promise of Jesus to Peter that "the gates of Hades shall not overpower" the church (Matt. 16:18). As Childs put it, "The church . . . is promised an eternal existence against all the forces of opposition."[42] But what assurance can there be in a promise like this if God has promised the same to Israel and, by all appearances at least, failed to keep it?

Paul was probably responding to a form of this question in the middle section of his letter to the Romans (9-11).[43] After a lengthy treat-

39. F. Van Segbroeck, "Les citations d'accomplissement dans l'Évangile selon Matthieu d'après trois ouvrages récents," *L'Évangile selon Matthieu*, pp. 107-30.

40. J. A. Ziesler, *Pauline Christianity* (New York: Oxford U., 1983), p. 64.

41. Cf. Walther Eichrodt, "In the Beginning," *Creation in the Old Testament*, ed. Bernhard H. Anderson (London: SPCK, 1984), p. 70.

42. Brevard S. Childs, *The New Testament as Canon* (Philadelphia: Fortress, 1985), p. 177.

43. Cf. W. S. Campbell, "The Freedom and Faithfulness of God in Relation to Israel," *Journal for the Study of the New Testament* 13 (October 1981):27-45.

ment of the doctrine of salvation he concluded by stressing that nothing "shall be able to separate us from the love of God, which is in Christ Jesus our Lord" (Rom. 8:39). He then addressed immediately the place of Israel in salvation-history and affirmed that God's Word had not failed (Rom. 9:6), a fact that some must have questioned. It was a problem that demanded an answer, for if God had abandoned Israel what certainty could the Christian have in the promise that nothing "shall be able to separate us from the love of God"? It was a problem that threatened to undermine his doctrine of salvation.

Paul proceeded to defend the faithfulness of God and His Word in several ways, making liberal use of the OT in the process. His response constitutes a theodicy, broadly defined as the attempt to defend the righteousness of God in the face of circumstances that seem to call that righteousness into question.[44] In the case of Israel it is the apparent unfaithfulness of God to the covenant promises that is problematic. As Crenshaw noted, "the covenant relationship exacerbated the problem of theodicy, for the Lord confessed a personal interest in Israel's destiny."[45] The problem is summed up in Gideon's reply to the angel of the Lord: "If the Lord is with us, why then has all this happened to us? And where are all His miracles which our fathers told us about, saying, 'Did not the Lord bring us up from Egypt?' But now the Lord has abandoned us and given us into the hand of Midian" (Judg. 6:13). Christians in Matthew's day may also have thought that Israel looked like an abandoned people.

But Matthew's fulfillment texts serve, in part, to show how the plan of God was carried out in the life and ministry of Jesus. The circumstances of His birth, the flight to Egypt, the return to Galilee are all portrayed as events in accordance with God's plan.[46] Even when the disciples desert Him and He is taken by His foes, it is in accordance with the plan of God ("that the Scriptures of the prophets may be fulfilled," Matt. 26:56).

---

44. James L. Crenshaw defined theodicy as "the attempt to pronounce a verdict of 'not guilty' over God for whatever seems to destroy the order of society and the universe" ("The Shift from Theodicy to Anthropodicy," *Theodicy in the Old Testament* [London: SPCK, 1983], p. 1). Walther Eichrodt similarly proposed that theodicy represented an "attempt to balance the present state of the world, with its physical and moral evils, with the all-inclusive government of a just and beneficent God" ("Faith in Providence and Theodicy in the Old Testament," *Theodicy in the Old Testament*, p. 27).

45. Crenshaw, "The Shift from Theodicy to Anthropodicy," p. 5.

46. Cf. Krister Stendahl, "Quis et Unde? An Analysis of Matthew 1-2," in *The Interpretation of Matthew*, ed. Stanton, p. 58.

This assurance of God's plan being fulfilled has relevance also to the question of Israel's future. According to God's messenger, Jesus will save His people from their sins (1:21). But who are "His people"?[47] According to Bornkamm, "this can hardly be taken to mean Jewish people in the context of the first gospel."[48] He adduced no support for this assertion, however, possibly because the use of the term "people" (*laos*) elsewhere in Matthew (13 times) stands almost uniformly against such a conclusion.[49]

The next fulfillment citation at Matthew 2:6 is a case in point. In the quotation, Jesus is identified as the one who will "shepherd My people, Israel." According to Matthew, Jesus tells the disciples that He has come to fulfill the law and the prophets (5:17). He twice identifies Israel as the focus of His mission (10:6; 15:24). And yet it is Israel whom Matthew shows crying out "His blood be on us and on our children" (27:25). An indication of who bears responsibility for what is done could not be more clear.[50] Does Matthew intend his readers to conclude that in regard to Israel the plan of God has been frustrated or gone awry? The fulfillment theme in Matthew suggests otherwise, and leads the reader to think that though the prospects for Israel are presently grim, the plan of God for Israel will be fulfilled.

Two further lines of thought also suggest that Matthew entertains hope for Israel's salvation. One involves the necessity of an ongoing mission to Israel and the other the expectation that the mission will ultimately meet with a positive response.

Matthew's Commission to Israel

That the mission to Israel would continue is implied in the several unqualified commissions given to the disciples at various points in the gospel. They are called to be "fishers of men" (4:19). They are a "light to the world" (5:14). And they are to "make disciples of all nations"

---

47. Apparently the editor of the Curetonian Syriac version (5th c.) saw this as a problem which he resolved by substituting "world" for "his people."

48. Günther Bornkamm, "The Risen Lord and the Earthly Jesus," in *Tradition and Interpretation in Matthew*, p. 325.

49. Only the last reference (Matt. 27:64, "Otherwise, his disciples may come and steal the body and tell the people that he has been raised from the dead" [NIV]) is ambiguous and even here it is doubtful that the Jewish leadership is concerned about anything but Jewish reaction to the resurrection.

50. Cf. Hans Kosmala, "'His Blood on Us and on Our Children,'" *Annual of the Swedish Theological Institute* 7 (1968-69):94-126.

(28:19).[51] Yet alongside these general (or universal) commissions are several references to a specific (or particular) ministry to Israel. The disciples' early mission to Israel recorded at 10:5-6, though expanded subsequently at 28:19, is never rescinded. Unlike Luke (9:10), Matthew never records the return of the disciples from this mission. In fact, at 10:23 the disciples are told that they will not finish the mission to Israel until the Son of man returns. And at 23:34, after a sevenfold pronunciation of woe on religious leaders, Matthew shows Jesus still affirming a mission to Israel (using the present tense verb: "I am sending").

Though the mission to Israel is associated with opposition and persecution (10:17; 23:34), Matthew also offers hope that a positive response may be found. Two passages are noteworthy in this regard. In the first instance, Matthew records Jesus' promise to the disciples that they will one day judge the twelve tribes of Israel (19:28, cf. Luke 22:30).

In a study of the intention of Jesus and His relationship to Judaism, Sanders found Matthew 19:28 to be a text that showed that "Jesus looked for the restoration of Israel."[52] After surveying Jewish literature relevant to this period, he concluded that "the hope that seems to have been most often repeated was that of the restoration of the people of Israel,"[53] a hope in which the number twelve served to "symbolize the inclusion of all Israel in the coming kingdom."[54]

Even Philo, despite his inclination to allegorize aspects of Jewish belief, shared this hope and looked forward to the day when "the cities which now lay in ruins will be cities once more,"[55] indicating as well that he conceived of the kingdom in what might be called "this-worldly" terms.[56] It is the conclusion of Sanders that "the kingdom expected by Jesus . . . is like the present world—it has a king, leaders, a temple, and twelve tribes."[57]

Since Matthew 19:28 coheres with a widespread Jewish expectation of national restoration, the anticipated role of the disciples may be

51. The commission to "all nations" in Matt. 28:19 has been interpreted to signify the exclusion of Israel from the church's task by Douglas R. A. Hare and Daniel J. Harrington, "'Make Disciples of All the Gentiles' (Mt 28:19)," *Catholic Biblical Quarterly* 37 (July 1975):359-69. But cf. John P. Meier, "Nations or Gentiles in Matthew 28:19?" *Catholic Biblical Quarterly* 39 (January 1977):94-102.
52. E. P. Sanders, *Jesus and Judaism* (Philadelphia: Fortress, 1985), p. 103. Cf. B. F. Meyer, *The Aims of Jesus* (London: SCM, 1979), pp. 134-36, 154.
53. Sanders, *Jesus and Judaism*, p. 87.
54. Ibid., p. 104.
55. Philo, *De Praemiis et Poenis*, p. 168.
56. This was the view of the Qumran sectarians as well. Cf. Talmon, *The World of Qumran from Within: Collected Studies*, p. 300.
57. Sanders, *Jesus and Judaism*, p. 232.

considered in light of that context as well. In the OT the ruler or governor could be described as functioning as a judge (e.g., 2 Kings 15:5; Ps. 2:10; Isa. 1:26). This view of the role is also found in Jewish literature such as 1 Maccabees (9:73) and the Psalms of Solomon (16:27; 17:29).[58] It is also similar to the role envisioned in Revelation 20:4, where those who sit on thrones are given the authority to judge and are said to reign with Christ for 1,000 years.[59] Jewish literature also reflects the idea of an earthly messianic reign which precedes the eternal state (though of varying duration),[60] and it seems to be with reference to such an era that the disciples' future role as judges is referred to at Matthew 19:28.[61]

This authority is to be exercised in relation to Israel, which means the Jews and not the church. Interpreters may refer to the church as a "new Israel"[62] or "true Israel"[63] but Matthew[64] and other NT writers did not do so. The distinction that the NT maintains between the two has been set out well by Wilder,[65] Richardson,[66] Davies,[67] and Cranfield.[68]

58. Horbury suggests that the governmental role for the disciples referred to in Matt. 19:28 is based on the traditional role of the *phylarchs*, the princes of the 12 tribes, whose rule over a restored Israel finds mention in Qumran texts (1QM 3:3; 5:1-2) and the *Testament of the Twelve Patriarchs* (TJudah 25:1-2; TBenj 10:7) (William Horbury, "The Twelve and the Phylarchs," *New Testament Studies* 32 [1986]:503-27, esp. pp. 512, 524).

59. That the conceptual antecedents to this text are to be found in the OT and Jewish literature is generally recognized (cf. J. Massyngberde Ford, *Revelation: Introduction, Translation, and Commentary*, The Anchor Bible [New York: Doubleday, 1975], pp. 350-54). On the meaning of "judging," "reigning," and "sitting on thrones" as synonymous ideas based on Dan. 7, see Pierre Prigent, *L'Apocalypse de Saint Jean*, 2d ed. (Geneva: Labor et Fides, 1988), p. 310. See also the request of James and John to sit beside Jesus in the kingdom (Mark 10:37).

60. Cf. J. W. Bailey, "The Temporary Messianic Reign in the Literature of Early Judaism," *Journal of Biblical Literature* 53 (July 1934):170-87.

61. See the preceding context of the parallel passage in Luke 22:24-27, which is concerned with the proper exercise of authority. For Matthew, judgment in the sense of determining individual destiny is a prerogative of Jesus (the Son of man) (e.g., 16:27; 25:31-46).

62. Cf. Hummel, *Die Auseinandersetzung zwischen Kirche und Judentum im Matthäusevangelium*, pp. 156, n. 72; 160.

63. Cf. Trilling, *Das wahre Israel*, pp. 138, 162, 213.

64. Matthew seems to distinguish Israel and the church throughout the gospel (cf. 8:10; 10:6; 15:24; with 16:18; 18:17; 21:43).

65. A. N. Wilder, "The Church and Israel in the Light of Election," *Texte und Untersuchungen zur Geschichte der altchristlichen Literatur* 102 (1968):352-53.

66. Peter Richardson, *Israel in the Apostolic Church* (London: Cambridge U., 1969).

67. W. D. Davies, "Paul and the People of Israel," *New Testament Studies* 24 (1977):4-39.

68. C. E. B. Cranfield, *A Critical and Exegetical Commentary on the Epistle to the Romans* (Edinburgh: Clark, 1976-79), 2:448. Cf. Karl Hermann Schelkle, "Israel und Kirche im Neuen Testament," *Die Kirche des Anfangs*, ed. Rudolf Schnackenburg, et al. (Freiburg: Herder, 1978), pp. 607-14.

This exercise of authority is to take place in the "regeneration" (*palingenesia*), an era yet future.[69] Philo uses this term in connection with the renewal of the world generally, such as after the Flood,[70] or after destruction by fire.[71] Josephus uses it more particularly in a discussion of the restoration of the land of Israel after the Exile.[72] The prophecy of Isaiah gives particular expression to this expectation of a renewal and restoration of the land and people of Israel (e.g., Isa. 49:5-13; 56:1-8; 60:1-22; 66:18-24), and it is reflected as well in the literature of Judaism (e.g., Tobit 13:16-17; 14:5-6; *Jub.* 1:15-17, 26-28; 1QM 2:2-7).[73] Gundry seems to be correct when he concludes that the word "regeneration" (*palingenesia*) in this context refers to "Israel's renewal when God fully establishes his kingdom on earth."[74] According to Kümmel, the saying recorded at 19:28 was Jesus' way of assuring the disciples that He would win the people of Israel to whom He had been sent.[75]

Another example of this expectation may be found in Matthew 23:39 (cf. Luke 13:35). Jerusalem will not see Jesus again until they say, "Blessed is the one who comes in the name of the Lord" (Ps. 118:26). According to Beare, "As Matthew has placed it, it can only be an anticipation of his coming in power and glory. The city will then acclaim him."[76] The quotation is taken from a psalm that refers to God's chastening of Israel, almost to the point of death (v. 18). The main theme of the psalm is, however, a celebration of God's goodness and steadfast love which is "everlasting" (vv. 1, 29). The quotation thus serves as a reminder that the chastening of Israel does not mean it has been abandoned by God. The cited words also imply that Israel's restoration will be associated with repentance, expressed in the acknowledgement that Jesus is indeed God's anointed. Repentance, too, is a theme commonly connected with

69. Cf. *Theological Dictionary of the New Testament*, s.v. *palingenesia*, by Friedrich Büschel, 1:686-89; F. W. Burnett, "*Palingenesia* in Matt. 19:28: A Window on the Matthean Community?" *Journal for the Study of the New Testament* 17 (February 1983):60-72.

70. Philo *De Vita Moses* 2.65.

71. Philo *De Aeternitate Mundi* 9, 47, 76, 85, 93, 99, 103, 107.

72. Josephus *Antiquitates Judaicae* 11.66.

73. See also the literature discussed by Sanders, *Jesus and Judaism*, pp. 75-88, 95-98.

74. Robert H. Gundry, *Matthew: A Commentary on His Literary and Theological Arts* (Grand Rapids: Eerdmans, 1982), p. 392.

75. Werner Georg Kümmel, *Promise and Fulfillment: The Eschatological Message of Jesus*, 2d ed. (London: SCM, 1961), p. 47. See also Trautmann, who regards the disciples' mission to "the lost sheep of the house of Israel" at 10:6 as meant to show that it is God's will to include all Israel in the eschatological kingdom (Maria Trautmann, *Zeichenhafte Handlungen Jesu: ein Beitrag zur Frage nach dem geschichtlichen Jesu* [Würzburg: Echter Verlag, 1980], p. 228).

76. Beare, *The Gospel According to Matthew: Translation, Introduction, and Commentary*, p. 461.

the restoration of Israel in the literature of Judaism.[77] The quotation, therefore, expresses a note of hope[78] that the rejection of Jesus as Messiah, which Matthew has portrayed, is not Israel's last word concerning Him, nor is the pronouncement of woe God's last word concerning them.

CONCLUSION

In sum, Matthew does underscore the obduracy of Israel in its failure to respond to Jesus as the Messiah. But he also develops the theme of God's faithfulness to His Word, which includes by implication the promises made to Israel. In that context, Matthew also encourages a continuing mission to Israel as a means to the realization of the hope that one day Israel will be restored. His record of Jesus' word in 19:28 is a confident assertion that this restoration will indeed take place. When that statement is taken in conjunction with 23:39 the expectation is given further definition: It is at His second coming that Jesus will be welcomed by repentant Israel as its rightful King. The heir of David will then establish His glorious throne on the earth and reign over His people. Such is the future of Israel according to Matthew.[79]

---

77. Cf. Ephraim E. Urbach, *The Sages, Their Concepts and Beliefs*, 2 vols. (Jerusalem: Magnes, 1975), 1:668-72; Sanders, *Jesus and Judaism*, pp. 106-13.

78. So Dale C. Allison, "Matt. 23:39 = Luke 13:35b as a Conditional Prophecy," *Journal for the Study of the New Testament* 18 (June 1983):75-84; Graham N. Stanton, "The Gospel of Matthew and Judaism," *Bulletin of the John Rylands Library* 66 (Spring 1984):257-76.

79. The substance of this article was presented to the Kolloquim für Graduierte, Universität Tübingen, in January, 1991. The author extends his thanks to the participants, especially Prof. O. Betz, for a cordial and complimentary reception.

10

EVIDENCE FROM ACTS

DARRELL L. BOCK
Professor of New Testament Studies
Dallas Theological Seminary

To speak of "premillennialism in Acts" might appear odd, for Luke does not use the term "premillennial," nor does he in fact refer to a "millennium." But the phrase is defensible.

Theological teaching can be viewed from three perspectives. First, there is the text's meaning to its author and original recipients. Second is examining the contribution of a given writer in the development of a doctrinal category building on what has preceded and awaiting what shall come later. This task is called biblical theology. Third comes the attempt to synthesize and organize the various writings of Scripture into unified categories of truth. This is the task of systematic theology. It draws on revelation as a whole and produces appropriate, descriptive categories drawn from the Bible's teaching, but not necessarily limited to its terminology. This discipline can create new categories to summarize whole concepts and use terminology that is absent from Scripture to "name" the concept (e.g., the Trinity). Similarly, later biblical writers sometimes create new categories or terms, which can be associated with concepts used by earlier writers, even though the earlier writer did not use the terms in question or handle the area with the specificity of a later writer (e.g., Millennium).

Systematics assumes that one mind (God) ultimately stands behind the writings of the Bible. The various writings of the Bible complement one another and can be brought together into a unified whole.

Such is the case for this topic. When we discuss "premillennialism" in Acts, we are speaking from the perspective of the third discipline, systematics, since it is Revelation 20 that brings this idea into our eschatology. At the level of the second discipline, biblical theology, we can speak about the nature of Jesus' return, the nature of Jesus' future rule, and its relationship to Luke's view of the kingdom.[1] Luke does discuss such ideas and clearly relates them to the endtime activity of God. When we discuss premillennialism in Acts, we are looking at how Luke saw the final stages of Jesus' rule.

One other factor also impacts the approach to this question. Luke-Acts is really one volume. To speak about the teaching of Acts, we need the background of Luke. A brief look at a few texts in Luke will set the stage to view the picture of Jesus' return and the kingdom in Acts. The relevant passages in Acts are the teaching of Acts 1 and 3, the perspective of Acts 2, and the view of Acts 15.

THE BACKGROUND OF THE
KINGDOM REFERENCES IN ACTS

For Luke, Jesus is the fulfillment of a long-held hope. The infancy material brings this out clearly when Jesus' birth is described as the first step in fulfillment of promises made to David (Luke 1:31-33). God will put this child on David's throne and He will rule the house of Jacob forever. This announcement by the angel Gabriel was the first heavenly commentary on Jesus' birth to be noted by Luke. It firmly links the task of Jesus to the nation Israel. Jesus' authority, once established over Israel, will never end (v. 33). The language here is purely national. There is no hint that Israel and Jacob refer to anything else than the ancient people of God descended from the patriarch. Further texts in the infancy material confirm this conclusion.

The remarks of Mary in the Magnificat reaffirm the Israelite hope (Luke 1:51-55). Mary expressed the conviction that this child represents the presence of God's salvation. The theme is found in verse 47 where she praises God her Savior. Again the images were tied to national hope. Blessing comes to "those who fear Him" (v. 50b).[2] Then Mary described

---

1. For a full development of Luke's view of the kingdom, see Darrell L. Bock, "The Reign of the Lord Christ," *Dispensationalism, Israel and the Church*, ed. Craig A. Blaising and Darrell L. Bock (Grand Rapids: Zondervan, 1992).

2. The translation of Scripture passages used throughout this article is that of the author.

a series of reversals that God will perform. The proud are scattered, the mighty are put down, the lowly are exalted, the hungry are filled with good things, and the rich are sent away empty (vv. 51-53).[3] Lest this language be interpreted broadly, Mary identified the ones she saw as blessed, and spoke of God helping His servant Israel and remembering His mercy as He promised to Abraham and "our" fathers forever.[4] This is the language of Israelite hope, as given in the covenant promises. Mary hoped for victory over those who act against the nation.[5]

Zacharias's hymn, the Benedictus, is no different in force. In Luke 1:68-79, John the Baptist's father spoke under the inspiration of the Spirit (v. 67). He spoke about God visiting His people through a Davidic "horn," just as He promised in the prophets of old (1 Sam. 2:10; Ps. 132:17; Ezek. 29:21).[6] The salvation is explained as being saved from enemies and those "who hate us." Salvation is the performance of mercy promised to "our fathers." It is God's way of remembering the holy covenant, the oath to Abraham. This is national hope, pure and simple.[7]

The infancy material is like an overture to a symphony. It introduces fundamental themes of Luke-Acts. One of the basic themes is that

3. The verb tenses of these statements are aorist, a fact that has caused no lack of controversy. The most natural way to take these verbs is as prophetic aorists. The future is so certain that it can be portrayed as past. The verbs act like iterative perfects from Hebrew. See Earle E. Ellis, *The Gospel of Luke*, The New Century Bible (London: Oliphant, Marshall, and Scott, 1974), p. 76; and I. Howard Marshall, *Commentary on Luke*, New International Greek Testament Commentary (Grand Rapids: Eerdmans, 1978), p. 84.

4. Old Testament allusions dominate the language of these verses. Among the passages alluded to are: (1) God's arm and power—Deut. 3:24; 4:34; 7:19; Pss. 44:3; 89:13; 118:15; Isa. 51:9; 53:1; (2) God's dispersing the arrogant—Num. 10:35; 1 Sam. 2:4-10; Pss. 68:1; 89:10; (3) the people of God as oppressed and humble—Pss. 9:12-13, 17-20; 10:1-4; 12:1-5; 18:25-29; (4) filling the hungry with good things—1 Sam. 2:5; Pss. 107:9; 146:7; (5) sending the rich away empty—1 Sam. 2:5; Job 15:29; Jer. 17:11; (6) Israel as the Servant—Isa. 41:8-9; 42:1; 44:1, 21; 45:4; 48:20; 49:3; and, of course, (7) the passages of the Abrahamic promise alluded to are Gen. 12:1-3; 17:7-8; 18:18; 22:17-18; 26:3-4; Ex. 2:24; Mic. 7:20. Mary's language is that of the national hope of the ages.

5. F. Godet remarks that the lack of Christian expression in the hymn argues against a setting after Jesus' ministry. Mary praises God as a good pious Jew (*A Commentary on the Gospel of Luke*, 2d ed., 2 vols. [1870; reprint, Edinburgh: Clark, 1976], 1:107).

6. The reference to "the prophets from of old" is the first of many general allusions back to the hope of the Hebrew Scriptures in Luke (Luke 18:31; 24:25, 27, 44; Acts 3:18, 21; 10:43; 13:27; 15:15; 24:14; 26:22, 27; 28:23). The hope of those texts is the hope of these saints. The topics that the prophets address in these Lucan texts differ from passage to passage. The subjects range from the suffering, resurrection, and return of Christ to the hope of the believer for resurrection. The point Luke is making is that fundamental truth and promise about God's plan is found in the writings of the prophets. The uses in Acts 3:18, 21 will become particularly important to our theme.

7. Again OT language permeates: (1) salvation—2 Sam. 22:18; Pss. 18:17; 106:10; (2) "those who hate us"—Pss. 18:17; 106:10; and (3) to remember mercy—Gen. 24:12; Judg. 1:24; 8:35; Ruth 1:8; Mic. 7:20.

Jesus as the promised Davidic seed is the fulfillment of the hope of Abraham. One of the aspects of that hope is that the nation Israel will experience salvation. This salvation is not limited to a spiritual dimension. The hope is seen in Luke 1-2 as executed on the earth for the nation.

But this is early in the story of Jesus. Does this hope change? Is it altered later in the gospel of Luke? Does it become consumed by the universal hope that Jesus' ministry ultimately embraces?

There is no doubt that the plan about the kingdom becomes more complex as Luke's gospel account develops. There are texts where the kingdom is said to be near or to have arrived (10:9, 18-19; 11:20-23; 17:21; 19:14-15 [where the Master of the parable, who pictures Jesus, receives a kingdom before his return]; 22:69 [where Jesus says He will sit at God's side "from now on"]). When it comes to the kingdom, consummation seems to have come in some texts, while in others it is still anticipated.[8] How can this be? Peter in Acts 2 gives the key exposition of the significance of this "arrival" strand of kingdom hope. We will look at it later. What is clear is that the kingdom "arrives" in some sense now. Aspects of it are present with Jesus' first coming. Debate exists as to how much presence there is, but a look at Luke 11:20-23; 17:21; and 22:69 makes it clear that Luke placed the coming of the kingdom in an "already"/ "not yet" form.[9] He did not look at the kingdom as an "either"/"or" affair that was either all here or entirely absent. Rather it comes in stages. That is why there are two kinds of kingdom texts in Luke-Acts. Acts 2 will only confirm this picture for arrival, while Acts 3 will stress what is left to occur in the consummation. What is clear is that the kingdom is a "both/ and" kind of hope. Some of the hope has come and some is left to come.

But did the more earthly elements of the old hope get lost, redefined, or clarified in the development of a present phase of fulfillment that is not so focused on Israel? Was the Israelite hope transformed into a universal hope or transcended by it, so that a kingdom involving Israel becomes superfluous, being swallowed up in God's gracious dealings with all men and being fulfilled there? Or was the earthly hope always

8. Two great texts where the kingdom is anticipated in Luke's gospel are 17:22-37 and 21:25-28; these are but two of the more prominent texts among several.

9. Views here range from declaring that only "the King is present" to declarations that the entire kingdom promise has come. The former approach often tries to argue that though the King has come, the kingdom has not. The texts mentioned here are discussed in detail in Bock, "The Reign of the Lord Christ," as mentioned in note 1. We prefer to see Jesus as seated and reigning in an initial fulfillment of Davidic hope. The reign today primarily involves authority over salvific benefits, but the sovereignty of Jesus extends over all men, which is why the gospel can be offered to all and why all men will be subject to judgment by Jesus. Regardless of how one sees the details, it cannot be denied that Luke's portrait of the kingdom plan develops in detail as his two volumes proceed.

designed to be fulfilled in the execution of Jesus' universal task, so that once Israel lost her central place, the hope of a kingdom for her was gone or was continued only in relationship to the program for all men?[10]

Two texts in Luke suggest Israel still has a major role in God's plan, though the clear answer to these questions emerges from Acts.

(1) The first text comes from the last meal of Jesus with His disciples. In these last moments, as Jesus prepares to depart and face death, He makes some final remarks about the future. Luke 22:16 contains a curious statement. Jesus says that He will not "eat it" until "it" is fulfilled in the kingdom of God. Jesus alludes in the first use of "it" to the Passover meal that He is sharing for the last time before His death. This text says that Jesus will not eat "it," that is the Passover meal, until it is fulfilled in the kingdom. The reference to fulfillment in the kingdom is an allusion to the future consummation of the promise as experienced at the eschatological banquet table.

Luke 22:18 makes it clear that this event occurs and is fulfilled when the kingdom "comes." It is then that Jesus will drink again from the vine. The Luke 22:18 remark is parallel to Luke 22:16. Now the only antecedent for "it" in Luke 22:16 is the Passover meal. Here is a commemorative Israelite feast that will be transformed in the eschaton into a victory celebration. Sacrifices will commemorate not only the picture of salvation, the Exodus, but also the sacrificial death of Jesus that accom-

---

10. We must be careful not to view all amillennialists as holding to the same eschatological detail. Recently three distinctive emphases have developed.

(1) Some amillennialists see Israel as having forfeited her hope when she rejected Christ. The church is the new Israel and has taken her place permanently in God's plan. This might be called classic amillennialism.

(2) Others see the kingdom promise of Israel as taking on a more spiritual quality as revelation progresses. The hope was always intended to be seen in these more spiritual terms. Israel shares in the hope, but it is the hope of all in which she shares.

(3) Others see an earthly, eternal kingdom in which Israel has a role. This fulfills the OT hope literally, since it is a kingdom on earth. With this third strand of amillennialism, premillennialists have two differences. (a) The premillennialist sees a 1,000-year kingdom preceding the eternal state. (b) The premillennialist emphasizes the central role of Israel more. But the gap between premillennialism and amillennialism is much smaller with this third approach than with the other two. For examples of this variety, see Anthony Hoekema, *The Bible and the Future* (Grand Rapids: Eerdmans, 1979) and some of the essays in *Continuity and Discontinuity: Perspectives on the Relationships Between the Old and New Testaments—Essays in Honor of S. Lewis Johnson*, ed John S. Feinberg (Westchester, Ill.: Crossway, 1988). In this latter volume, dispensationalists, premillennarians, and amillennarians dialogue in essays in which each side addresses the same topic.

Some amillennarians are not so happy with these recent differentiations in the amillennarian camp. This complaint has been made, for example, by Mark W. Karlberg, "Reformed Interpretation of the Mosaic Covenant," *Westminster Theological Journal* 43 (1980-81):1-57; and "Legitimate Discontinuities Between the Testaments," *Journal of the Evangelical Theological Society* 28 (1985):9-20.

plished salvation. The imagery is still very Israelite in character, with a meal present that has sacrificial elements attached to it.

The text is significant, because it suggests that at least some sacrificial elements will exist in the end. These sacrifices are transformed in the final age, but they are still there. They do not look forward as the sacrifices of the OT did, but they look back, like the Passover did to the Exodus. This is not a full blown, earthly kingdom hope, so the passage cannot be made to say too much, but it is evidence of the transformed remnants of the old structure, a feast of the nation celebrated with a new richness of meaning. The use of such sacrifices and meals is not a reversion to Law, nor is it a sacrifice for sin, which the book of Hebrews makes clear is no longer needed, but it is the continued portrayal of hope with a line of continuity that looks back to the origins of promise. They commemorate and memorialize God's faithfulness through the ages. At this meal, Jews and Gentiles will be present (Luke 13:29-30), but the roots of celebration extend back into Israelite promise.

(2) The second text is Luke 22:30. Here the eschatological banquet is alluded to again in the promise to the eleven that they are to sit at Messiah's table in the kingdom eating and drinking. Yet another promise also appears. They are also to sit on thrones judging the twelve tribes of Israel. Here is authority granted to the eleven to exercise judgment over the nation. Clearly, the nation is still in view as being an entity and having a future. This authority parallels authority already received, as Luke 22:29 makes clear. Jesus assigns a kingdom to the eleven here, because He has already been assigned a kingdom by God. This assignment to the eleven in verse 29 is made in the present era, since the verb is present tense. In verse 30 reference is made to the future when they will sit at the banquet table and exercise future authority over Israel. "Already"/ "not yet" appear side by side here. The authority the eleven will exercise in the future is like that described in Acts. One institution (the church) mirrors the other (the future authority over Israel), but they belong to two related but distinct kingdom phases. The phases can be studied as a unit or as distinct entities. Both emphases need to be present to keep the biblical balance.

If the impression of a future for Israel seems farfetched, we need only look to the next key passage of Acts 1 to see that this was the category in which the eleven still operated after Jesus' eschatological discourses and His resurrection. They still ask in Acts 1:6 if this is the time that Jesus will restore the kingdom to Israel. From Zacharias in Luke 1 to the time of the ascension in Acts 1, those who followed Jesus never gave up the hope they had been taught to expect from the Law and prophets.

They never gave up hope of a kingdom related to Israel. The suggestion of a future for Israel emerges as still present by the time one reaches Acts. Now the question is: Does Acts enlighten us any more about this theme?

THE DISCUSSION OF THE
KINGDOM REFERENCES IN ACTS

ACTS 1/ACTS 3: A LINK

Acts 1:6-7 is usually treated by itself, and some regard Jesus as rejecting the premise of Israel's future that is present in the question. It is argued that Jesus' reply clearly shows that the disciples still lack understanding about God's plan. Jesus does not answer the question directly but, it is suggested, He did show that the eleven were operating on the wrong assumptions when they still held out hope for Israel. Is that correct? Our thesis is that Acts 1 must be read together with Acts 3, for in Acts 3, Peter gives an inspired speech that explains in detail what Jesus' return involves. It is in Acts 3 that the most important statement related to our topic occurs. It is also there that the unity of perspective between Luke and Acts becomes clear.

In Acts 1 Jesus is concerned with teaching His disciples about the kingdom (v. 4). Even after this summary teaching, the disciples still asked Him about the restoration of Israel, "Lord, will you at this time restore the kingdom to Israel?" (v. 6). The term they used for time was *chronos*. Jesus' reply was more specific, but does not answer the question. He said that it was not for them "to know times or seasons which the Father has fixed by his own authority" (v. 7). He uses the terms *chronos* and *kairos*. Jesus spoke of two periods, not one. Yet He does not answer the question. But the passage has one more point. When Jesus departed the angel said that He will "come in the same way you saw Him go into heaven" (v. 11). Can we not deduce that the restoration takes place with Jesus' return?

This is where Acts 3 fits. Here Peter explains what he learned in Acts 1. He appealed to the Torah at the end of his speech. Peter alluded to Deuteronomy 18:15, Leviticus 23:29, and Genesis 22:18 as he made his call for response in light of national covenant promises (Acts 3:22-26). Before he made this appeal, Peter reviewed Jesus' career for his audience, which is clearly identified as Israelite in verse 12. Peter explains to them that the healing of the lame man is a sign that God has glorified His servant Jesus (v. 13*a*). This Jesus is the same one "you" delivered up and denied in the presence of Pilate, when Pilate was ready to release Jesus —an allusion to Luke 23:1-25 (Acts 3:13*b*). Peter continued that "you" denied the holy and righteous one and asked for a murderer to be grant-ed to "you" (v. 14). "You" killed the author of life, whom God raised from the dead, a resurrection to which Peter and those with him are witnesses (v. 15). By faith in His name, the lame man was strong, and through Jesus the man received health in the presence of "you" all (v. 16).

Peter concluded his review of recent events and issued a call by "excusing" their action as being one of ignorance, just as Jesus did on the cross when He asked the Father to forgive His executioners, for "they know not what they do" (Luke 23:34). Peter remarked that both "you" and "your rulers" acted in ignorance (Acts 3:17). But all "God foretold by the mouth of all the prophets, that His Christ should suffer, He thus fulfilled" (v. 18). Here Peter said that recent events were dis-cussed and promised in the whole of the prophets. Luke uses his general reference to the whole of the prophets to make the point. The rest of Luke-Acts makes clear which passages made such promises.

After his indictment against the nations' citizens and leaders, Pe-ter moved to the solution. Peter called on the crowd to repent and turn, that "your" sin might be blotted out (v. 19a). In addition, times of re-freshing might then come from the presence of the Lord (v. 19b). The term Luke used here for the times of refreshing is *kairoi*, the same term Jesus added in Acts 1:7 to the question of the disciples. Here is a verbal link to Acts 1 that shows the texts belong together.[11] It is the first of two such links in the chapter. The second is the reference to restoration, using a form of the term *apokathistēmi* (cf. 1:6 with 3:21). Another con-sequence is that God might send Jesus, the Christ appointed for "you" (3:20). Now the only possible referent for "you" is the Israelite men of the audience. Peter said Jesus is Israel's hope.

---

11. In "The Reign of the Lord Christ," we argued that this term was a technical time reference to the first period of the eschaton, what we have called the "already" peri-od. This can be supported by two points.

(1) Luke 21:24 refers to the current era as the "times of the Gentiles," using the term *kairoi*, the same term as appears here.

(2) When the disciples asked about the future era, they used the term *chronos*, to which Jesus added a reference to a seeming second period He called *kairous*. In addition, when the disciples asked about the restoration to Israel, they used a form of the word *apokathistēmi*, which also is the word used when Peter spoke of the events after the return in Acts 3:20. These terms are used with some consistency and suggest that Luke had technical terminology to refer to the two parts of the eschaton, the "already" (*kairos*) and the "not yet" (*chronos* and *apokathistēmi*). If so, the re-freshing of Acts 3:19 is an allusion to the *present era*.

Even if this technical terminology is not present, the point to be made from Acts 3:21 stands. The presence of technical terminology makes the case stronger, but it is not a key point in the argument. Also clear is the fact that Acts 1 and 3 are linked together conceptually. Peter learned from the events of Acts 1 and yet he still spoke of *Israel's* hope.

But there is more. Here is where we see that Acts 1:11 and Acts 3 belong together and that Peter learned from the ascension what the sequence of events was. He said that heaven must receive this Christ until the "times of the renewal of all things" (3:21). Peter's language repeats the language of the disciples' question of 1:6. Both *chronos* and a form of *apokathistēmi* reappear here. In other words, heaven holds Jesus until the time of Israel's restoration. The deduction that the angels' remark in 1:11 alludes to Israel's restoration stands.

Acts 3 adds that this restoration of all things is something that "God spoke about by the mouth of his prophets of old" (v. 21). Here is Luke's generalized appeal to the ancient Scripture as teaching this hope. One can read about it throughout the Holy Writings. The texts in view, as in the case of other such generalized appeals, include passages noted by Luke elsewhere. This hope is not redefined or clarified in the new era in a way that old promises are lost. It is the hope of the ages for the nation. It is the restoration of order with Israel having a central role. It is, to match the language of Acts 1:6 to which the terminology here alludes, the restoration of the kingdom to Israel. What Gabriel promised to Mary, what Mary hoped for, and what Zacharias predicted of Jesus in Luke 1-2 is what Peter hoped for here. There is a kingdom hope that applies to Israel and that is explained in what is now called the OT.[12] The existence of the church has not canceled the hope for Israel.

The view defended here has been challenged. Waltke has argued that there is no clear passage in the NT that teaches the restoration of a kingdom to Israel.[13] In discussing Acts 3:19-21, Waltke cites F. F. Bruce who limits the point to Peter's call to Israel to reverse the verdict of Passover eve, stating how different history would have been had the Jews responded to Peter, and how much more quickly the end might have come. Bruce adds that one cannot discuss the "might-have-beens" of history.[14] Yet there is no real contingency in Acts 3. The uncertainty is when

12. The case for continuing to read OT promise in OT categories is made by John Feinberg, "Systems of Discontinuity," in *Continuity and Discontinuity*, pp. 76-79, where he argues that OT unconditional promises that were not fulfilled in the first coming of Christ are still to be fulfilled. Fulfillment in the church does not equal fulfillment for Israel. As he says, "The unconditionality of the promises to Israel guarantees that the NT does not even implicitly remove those promises from Israel." Or again, "Unconditional promises are not shadows." He also notes that there is no single pattern in how the NT uses the OT. This means that just because one writer applies an OT promise to the church does not mean that the promise's role is over for Israel, since aspects of such promises still await fulfillment.
13. It is interesting how Bruce K. Waltke's article in the same volume, "Kingdom Promises as Spiritual," pp. 274-75, moves quickly past Acts 3:19-21, calling it ambiguous.
14. F. F. Bruce, *Commentary on the Book of Acts* (Grand Rapids: Eerdmans, 1979), pp. 91-93. Bruce's revised edition of *Acts* lacks this remark.

Jesus returns; but that He is returning, there is no doubt. Heaven holds Jesus until He returns. Then the things promised will occur.

Now Waltke argues that no passage teaches the restoration of national Israel. We beg to differ, having noted numerous texts in Luke-Acts that point in this direction by referring to a Davidic king on the throne over the house of Jacob, the presence of a sacrificial feast, or the mention of restoration itself. F. F. Bruce ties Acts 3 to the regeneration of Matthew 19:28, but that text parallels Luke 22:30 and so does not answer the question, since the nature of the future period seems clearly to involve Israel. A better guide to the force of this remark is Acts 1:6. Waltke's additional argument that Romans 11 refers to a mediatorial kingdom clouds the issue. The kingdom of the future is mediatorial, but also it is earthly, with a king, and with enemies removed as well. This is not an either/or issue, but a both/and issue.

Such differences are small but important. At stake are God's promises and the trustworthiness of His Word in commitment to Israel about a land and a kingdom. The "not yet" realization which Waltke sees resolved just in an eternal, future kingdom, comes rather in two additional phases: a future, earthly kingdom that fulfills promises to Israel and the eternal kingdom in which she also participates. In this way God's promises are united in one package. There is a future fulfillment on earth, which includes fulfillment for Israel, and after that a heavenly fulfillment in the eternal state for all who believe.

To hold out for a future for Israel and for the constancy of OT promise does not mean that the period tied to Jesus did not clarify God's plan. We have demonstrated this by noting the "already" phase of fulfillment. But clarification and new revelation is not the same as omission or deletion. What became clear was that there was more to the plan, not that older parts were lost or that new revelation had dimensions which made earlier promises unnecessary. God works through the institution of the church now. He will work through the institution of a restored Israelite kingdom later. In that kingdom what Christ has accomplished for Jew and for Gentile will remain, but Israel will have the promises made to her fulfilled, including the promise of a kingdom in which her enemies are removed, so she can serve God freely (Luke 1:69-75).[15] God's grace and

---

15. Our point here is that each period centers in an institution through which blessing comes, and each period builds on what has gone before. In some cases old frameworks are replaced (e.g., the law of Moses and the barrier between Jew and Gentile). In others they are merely altered (e.g., Passover to eschatological banquet with the requisite sacrifices). For Israel to receive her promise of a kingdom does not mean the end of Jew-Gentile unity, since Gentiles still will have access to God through Christ. The Millennium is an administrative framework for blessing, and nationality will not determine membership; response to Christ will. But the reality is

promises remain true. What God said He would do for Israel, He will do. The major case for premillennialism in Acts is found in the Acts 1-Acts 3 link; but two balancing notes are needed to see the unity of God's kingdom program in Acts. So we turn to Acts 2 and then to Acts 15.

ACTS 2: A CURRENT REIGN

To say there is a hope for Israel is not to deny a current aspect to Jesus' rule or a current phase for the kingdom. Though the existence of the current form of the kingdom is tangentially related to our topic, the point needs to be made, because often premillennialists are accused of denying Jesus' current work and rule, looking only to the future. The balance of Luke-Acts requires a balanced presentation of Luke's portrait of the kingdom. Jesus will rule later, but He also rules now. The promise is fulfilled in phases, not all at once. There is continuity in the midst of discontinuities.

There are many significant points in Acts 2:14-39. We are concerned with only one. It is the linkage between Psalm 16 and Psalm 110 through Psalm 132. Some premillennialists see no OT fulfillment in Acts 2, only analogy. This underestimates Peter's point. Three fulfillments are clear and set the background for the relationship of the three psalms.

First, the use of Joel 2:28-32 is introduced with one of the clearest introductory formulas available: "This is that which is spoken" (Acts 2:16). It does not say "this is like that." Peter sees the coming of the Spirit as a fulfillment of the promise of Joel 2, just as the NT sees the coming of the Spirit as the inauguration of the New Covenant (2 Cor. 3; Heb. 8-10). Joel 2 is not completely fulfilled, for the day of the Lord has not yet come, but Pentecost represents another advance on the eschatological calendar.

Second, there is no doubt that Peter saw Psalm 16 as fulfilled in Jesus' immediate, bodily resurrection. His exposition in Acts 2:29-32 makes this point clear.

Third, his use of Psalm 110 shows that Peter saw a fulfillment of Psalm 110 in Jesus' ascension to God's right hand. This fulfillment is made clear by the repetition of the phrase "the right hand" in Acts 2:33 and in the citation of the psalm in verse 34. In short, the context contains several points of fulfillment in the present.

But the allusion to Psalm 132:11 is often missed in discussing the argument of this chapter. That text is alluded to in Acts 2:30, and it prom-

that much of the nation will respond at that time (Rom. 11:26) and the Son of David will reign physically on the earth. The statements of this note are synthetic and systematic in character. Luke-Acts does not have such detail.

ised that one "out of the fruit of his [David's] loins would sit on his [David's] throne." This language recalls Luke 1:32-33. The key term here is *kathisai* ("to sit"), for it appears in Acts 2:30 and reappears in the citation of Psalm 110 in Acts 2:34 (*kathou*, "sit"). One of the ways Jews showed fulfillment of an OT passage was to cite the language in alluding to a second passage, thus linking the two texts conceptually. So by his use of the verb "to sit" (Acts 2:30, 34) Peter links Psalm 132:11 (cited in 2:30) with Psalm 110 (cited in 2:34). He connects a clear "Davidic covenant" passage (Ps. 132:11 in its reference to 2 Sam. 7:12) not only with the resurrection of Christ but also with the ascension and "present session" of Christ. Peter insists that Christ's resurrection had been foreseen by the "prophet" David (Peter's citation of Ps. 16:8-11 in Acts 2:25-28), and His ascension and session were also prophesied by David (Peter's citation of Ps. 110:1 in Acts 2:34-35). In Acts 2 the only reason to mention Psalm 132 is to declare its inaugural fulfillment in the events tied to Psalm 110.

Once again, Psalm 132 reflects the promise of 2 Samuel 7:12. This citation from Samuel is known as the Davidic Covenant. What Peter has done, in a context replete with present fulfillment, is to link exaltation to God's right hand with initial fulfillment of the Davidic promise.[16] Being seated on David's throne (Ps. 132:11) equals being seated at God's right hand (Ps. 110:1). By linking these passages with Christ's resurrection and ascension (Acts 2:29-35), Peter declares the Davidic Covenant initially fulfilled, just as he declared the New Covenant initially fulfilled in citing Joel 2, and just as he will declare the Abrahamic Covenant initially fulfilled in Acts 3:25. Peter is interested in discussing more than a fulfillment in resurrection here. Peter is interested in saying that Jesus rules (He is Lord, 2:36) and that He will return to exercise decisive authority in judgment, as Peter's allusion to the day of the Lord shows (compare v. 20 with v. 40). The ascension represents only an initial fulfillment, because all the enemies of Jesus are not subdued yet (1 Cor. 15:20-28). But Jesus is not passive on the throne. He distributes spiritual benefits, and rites (like baptism) associated with salvation are performed in His name, that is, in His authority (Acts 2:32-33, 38).

There is an objection to this reading of Psalm 110. It is that Revelation 3:21 distinguishes between "my throne," on which the overcomer will sit, and the Father's "throne," on which Jesus currently sits. According to this view, the throne on which Jesus sits in Acts 2:33-34 (citing Ps.

---

16. The emphasis parallels Luke 22:69, where Jesus said to the Sanhedrin that "from now on the Son of Man will be seated at the right hand of the power of God." Here is another image of current rule, starting immediately.

110:1) is the Father's throne, not David's. The objection makes the point that to distinguish kinds of thrones is appropriate and that David's throne is not the point in Acts 2, because a heavenly throne is meant by Peter, namely God's throne, not an earthly one like David's.

The objection cannot stand. First, we must recall that the reference to a throne is to signify a rule (Ps. 110:1-2). This is what Peter in Acts 2 says Jesus is doing, when the apostle acknowledges that Jesus is Lord. Acts 17:30-31 makes a similar point, when it notes that Jesus already has been appointed. Peter's basis for Jesus' present enthronement is the Davidic promise in Psalm 110. That psalm is cited in the book of Hebrews to point out that Jesus is already a priest according to the order of Melchizedek as a result of His seating through exaltation. How can one allow the fulfillment of Melchizedekian priesthood for the present age (as based on the language of Ps. 110 by the writer of Hebrews) and then deny the present rule of Jesus in the present age (as based on the language of Ps. 110 by Peter)? This question is particularly appropriate since Peter connects Psalm 110 to a regal image (the Davidic throne), not a priesthood image. Psalm 110 is regal and messianic because that is exactly how Jesus introduces it in Luke 20:41-44. There He asks a question about David's Son, "the Christ." Jesus argues through this question that the more appropriate title is "Lord," as the use of Psalm 110 imagery in Luke 22:69 and Acts 2 shows.

Second, the distinction in Revelation 3:21 is really an equation, since Jesus' authority in John's writings comes from the Father and is given to His disciples through Jesus (John 13:20; 17:6-12, 23).[17] The throne the Father gives to Him is the rule that Jesus will share with the overcomers.[18]

Third, Revelation 3:7 says that Jesus has the "key of David."[19] The image is taken from Isaiah 22:22 and presents a parallel picture. In Isaiah Eliakim as the chief steward had the key to the door of the Davidic treasury and thus determined who could enter to see its treasures. That Christ is the one who now has "the key of David" indicates a present exercise of Davidic authority.

Fourth, the OT explicitly identifies David's (and Solomon's) throne with the Lord's throne (1 Chron. 28:5; 29:23-29; 2 Chron. 9:8). So the Lord's throne need not be just a "heavenly" throne.

---

17. This Johannine teaching is like Luke 22:29-30.
18. This type of equation is not unique to John. In Luke the servant imagery can be applied to Israel (Luke 1:54), to David (Luke 1:69), to Jesus (Acts 8:34-35), and to Paul and Barnabas (Acts 13:47). The role that Jesus has, His disciples share.
19. For a defense that Revelation parallels the "already"/"not yet" of Luke, see Bock, "The Reign of the Lord Christ."

The Davidic throne and the heavenly throne of Jesus at the right hand of the Father are one and the same, but there are two stages to the rule of that throne, so that the earthly, national character of OT promises is maintained, even though their scope is broadened in the NT to include universal, salvific blessing bestowed by the messianic king through the Holy Spirit.

The view of the kingdom defended here is not covenant premillennialism (as Ladd) for two reasons. First, this form of dispensational premillennialism sees the kingdom's present realm as relating primarily to the salvation benefits bestowed by Jesus through the Spirit, so that those who share the Spirit are a kingdom alongside other kingdoms, and these kingdoms are not to be confused. The kingdom today is not to be confused with any other social or political entity on earth. The kingdom today (the church) is the most important institution on earth, not because of the political power it yields, but because of the spiritual blessings it proclaims, the love it is to manifest to others, and the promises it is to pass on. Yet the kingdom still defers many aspects of the OT promises to the future millennium, rather than seeing final fulfillment now. Second, this form of dispensational premillennialism sees a fulfillment of the OT promises (as in Acts 3) that introduces national Israel directly and centrally back into God's working in the culmination.

Peter is clear to point out that the earthly character of Jesus' rule is not eliminated by what he asserts here. Rather his assertion of a "now"/"not yet" fulfillment of the Davidic throne promise is a development of the picture of Jesus' career much like the apostolic realization that Messiah would accomplish His work in two comings, not one. Thus Peter's association of Psalm 110 with the Davidic promise is not a hermeneutical leap that ignores OT promise, but reflects part of the Christian understanding about what God is doing through Jesus, an understanding made clear in the progress of revelation.

What does this mean? It means that for Luke the future kingdom tied to Israel is only a part of the total kingdom program. There is continuity between the eras, in the midst of discontinuity. There is an "already" phase and a "not yet" phase in the rule of Jesus. Premillennialism need not deny the former to have the latter. One other text needs brief treatment, since it also has been the subject of much criticism for the premillennial view. It is Acts 15.

ACTS 15: ANOTHER "ALREADY" ARGUMENT

Acts 15 has often been regarded as a text that is difficult for the premillennial view. Does not the argument for fulfillment here show that OT promise is reinterpreted or applied to the church in a way that makes a literal fulfillment for Israel unnecessary? Premillennialists have often responded that the application of Amos 9 really looks to the future and does not speak of a present fulfillment. Is that approach necessary for premillennialism to stand? Does seeing a current fulfillment in Acts 15 mean the death-knell for premillenialism? Our answer is no. One can see a present application and still argue that there is a future hope for Israel.

The key to this text is the use of Amos 9:11 (LXX) and the phrase in Acts 15:17, "all the Gentiles who are called by My name." The citation comes from James, who is reviewing events of the Jerusalem Council which was called to decide if Gentiles had to be circumcised. James relates Simeon's report about how "God first visited the Gentiles, to take out of them a people for His name" (v. 14). Obviously a connection exists between verse 14 and verses 15-17. The issue is, what is the nature of that connection?

The summary citation of James actually involves two passages and three ideas. The two OT texts are Amos 9:11 and Isaiah 45:21.[20] The three ideas are the rebuilding of the Davidic house, the Gentiles who are called by God's name, and the fact that this is the hope of the God who has made these things known from of old.

It is often argued by premillennialists that Amos looks to the rebuilding of the national kingdom in Israel, and thus any fulfillment of Amos is still strictly future, as far as James is concerned. James's argument is that what has happened to Peter should not surprise us, because we know that one day God will bring Gentiles into the rebuilt kingdom as Amos promised. Usually this view maintains that "after this" in Acts 15:16 should be located temporally after the events of the Gentile inclusion related in verse 14.

One problem with this view is the intervening introductory formula of verse 15. The verse reads, "And with this the words of the prophets agree, as it is written." The key to the passage comes in two points. (1) To what does "this" in the verse refer? (2) What does the verb "to

---

20. There may also be an allusion to Jer. 12:15, but this is uncertain. Many issues are beyond the concerns of our topic, such as why James would present a version of Amos that is like the Septuagint in a Jewish setting, especially a version whose meaning is somewhat distinct from that of the Masoretic text. But it must be remembered that the Septuagint was a respected translation for the Jews and only became suspect as Christians made such significant use of it. In addition, James's introductory formula is a broad reference to the prophets (Acts 15:15), like the references in Luke 1:70 and Acts 3:18, 21. His point is not made by this one text alone, but by other texts also that share the teaching of this passage. Had James been pressed there were many other texts to which he could have appealed (e.g., Isa. 2:2-4).

agree" mean? The only likely antecedent to "this" is the reference in verse 14 to the Gentile inclusion that Simeon had experienced. Efforts to tie the expression "this" to the beginning of verse 16 and the phrase "after this," so that a look to the future can be defended, are forced and go against the normal reading of such constructions. They also ignore the linkage within the citation that looks back to verse 14. The connection of "this" to past events is reinforced by the fact that the only part of the Amos citation that matches the exposition of James is the phrase "all the Gentiles who are called by My name" in verse 17, and it matches verse 14. The Gentile inclusion of verse 14 is what James is interested in noting. When James says that the prophets agree with "this," he is not looking forward, but backward to the events Peter just experienced. The verb *symphōnousin* ("they agree") means "to match," "to harmonize," or "to fit" (Matt. 18:19; 20:2, 13; Luke 5:36; Acts 5:9; related terms are in 1 Cor. 7:5; 2 Cor. 6:15). James is not looking to the future, but to the recent past, to current events. He is reading a text on kingdom expectation and is applying it to the current events as kingdom events. In sum, in the earliest church, OT texts were read as "kingdom texts," not as "first coming" and "second coming" texts, since the delay only became clear as time passed. We can separate these texts, but the earliest church did not. They saw them as a unit. The texts all dealt with "the kingdom." It is the erroneous equation by some that "kingdom" equals only "Millennium" that has made these OT texts difficult to interpret for premillennialism.

The rebuilt Davidic house alluded to in Amos is something Luke has already shown as accomplished in his allusions to the initial fulfillment of the Davidic hope. To do this Luke uses Psalm 132 and Psalm 110 in Acts 2. (Note also Acts 13:34, where these Davidic promises are offered directly to Paul's audience in the same context in which forgiveness and justification are discussed.) The Davidic house is in the process of being rebuilt and Gentiles are included. Such is the promise of the God of promise, as the end of the Amos 9 citation in Acts 15 suggests.

But does the reading of a present emphasis mean that premillennial hope is gone, since the initial phase of the kingdom and Davidic rule have come? Does it mean that the mystery teaching of the church, as something distinct from Israel, is lost, and that a future kingdom for Israel is irrelevant in the face of the universal scope of the church?

To rebuild the Davidic house does not mean that the newness of the church is lost. Peter speaks of the "beginning" himself in Acts 11:15, when he speaks of the gift of the Spirit. Something new happened in Acts 2 and Peter knew it. The Body of Christ is a fresh revelation and a newly born institution, having a fresh start and a fresh structure. The institution of the church was not predicted in the OT, but the renewing of the Davidic rule, the Spirit in the hearts of men, and blessing coming to all men through that hope were promised in the OT (Amos 9:11-12; Jer. 31:31; Ezek. 36:24; Gen 12:3). Initial fulfillment is not exhausted fulfillment. To have an "already" does not mean that one cannot have a "not yet" that completes promises on OT lines, while being in line with what the NT reveals. To have an initial fulfillment does not mean that new elements in the fulfillment are prohibited when the final fulfillment comes.

James simply said that what Peter experienced is what the prophets said would happen. They agree that Gentiles can bear God's name, even though they are Gentiles. They agree that there would be a Davidic renewal and that Gentiles would be involved. James said that this is what the prophets teach and this is what is happening. The conclusion was that circumcision was not necessary. A Gentile did not have to become a Jew to be a Christian. One only needed Christ, not Christ plus circumcision. Old things had passed away and new things had come; but with some sense of continuity with reference to promise. There was discontinuity and continuity side by side.

The NT has clarified the elements in this hope, as does Luke. The kingdom comes in stages. Some parts of that program are newly revealed. A new institution, the church, functions in Israel's place for a time, during the "times of the Gentiles" (Luke 21:24; Eph. 3:5-6; Acts 11:15). Messiah in the believer, the hope of glory, is new (Col. 1:27). But all the initial realization means is that God's plan is moving ahead; it has crossed another hurdle, but more remains to be fulfilled, just as the "Lord, who made these things known from of old" (Acts 15:18) promised. Acts 3 tells us that the "rest" comes just as the OT prophets promised. There is a future hope for Israel in Luke-Acts, just as there is a present form of the kingdom that is in line with what the OT promised. What the kingdom's coming in its present form demonstrated was that God's program had more stages and more institutions than were previously revealed. The NT and the hope of the new era are called new for reasons other than that they are more recent than the hope of the Law, the Psalms, and the Prophets.

CONCLUSION

We started by asking how one can speak of premillennialism in Acts, when Luke does not use the term. Here is the answer. What Luke reveals is a kingdom that has come and will come in stages: "already"/ "not yet." The "already" kingdom shows that God is rebuilding the house of David through a raised and reigning Jesus Christ (Acts 2). Gentiles also share in blessing, as God's promise and activity show (Luke 24:47; Acts 10-11, 15). The Abrahamic Covenant (Acts 3:22-26), Davidic Covenant (Acts 2:30-36), and New Covenant (Acts 2:16-39) have all received an initial fulfillment. Eschatological events have begun, but they move on into a future, more glorious fulfillment.

In the "not yet" kingdom, the eleven will rule with Jesus on thrones judging the twelve tribes of Israel (Luke 22:30). Jesus will celebrate a Passover feast, a memorial to the fulfillment of God's promises (Luke 22:16). As Mary hoped, the humble will be exalted and the proud will be thrown down from their thrones, just as God promised the fathers starting with Abraham (Luke 1:50-55). As Zacharias promised, those who fear God will be saved from enemies to serve God through the horn of David, just as the prophets of old predicted (Luke 1:68-74). Jesus, who currently sits on the throne of David (Acts 2:30-34), will rule over Israel forever, and of His kingdom there will be no end (Luke 1:32-33). In fact, Jesus sits in heaven, waiting to return to establish the restoration to Israel promised by the prophets (Acts 1:6-11; 3:19-21).

This is OT prophetic hope, pure and simple. It is what the God who made these things known of old promised, and He will bring it to pass. It is a matter of His Word. Revelation 20-22 defines this hope as the hope of the millennial rule followed by the eternal state of the new heaven and the new earth. Jesus returns to set up this rule in Revelation 19:11-21. He returns to bring about this climactic stage of Messiah's rule and of God's promise. Revelation gives us the time frame, the sequence, and the name. But Luke knows the concept.

11

EVIDENCE FROM ROMANS 9-11

S. LEWIS JOHNSON, JR.

Former Professor of Biblical and Systematic Theology
Trinity Evangelical Divinity School

On initial consideration one might reasonably conclude that Romans 9-11 has little direct reference to the millennial controversy. After all, the word "kingdom" is not even found in Paul's great theodicy, and there is no reference, of course, to the duration of the kingdom.

The chapters, however, are a studied attempt by the apostle to vindicate God's dealings with men from the standpoint of justice. They relate directly to what Dodd called "the divine purpose in history."[1] If that is so, then they bear rather closely on the doctrine of the messianic kingdom, for the messianic kingdom is a leading theme of the divine purpose as unfolded in the Scriptures.

To take this line of thought one step further, the central theme of the OT is the coming redeemer and His purpose through the Abrahamic, Davidic, and New Covenants to confer in grace eternal salvation on His chosen people Israel and the Gentiles. This sovereign and covenantal dealing with His people is the overarching theme of Romans 9-11 and,

---

1. C. H. Dodd, *The Epistle of Paul to the Romans* (London: Hodder and Stoughton, 1932), p. 161.

though the length of the kingdom is not a subject of the chapters, the kingdom itself is intimately related to the apostle's exposition.

The indirect reference of the chapters to the millennial controversy is clear and significant. First, as we shall see, the meaning of the term "Israel," a key eschatological point, finds clarification here.

Second, the hermeneutics of eschatology as it relates to the millennial question also finds clarification in Paul's use of Hosea in Romans 9:25-26, thought by some to be a troublesome passage for premillennialists.

Third, the most significant contribution of the section to the millennial controversy is the lengthy eleventh chapter with its climactic "and thus all Israel will be saved" (v. 26). The future of ethnic Israel, which seems to be taught plainly here, bears with weighty force on the question of an earthly kingdom of God. The contrary viewpoints of Anthony A. Hoekema,[2] G. C. Berkouwer,[3] Herman Ridderbos,[4] and other amillenarians will be considered at this point in the study.

Underlying all of this, fourth, is Paul's conviction of the relevance of the Abrahamic Covenant's provisions to the present age of Gentile salvation and to the future time of Israel's restoration (cf. 4:1-25; 9:5-13; 11:1, 11-32; Gal. 3:1-29). In that discussion it will be useful to consider the question: If an earthly kingdom including the land promised to Abraham is the teaching of the OT covenantal promises, why is there no specific repetition of the land promises of the Abrahamic Covenant in the NT? I hope to give a sufficient answer to that good question.

THE MEANING OF THE TERM "ISRAEL"

EXPOSITION OF THE OCCURRENCES OF THE TERM

Romans 9:6, 27, 31

The term "Israel" occurs five times in Romans 9. Two of its occurrences appear in verse 6, where Paul writes, "For they are not all Israel who are descended from Israel." It is sometimes thought that Paul in this statement says that believing Gentiles are to be found in the expression "all Israel." Thus, their salvation would justify his statement that the Word of God has not failed, "Israel" being broad enough to include both believing Jews and Gentiles.

2. Anthony A. Hoekema, *The Bible and the Future* (Grand Rapids: Eerdmans, 1979), pp. 139-47.
3. G. C. Berkouwer, *The Return of Christ*, trans. James Van Oosterom and ed. Marlin J. Van Elderen (Grand Rapids: Eerdmans, 1972), pp. 335-49.
4. Herman Ridderbos, *Paul: An Outline of His Theology*, trans. John Richard De Witt (Grand Rapids: Eerdmans, 1975), pp. 354-61.

That cannot be true. The idea is foreign to the context (cf. vv. 1-5). Rather the apostle is making the same point he has made previously in the letter (cf. 2:28-29; 4:12). The division he speaks of is within the nation. They "who are descended from Israel" refers to the physical seed, the natural, ethnic descendants of the patriarchs (from Jacob, or Israel). In the second occurrence of the word in verse 6 Paul refers to the elect within the nation, the Isaacs and the Jacobs. To the total body of ethnic Israel the apostle denies the term "Israel" in its most meaningful sense of the believing ethnic seed. Gentiles are not in view at all.[5]

As a matter of fact, the sense of the term "Israel" is clearly established by the meaning of the term "Israelites" in verse 4, and there it can only refer to the ethnic nation's members.

The two occurrences of the term "Israel" in verse 27 fall plainly within this sense, for the apostle there cites in merged form Isaiah and Hosea as support for the certainty of the fulfillment of the Abrahamic promises, though they may be enjoyed by the remnant only. "Israel" still refers to the ethnic nation.

Finally, in verse 31 the term has the same sense, referring to the nation's failure to find justification by faith.

Romans 10:19, 21

The two occurrences of "Israel" in Romans 10 are also clear references to ethnic Israel. In verse 19, asking if Israel has not known the truth, the apostle cites Deuteronomy 32:21 in proof of an affirmative answer. The citation is from the Song of Moses, delivered "in the hearing of all the assembly of Israel" just before entrance into the land (Deut. 31:30). Ethnic Israel is meant.

The second occurrence, in verse 21, is also part of the apostolic exegesis of the OT (cf. Isa. 65:1-2). The rebellious people to whom Yahweh had spread out His hands in appeal for repentance, as Isaiah wrote, Paul identifies as ethnic Israel. In fact, in Isaiah 65 the rebellious people are specifically distinguished from those who have responded in faith, presumably the Gentiles.[6]

---

5. Gutbrod comments, "On the other hand, we are not told here that Gentile Christians are the true Israel. The distinction at R. 9:6 does not go beyond what is presupposed at Jn. 1:47, and it corresponds to the distinction between *Ioudaios en tō kryptō* ('a Jew who is one inwardly') and *Ioudaios en tō phanerō* ('a Jew who is one outwardly') at R. 2:28 f., which does not imply that Paul is calling Gentiles the true Jews" (*Theological Dictionary of the New Testament*, s.v. "*Israēl*" [Israel], by Walter Gutbrod, 3:387). Or, as Dunn puts it, "Not all who can properly claim blood ties to Israel actually belong to the Israel of God (cf. Gal. 6:16)" (James D. G. Dunn, *Romans 9-16*, Word Biblical Commentary [Dallas: Word, 1988], 38:547).

6. Dunn, *Romans 9-16*, pp. 626, 631-32.

Romans 11:2, 7, 25, 26

The four occurrences of "Israel" in Romans 11 fall into the same category, referring to ethnic Israel. Verse 2 refers to Elijah's complaint to Yahweh regarding Israel. Paul reminds the Romans in verse 4 that God responded to the prophet that He had kept for Himself a remnant who had not bowed the knee to Baal. The context of 1 Kings 19:1-21, with its clear statement that Elijah was speaking of the nation (cf. v. 10), defines the term "Israel" in its ethnic sense.

The occurrence in verse 7 refers to the same entity, and the apostle makes the same distinction between the two elements within the nation—the elect, believing remnant and the unbelieving nation as a whole. The fact that the mass of the nation was hardened is supported by texts from the Law, the Psalms, and the Prophets.

The reference to "Israel" in verse 25, clearly defined by the statements made in verses 7-10 and in verses 11-15, where the nation's hardening and blinding are stated, can only refer to the ethnic nation of Israel (cf. the use of the verb "to harden" in v. 7 and the noun "hardening" in v. 25, both from the same root).

That brings us to the eleventh and final use of "Israel" in Romans 9-11. On the face of it, one would need clear and full justification for finding a different sense of the word in verse 26, particularly since the use here is closely related to the sense of the term in verse 25. The apostle adds the adjective "all" in verse 26 to make the point that he is speaking not simply of a remnant, but of the nation as a whole, "His people" as he puts it in verse 1. When we come to the interpretation of this section, the divergent interpretations of the term will be handled. One thing may be said: It is exegetically and theologically highly unlikely that the term "Israel," having been used 10 times for the nation in the theodicy of Romans 9-11, should now suddenly without any special explanation refer to "spiritual Israel," composed of elect Jews and Gentiles.

This spiritualizing interpretation cannot be supported by Galatians 6:16, as even Berkouwer admits. He writes, "But it is indeed open to question whether Paul, in writing to the Galatians, had in mind the church as the new Israel. The meaning may well be: peace and mercy to those who orient themselves to the rule of the new creation in Christ, and also peace and mercy be upon the Israel of God, that is, upon those *Jews* who have turned to Christ."[7] The people Paul is talking about in 11:26 are defined in verse 28 as those who "are beloved for the sake of the fathers."

---

7. Berkouwer, *The Return of Christ*, p. 344 (italics added). For a fuller treatment of Gal. 6:16 see my "Paul and 'The Israel of God': An Exegetical and Eschatological Case-Study," *Essays in Honor of J. Dwight Pentecost*, ed. Stanley D. Toussaint and Charles H.

CONCLUSION

In summary, Romans 9-11 contains 11 occurrences of the term "Israel," and in every case it refers to ethnic, or national, Israel. Never does the term include Gentiles within its meaning. The NT use of the term is identical with the Pauline sense in this section.

THE USE OF THE PROPHET HOSEA

THE NEW TESTAMENT CONTEXT OF THE CITATION

The apostle, having unfolded his magnificent account of God's glorious plan of salvation in Romans 1-8, finds it necessary to explain the almost complete absence of Israel in that account (cf. 2:17-29; 3:1-8). In fact, Israel has been the most rebellious entity in the story. That, however, presents a problem. It might seem that either Paul's message is true and the Jewish promises are nullified, or the promises still hold and Paul's gospel is false, and Jesus Christ is a messianic imposter.[8] Paul's answer, of course, is not an either/or, but a both/and. His gospel is true, and the promises to Israel are still in effect.

Romans 9-11, then, is not parenthetical, or an excursus. The argument of the preceding chapters is not yet complete. The indictment of Israel in 2:1-29 and particularly the apostle's question in 3:1, "Then what advantage has the Jew?" cry out for explanation in the light of the unconditional Abrahamic promises. Further, in the light of Paul's description of the gospel of God as "concerning His Son, who was born of a descendant of David," and that the Son was "Jesus Christ [= Messiah] our Lord" (cf. 1:3-4), it is clear that in the apostle's mind the gospel is unintelligible without a full exposition of its relation to Israel, God's people. Thus, Romans 9-11, where that exposition is found, is "an integral part of the working out of the theme of the epistle."[9]

One might ask the question, "But why should the theodicy be put here, after chapters 1-8, rather than after 12:1–15:13?" Perhaps the apostle realized that the great stress on God's sovereign elective purpose

---

Dyer (Chicago: Moody, 1986), pp. 181-96. It is unfortunate that the NIV rendering of the text still follows what Berkouwer calls "the spiritualizing interpretation." It should be abandoned for, like the emperor, it has no clothes.

8. F. Godet, *Commentary on St. Paul's Epistle to the Romans*, trans. A. Cusin (Edinburgh: Clark, 1882), 2:127.

9. C. E. B. Cranfield, *A Critical and Exegetical Commentary on the Epistle to the Romans*, International Critical Commentary (Edinburgh: Clark, 1979), 2:445. Beker is right in saying that the chapters are "a climactic point in the letter" (J. Christiaan Beker, *Paul the Apostle: The Triumph of God in Life and Thought* [Philadelphia: Fortress, 1980], p. 87).

and the believer's certainty of hope in Romans 8:28-39 might be rendered questionable by Israel's rejection. After all, if God might be frustrated in any aspect of His purpose (such as Israel), as it might appear from Israel's history, then is His purpose a reliable ground for our faith? It is eminently necessary that Paul respond to that problem. Romans 9-11 is his answer. As Beker says, "Israel's betrayal does not thwart Israel's destiny in the plan of God."[10] Further, not only does Israel's failure not cancel the promises made to her (cf. 3:1-8), the facts are that, if the Gentiles are to share the promises of God, then they must get them through Abraham or they will not get them at all.[11] That is how far wrong those are who take the position that the church has supplanted Israel forever.[12]

After expressing his sorrow over Israel's failure (9:1-5), Paul proceeds to explain that their falling away has its analogy in the biblical history itself (9:6-13). The divine dealings with Isaac and Ishmael and Jacob and Esau indicate that there is an elective purpose of God being accomplished within the history of salvation. The natural seed of Abraham inherit only if they are also the products of the divine elective purpose. The apostle finds the matter illustrated in two passages in the OT: Genesis 25:23 and Malachi 1:2-3.

Of course, Paul's line of reasoning raises the common question, "Is God righteous in His sovereign choice?" The apostle's answer takes the form of replies to two rhetorical, or diatribe-like, questions (vv. 14, 19), one looking at the matter from the Godward side, and the other from the manward side. He affirms God's right to show mercy and to harden (vv. 14-18), and he denies that God is responsible for man's lost and rebellious condition (vv. 19-24).[13]

After the illustration of God's sovereign autonomy in the potter and the clay, he points out that, in fact, God has been long-suffering in order to demonstrate His wrath and His mercy on both Jews and Gentiles (vv. 22-24). What, then, remains of their complaints?[14] To be God is to exercise mercy against the background of wrath to whomever He

10. Beker, *Paul the Apostle*, p. 88.

11. Cf. Paul J. Achtemeier, *Romans*, Interpretation: A Bible Commentary for Teaching and Preaching (Atlanta: Knox, 1985), p. 79.

12. Dunn suggests that the church is a "subset of Israel" in the light of Paul's grafting illustration in chap. 11 (*Romans 9-16*, p. 520).

13. For an interesting and helpful study of Rom. 9:1-23 one should consult John Piper's *The Justification of God* (Grand Rapids: Baker, 1983). One of the delights of this book is its recourse to exegesis in the solution of the great problem of divine election and human responsibility.

14. This sentence is supplied as the apodosis of the condition begun with the *ei* of v. 22, a common enough phenomenon in Greek (cf. Cranfield, *A Critical and Exegetical Commentary on the Epistle to the Romans*, 2:492-93).

pleases apart from any contraints that arise outside His sovereign will. That is His glory and His name.[15]

At this point Paul calls forth the witness of prophecy to show that the Scriptures have predicted that vessels of mercy were to come from both Gentiles and Jews, and that the majority of the nation Israel was to become vessels of wrath (vv. 25-29). The expression, "not from the Jews only," would have been troublesome to many Jewish readers, for it might have implied that the mass of God's ancient people were left in unbelief. "Did Jewish prophecy," Liddon asks, "anticipate this state of things, which placed Gentiles and Jews, religiously speaking, each in a new position?"[16]

THE OLD TESTAMENT CONTEXT OF THE CITATION

Hosea, the prophet of unconditional love, ministered to the Northern Kingdom in the turbulent era of the 8th century B.C. By divinely designed marital sufferings he played out in his own experience the unfaithful straying of Israel from Yahweh and Yahweh's conquering love, of which Calvary is the ultimate exposition. Israel's sin is represented by its ugliest figure, harlotry, and God's love by its counterpart, selfless, forgiving, faithful love.

The passages cited freely by Paul come from Hosea 2:23 and 1:10. They both appear to affirm the restoration of ethnic Israel after an indefinite time of discipline to their ancient "favored nation" status. The disastrous opening oracles of Hosea 1 are astoundingly reversed, and the pained appeal of a forgotten God in Hosea 2, followed by unsparing discipline, issues in eternal covenantal union. "The mood," Kidner says, "is that of the great parable, as though to say, 'These my sons were dead, and are alive again; they were lost, and are found.'"[17]

The apostle's citation is a merged one that contains some interesting variations from the OT Hebrew and Greek texts, but basically follows the Greek Septuagint text.[18]

---

15. Piper, *The Justification of God*, pp. 203-5.
16. H. P. Liddon, *Explanatory Analysis of St. Paul's Epistle to the Romans* (reprint, Zondervan, 1961), p. 171.
17. Derek Kidner, *Love to the Loveless: The Message of Hosea* (Downers Grove, Ill.: InterVarsity, 1981), p. 25.
18. I do not have the space to list and discuss all the modifications of the OT Hebrew and Greek texts in Paul's merged citation. One variation is significant. The apostle in v. 25, citing Hosea 2:23, modifies the verb "I will say" to "I will call," thus making a clear connection with the "called" of Rom. 9:25-26. The threefold use of the verb "to call" (*kaleō*), underlines the sovereign, effectual grace in the nation's future restoration (cf. Rom. 8:30).

The critical point for millennialism is the Pauline hermeneutical handling of the OT passages. It is at this point that premillennialism's claim that one should follow a grammatico-historico-theological method in the interpretation of prophetic passages has come under spirited attack. Premillennialists have claimed that this method of interpretation leads inevitably to a literal kingdom of God on this present, though renewed, earth.Amillennialists have disputed this "literal," or "normal," use of the OT by the NT authors. It is their contention that the NT writers, while generally following a literal approach, nevertheless in certain crucial NT eschatological passages have followed the principle of "spiritualizing," or reinterpretation of the OT passages. Premillennialists, therefore, often accuse amillennialists of following "a dual hermeneutic," that is, of following a grammatico-historical sense generally, but a spiritualizing hermeneutic in eschatology. I am not sure the accusation is a fair one. What amillennialists are saying is simply this: We follow a grammatico-historical method always, but in handling eschatological passages in a grammatico-historical sense it becomes plain that often the NT authors give a "spiritualized" sense to OT texts. They "reinterpret" them, and we are obligated by grammar and history to follow them in what they do.

Premillennialists deny that the NT authors spiritualize, or reinterpret, OT texts. That is really the focus, it seems to me. Does the NT, for example, apply OT promises made to ethnic believing Israel to the NT church (cf. Acts 15:13-18; Gal. 6:16)?

We cannot settle this question, as many hermeneutical manuals attempt to do, by theological logic alone. Greg Bahnsen's counsel is correct, "The charge of subjective spiritualization or hyperliteralism against any of the three eschatological positions cannot be settled in general; rather the opponents must get down to hand-to-hand exegetical combat on particular passages and phrases."[19] That is to the point, and that is what must be done by premillennialists, if they wish to prevail. The meaning of the sacred text is to be found by the perusal of the sacred pages themselves. It is from them that our hermeneutics must originate. *Scriptura ex Scriptura explicanda est*, or *interpretatio ex Scriptura docenda est* ("Scripture is to be explained by Scripture," or "interpretation is to be taught by Scripture").

VARIOUS INTERPRETATIONS OF ROMANS 9:25-26

The late George Ladd was a premillennialist who contended that the NT authors spiritualized, or reinterpreted, the OT texts. He said,

19. Greg Bahnsen, "The Prima Facie Acceptability of Postmillennialism," in *Journal of Christian Reconstruction* 3 (Winter 1976):57.

"The fact is that the New Testament frequently interprets Old Testament prophecies in a way not suggested by the Old Testament context."[20] He also claimed that there were "unavoidable indications" that promises made to Israel are fulfilled in the Christian church.[21]

One would naturally like to know the passages on which Ladd has built his thesis, and he has given us his principal ones. It would be unfair to spend time on the first two examples, for they are so easily refuted, namely, the use of Hosea 11:1 in Matthew 2:15 and Isaiah 53:4 in Matthew 8:17. His third example is the citation we are studying, that of Hosea 2:23 and 1:10 in Romans 9:25-26. He obviously thought this was a clinching text, for he calls it "a most vivid illustration"[22] of the principle. To its interpretation we now turn.

The questions at issue are these: (1) To whom do the passages in Hosea refer? and (2) To whom are they referred in the NT?

As far as the first question is concerned, the context of Hosea seems to make it plain that the Northern Kingdom of Israel is indicated by the phrase "not my people" (Gk. *ou laos mou*, vv. 25, 26). Commentators overwhelmingly favor this.

A few students have suggested that, in the light of Israel's apostasy in Hosea's day, God had now taken the position that they were as the Gentiles, having no claim any longer on Him at all (cf. Rom. 3:1-8; 9:6). Such an abandonment of the nation as a whole does not seem contemplated by Hosea (cf. Hos. 3:1-5) or Paul (cf. Rom. 11:1-36).[23]

As far as the second question is concerned, there are several ways of taking Paul's usage.

First, as Ladd does, we may refer the Hosea verses about Israel to the church. If this is so, then those who espouse a consistent grammatico-historico-theological interpretation of the Bible would have to modify their position.

Aside from Ladd, there are others who take the view that Paul changes Hosea's sense of the texts. C. H. Dodd comments,

20. George Eldon Ladd, "Historic Premillennialism," in *The Meaning of the Millennium: Four Views*, ed. Robert G. Clouse (Downers Grove, Ill.: InterVarsity, 1977), p. 20.

21. Ibid., p. 27.

22. Ibid., p. 23.

23. Andersen and Freedman may be right in claiming, "In Deut. 32:21 unidentified foreigners are gathered under the head of *lō'-'ām*, 'a non-people.' What we have in Hos. 1-2 is not a negation of *'ammî*, 'my people,' but a suffixation of the noun compound *lō'-'ām*, i.e., my 'non-people.' In the latter case ownership is still claimed, but Israel is no better than the heathen" (Francis I. Andersen and David Noel Freedman, *Hosea: A New Translation with Introduction and Commentary*, The Anchor Bible [Garden City, N.Y.: Doubleday, 1980], p. 198).

When Paul, normally a clear thinker, becomes obscure, it usually means that he is embarrassed by the position he has taken up. It is surely so here. . . . It is rather strange that Paul has not observed that this prophecy referred to Israel, rejected for its sins, but destined to be restored: strange because it would have fitted so admirably the doctrine of the restoration of Israel which he is to expound in chap. xi. But, if the particular prophecy is ill-chosen, it is certainly true that the prophet did declare the calling of the Gentiles.[24]

Ernst Käsemann's comment, "With great audacity he takes the promises to Israel and relates them to the Gentile-Christians,"[25] is unclear, for he does not really tell us how the passages are related to the Gentiles. Are they related typically, analogically, or by direct application?

There are things to be said for this position. For one thing, the following sentence's opening *de* ("and," NASB) can be translated "but." Taken with the phrase, "concerning Israel," it might appear to contrast Israel to the preceding clauses about Gentiles. Furthermore, the pattern of preference for the "non-nation" in Romans 10:19-20 followed by judgment on Israel in verse 20 is similar. The "non-nation" there is a reference to the Gentiles (cf. 10:19; 11:11, 13). In addition, Peter, it is thought, has the same view of Hosea 2:23 (cf. 1 Pet. 2:10).

Second, others, wishing to maintain Hosea's reference to Israel as in some way harmonious with Paul's reference to the Gentiles, have seen the Pauline usage of Hosea's words concerning Israel as an application by way of analogy to the Gentiles. No claim of fulfillment in Gentile salvation is made. This is the view of scholars with no premillennial bias, such as Sanday and Headlam,[26] and John Murray.[27] Charles Hodge, also with no premillennial bias, has pointed out that verses spoken of the ten tribes are

applicable to others in like circumstances, or of like character. . . . This method of interpreting and applying Scripture is both common and correct. A general truth, stated in reference to a particular class of persons, is to be considered as intended to apply to all those whose

---

24. C. H. Dodd, *The Epistle to the Romans* (New York: Harper, 1932), pp. 159-60.

25. Ernst Käsemann, *Commentary on Romans*, trans. and ed. Geoffrey W. Bromiley (Grand Rapids: Eerdmans, 1980), p. 274.

26. William Sanday and Arthur C. Headlam, *A Critical and Exegetical Commentary on the Epistle to the Romans*, International Critical Commentary (Edinburgh: Clark, 1895), p. 264. They write, "St. Paul applies the principle which underlies these words, that God can take into His covenant those who were previously cut off from it, to the calling of the Gentiles. A similar interpretation of the verse was held by the Rabbis."

27. John Murray, *The Epistle to the Romans*, New International Commentary on the New Testament (Grand Rapids: Eerdmans, 1965), 2:38. Murray states that "Paul finds in the restoration of Israel to love and favour the type in terms of which the Gentiles become partakers of the same grace."

character and circumstances are the same, though the form or words of the original enunciation may not be applicable to all embraced within the scope of the general sentiment.[28]

In support of this view is the comparative force of the introductory formula "as He says also in Hosea." There is an analogy between the calling of the Gentiles at the present time and Israel's future calling as sons of the living God. In addition, the threefold occurrence of the concept of the efficacious call (vv. 24, 25, 26), obviously connected, underlines the heart of the analogy. In fact, as the apostle points out in the chapter, the present calling of the remnant (vv. 7, 11-12; 8:28-30; 11:5) is, indeed, an earnest of the calling of the mass.

So, to sum up this analogical view, the elective calling of the unbelieving Gentiles finds its counterpart in the future calling of the mass of unbelieving ethnic Israel. Both are works of grace from God. This view, in my opinion, is a legitimate view.

But, third, I suggest a more appropriate view, also analogical, but centered in a different correspondence and grounded more soundly in the chapter's context. The stress of the apostle in chapter 9 does not lie in God's call of both Jews and Gentiles, though, of course, that is true. The real point is Paul's desire to show from salvation history that God has had a sovereign elective purpose of grace in His dealings with Israel (cf. vv. 6-13). Why is the mass of Israel missing from the elect people of God whose spiritual status has been so marvelously set forth in chapters 1-8? God's elective purpose is the primary cause. The mention of the Gentiles in verse 24 is only incidental at this point. It is the sovereign purpose of grace in the salvation of both Israel and the Gentiles that is the point. In other words, the analogy is not a national or ethnic one; it is a soteriological one. It is not so much the fact of the calling of the Gentiles now and the future calling of Israel that forms the analogy. It is rather the manner of the calling of the Gentiles and the manner of the future calling of Israel that forms the analogy. Paul thus lays stress from Hosea on the electing grace of the calling of both the Gentiles in the present time and the mass of ethnic Israel in the future. This is the point that he finds in Hosea, and it is most appropriate.

The use of the verb "to call" supports the point, emphasizing the fact that God's effectual calling in elective grace is true both in the salvation of the Gentiles today and in the salvation of ethnic Israel in the

28. Charles Hodge, *Commentary on the Epistle to the Romans* (reprint, Grand Rapids: Eerdmans, 1950), pp. 326-27. It would unnecessarily enlarge the apparatus to cite others who hold the same view.

future. Therein lies the resemblance, the analogy, the apostle sees in the present situation and in Hosea's texts.

The mention of the salvation of the Gentiles in verse 24 is very appropriate, but their admission into the people of God is itself an act of divine sovereign grace which is Paul's theme. In this respect their call is analogical to the call of both Israel's remnant (cf. 11:5) and the future ethnic mass of believers at the time of the Messiah's coming (11:25-27).

A careful study of Hosea's references will lead the reader to the conviction that no passage could better and more tenderly extol God's sovereign electing mercy in His compassionate courting and winning of the adulterous wife. He takes the initiative, "allures" her, "speaks comfortably" to her, and triumphantly brings her to songs of salvation grace as in the days of the Exodus. His advances, His efforts to win her back, and His final success are the results of His purpose. The fragment from Hosea 2:23, "I will call those who were not My people, 'My people,' and her who was not beloved, 'beloved,'" if one is conscious of its context, underlines the great principle of sovereign mercy.

It should also be noted that, while Paul mentions the Gentiles' salvation in verse 24, which is in harmony with his theme of sovereign electing mercy, nevertheless his chief interest is in Israel, as the final verses of the chapter indicate (vv. 27-33).[29]

The two passages from Hosea 2:23 and 1:10 illustrate God's royal sovereignty in the rejection and reception of men, Paul's immediate theme. The sovereignty itself is set forth more clearly in the first part of the merged citation, while the second states the glorious result of it in Israel's history more clearly than in the first.[30]

Ladd and others have made a mistake in their initial analysis of the context, thinking that Paul is arguing primarily the relationship of Jews and Gentiles in the divine purpose. That theme will be more on the apostle's mind in chapter 11. But in chapter 9 the subject is God's sovereign dealing with Israel. His usage of Scripture aptly illustrates his purpose.

We conclude, then, that there is no legitimate reason to deny to Paul an analogical use of Hosea to support the manner of the calling of the remnant of Israel and the Gentiles in his day. The truth of the divine gracious calling unites the continuing work of God through the ages.

Ladd's best example fails of demonstration, and with it the contention that the OT Scriptures are on occasion "reinterpreted" in the

29. The *de* of v. 27 is not adversative, as if the preceding verses are about Gentiles, but is continuative, properly rendered by "and" (NASB).

30. Cf. Franklin Johnson, *The Quotations of the New Testament from the Old Considered in the Light of General Literature* (London: Baptist Tract and Book Society, 1896), pp. 354-55.

210

New. More recently Clark Pinnock has written, "Let us by all means begin with the original sense and meaning of the text," adding in a new paragraph, "But when we do that, the first thing we discover is the dynamism of the text itself. Not only is its basic meaning forward looking, the text itself records a very dynamic process of revelation, in which the saving message once given *gets continually and constantly updated, refocussed, and occasionally revised*."[31] However, there are no "crucial reinterpretations" of the OT in the New, as Pinnock claims,[32] only inspired interpretations, the Holy Spirit being the final arbiter in biblical interpretation. As John Ball wrote in the 17th century, "We are not tyed [sic] to the expositions of the Fathers or councels [sic] for the finding out the sense of the Scripture, the Holy Ghost speaking in the Scripture, is the only faithful interpreter of the Scripture."[33] This is the watchword of historic orthodoxy.

THE FUTURE OF ETHNIC ISRAEL

THE CHAPTER CONTEXT OF ROMANS 11:25-27

Two relatively recent books, one authored by the late Anthony A. Hoekema and the other one to which he has made a significant contribution, have enabled Hoekema to emerge as the leading defender of amillennialism in our day. That prominence is well-earned, for his works are soundly argued, clearly written, and represent a significant advance over the older works from the amillennial position.[34]

It must, however, be pointed out that he has primarily simplified an approach popularized in the Netherlands among such Dutch scholars as Herman Ridderbos of Kampen and G. C. Berkouwer of Amsterdam, who have been followed in the United States by their spiritual compatriots, such as William Hendriksen, Palmer Robertson, and Charles Horne. Crucial to the views of these men is the question of the future of ethnic Israel, and it is to this significant eschatological issue that we now turn.

---

31. Clark H. Pinnock, "The Inspiration and Interpretation of the Bible," *TSF Bulletin* 4 (October 1980):6 (italics added).

32. Ibid.

33. Cited in Charles Augustus Briggs, *General Introduction to the Study of Holy Scripture* (reprint, Grand Rapids: Baker, 1970), p. 460. Briggs notes that John Wycliffe, the morning star of the Reformation, echoed the thought, "The Holy Spirit teaches us the sense of Scripture as Christ opened the Scriptures to His apostles" (p. 455).

34. Cf. Hoekema, *The Bible and the Future*; Robert G. Clouse, ed., *The Meaning of the Millennium: Four Views* (Downers Grove, Ill.: InterVarsity, 1977), 223 pp.

Berkouwer excused a separate chapter on Israel in his *The Return of Christ* for two reasons: First, the renewed attention given to Israel due to "the tragic outbursts of antisemitism in our age,"[35] and second, the rise of the Jewish state in Palestine.

We might add a third reason, namely, the importance of the question of the future of ethnic Israel for amillennial eschatology. If ethnic Israel has a future in biblical teaching, then how is it possible to deny to her a certain preeminence in the kingdom of God? The same passages in the OT that point to her future point also quite plainly to her preeminence in that day.

So we come to Romans 11, the one chapter in which Paul discusses "thematically" the future of Israel.[36]

As we have suggested, in Romans 1-8 the apostle has described an elect company's emergence from sin by divine grace, but Israel is missing from among them. Why? In the heart of the book Paul makes three points in reply.

First, Israel's failure is due to spiritual pride and self-sufficiency, which a careful reading of the Scriptures with their doctrine of divine elective grace might have prevented (cf. 9:6-13, 31, 33; 10:3, 21). Chapter 9 stresses the divine election, while chapter 10 emphasizes Israel's human responsibility.

Second, in chapter 11 a consideration of the existence of the remnant of believers in Israel leads to the conclusion that Israel's failure is not total (cf. vv. 1-10).

Third, since Israel still has "the oracles of God" (cf. 3:2, their "advantage"), her failure is not final (cf. 11:11-32). Her future is glorious and, through her, the Gentiles' future is glorious, too. The temper of Paul is that suggested by Lüthi, "The joy in the House of the Father at the return of the prodigal son will always be tempered as long as the elder brother refuses to come in."[37]

Israel's failure is not total (vv. 1-10)

The Pauline question (v. 1*a*), introduced by "then," is followed by the Pauline answer (vv. 1*b*-6) and the logical conclusion (vv. 7-10). General apostasy is not contrary to the existence of a remnant, to whom God has been faithful. The failure of the mass is traceable to Israel's perverse attempt to gain acceptance by works and to the divine election (vv. 6-7).

---

35. Berkouwer, *The Return of Christ*, p. 323.
36. Nils Alstrup Dahl, *Studies in Paul: Theology for the Early Christian Mission* (Minneapolis: Augsburg, 1977), p. 137.
37. Walter Lüthi, *The Letter to the Romans: An Exposition*, trans. Kurt Schoenenberger (Richmond: Knox, 1961), p. 153.

Israel's failure is not final (vv. 11-32)

In this section Paul makes three points. First, a final fall for God's people is unthinkable and blasphemous (cf. 3:1-8). Second, the falling away of the mass of Israel has led to the divinely intended Gentile salvation (vv. 11-12). Third, arguing from the logic of the situation, Paul says that if the fall of the mass of Israel has meant "the reconciliation of the world," their recovery must result in tremendous world blessing, something like life from the dead (vv. 13-15, cf. v. 12).

To illustrate the situation, the apostle unfolds his great parable of the olive tree (vv. 16-24). Its intent is to warn the Gentiles against pride and arrogance and to remind them that, though they have inherited with Israel's believing remnant the covenantal blessings, they will suffer the same fate as the mass of Israel if they do not continue in faith. The parable closes with a massive a fortiori argument for the restoration of national Israel (vv. 23-24).

That leads into the prophecy of restoration of the mass of the nation to salvation (vv. 25-27). Paul has up to this point shown that Israel's restoration in the purpose of God is both *possible* (faith is the lone condition) and *probable* (it is more likely than Gentile salvation, which has occurred). He now shows that it has been *prophesied.* The free citation of verses 26b-27, taken from Isaiah 59:20-21; 27:9; Psalm 14:7 (13:7, LXX), and probably from Jeremiah 31:33-34 also attests it.

The preceding verses (Rom. 11:11-27) have raised the question of the broad sweep of the plan of God for the nation and the nations, and the apostle obliges his readers by surveying the divine purpose. The final balanced sentence is a kind of "reiteration and confirmation"[38] of verses 11-27. The end of the road for both Jew and Gentile is God's mercy, and for each of them the road leads to it through disobedience (vv. 28-32).

The doxology (vv. 33-36)

Paul, caught up in the spirit of Wesley's "Love Divine," is also "lost in wonder, love and praise." He concludes the chapter with a doxology, a *Hymnus*[39] cast in OT language (cf. Isa. 40:13; Job 41:11 [v. 3, MT]). After extolling the inscrutable wisdom and knowledge of God, he mentions His independent sovereignty as the sufficient answer to the preceding questions. As one might expect, he concludes on the note of the ineffable glory of God in verse 36. He is the source, the means, and the goal of all the divine acts of creation, providence, and redemption

---

38. William G. T. Shedd, *A Critical and Doctrinal Commentary on the Epistle of St. Paul to the Romans* (reprint, Grand Rapids: Zondervan, 1967), p. 351.

39. Otto Michel, *Der Brief an die Römer*, 14th ed. (Göttingen: Vandenhoeck & Ruprecht, 1978), p. 359.

(cf. Dan. 2:21; 4:35). As someone has said, "We have learned Paul's meaning only when we can join in this ascription of praise."

THE CRUCIAL QUESTIONS OF ROMANS 11:25-27

The interpretation of kai houtōs *("and thus," v. 26)*

Among the warmly debated words and phrases of the passage is the sense of *kai houtōs* in verse 26. F. F. Bruce, for example, has consented to a temporal sense for *houtōs*, claiming that the force is well attested.[40] It is, however, a rarer use of the adverb (cf. 1 Cor. 11:28; Gal. 6:2).

Others have suggested an inferential force. The sense is good, but again there is little support from usage (cf. Gal. 6:2).[41]

A third possibility is to take the *houtōs* as correlative with the following *kathōs* ("just as";[42] cf. Luke 24:24; Phil. 3:17). The sense would be this: And so all Israel shall be saved, just as the prophetic words indicate. The sense is good.

Finally, the majority of the commentators have given the phrase a comparative force, translating it by "and so," or "and in this manner," that is, the manner indicated in the preceding context (vv. 1-24 or 25). But there is disagreement over the force of the preceding context, so two views have been taken of the meaning of the comparative force. On the one hand, Berkouwer, together with Hendriksen, Horne, Ridderbos, and Robertson, refers the expression to the remnant of Jewish believers being saved in this age. It is in this way that all Israel shall be saved. The method is that of Gentile provocation to jealousy, a continuing process throughout the age between the two comings of Christ. Thus, according to these scholars, there is no future for ethnic Israel in the sense of a great national conversion at the end of the present age.[43]

---

40. F. F. Bruce, *The Epistle of Paul to the Romans: An Introduction and Commentary*, Tyndale New Testament Commentaries (Grand Rapids: Eerdmans, 1963), p. 222. Barrett evidently agrees, seemingly approving the rendering, "when this is done" (C. K. Barrett, *A Commentary on the Epistle to the Romans*, Harper's New Testament Commentaries [New York: Harper, 1957], p. 223).

41. Murray, *The Epistle to the Romans*, 2:96.

42. Henry George Liddell and Robert Scott, *A Greek-English Lexicon*, new ed. rev. and augmented by Sir Henry Stuart Jones and Roderick McKenzie (Oxford: Clarendon, 1940), p. 1277.

43. Berkouwer, *The Return of Christ*, pp. 335-49. There are some differences of opinion among the Dutch group of scholars. Some do expect an eschatological salvation to some extent, like Ridderbos, who says, "Nevertheless, with however much justice Berkouwer places the emphasis on the 'now' of 11:30, this does not alter the fact that 'all Israel will (only) be saved when the *pleroma* of the gentiles shall have come in.' That speaks of the final event: *plērōma* here has a future-eschatological sense, just as in v. 12, and *pas Israēl* is synonymous with it (= *to plērōma autōn*; v. 12)" (Ridderbos, *Paul: An Outline of His Theology*, p. 359, n. 71; cf. pp. 354-61).

On the other hand, Sanday and Headlam and others refer the phrase to the entrance of the Gentiles into the community of the saved. The phrase would normally refer to the nearest antecedent, which is the salvation of the whole number of the Gentiles (v. 25), rather than the more distant reference to Jewish salvation. It is Jewish hardening and Gentile salvation in the immediate context, not Jewish salvation. By provocation to jealousy through the salvation of all the Gentiles Israel shall come to salvation herself. One of the failures of the "Dutch" view is at this point.

An important consideration is the future tense of the verbs, "shall be grafted" (v. 24) and "will be saved" (v. 26). The future is ordinarily aoristic in force, that is, it refers then to an event, which would be more compatible with a future national conversion than a continuing one, although the point is not decisive. The final solution is related to other questions yet to be considered.

The meaning of pas Israēl ("all Israel," v. 26)

The term, if read without consideration of biblical usage, might be thought to refer to all Israelites without exception, but the usage of the term and the teaching of the Scriptures argue to the contrary. It means in usage *Israel as a whole*, not necessarily every individual Israelite (cf. 1 Sam. 7:2-5; 25:1; 1 Kings 12:1; 2 Chron. 12:1-5; Dan. 9:11). The clues to its force are not only the sense of people (Rom. 11:1), but also the nature of the rejection of the Messiah by the nation, a rejection by the nation as a whole (the leaders and the great mass of the people, but not every Israelite). This usage, as is well-known, is found in rabbinic literature. The Mishnah tractate *Sanhedrin* (x. 1) says, "All Israel has a share in the world to come," and then enumerates notable exceptions in a rather lengthy list, including Sadducees, heretics, magicians, the licentious, and others. Thus, Paul affirms that ethnic Israel as a whole will be saved.

The composite citation from the Old Testament

After the declaration of Israel's restoration, Paul gives the biblical attestation. It is a free citation from Isaiah 59:20-21; 27:9; Psalm 14:7; and perhaps Jeremiah 31:33-34 as well. The blend of passages is designed to support the statement, "and thus all Israel will be saved." The citation makes this simple point: the deliverer will save Israel at His advent (cf. Acts 3:19-21; 2 Cor. 3:16).

The most remarkable thing about the blend of texts is their foundation in the unconditional (= unilateral) covenants of Israel. In verse 26*b* Paul refers to Isaiah 59:20, a messianic passage about the coming of the deliverer. The Davidic Covenant is evidently before the apostle. In verse 27*a* Isaiah 59:21 is in Paul's thought, and that text is, in turn, "a renewal of the words of God to Abram in Gen. xvii. 4."[44] Thus, the Abrahamic Covenant finds its fruition here, too. Finally, in verse 27*b*, either Isaiah 27:9 or Jeremiah 31:33-34 is referred to, but the reference to forgiveness of sins makes it fairly plain that the New Covenant is in view (cf. Isa. 59:21). All the unconditional covenants are fulfilled at that time.

THE PRINCIPAL INTERPRETATIONS OF ROMANS 11:25-27

The interpretation of John Calvin

Almost all premillennialists and some important postmillennialists, such as Charles Hodge and John Murray, affirm the future of ethnic Israel. And even some amillennialists affirm that their view does not exclude such a future for Israel. Anthony Hoekema writes of the possibility of a large-scale conversion of the Jews in the future.[45] While Romans 11 has little to say directly concerning the millennial question, it is difficult to see how it is possible to fit a future for ethnic Israel into the amillennial view of the future. The reason for this is simple: the same passages that declare a future for ethnic Israel also speak of Israel's preeminence among the nations in the kingdom of God. But how can an amillennialist admit a preeminence for Israel in his view of the future, that is, in the new heavens and the new earth?

John Calvin took the term "Israel" to mean here the church, composed of both Jews and Gentiles. He writes,

> Many understand this of the Jewish people, as if Paul were saying that religion was to be restored to them again as before. But I extend the word *Israel* to include all the people of God, in this sense—"When the Gentiles have come in, the Jews will at the same time return from their defection to the obedience of faith. The salvation of the whole Israel of God, which must be drawn from both, will thus be completed, and yet in such a way that the Jews, as the firstborn in the family of God, may obtain the first place."[46]

Calvin claimed Galatians 6:16 supported his view.

---

44. Franz Delitzsch, *Biblical Commentary on the Prophecies of Isaiah*, trans. James Martin, 3d. ed. (Edinburgh: Clark, 1877), 2:408. For further comments on the use of the OT here see Michel, *Der Brief an die Römer*, pp. 355-56; Joseph Huby, *Saint Paul: Épître aux Romains* (Paris: Beauchesne et ses Fils, 1957), pp. 402-3; Ulrich Wilckens, *Der Brief an die Römer* (Köln: Benziger Verlag, 1980), 2:256-57; Cranfield, *A Critical and Exegetical Commentary on the Epistle to the Romans*, 2:576-77; Dunn, *Romans 9-16*, pp. 682-83; Matthew Black, *Romans* (Greenwood, S.C.: Attic, 1973), pp. 147-48, and others.

45. Hoekema, *The Bible and the Future*, pp. 146-47.

46. John Calvin, *The Epistles of Paul the Apostle to the Romans and to the Thessalonians*, trans. Ross Mackenzie, ed. David W. Torrance and Thomas F. Torrance (Grand Rapids: Eerdmans, 1961), p. 255.

There are compelling objections to Calvin's view. First, the usage of the term "Israel" in the NT is against it. As we have pointed out, never does the term refer to Gentiles, not even in Galatians 6:16. Historically the view is weak, since there is no evidence that the church was identified with Israel before A.D. 160. Further, in the special context of Romans 9-11 "Israel" is mentioned 11 times and, as we have shown, in not one of the cases are Gentiles in view. And, finally, such a sense would introduce hopeless confusion into the interpretation of verses 25 and 26. If "Israel" refers to spiritual Israel, composed of Jews and Gentiles, what is the meaning of "hardening in part has happened to Israel"?

The "Dutch" interpretation

We have referred above in the brief survey of Paul's argument in Romans 11 to the view of the chapter offered by well-known interpreters from the Netherlands, such as Berkouwer and Ridderbos, and others influenced by them. Among the latter perhaps Hoekema is the most important. It is the contention of these for the most part that Paul refers to the remnant of elect Jews that are saved throughout the centuries by provocation to jealousy through Gentile salvation. Hendriksen's principal point is that Romans 9-11 contains one important idea, namely, "that God's promises attain fulfilment not in the nation as such but in the remnant according to the election of grace."[47] Is it not rather that Israel's covenantal promises are not forgotten, because there is a remnant being saved now, while the future holds promise of the fulfillment of the promises in the salvation of the nation as a whole? Hendriksen's other strong point is that the "and so" must be interpreted in the light of the immediately preceding context, a point well taken. He then contends that the point of the context is that the hardening of Israel is not complete and never will be. The mystery is that in every age elect Jews will be saved by grace until "all Israel" is saved.[48] In my opinion there are weighty objections to this view, and I will seek to indicate them against the views of Hoekema and Hendriksen primarily.

First, it must be kept in mind constantly that the passage has to do with Israel as a nation, as a people (cf. 10:21; 11:1). As a people they have been rejected, they have fallen away, and the mass of the people, the majority, have rebelled and have been hardened (11:7, 12, 15). The figures of the passage are collective in nature, not individualistic in nature—"people" (10:21; 11:1) and "olive tree" (11:16-24). A reversal of

47. William Hendriksen, *Israel and the Bible* (Grand Rapids: Baker, 1968), p. 49.
48. Ibid., p. 51.

the present situation in this collective sense is an important ingredient of the text (cf. vv. 12, 15, 23; "again").

Hoekema, whose defense of the "Dutch" view is found in his excellent book on eschatology, takes "all Israel" to be simply the sum of all the remnants of Jewish believers in the church throughout history. But the sum of the remnants cannot equal "all Israel," as the usage of the term indicates. The sum of the remnants through the ages is still the remnant within Israel.

Second, there are two related concepts in the passage that militate against Hoekema's view. (1) There is the concept of a reversal of fortune for the nation (vv. 7, 11-12, 15, 23-24). In Hoekema's view there is simply the continual saving experience of a minority of Jews down through the history of the church. (2) The other concept is that of a future transformation of Israel's status before God. The note of the future change is found in the same texts, with the addition of verses 25-27.

Third, if all that Paul means in this section is that there is taking place a constant grafting in of believing Israelites into the olive tree, since this would have been a rather obvious truth, why would the question, "God has not rejected His people, has He?" ever have arisen in the first place?

Fourth, the a fortiori argument of verse 12 and the statements in verses 11, 14-15, taken together with the future sense of the passage, support the doctrine of the future of ethnic Israel. The views of Berkouwer and Hendriksen have no real "casting away" and "receiving," no imposition of judicial hardening and no lifting of it. And, further, the uses of "their" (*autōn*) in verses 12 and 15 must refer to different entities, at one time to the mass of the fallen, and then to the remnant of the elect. And, finally, since the verses clearly suggest consequences for the whole world of the salvation of the Israel under discussion, it may be asked reasonably: Why does the conversion of a Jewish remnant, one by one in the "trickle down theory" of the Dutch, lead to such undreamed of abundance in the conversion of the Gentiles? Why does not this happen when individual Gentile elect persons are converted one by one? The Dutch view finds it difficult in the extreme to explain why Paul is so concerned with Israel, when they are no different from anyone else.

Fifth, Hoekema equates the continuing "remnant" with "all Israel," but the context of the chapter certainly seems to contrast them (cf. 10:21; 11:1, 5, 7, 26). And, as was noted earlier, Paul contrasts the two entities in time also, one being now (v. 5), and the other future (vv. 23-24, 26).

Sixth, in verse 23 Paul says that Israel will be grafted in "again." If this is said of the remnant, as Hoekema says, how can this take place? The remnant of elect, being part of the tree, were never broken off (v. 17). The grafting in again of Israel must be, then, the grafting in again of those broken off, the mass of the nation, or the nation as a whole, "His people." They have been cast away but will be received again by virtue of the faithfulness of God to the covenantal promises made to them.

Seventh, the interpretation of Berkouwer and the others destroys the climactic element in Paul's statement that "all Israel will be saved." If all that is meant is that all the elect of national Israel will be saved, as Hoekema appears to claim, then the conclusion is insipid and vapid. Why, of course, the elect will be saved.[49]

Eighth, finally, while there is reason for honest difference of opinion over this,[50] the Scripture citation from Isaiah 59:20-21 and 27:9 does not agree with the "Dutch" view, for the citation in its most prominent sources refers to the messianic salvation at the second advent, not the first advent and the time that intervenes up to the second advent.

CONCLUSION

We therefore conclude that the history of God's dealings with ethnic Israel as set out in Romans 11:1-10, the logic of Israel's reversal of fortune in verses 11-15, supported by the illustration of the olive tree and the regrafting of the natural branches of ethnic Israel into it "again" in verses 16-24, and the prophecy of the salvation of "all Israel" in verses 25-27 combine to establish the future of ethnic Israel as a glorious hope of both Israel and the church.

W. D. Davies, in his significant presidential address at the meeting of *Studiorum Novi Testamenti Societas* at Duke University in August, 1976, emphasized some important points that are true to Paul's thought here. Covenantal forgiveness will take place at the parousia for Israel. That will be the consummation of genuine Judaism itself. The "advantage" of Israel still obtains (cf. Rom. 3:1-2)—priority without superiority. There is a continuity between the olive tree and the root of Abraham, between the patriarchs (v. 28) and the nation. Fundamental to the fulfillment of the promises is the faithfulness of God. While the Gentiles partake of the promises, Israel still has a "favored nation" status; it is "their own olive tree" (v. 24). And, finally, it is the Lord God who is responsible for the consummation of the program.[51]

49. Murray, *The Epistle to the Romans*, 2:97. Robertson seeks to answer this, laying stress on the manner of Israel's salvation, but the attempt does not succeed in my opinion. Cf. O. Palmer Robertson, "Is There a Distinctive Future for Ethnic Israel in Romans 11?" in *Perspectives on Evangelical Theology*, ed. by Kenneth S. Kantzer and Stanley N. Gundry (Grand Rapids: Zondervan, 1979), pp. 219-21.

50. Hendriksen (*Israel and the Bible*, p. 48) sees the references as pointing to the first advent, but the majority of orthodox commentators who comment on the citation refer the texts to the second advent.

51. W. D. Davies, "Paul and the People of Israel," *New Testament Studies* 24 (October 1977): 25-39.

THE COVENANT OF AN EARTHLY KINGDOM

THE ABRAHAMIC COVENANT: ITS PERMANENCE

"Abraham is . . . the greatest human character in the Bible," said Donald Grey Barnhouse some years ago.[52] Barnhouse's reasons for the patriarch's greatness included the frequency of his name in the NT. Outside of such expressions as "Moses says," or "Moses wrote," Abraham's name stands fourth behind Paul, Peter, and John the Baptist in frequency of mention. Further, Abraham's encounter with God is the pattern of justification by faith (cf. Gen. 15:6; Rom. 4:1-25). Rabbinic theology's failure is related to its views of the precedence of Moses over Abraham, as well as its failure to see divine grace in Abraham's justification. In an ancient midrashic work (*Mekilta* 40*b*) it is said that Abraham was justified by "the merit of faith." Finally, Abraham's life became the NT pattern of the life of faith (cf. Heb. 11:8-19).

The Abrahamic Covenant has a corresponding importance in biblical eschatology. Premillennialists have laid great stress on its nature and provisions, sometimes claiming that the correct interpretation of its content really settles the argument over the question of a kingdom of God on the earth. It is, therefore, rather revealing that Hoekema has no detailed treatment of the significance of the biblical covenants for eschatology.[53]

The promises that God gave Abraham were threefold: (1) personal promises to the patriarch (Gen. 12:2, "make your name great"); (2) national promises to Abraham's ethnic believing seed, the stress resting on the grant of land (12:1; 13:14-17; 15:7; 17:8); and (3) universal promises to Abraham's Gentile seed (12:3; Gal. 3:7,16, 29; Matt. 1:1). At the last, Christ is the "in you" fulfillment.

The promises were unconditional promises, that is, dependent ultimately on God's sovereign determination, as the striking ratification of the covenant indicated (Gen. 15:7-21). While there are several important features of the ratification, the most outstanding feature is the peculiar action of God. In other covenants of this nature both parties walked between the pieces of the animals. In this instance, however, God symbolically walked between the pieces, and Abraham was not invited to follow. The meaning is clear: This covenant is not a conditional covenant in which certain duties rest finally on man alone. God undertakes to fulfill the conditions Himself, thus guaranteeing by the divine fidelity to His Word and by His power the accomplishment of the covenantal

---

52. Donald Grey Barnhouse, *God's Remedy* (Wheaton, Ill.: Van Kampen, 1954), p. 351.
53. While Hoekema in his chapter on "The New Earth" (*The Bible and the Future*, pp. 274-87) has some things to say concerning Abraham's promises, one of the most disappointing features of his work is the absence of a treatment of the covenants and eschatology.

promises. Ridderbos vividly describes the unilateral nature of the event: "Abraham is deliberately excluded—he is the astonished spectator (cf. Gen. 15:12, 17)."[54] Even the faith that Abraham would exercise is the product of divine, efficacious grace.

The remainder of the Bible is concerned with the ongoing fulfillment of these promises. In the OT, as the promises receive expansion by the Davidic and New Covenants, many prophetic passages assure the readers of Scripture of their continuing validity (cf. Isa. 11:1-11; Jer. 16:14-15; 23:3-8; 33:19-26; Hos. 1:1–2:1 [2:3, Heb.]; Amos 9:11-15; Mic. 4:1-7; 5:1-9; 7:18-20).

Micah 7:18-20 is particularly striking. The final section of this great prophecy shifts to a more lyrical, or hymnic style.[55] It is a choral piece of devotion, a doxology for the noble character of a God who forgives and delights in constant love (v. 18, *ḥesed*). "Micah" means "Who is like (Yahweh)?" and fittingly the last section of the book begins reminiscently, "Who is a God like Thee?" (v. 18). This kind of rhetorical question is usually reserved for His mighty acts (cf. Ex. 15:11).

The challenge is thrown out in verse 18. The book had begun with Yahweh's advent in wrath against the peoples of the earth (1:1-5). It concludes with a magnificent choral promise of His faithfulness and unchanging love to Jacob and Abraham. The prophet was convinced of the impossibility of the frustration of God's covenant promises.

The cause of the challenge is set out in verses 19-20. Here is the theology undergirding the preceding context. As Allen says, "They have come in repentance, but that is not enough to win back the blessing of God. He is no petulant princeling to be wooed away from a fit of capricious temper. Nothing they can do will avail of itself to secure God's acceptance. The sole ground of their hope lies in the noble character of God as one who forgives, forgets, and offers a fresh beginning."[56] Micah finds his deepest ground of confidence in the patriarchal promises (Ps. 105:8-11). God's ancient word of grace in His elective promises to Abraham and his seed is expressed in verse 20 as "Thou wilt give truth [*ʾĕmet*] to Jacob and unchanging love [*ḥesed*] to Abraham." "Jacob" and "Abraham" are used representatively as corporate objects of God's grace (the latter is unparalleled as a name for the people in the OT[57]). God's un-

54. Herman N. Ridderbos, *The Epistle of Paul to the Churches of Galatia*, New International Commentary on the New Testament (Grand Rapids: Eerdmans, 1953), p. 131, n. 2.
55. Delbert R. Hillers, *Micah* (Philadelphia: Fortress, 1984), p. 91.
56. Leslie C. Allen, *The Books of Joel, Obadiah, Jonah, and Micah*, New International Commentary on the Old Testament (Grand Rapids: Eerdmans, 1976), p. 401.
57. Cf. Hillers, *Micah*, p. 91; James Luther Mays, *Micah: A Commentary* (Philadelphia: Westminster, 1976), p. 168.

frustratable loyal love is expressed no more pointedly anywhere else in the prophetic literature. Thus did the prophets understand the Abrahamic Covenant.

To the NT authors the Abrahamic Covenant is still in force.[58] Passages of significance include Luke 1:46-55, 67-80, where in verses 55 and 73 a clear indication of the continuing validity of the covenant is affirmed, and that in spite of the apostasy of the prophetic age that has intervened. Further, there is no indication that the promises of the land are not included. The swearing of the oath in Zacharias's prophecy (Luke 1:73) is related to Genesis 22:16-18, and Israel's supremacy in the age to come is indicated by the clause, "and your seed shall possess the gate of their enemies" (Gen. 22:17).

THE ABRAHAMIC COVENANT: ROMANS 11

Romans 9-11 is filled with references to the Abrahamic Covenant (cf. 9:4-5, 6-13, 25-26; 10:19 [Deut. 32:9, 18, 29, 36, 43]), but the most important section is Romans 11:11-27. We have already sought to show that the passage clearly points to the future of ethnic Israel, and that the merged citation in verses 26-27 includes a reference to the Abrahamic Covenant as fulfilled at the time of the second advent of the Messiah.

THE ABRAHAMIC COVENANT: ITS EARTHLY KINGDOM

Two questions deserve some answer. The first is: "What about the land promises? They are not mentioned in the NT. Are they, therefore, canceled?" In my opinion the apostles and the early church would have regarded the question as singularly strange, if not perverse. To them the Scriptures consisted of our OT, and they considered the Scriptures to be living and valid as they wrote and transmitted the NT literature. The apostles used the Scriptures as if they were living, vital oracles of the living God, applicable to them in their time. And these same Scriptures were filled with promises regarding the land and an earthly kingdom. On what basis should the Abrahamic promises be divided into those to be fulfilled and those to remain unfulfilled?

Also remember that Peter urged the church to recall both the words of the prophets and the things spoken by the apostles, obviously with a view to adherence to them (cf. 2 Pet. 3:1-2). So far as I can tell, Papias, Irenaeus, Justin, and others knew no such division of the prophecies.

---

58. Leon Morris has pointed out that the NT sees the covenant as still being in force in three of its four occurrences, and possibly in the fourth occurrence as well (*The Apostolic Preaching of the Cross* [Grand Rapids: Eerdmans, 1955], p. 93).

Finally, there is no need to repeat what is copiously spread over the pages of the Scriptures. There seems to be lurking behind the demand a false principle, namely, that we should not give heed to the OT unless its content is repeated in the New. The correct principle, however, is that we should not consider invalid and worthy of discard any of the OT unless we are specifically told to do so in the New, as in the case of the law of Moses (the cultus particularly).[59]

The second question is this: Were not the land promises fulfilled in OT times, both regarding the multiplied seed (cf. 1 Kings 4:20; 1 Chron. 27:23; 2 Chron. 1:9; Heb. 11:12 [partial fulfillment is conceded by all]) and the land (cf. 1 Kings 4:21)? The answer is plain: Israel never had anything but an incomplete and temporary possession of the land. Some premillennialists believe the boundaries of Genesis 15:18 were attained only in David's reign, "and then as an empire rather than a homeland."[60] The prophets, however, were ignorant of this "fulfillment," and long after the incomplete and temporary possession of the land looked on to the fulfillment of the land promises (Amos 9:13-15).

I see no compelling reason why our Lord's counsel should not be heeded. We, too, with the apostles and prophets, send our petition heavenward, "Thy kingdom come."

---

59. Gordon H. Clark first called my attention to this (cf. *Biblical Predestination* [Nutley, N.J.: Presbyterian & Reformed, 1969], p. 12).

60. Derek Kidner, *Genesis: An Introduction and Commentary*, Tyndale Old Testament Commentaries (Chicago: InterVarsity, 1967), p. 125.

12

EVIDENCE FROM 1 CORINTHIANS 15

D. EDMOND HIEBERT

Professor Emeritus of New Testament
Mennonite Brethren Biblical Seminary

F irst Corinthians 15 is justly famous as "the resurrection chapter." It presents the most elaborate development of bodily resurrection in all Scripture. It was Paul's inspired answer to the heresy in the Corinthian church which denied the reality of bodily resurrection as inconsistent with prevailing philosophical conceptions.

In dealing with this heresy Paul reminded the Corinthian believers of the content of the gospel which he had preached to them and which they had accepted in faith. Of first importance in that message was the reality "that Christ died for our sins according to the Scriptures, and that He was buried, and that He was raised on the third day according to the Scriptures," and that His appearances to many after His resurrection verified that He had indeed arisen from the dead (vv. 1-10). This, Paul reminded them, was the uniform apostolic message and the accepted faith of the Christian church (v. 11).

In verses 12-19 Paul set forth that Christ's resurrection was essential for the soteriological function of Christianity. He did so, negatively, by drawing out the inevitable tragic consequences "if" Christ has not been raised from the dead. In verses 20-28 Paul declared the positive reality of Christ's resurrection and unfolded its foundational function in the resurrection of believers in the future. In its very nature the resurrection of Christ is eschatological; its denial undermines the entire eschatological program.

First Corinthians 15 was not meant to be a systematic treatise on eschatology but was intended to answer the difficulties of the readers concerning the Christian doctrine of the resurrection. Paul's central concern is to show that bodily resurrection is at the very heart of the entire soteriological-eschatological program.

It is our purpose here to center attention on 1 Corinthians 15:20-28 in an effort to discern more precisely its eschatological message. It is recognized that equally devout and diligent students of Scripture will arrive at different views relative to the order and implications of the varied elements in the eschatological program. Proponents of their respective views must avoid attributing unworthy motives or insincerity in exegesis to those with whom they differ. Nor should the defense of any precise eschatological view cause the student of prophecy to miss the present ethical and practical impact of our blessed hope centered in the anticipated return of our Savior and Lord, Jesus Christ.

THE FOUNDATION OF THE RESURRECTION PROGRAM
(1 COR. 15:20-22)

CHRIST, THE RISEN ONE (v. 20a)

No eschatological projections can claim to be acceptable as valid apart from a committal to Paul's ringing declaration, "But now Christ has been raised from the dead" (*Nuni de Chrīstos egēgertai ek nekrōn*). The opening words, "But now," abruptly terminate Paul's hypothetical enumeration in verses 13-19 of the tragic results if Christ did not rise from the dead. They introduce a joyous outburst, confidently declaring the contrasting reality to the dreary picture just presented.

The expression "from the dead" (*ek nekrōn*) indicates that "Christ's resurrection was a *resurrection out of*, whereby many dead remained in their graves. And that is why *ek* is always used for His resurrection."[1] The plural noun *nekrōn*, "dead ones," rather than *thanatos*, "death," as in verses 21, 54, 55, makes clear that the risen Christ is contrasted to physically dead human beings. He arose with a deathless body no longer subject to physical death (Rom. 6:9-10). The particular "dead ones" Paul has in mind here are believers and not the unbelieving dead. This becomes clear in verse 20b where Paul specifies that "the dead" are

---

1. Harry Bultema, *Maranatha! A Study of Unfulfilled Prophecy*, trans. Cornelius Lambregtse (Grand Rapids: Kregel, 1985), p. 135.

"those who are asleep" (*tōn kekoimēmenōn*), a common Pauline expression for believers who have died (cf. 1 Cor. 15:6, 18; 1 Thess. 4:13-15). The apostle is dealing in this chapter with resurrection "in Christ" (v. 22b) and not resurrection in general.[2]

CHRIST, THE FIRST FRUITS (v. 20b)

Verse 20 contains the last direct reference to the personal resurrection of Christ in this chapter, yet the appositional identification, "the first fruits of those who sleep," indicates that for Paul everything that follows is inseparably grounded in that reality. Paul's purpose in using this OT designation lies in its function as the pledge and guarantee of the coming harvest. "In his usage," Fee points out, "the metaphor functions similarly to that of the 'down payment' or 'earnest money' of the Spirit in 2 Cor. 1:22 and 5:5 (cf. Eph. 1:14); both serve as a present pledge on the part of God for the final eschatological harvest or payment."[3]

The figure of "the first fruits" (*aparchē*)[4] is grounded in the OT law which designated that the first ripe sheaf of the harvest belonged to God and was to be offered to Him before the rest of the harvest could be used (Lev. 23:9-11, 14). It was to be offered the first day after the Sabbath during Passover, the very day Christ arose from the dead, hence the aptness of the figure. The sheaf offered in the Temple was the same in kind as the rest of the harvest; the figure does not imply that those who constitute the coming harvest are intrinsically the same in their own nature as the incarnate Son of God; rather, as united to Him by their faith, they will be raised with a deathless body like His own.

In Romans 16:5, 1 Corinthians 16:15, and 2 Thessalonians 2:13 Paul uses the term *aparchē* ("first fruits") of the first converts of a province or geographical area as constituting the promise of the coming harvest for the Lord in the area. Here the figure declares that the resurrection of believers is fully assured by the resurrection of Christ as "the first fruits." As Christ arose, so must His people. But His resurrection with a deathless body establishes His uniqueness as the first fruits of "those who are asleep" (*tōn kekoimēmenōn*, "those having fallen asleep"). The term is a transparent metaphor of physical death. The passive participle indicates that as members of a mortal race, believers' bodies have succumbed to the ravages of physical death. Jesus Christ in His

---

2. This is not to say that Paul did not believe in the ultimate resurrection of all men (cf. Rom. 2:5-10; Acts 24:15).

3. Gordon D. Fee, *The First Epistle to the Corinthians*, New International Commentary on the New Testament (Grand Rapids: Eerdmans, 1987), p. 749.

4. Our English versions use the idiomatic plural, "first fruits," but in the Greek the collective singular is always used.

incarnation identified Himself with mortal humanity; but in His resurrection He was the first to rise from the dead with a deathless body. In the OT some individuals were raised from the dead, and Jesus Himself raised some during His earthly ministry, but all these were simply resuscitations; those raised remained subject to physical death at a later time. In His resurrection with a deathless body, Christ became "the first born from the dead" (Col. 1:18), having established His mastery over death. The uniqueness of His resurrection fully qualified Him to be the foundation and head of the resurrection program.

CHRIST, THE FEDERAL HEAD (vv. 21-22)

Verse 21 gives the reason (*gar*) why Christ is the first fruits in relation to those who have fallen asleep in Christ. The reason is that of federal headship which Paul expounds more fully in Romans 5:12-21. Verse 22 explains (*gar*) that the "man" bringing death to all connected with (*en*) him is Adam and the "man" bringing resurrection life to all connected with (*en*) Him is Christ. The point is that whereas Adam has brought death to all men (for all men are "in Adam"), Christ will bring resurrection life to all who are His (for only believers are "in Christ"). Hence Christ is established as the first fruits of the believing dead.[5]

THE STAGES IN THE RESURRECTION PROGRAM (1 COR. 15:23)

Having established Christ's resurrection as the historical foundation and guarantee of the resurrection program (vv. 20-22), Paul next dealt with the sequence of future events in relation to the resurrection program. Verse 23 specifies certain stages in the program.

The opening words, "But each in his own order," imply a differentiation and distinctness in the resurrection events, yet an underlying unity in those events. "Each" (*Hekastos*) looks back to "all shall be made alive" (*pantes zōopoiēthēsontai*) just before and implies an orderly sequence in dealing with them. The word "order" (*tagma*) in classical Greek was almost exclusively a military technical term for a body of

---

5. It should be noted that a number of evangelical scholars take the parallel uses of *pantes* in v. 22 as referring to universal resurrection rather than universal resurrection "in Christ." So Robert D. Culver, "A Neglected Millennial Passage from Saint Paul," *Bibliotheca Sacra* 113 (April 1956):144-45; B. B. Warfield, *Biblical Doctrines* (New York: Oxford, 1929), p. 621; Wilber B. Wallis, "The Problem of an Intermediate Kingdom in 1 Corinthians 15:20-28," *Journal of the Evangelical Theological Society* 18 (Fall 1975):234-37. The decision on this issue, however, does not affect the implications of the passage for the millennial kingdom.

troops. In later Greek it came to be applied to any sort of group, military or civilian.[6] Two resurrection groups are specified in verse 23.

"CHRIST THE FIRST FRUITS" (v. 23b)

The first *tagma* ("group") consisted of Christ as the "first fruits," indicating more would follow. The presentation of the "first fruits" on the first day after the Passover sabbath was not a single stalk of grain but a sheaf consisting of a number of ears. This would suggest that this first *tagma* in the resurrection program, like the following *tagma*, involved more than one individual. Matthew 27:52-53 informs us that after Christ's resurrection a number of "the saints" came forth from their tombs around Jerusalem and appeared to many in the city. Nothing further is revealed concerning them, but it seems that the purpose of their resurrection was to provide further verification of Christ's resurrection and to give a foretaste of what His resurrection meant for His people. It is probable that their resurrection was not merely a resuscitation; following Christ's resurrection, they too experienced a bodily resurrection like Christ's to complete the figure of the first fruits. Like Christ, they too were raised *ek nekrōn* ("from the dead"), thus fully completing the figure of the first fruits.[7]

"THOSE WHO ARE CHRIST'S AT HIS COMING" (v. 23c)

In contrast with the first *tagma* which is past, the second is future and will consist of those who belong to Christ (i.e., believers, cf. 3:23; Gal. 3:29; 5:24) when He returns. The noun *parousia* ("coming" or "presence") is one of the important NT terms for the return of Christ. It involves both the thought of arrival and consequent presence with (cf. 1 Cor. 16:17; 2 Cor. 7:6-7; Phil. 2:12). In verses 51-57 Paul elaborated on the eschatological consequences connected with Christ's return for His own.

The temporal adverb *epeita* ("after that") encompasses the time between Christ's resurrection and return. Thus the first two groups in the resurrection program are separated by over 1900 years.

THE CONSUMMATION OF THE RESURRECTION PROGRAM
(1 COR. 15:24-28)

Here the crux of the millennial issue is reached. By the indefinite phrase, *eita to telos* ("then [comes] the end"), which begins verse 24,

---

6. *A Greek-English Lexicon of the New Testament and other Early Christian Literature*, 2d Eng. ed., revised and augmented by F. Wilbur Gingrich and Frederick W. Danker (Chicago: U. of Chicago, 1979), pp. 802-3.

7. For a further discussion see D. A. Carson, "Matthew," in *The Expositor's Bible Commentary* (Grand Rapids: Zondervan, 1984), 8:582.

does Paul establish an interval between Christ's coming and the consummation? If so then Paul, at the very least, leaves room for an end-time millennial kingdom. Or does the apostle mean that "the end" occurs at Christ's coming which, of course, leaves no room for a millennial reign of Christ? Our exegesis will give emphasis to this question.

THE FACT OF THE CONSUMMATION (v. 24)

Like the preceding *epeita* (v. 23), the temporal adverb *eita* most likely implies an interval of time between the coming of Christ and the end. While it is true that *eita* can refer to immediately consequent events (cf. John 13:5; 19:27; 20:27), Paul consistently used *eita* to denote clearly distinct events separated by intervals of time. In verses 5 and 7 of this chapter Paul used *eita* to note separate post-resurrection appearances of Christ. In 1 Timothy 2:13 *eita* marks the interval between the creation of Adam and Eve (cf. 1 Tim. 3:10 [only other use]). If *epeita*, a closely related word, can mark an interval of over 1900 years in the previous verse, may not *eita* allow for a 1,000-year interval in verse 24? Subsequent evidence from the passage will show that this is not only possible, but the most probable understanding of Paul's meaning.

What does Paul mean by "the end" (*to telos*)? Is this primarily a reference to a third *tagma* or resurrection group? If so, then *to telos* must be translated "the rest, remainder" or in an adjectival sense, "the end [resurrection]." But it is questionable whether *to telos* ever carried these meanings.[8] In fact Paul described what he meant by "the end" with the two *hotan* ("when") clauses in verse 24. The tense change between the two clauses is significant. "The aorist subjunctive of the second *hotan* clause indicates that the destruction of Christ's enemies is prior to the event of the first *hotan* clause, the delivering over of the Kingdom at the *telos*: the delivering follows the subjugation."[9] Therefore, by "the end" Paul means an end period,[10] which includes Christ's conquest of enemy

8. Cf. *A Greek-English Lexicon of the New Testament and Other Early Christian Literature*, pp. 811-12. Barrett comments: "It cannot be said that attempts (notably Leitzmann's) to demonstrate this meaning [rest, remainder] have succeeded (see Kummel, Allo, Hering, and others). Even if the meaning stood out clearly in the two or three passages in which it is supposed to occur (and it does not), these would be worth little against the very many passages where the meaning is simply *end*" (C. K. Barrett, *A Commentary on the First Epistle to the Corinthians* [New York: Harper, 1968], p. 356).

9. Wallis, "The Problem of an Intermediate Kingdom in 1 Corinthians 15:20-28," p. 230. Wallis goes on to point out that the same sequence is seen again in v. 28.

10. Similar to *tē santeleia tou aiōnos* in Matt. 13:40, 49; 24:3, 6, 14; 28:20. Cf. Archibald Robertson and Alfred Plummer, *A Critical and Exegetical Commentary on the First Epistle of St Paul to the Corinthains*, International Critical Commentary (Edinburgh: Clark, 1914), p. 354. Cf. the discussion by Wallis, "The Problem of the Intermediate Kingdom in 1 Corinthians 15:20-28," p. 231.

powers[11] followed by the handing over of the kingdom to the Father. The significance for the millennial issue is summarized well by Wallis, "Therefore, since there is a sequence clearly marked, the *telos* cannot be simultaneous with the Parousia. Because the *telos* is preceded by the destruction of enemies, and the destruction of enemies cannot be put before the Parousia, the *telos* must stand beyond the Parousia and judgment."[12]

Thus the most probable meaning of *eita* and *to telos* in verse 24 lends evidence to a time gap between the coming of Christ and the end, which allows for a millennial reign of Christ, the very kingdom (*tēn basileian*) mentioned in verse 24.

THE EXPLANATION OF THE CONSUMMATION (vv. 25-28)

With the *gar* of verse 25 Paul explained the reason why Christ cannot hand over the kingdom until the end. It is necessary (*dei*) that Christ[13] exercise His sovereignty over the earth until all His enemies (the "all rule and all authority and power" of v. 24) are subjugated. This will take a period of time, as the present tense infinitive, *basileuein* ("reign"), implies. The mention of "death" as "the last Enemy" (v. 26)[14] indicates that Christ's reign involves a series of conquests, and is not simply one final conquest at His parousia. The adjective "last" stands forward in the Greek text of verse 26, underlining that death is the last in a series of enemies which His reign must render inoperative. Clark comments: "His reign takes time, and it seems that it is a time of war."[15]

Of course the crucial question for the millennial issue is: When does this reign of Christ take place? The flow of Paul's argument in verses 24-25,

---

11. The triple designation of enemies, "all rule and all authority and power," "should not be limited to *angelic powers*, or *demons*," for it "embraces *all* forces oppugnant to God, on earth or above it, whether they exercise *princely sway* (*archen*) or *moral authority* (*exousian*) or *active power* (*dunamin*)" (G. G. Findlay, "The First Epistle of Paul to the Corinthians," in *The Expositor's Greek Testament* [Grand Rapids: Eerdmans, n.d.], 2:926).

12. Wallis, "The Problem of an Intermediate Kingdom in 1 Corinthians 15:20-28," p. 231.

13. The question of whether the subject of *thē* ("has put") is the Father (so Ps. 110:1) or the Son (better with the syntax and context) is rendered less crucial by the use of Ps. 8:6 in v. 27, which makes clear that the Father and Son join in a co-sovereignty over the earth. Ultimately it can be said that both are reigning.

14. Physical not spiritual death is in view in the context, and the indication seems to be that physical death will continue through the millennial period (cf. discussion of Isa. 65:20 in Jeffrey L. Townsend, "Is the Present Age the Millennium?" *Bibliotheca Sacra* 140 [July-September 1983]:209-10). The overcoming of the last enemy, death, may hint at a resurrection of millennial saints at the end of the thousand years.

15. Gordon H. Clark, *First Corinthians: A Contemporary Commentary* (Nutley, N.J.: Presbyterian & Reformed, 1975), p. 266.

as indicated by *eita . . . hotan* (with the present subjunctive, *paradidoi*, "delivers up") . . . *hotan* (with the aorist subjunctive, *katargēsē*, "has abolished") . . . *gar*, suggests that the reign in verse 25 refers to the period of conquest in the second *hotan* clause of verse 24. If so, Christ must reign after the parousia and before the *telos*. "The *telos* cannot be made simultaneous with the Parousia."[16]

A convincing confirmation of this time-sequence comes from the realization that Paul employs Psalm 110:1 in verse 25*b* and Psalm 8:6 in verse 27*a*. The writer to the Hebrews makes similar use of these same two passages from the Psalms in Hebrews 1:13 (Ps. 110:1) and 2:8 (Ps. 8:6).[17] Wallis has argued persuasively that the parallel use of these Psalms in 1 Corinthians 15 and Hebrews 1 and 2 allows the passages to comment on one another. He writes,

> Hebrews emphasizes the fact that the subjugation of all things is yet future [so not prior to the parousia], though a decisive point in the total redemptive plan has been reached in the suffering and death of the Son. Hebrews calls the situation in the future "the world to come." On the other hand, I Corinthians makes it clear that that situation is a time when Christ reigns and overcomes His enemies [so it is not the eternal state].[18]

In a subsequent article, Wallis concludes,

> Here then is the answer to the question as to the position of the reign indicated in I Corinthians 15:25; Christ must reign, but when? Is He now reigning in the eschatological sense intended, or will that reign commence at the Parousia? Hebrews gives a decisive answer in the *mellousan* ["coming"] of 2:5 and in the *oupo* ["not yet"] of 2:8: the reign and conquest of enemies must needs be, but it lies in the future, at and after the Parousia.[19]

The *gar* ("for") of verse 27 introduces the reason why death will be abolished—all things will be subjected to the consummate man, the Messiah, according to Psalm 8:6. In verse 27 Paul connected the universal

16. Wallis, "The Problem of an Intermediate Kingdom in 1 Corinthians 15:20-28," p. 233.
17. The unity of thought in Heb. 1 and 2 is ably defended by Wallis: "The assumption that the subjugation of the world to come of 2:5 is closely related to the subjugation of enemies of 1:13 explains both the resumptive reference to angels and the explanatory remark 'about which we are speaking'" (Wilber B. Wallis, "The Use of Psalms 8 and 110 in I Corinthians 15:25-27 and in Hebrews 1 and 2," *Journal of the Evangelical Theological Society* 15 [Winter 1972]:27).
18. Ibid., p. 28.
19. Wallis, "The Problem of an Intermediate Kingdom in 1 Corinthians 15:20-28," p. 241.

rule of the Son with the initial crowning of "man" as king over the earth, as lyrically portrayed in Psalm 8. In the words of Bruce, "In Ps. 8.5-8, which reflects the creation narrative of Gen. 1.26-30, it is man that is vested with dominion over all things, but Paul, like the writer to the Hebrews, applies the psalmist's language to Christ as the last Adam, the 'son of man' who retrieved the situation which the first Adam lost."[20] As the self-seeking, rebellious actions of the first Adam brought this world under the domination of Satan, sin, and death, so the last Adam, in voluntary obedience to the Father's commission, will continue His reign until He has effectively "put all things in subjection under His feet." The true solution to earth's death-terminating enslavement will ultimately be brought to completion through the incarnate Son of God. "When He says, 'All things are put in subjection,'" (v. 27*b*) records the Son's joyous proclamation when His mediatorial assignment finally has been fulfilled.

When the divine purpose behind the mediatorial kingdom of the Son has been realized, then the incarnate Son, who ever delighted to do the will of the Father (Ps. 40:8; John 5:30; 6:38), will voluntarily turn over the authority of the kingdom to the Father (v. 28). Thus He will voluntarily subject Himself to the Father who had placed all things in subjection to the Son. The reference is to the Son's termination of His distinctive messianic mission. This action of the Son, voluntarily subjecting Himself to the Father, is not in addition to, but distinct from the "all things" that the Son has brought into subjection. It is a matter of function, "that God may be all in all" (v. 28*c*). Then the exercise of the distinctive functions of the individual members of the Godhead, during the varied stages of the whole redemptive program, will no longer be needed. The Son's action will openly exhibit the unity of the Godhead.

Christ's act of turning the kingdom over to the Father does not mean that He will cease to reign, for "His kingdom will have no end" (Luke 1:33; cf. Heb. 1:8; Dan. 7:13-14). Rather, as Barnes points out, He will surrender to the Father "that power only which he had *as* Mediator; and whatever part in the administration of the government of the universe he shared as Divine before the incarnation, he will *still* share, with the additional *glory* and *honour* of having redeemed a world by his death."[21]

The final achievement of the goal "that God may be all in all" does not imply that the distinctions in the members of the Godhead will be eliminated. Rather it expresses the loyal purpose of the Son "whose

20. F. F. Bruce, *1 and 2 Corinthians*, New Century Bible (London: Oliphants, 1971), p. 147.
21. Albert Barnes, *Notes on the New Testament, Explanatory and Practical, I Corinthians*, ed. Robert Frew (Grand Rapids: Baker, 1962), p. 298 (italics his).

submission exhibits the unity of the Godhead (cf. John x.30-36, xvii.23), and constitutes itself the focus and uniting bond of a universe in which God's will is everywhere regnant and His being everywhere immanent."[22] Thus the kingdom does not end, rather the temporal kingdom of the Son as mediator is merged into the eternal kingdom of the Godhead.

CONCLUSION

In 1 Corinthians 15:20-28 Paul affirms the bodily resurrection of believers by showing its necessary link to the resurrection of Christ. The bodily resurrection of Christ guarantees the bodily resurrection of dead Christians as well as Christ's final triumph over all things, including death.

Our exegesis has shown that it is not only possible but probable that Paul understood this final triumph to take place during the millennial reign of Christ. To sum up the principal evidence, Paul's use of *epeita* ("after that") and *eita* ("then") in 1 Corinthians 15:23-24, the syntax of 15:24-25, and the parallel use of Psalms 8 and 110 in 1 Corinthians 15 and Hebrews 1 and 2 all point to the understanding that when Paul mentioned a kingdom and reign in 15:24-25, he referred to the reign of Christ on this earth following His return and prior to the eternal state, a time that Revelation 20:4-6 calls "the thousand years."

22. Findlay, "The First Epistle of Paul to the Corinthians," p. 930.

13

EVIDENCE FROM REVELATION 20

HAROLD W. HOEHNER
Professor of New Testament Studies
Dallas Theological Seminary

When reading Revelation 20:1-7, one immediately notices the six-fold mention of 1,000 years. The obvious question is: How does one interpret the 1,000 years? There have been two basic answers. Some think that the 1,000 years must be taken literally; that is, a 1,000-year period exists after the coming of Christ to earth and before the time of the eternal state described in Revelation 21-22. The majority of those who hold this position of a literal 1,000 years are premillennialists.[1] The only others who hold to the literal 1,000 years are the very few postmillennialists who maintain that Christ's second coming takes place after the 1,000-year period.[2] The other major view held by

1. Cf. George E. Ladd, *Crucial Questions About the Kingdom of God* (Grand Rapids: Eerdmans, 1952), pp. 135-50; John F. Walvoord, *The Millennial Kingdom* (Findlay, Ohio: Dunham, 1959), pp. 113-334; George Eldon Ladd, "Revelation 20 and the Millennium," *Review and Expositor* 57 (April 1960):167-75; Jack S. Deere, "Premillennialism in Revelation 20:4-6," *Bibliotheca Sacra* 135 (January-March 1978):58-73; Jeffrey L. Townsend, "Is the Present Age the Millennium?" *Bibliotheca Sacra* 140 (July-September 1983):206-24; John F. Walvoord, "The Theological Significance of Revelation 20:1-6," in *Essays in Honor of J. Dwight Pentecost*, ed. Stanley D. Toussaint and Charles H. Dyer (Chicago: Moody, 1986), pp. 227-38.

2. Cf. Loraine Boettner, *The Millennium* (Philadelphia: Presbyterian and Reformed, 1957), pp. 3-105; David Chilton, *The Days of Vengeance: An Exposition of the Book of Revelation* (Ft. Worth, Tex.: Dominion, 1987), pp. 480-529.

amillennialists denies a literal 1,000-year period and sees Revelation 20 as referring to an undetermined period of time beginning with the the first advent of Christ and ending with His second advent.[3]

At face value John speaks of a 1,000-year reign of Christ. Why have some accepted it literally while others have not? How did these two very different interpretations develop? Once these questions are answered, it remains to be seen which view has the best exegetical support. This must be tested in the light of current discussion on this passage.

THE HISTORICAL INTERPRETATIONS OF 20:1-10[4]

ANCIENT INTERPRETERS

Papias (A.D. 60-130), who according to Irenaeus was a disciple of the apostle John and a companion of Polycarp,[5] held to a literal 1,000 years. Although he wrote extensively, none of his works are extant, and so we must gather his material from those who quoted him. According to Irenaeus, Papias attributed a millennial saying to Jesus.[6] Eusebius spoke disparagingly of Papias's acceptance of a literal, earthly 1,000-year reign of Christ.[7] Jerome (347-420) stated that Papias, along with Irenaeus, Apollinarius, Tertullian, Victorinus, and Lactantius, promulgated the Jew-

---

3. Cf. W. Hendriksen, *More Than Conquerors* (Grand Rapids: Eerdmans, 1940), pp. 221-32; Oswald T. Allis, *Prophecy and the Church* (Philadelphia: Presbyterian and Reformed, 1945), pp. 3-5; Ray Summers, "Revelation 20: An Interpretation," *Review and Expositor* 57 (April 1960):176-83; Philip Edgcumbe Hughes, *Interpreting Prophecy* (Grand Rapids: Eerdmans, 1976), pp. 122-26; M. Eugene Boring, *Revelation* (Louisville: Knox, 1989), pp. 202-8; idem, *The Book of the Revelation* (Grand Rapids: Eerdmans, 1990), pp. 208-16; M. Robert Mulholland, Jr., *Revelation* (Grand Rapids: Zondervan, 1990), pp. 307-11.

4. The limited scope of this article allows only a cursory treatment of the history of interpretation of this passage. For a more thorough discussion of the early church's view of the thousand-year reign, consult Hans Bietenhard, "The Millennial Hope in the Early Church," *Scottish Journal of Theology* 6 (1953):12-30, which is a condensation of his doctoral dissertation *Das tausendjährige Reich. Eine biblisch-theologische Studie*, 2d ed. (Zurich: Zwingli-Verlag, 1955); Jean Daniélou, "The Theology of Jewish Christianity," in *A History of Early Christian Doctrine before the Council of Nicaea*, trans. and ed. John A. Baker (Philadelphia: Westminster, 1964), 1:377-404. These two scholars are extremely helpful in summarizing the various views throughout the early centuries. More recently Charles E. Hill, "Regnum Caelorum: Chiliasm, Non-Chiliasm and the Doctrine of the Intermediate State in the Early Church" (Ph.D diss., U. of Cambridge, 1988 [soon to be published by Oxford U.]), covers some of the same material but with a definite antimillenarian bias.

5. Irenaeus *Adversus Haereses* 5.33.4; Eusebius *Historia Ecclesiastica* 3.39.1.

6. Irenaeus *Adversus Haereses* 5.33.4.

7. Eusebius *Historia Ecclesiastica* 3.39.11-12.

ish tradition of the millennium.[8] The Epistle of Barnabas (ca. 130) speaks of the six days of the week and that on the seventh day God made an end and rested and sanctified it. The six days correspond with the creation being completed in 6,000 years,[9] and by implication the seventh day corresponds to the seventh 1,000-year period and the eighth day is the beginning of a new world.[10] Although the reasoning is confusing, the 1,000 years are taken literally in the Epistle of Barnabas.

Another early Christian interpreter was Justin Martyr (100-165). He states: "But I and every other completely orthodox Christian feel certain that there will be a resurrection of the flesh, followed by 1,000 years in the rebuilt, embellished, and enlarged city of Jerusalem, as was announced by the prophets Ezekiel, Isaiah, and others."[11] Then he quotes Isaiah 65:17-25, which speaks of the Millennium, and he comments:

> Now, by the words, "For as the days of the tree of life, so shall be the days of my people, and the works of their hands shall be multiplied," we understand that a period of one thousand years is indicated in symbolic language. When it was said of Adam that "in the day that he eats of the tree, in that he shall die" [Gen 2:17], we knew that he was not 1,000 years old. We also believe that the words, "The day of the Lord is 1,000 years" [Ps 89:4], also led to the same conclusion. And, further, a man among us named John, one of Christ's Apostles, received a Revelation that the followers of Christ will spend 1,000 years in Jerusalem, after which will come to pass the universal, and, in a word, eternal resurrection of all at once, followed by the judgment.[12]

Along the same line of reasoning as given in the Epistle of Barnabas, Irenaeus (130-202) concluded that there would be a millennial paradise after 6,000 years.[13] Irenaeus saw the seventh millennium with the messianic kingdom: "When this Antichrist shall have devastated all things in this world, he will reign for three years and six months, and then the Lord will come from heaven in the clouds, sending this man and those who follow him into the lake of fire, but bringing in for the righteous the times of the kingdom, that is, the rest, the hallowed seventh day."[14] Iren-

---

8. Jerome *De Viris Illustribus* 18.
9. It is interesting to note that although the early interpreters tend to mention the six thousand years, Revelation mentions only the thousand years and nothing of six thousand years that precede it. Cf. Robert M. Johnston, "The Eschatological Sabbath in John's Apocalypse: A Reconsideration," *Andrews University Seminary Studies* 25 (Spring 1987):48.
10. Epistle of Barnabas 15.3-9.
11. Justin Martyr *Dialogus cum Tryphone Judaeo* 80.4.
12. Ibid., 81.3-4.
13. Irenaeus *Adversus Haereses* 5.28.3.
14. Ibid., 5.30.4.

aeus argued against allegorical interpretations of the messianic kingdom in the prophecies in Isaiah and applied those prophecies to the Millennium.[15]

Tertullian (160-230), a lawyer and an ardent Christian apologist who lived in Carthage, also defended an earthly kingdom that would last 1,000 years.[16] He states:

> For we do profess that even on earth a kingdom is promised us but this is before we come to heaven, and in a different polity, in fact after the resurrection, for 1,000 years, in that city of God's building, Jerusalem brought down from heaven, which the apostle declares is our mother on high and when he affirms our citizenship is in heaven, he is evidently locating it in some heavenly city. . . . This is the manner of the heavenly kingdom: within the space of its thousand years is comprised the resurrection of the saints, who arise either earlier or later according to their deserts after which, when the destruction of the world and the fire of judgment have been set in motion, we shall be changed in a moment into angelic substance, by virtue of that supervesture of incorruption and be translated into the heavenly kingdom.[17]

Tertullian was arguing against Marcion, who thought that the OT God of the Jews was an inferior being who was bound up in the material world and that Jesus had come to reveal the true God. Marcion felt that the Jews would have their own messianic kingdom in Palestine, but that was not for Christians. Tertullian argued that though the believer belongs to a heavenly city, there is still going to be an earthly manifestation of that city as a part of the 1,000-year kingdom. He argued for two physical resurrections at the end of the church age, with the Millennium between them.[18]

Hence, we see in the first 150 years of the church a belief in a literal 1,000-year reign of Christ on earth. But this was about to change from two different fronts: the friends and foes of literal interpretation. The friend of literal interpretation was the Gnostic heretic Cerinthus (ca. 100), who taught that the 1,000-year marriage feast would be the indulgence of the flesh, that is, eating, drinking, and marrying.[19] Although he was a heretic, his view of a sensual chiliasm became associated with all who held to an earthly millennium. It was guilt by association.

15. Ibid., 5.35.1.
16. Contra Tsirpanlis, who states that Tertullian was not a chiliast (Constantine N. Tsirpanlis, "The Antichrist and the End of the World in Irenaeus, Justin, Hippolytus and Tertullian," *Patristic and Byzantine Review* 9 [1990]:15).
17. Tertullian *Adversus Marcionem* 3.24.3, 6.
18. Cf. Tertullian *De resurrectione carnis* 25; cf. also 19.
19. Eusebius *Historia Ecclesiastica* 3.28.2, 5; 7.25.3.

The literal interpretation of the 1,000 years came into disrepute with the foes of literal biblical interpretation. Under the influence of Hellenism and the Jewish allegorist Philo (20 B.C.-A.D. 54), the allegorical interpretation of the Scriptures became the legacy of Alexandrian thought. This thought continued among the Christian scholars in Alexandria. Clement of Alexandria (A.D. 155-215) did not speak directly to the issue of the 1,000-year reign. However, Origen (185-254) felt that those who held to a literal fulfillment of the promised earthly kingdom were simpletons who rejected the labor of thinking and wanted to have the pleasures and indulgences of the body.[20] Origen felt that a life of flesh and blood after the resurrection was absurd because 1 Corinthians 15:44 specifically promises the resurrection of a "spiritual body" and because verse 50 states that "flesh and blood shall not inherit the kingdom of God."[21] The idea that after the resurrection there would be marriage and the procreation of children living in an earthly city of Jerusalem rebuilt with precious stones was a regression back to Judaistic ideas, whereas the Christian did not place his hope in an earthly kingdom because he was a man of the Spirit and would look to a heavenly kingdom.

Origen's view was not uncontested. Nepos of Arsino (first half of the 3d century), bishop of Egypt, opposed allegorization of the promises. Eusebius stated that Nepos interpreted the promises of the Scriptures after a Jewish fashion and assumed that "there will be a kind of millennium on this earth devoted to bodily indulgence."[22] It is interesting to notice that the allegorists portrayed the literalists as holding to Christ's reigning over a literal earthly kingdom with His subjects living in sensual luxury. However, most literalists did not portray the people in Christ's kingdom as living sensually but as living normal physical lives that include eating and drinking as well as marrying because it was described in this manner in the OT.

Nepos published two works entitled *On Promises* and *Refutation of the Allegorist*. Dionysius (200-265), bishop of Alexandria, attacked his views. After Nepos died, Dionysius convinced the clergy of Arsino not to accept Nepos's literal view of the millennial kingdom,[23] for Dionysius thought that one cannot understand the Apocalypse in a literal sense.[24] In the same vein Eusebius (260-340), bishop of Caesarea, advocated understanding prophecies mystically and symbolically. He berated Papias as a

20. Origen *De Prinicipiis* 2.11.2; cf. also, *Commentariorum in Evangelium Matthaeum* 17. 35 [commenting on Matt. 22:29]; *In Canticum Canticorum* prologus.
21. Cf. Origen *De Prinicipiis* 2.10.3.
22. Eusebius *Historia Ecclesiastica* 7.24.1.
23. Ibid., 7.24.1-25.5.
24. Ibid., 7.25.6.

man of very little intelligence because he read the apostolic accounts in a perverse (i.e., literal) manner so that he saw a literal, earthly, 1,000-year reign of Christ.[25]

However, Methodius of Olympus (d. 311) thought that the seventh day of creation corresponded to the seventh millennium where, after the first resurrection, Christians will spend 1,000 years with Christ on the earth in celebrating the true feast of Tabernacles. After this comes the eighth millennium, which will be heaven.[26] Furthermore, Apollinarius (310-390), bishop of Laodicea in Syria, famous for his part in the Arian controversy, was also a millenarian. Although he was a prolific writer, very little has survived under his own name and his eschatological views are given by Epiphanius and Basil. Apollinarius believed that there would be a 1,000-year reign that would be Judaistic in nature where the resurrected believer would live in a way similar to the present age and would need to keep the OT law. After the 1,000-year period there would be heaven.[27] His millennial views continued with his disciples, but with their demise millennialism disappeared from the Eastern church.[28]

In the Western church Commodianus (middle 3d century?) saw the Millennium as the last 1,000 years of a 7,000-year scheme. It will be a period of peace in which the Antichrist is defeated by Christ and all evil is purged. It will also be a time of prosperity in which the resurrected saints will marry and have children. The heavenly Jerusalem will be the centerpiece of the Millennium.[29] Also Victorinus (d. 304), bishop of Pettau, followed in the same vein of thought, believing in a 1,000-year reign of Christ where Satan was bound at Christ's first advent and then after the 1,000 years he is released for a season of three years and six months to seduce the nations.[30] Victorinus is confusing because he says that the 1,000 years began with Christ's first advent and that the binding of Satan is the devil's exclusion from the hearts of the believers and his possession of the wicked, in whose hearts he is shut in a profound abyss. And yet he takes the 1,000 years literally. He was considered by Jerome a chiliast of a better sort.[31]

25. Ibid., 3.39.7.
26. Methodius *Synposion* 9.1.
27. Epiphanius *Panairion* 77.36.5; 38.1; Basil *Epistula* 263.4.
28. Bietenhard, "The Millennial Hope in the Early Church," p. 23.
29. Commodianus *Instructiones Adverses Gentium Deos* 1.29; 2.1-3, 39; cf. *Carmina apologeticum* 45. 791.
30. Victorinus *Scholia in Apocalypsin beati Jonnis* 20.1-3.
31. Jerome was thoroughly familiar with Victorinus's millennial views because he had reedited Victorinus's commentary on Revelation. This is an interesting phenomenon because he was reediting a work with which he basically disagreed.

Another who continued in this tradition was Lactantius (240-330), who used OT prophecies and the Sibylline Oracles as support for Christ's millennial reign. Lactantius thought that that golden age will be a literal fulfillment of OT prophecies in the future and that one should not spiritualize them by seeing their fulfillment in the present time. At the end of the present age will be a period of 1,000 years of peace and prosperity when Satan will be bound. After the 1,000 years Satan will be released for a short season, the new heaven and the new earth will be created, saints will be transformed, and the wicked will suffer eternal punishment.[32]

The demise of chiliastic thinking in the Western church, however, came with Jerome and Augustine. Jerome (347-420) thought that the millennialists depended on Jewish exegesis.[33] He was opposed to the restoration of the Jews and Jerusalem and the idea of a 1,000-year earthly reign of Christ.[34] Bietenhard says: "For Jerome Chiliasm and Judaism are identical. He removes the very foundation of Chiliasm by spiritualizing the Apocalypse. He hesitates to condemn the doctrine outright, for he can see that it was held by many Fathers."[35] He thought that the church age is the 1,000 years of Revelation 20 and that Satan is presently bound and cannot tempt the church but will be loosed for three and one-half years. In his commentary on Daniel, Jerome says the Jewish interpreters were wrong to see as belonging to Israel the messianic kingdom that comes after the four Gentile kingdoms.[36] Later in the same work, Jerome makes a strong attack against an earthly 1,000-year kingdom when he interprets Daniel's statement in 7:18 that the saints will take the kingdom. He states that the four preceding kingdoms are earthly in character "but the saints will never possess an earthly kingdom, but only a heavenly. Away, then, with the fable about a millennium."[37]

One of the great men of the church was Augustine. But it was Tyconius (d. 400), a Donatist, who laid the ground work for the Western church. Bonner notes that Tyconius "helped to adapt the allegorical method of interpreting Scripture, so popular in the East, to the service of

32. Lactantius *Divinarum institutionum* 7.14, 22, 24, 26; *Epitome Divinarum institutionum* 72.

33. Jerome *Commentariorum in Isaiam prophetam* 18. Prologue (introductory comments before Isa. 65).

34. Jerome *Commentariorum in Jeremiam prophetam* 4.19 (commenting on Jer. 19:10-11).

35. Bietenhard, "The Millennial Hope in the Early Church," p. 26.

36. Jerome *Commentariorum in Danielem prophetam* 2.40; cf. also *Commentariorum in Zachariam prophetam* 3.14 (commenting on Zech. 14:9-11).

37. Jerome *Commentariorum in Danielem prophetam* 7.17, 18.

western theology."[38] Tyconius's influence on Augustine's view of the Millennium was enormous. Bietenhard says that Tyconius's "view dominated the exegesis of Rev. 20 for the next 1,300 years, mainly because Augustine took it over from his Donatist opponent and clothed it with his authority. In the form given it by Augustine it has had an influence which has persisted right up to the present time, especially in Roman Catholic circles."[39] Tyconius, in his combining the spiritualizing method of the Alexandrians and the recapitulation method of Victorinus, put an end to chiliastic eschatology in the Latin churches for centuries.[40]

Tyconius did not take numbers very seriously. In the chapter on "Times" in his *Book of Rules*, which outlines the seven rules of interpretation, he said that the world's age is six days or 6,000 years and that the sixth day is the 1,000 years when the Lord was born, suffered, and rose again. The seventh 1,000-year period is the 1,000 years of the first resurrection and would be the church age. He thought that through the number twelve, 144,000 has reference to the whole church. And he went on to say that all the nations are indicated in the 12 tribes because Jesus said that "you will judge the twelve tribes of Israel" (Matt. 19:28), and since the part represents the whole, the 12 tribes refer to the whole world. Another example of his use of numbers is that the 1,260 days of Revelation 11:3 are to be multiplied by 100, making 126,000 days or 350 years. He did the same with the 42 months, making it equal 4,200 months or 350 years, and the time, times, and half a time would equal 350 years.[41] Tyconius felt that Christ's second advent would be 350 years after the crucifixion, that is, around A.D. 380.[42]

Augustine (354-430) wrote extensively on the 1,000 years of Revelation 20.[43] In his early days as a Christian, Augustine believed that the saints after their death would enter the seventh day, which was a period of millennial rest and happiness on earth before entering the eighth day, namely, heaven itself.[44] Augustine clearly states the reason he left this position:

38. Gerald Bonner, *Saint Bede in the Tradition of Western Apocalyptic Commentary*, Jarrow Lecture 1966 (Jarrow on Tyne, 1968), pp. 4-5.
39. Bietenhard, "The Millennial Hope in the Early Church," p. 28.
40. R. H. Charles, *Studies in the Apocalypse*, 2d ed. (Edinburgh: Clark, 1915), p. 12.
41. Tyconius *Liber Regularum* 5.
42. Ibid., cf. Wilhelm Bousset, *Die Offenbarung Johannis*, 5th ed. in Kritsch-exegetischer Kommentar über das Neue Testament (Göttingen: Vandenhoeck & Ruprecht, 1906), pp. 57-58; Gerhard Maier, *Die Johannesoffenbarung und die Kirche*, Wissenschaftliche Untersuchungen zum Neuen Testament, vol. 25 (Tübingen: J. C. B. Mohr, 1981), p. 119.
43. Augustine *De Civitate Dei* 20.7-13.
44. Ibid., 20.7; 22.30; Sermo 259.2.

But since they say that those who are to rise again will enjoy a holiday of most immoderate carnal feasts, in which food and drink will be so plentiful that not only will they observe no limits of moderation but will also exceed all bounds even of incredulity, all this can be believed only by the carnally minded. Those who are spiritually minded call those who believe these things, in Greek, chiliasts, and we may in Latin translate the term literally as "millenarians."[45]

Augustine interpreted the 1,000 years as having reference to the whole church age, namely, the period between the two advents of Christ.[46] Satan is bound during this period so that he will not lead astray the nations, namely the church. But Satan will be loosed for a short time, three and one-half years, at the end of the church age to test the church, but by God's grace the believers will not yield to Satan.[47] According to Augustine, the kingdom of Christ and the kingdom of heaven is the church, with a mixture of tares in the present age, as well as the future kingdom at the end of this world, where there are no tares.[48] Augustine is somewhat confusing about the resurrections. He states, on the one hand, that the first resurrection refers to the resurrection of the soul (viz., regeneration) in the present time and that the second resurrection refers to the resurrection of the body at the end of the world.[49] On the other hand, he says that the first resurrection is at the end of the 1,000 years, namely, the present age; and the second death has no power over these and the second resurrection will issue into the second death.[50] In short, Augustine did not take the 1,000 years literally but thought it refers to the present age with Satan bound.

In conclusion, the early church believed in the literal 1,000-year reign of Christ on earth. Due to the influence of Philo, the church of Alexandria adopted an allegorical interpretation of Scripture. This hermeneutic was propelled primarily by Origen's enormous influence. He felt that those who took the Scripture literally did not want the strenuous exercise of thinking and wanted to have the pleasures of the fleshly life. Bietenhard summarized it well: "For Origen the Chiliasts were visionaries, deluded fools, and what was worse, literalists."[51] Though this view was contested, it infiltrated the Western church through Jerome and Augustine. On the one hand Jerome felt that holding to a literal

45. Ibid., 20.7.
46. Ibid., 20.7, 9.
47. Ibid., 20.7-8.
48. Ibid., 20.9.
49. Ibid., 20.6, 10.
50. Ibid., 20.7, 9, 10.
51. Bietenhard, "The Millennial Hope in the Early Church," p. 20.

1,000-year reign of Christ on earth was Judaistic, whereas Augustine thought it was believed by carnally rather than spiritually minded persons. However, throughout history there were those who held to the literal 1,000-year rule of Christ on the earth. The real issue is one of consistent hermeneutics.

MODERN INTERPRETERS

Centuries after Augustine's time there was very little discussion of the 1,000-year reign of Christ. There was some revival of the chiliastic interpretation in the twelfth and thirteenth centuries, and in the thirteenth and fourteenth centuries the Apocalypse was used against the Church of Rome, with the papacy being identified with the Antichrist. This led to many fanciful interpretations.[52] In the sixteenth century with the entrance of the Reformation, Luther adopted the historical method of seeing the book of Revelation as unfolding history down to the present time. With the Augsburg and Helvetic Confessions, chiliasm was considered a Judaistic heresy.[53] However, opposition to an interpretation does not guarantee continuity of another interpretation. In the next few centuries there were all sorts of bizarre interpretations. This continued in a different direction with the rise of literary criticism. With the excesses in interpretations, the nineteenth- and twentieth-century interpreters generally fall within four schools of thought. The preterist or contemporary-historical school sees the major prophecies of Revelation fulfilled in the destruction of Jerusalem (A.D. 70) or the fall of the Roman Empire (476). The second view is the historicist school, which sees the prophecies fulfilled from John's time until the end of time. The third school is the idealist or symbolic school, which sees the imagery as illustrations of the struggle between the kingdom of God and the forces of evil. The final interpretation is the futurist school, which understands Revelation 4-19 as occurring at the end time leading to the return of Christ.

With regard to Revelation 20, the first three schools do not take the 1,000 years literally, whereas the futurist school views Christ's messianic kingdom as being on earth for a period of 1,000 years. Hence, we have come full circle with the interpretations of the early church. Either we accept or reject the idea of a literal 1,000-year reign of Christ on earth. We now turn to the interpretation of Revelation 20:1-10.

---

52. Charles, *Studies in the Apocalypse*, pp. 12-27.
53. Ibid., pp. 27-30; cf. Douglas McC. Lindsay Judisch, "Premillennialism and the Augustana," *Concordia Theological Quarterly* 47 (July 1983):241-45.

AN EXEGETICAL INTERPRETATION OF 20:1-10

Some interpreters think that Revelation 20:1-10 recapitulates of 19:11-21[54] rather than follows in a chronological progression from the previous context. However, before one observes the text, the context must be considered.

CONTEXT OF 20:1-10

In Revelation 20:2 mention is made of an angel laying hold of and binding for 1,000 years the dragon, the ancient serpent, who is the devil and Satan. Of the 29 times these four designations are used in the book, "Satan" and "devil" are used a total of six times before chapter 12 in connection with the seven churches (2:9, 10, 13, 24; 3:9). The other uses of the four designations are between Revelation 12:3 and 20:10. The only other places all four designations (dragon, serpent, devil, and Satan) are used together are 20:2 and 12:9. Hence, the context of 20:1-10 begins in chapter 12.

The context of Revelation 12-19 can be divided into three parts: (1) 12:1–16:21 describes the instruments involved in the Tribulation; (2) 17:1–19:5 describes the institution in the Tribulation; and (3) 19:6-21 discloses the intervention of Christ in world history.

The first part

This section reveals the instruments involved in the Tribulation (12:1–16:21). In 12:3-4 the dragon wanted to destroy the child of the woman. Expositors agree that the dragon is Satan as seen in 12:9 and the child is Christ as clearly seen in 12:5. In 12:7-9 Michael and his angels cast Satan, the deceiver of the whole inhabited earth, and his angels out of heaven down to the earth. With Satan cast out of heaven there is to be great rejoicing in heaven, but there is only woe for the earth and sea. Satan is on the earth and he knows he has only a short time to vent his wrath. In fact it is stated that the woman (most likely Israel) will be protected from Satan's persecution for 1,260 days (12:6) or a time, times, and half a time (12:14). This period of 1,260 days is also given in 11:3 and is described as being 42 months in 11:2. Hence, it is a description of a three-and-one-half year period in which Satan will operate on earth against the saints. This three-and-one-half year persecution is also given in Daniel 7:25 and 12:7, and this corresponds to 9:27, where the persecution is the last half of a unit of seven years.

---

54. Hendriksen, *More Than Conquerors*, pp. 221-23; Leon Morris, *The Revelation of St. John*, 2d ed. (Grand Rapids: Eerdmans, 1969), pp. 227-28; R. Fowler White, "Reexamining the Evidence for Recapitulation in Rev 20:1-10," *Westminster Theological Journal* 51 (Fall 1989):319-44.

In Revelation 13:2, 4 the dragon empowers a beast, and both the dragon and the beast are worshiped by mankind. The beast is given authority for 42 months (13:5), which corresponds to the 1,260 days or a time, times, and half a time mentioned above. In 13:11 another beast, who is also identified as the false prophet (16:13), appears and speaks like a dragon. Hence in chapter 13 the first and second beasts work in conjunction with the dragon. Chapter 14 is an interlude of joy and judgment.

In 15:1–16:12 John describes the judgment of the bowls, and in 16:13-16 there is an interlude before the seventh bowl (16:17) is poured out. In 16:13 the dragon is mentioned again, and he is mentioned in connection with the (first) beast and the (second) beast who is identified as the false prophet. They are seen as the unholy trinity, namely, Satan is posing as God the Father who is in heaven, the first beast is posing as Christ appearing to have been slain (13:3), and the second beast, the false prophet, is masquerading as the Holy Spirit because he never speaks of himself but always does things to point to the the first beast (13:12-17; 14:11; 16:2) as the Holy Spirit does in relationship to Christ (John 16:13-14).

The second part

This section describes the institution in the Tribulation (17:1–19:5) where the city and commerce of Babylon fall.

The third part

Christ will return with the full display of His power (19:6-16) and the annihilation of the kings and commanders who war against the saints. Finally the beast and the false prophet are thrown into the lake of fire (19:17-21). The two beasts first mentioned in chapter 13 are now in chapter 19 cast into the lake of fire.

Having read of the rise, actions, and end of the two beasts in chapters 12-19, the reader would want to know about the end of the dragon. This is given in 20:1-10. The dragon was introduced as the one cast out of heaven and thrown to the earth in 12:3-17. He is next mentioned in 16:13 in connection with the beast and the false prophet, namely, the unholy triad. Finally, the dragon is mentioned in 20:1-10 with regard to his being bound in the abyss for 1,000 years, released for a short time, and finally cast into the lake of fire where the beast and the false prophet are.

Another element in the context of 20:1-10 is Christ's role in Revelation 12-20. With the casting out of Satan from heaven there was rejoicing in heaven about the authority of Christ (12:10). In chapters 12-18 there is the war between the unholy trinity and the world, especially against the saints (12:17; 14:12; 17:6). Not until chapter 19 is Christ mentioned again, and this is in connection with His second coming, when He destroys the kings and commanders and casts the first beast and the false prophet into the lake of fire. In 20:1-6 Satan is bound for 1,000 years, and during that time Christ reigns. According to 20:7-10, when the 1,000 years are completed, Satan is released for a short time and then is cast into the lake of fire with the beast and the false prophet. Though John does not say who casts Satan into the lake of fire, it is most probably Christ in order to demonstrate complete victory over His ardent foe and that Christ is the Lord of the universe.

In conclusion, Revelation 20:1-10 seems to fit well chronologically after the events of 19:11-21. Revelation 12-19 describes the struggle of Christ and His saints against the forces of evil headed by Satan, the beast, and the false prophet with the kings of the earth. When Christ returns there is the defeat and the destruction of the kings and the armies who were aligned with the beast and the false prophet as well as the casting of the beast and false prophet into the lake of fire. However, there is nothing in the text about the final outcome of Satan, the archenemy of Christ. Revelation 20:1-10 serves as the final piece of the puzzle in the defeat and ultimate punishment of the utmost enemy of Christ and His saints. Therefore, in order to make sense of the culminating victory of Christ and the conclusive defeat of Satan, Revelation 20:1-10 is a logical and chronological necessity to chapters 12-19.[55]

TEXT OF 20:1-10

A threefold development characterizes Revelation 20:1-10: (1) the binding of Satan (20:1-3); (2) the resurrection of the Tribulation saints (20:4-6); and (3) the doom of Satan (20:7-10). After observing the text, we will consider the view that this passage is a recapitulation of 19:11-21.

The binding of Satan (vv. 1-3)

John begins chapter 20 with the binding of Satan. The introductory words "and I saw" (*kai eidon*), used 32 times in the book, usually denote the next vision seen by John (e.g., 13:1, 11; 14:1, 6, 14; 15:1; 16:13; 17:3; 19:11, 17, 19; 20:4, 11, 12; 21:1). Though these words are not as forceful a chronological marker as "after these things I saw" (*meta tauta*

---

55. From a different viewpoint and pattern, see Michel Gourgues, "The Thousand-Year Reign (Rev 20:1-6): Terrestrial or Celestial?" *Catholic Biblical Quarterly* 47 (October 1985):676-81.

eidon; 4:1; 7:9; 15:5; 18:1) or "after these things I heard" (*meta tauta ēkousa*; 19:1), they do show chronological progression. As mentioned above, Satan was cast out of heaven and thrown down to the earth (12:7-9) and has been working in conjunction with the beast and the false prophet (chaps. 12-18). Christ returns (19:11-19) and destroys both the beast (and his followers) and the false prophet (19:20-21), and then He must deal with Satan (20:1-10). This shows not only the negative aspects of Christ's coming in the defeat of the enemies but also the positive aspects, Christ's reign over the earth in place of the rule of the beast. Hence, these introductory words integrally relate 20:1-3 to 19:20-21.[56]

In verses 2 and 3 John stated that an angel has the key to the abyss and a large chain and lays hold of the dragon, the ancient serpent, who is the devil and Satan, binds him, and throws him in the abyss for 1,000 years in order that he might not deceive the nations any longer. Although there is symbolic language here, we should not dismiss it as having no real meaning. The use of a key and a chain denotes binding. The abyss is mentioned earlier in the book as the place of the demonic world and Satan (9:1-2, 11; 17:8). Shutting and sealing the abyss denotes the security that he will not deceive the nations any longer.

Three things deserve special attention regarding verses 2-3: the interpreting of the 1,000 years in a literal manner, the binding of Satan during the 1,000 years, and the releasing of Satan for a short time after the 1,000 years.

As mentioned above, the demise of a literal intrepretation of the 1,000 years was due to seeing them as a time of fleshly overindulgence. This brought the idea of a millennium into disrepute. Furthermore, under the influence of Hellenism and Philo's allegorical interpretation of the Scriptures, the Alexandrian school allegorized the 1,000 years. They believed the 1,000-year reign of Christ was Judaistic and that believers were to inherit a heavenly kingdom and not an earthly kingdom. Augustine thought Satan was bound during Christ's ministry, based on Luke 10:18: "I was watching Satan fall from heaven like lightning," and that the binding would continue until Christ's second advent. Those who deny a literal 1,000-year reign of Christ on the earth think it refers to Christ's present rule in the believers on earth[57] or His present reign with the saints in heaven.[58]

56. Alan Johnson, "Revelation," *The Expositor's Bible Commentary*, 12 vols., ed. Frank E. Gaebelein (Grand Rapids: Zondervan, 1981), 12:581.

57. Augustine *De Civitate Dei* 20.9; Floyd E. Hamilton, *The Basis of Millennial Faith* (Grand Rapids: Eerdmans, 1942), pp. 134-35.

58. R. C. H. Lenski, *The Interpretation of St. John's Revelation* (reprint, Minneapolis: Augsburg, 1963), pp. 583-90; Hendriksen, *More Than Conquerors*, pp. 230-32; Morris, *The Revelation of St. John*, pp. 230-31; Hughes, *The Book of the Revelation*, p. 212.

There are problems in rejecting a literal 1,000 years for the binding of Satan and the reign of Christ on earth. First, six times in this context John stated that there will a be a 1,000-year period in which Satan is bound and Christ rules over the earth. It is noteworthy that John was consistent in his use of the 1,000 years. In verses 2-5 the description of the vision of the 1,000 years is in the aorist tense, whereas the interpretation of the vision in verses 6-7 is in the future tense. Therefore, what is in vision form will actually take place in the future.

Second, there is no reason to interpret the 1,000 years as anything other than that. Whenever the number "thousand" is used in Revelation, it refers to something definite. For example, the 144,000 (Rev. 7:4-8; 14:1, 3) must be taken literally because John states that they are made up of 12,000 from each of the 12 tribes of Israel. These are real numbers that must be taken literally. When John speaks of the 1,260 days (11:3), the immediately preceding verse indicates that this is the same as 42 months. Forty-two months having 30 days equals 1,260 days (cf. 12:6; 13:5). In addition, when John states that 7,000 are to be killed in an earthquake (11:13) or that the blood of the carnage will cover the length of 1,600 stadia (14:20) or that the measurement of the new Jerusalem will be 12,000 stadia in length (21:16), it would be reasonable to conclude that he used the numbers literally. There is nothing in the context to indicate otherwise.

Third, whenever there is reference to a time period like days (1:10; 2:10, 13; 4:8; 6:17; 7:15; 8:12; 9:6, 15; 10:7; 11:3, 6, 9, 11; 12:6, 10; 14:11; 16:14; 18:8; 20:10; 21:25) or months (9:5, 10, 15; 11:2; 13:5; 22:2), they are always to be taken literally. There is no reason for not making the same application for years. Some commentators would deny a literal 1,000 years by citing 2 Peter 3:8, where 1,000 years is equated with one day. However, there is no connection between this passage and Revelation 20, and the reference in 2 Peter 3 depends on the literal meaning of 1,000 years in that 1,000 years with men is like one day from God's eternal viewpoint.[59]

Fourth, the 1,000 years denotes a definite period of time because in the context John describes Satan's release from the abyss by the indefinite phrase "a short time" (20:3). Hence, John uses in the same verse definite terms for a definite period of time and indefinite terms for an indefinite period of time.[60] Therefore, the 1,000 years are to be taken literally.

Therefore, the most natural way to take the 1,000 years is literally. Its denial came about because it was depicted as a time of overindulgence

---

59. Walvoord, "The Theological Significance of Revelation 20:1-6," p. 231.
60. Townsend, "Is the Present Age the Millennium?" p. 214.

of the flesh and because the allegorical interpretation of Scripture had become the dominant school of thought. The denial of a literal 1,000 years is not because of the exegesis of the text but a predisposition brought to the text. Even in modern times scholars like Kline think the concept of a literal millennium is incompatible with the Reformed view of the covenant of common grace.[61] However, this is forcing a text to conform to a certain predisposition rather than letting the text speak for itself. In examining Revelation 20, the most natural interpretation is to take the 1,000 years literally.

A second major item to be discussed is the binding of Satan for 1,000 years. It is thought by some commentators that Satan's binding occurred at Christ's first advent and will continue until His second advent.[62] It is thought that the casting out of Satan from heaven in Revelation 12:7-9 parallels Luke 10:18-19 when the 70 disciples returned and Jesus said, "I saw Satan fall like lightning from heaven. Behold, I have given you authority to tread upon serpents and scorpions, and over all the power of the enemy and nothing shall harm you." Hence, Satan is bound during this present age until the second advent of Christ.

However, to say that Satan is bound in the present age contradicts several NT passages. In the time of Christ, even after Luke 10:18, Satan entered Judas in connection with his betrayal of Jesus (Luke 22:3; John 13:27), and he tried to control Peter (Luke 22:31). Christians are warned to be on the alert, for the devil is prowling like a roaring lion seeking whom he may devour (1 Pet. 5:8). This activity is seen when Ananias's heart was filled with Satan (Acts 5:3). Satan is the one who blinds unbelievers to the gospel (Acts 26:18; 2 Cor. 4:3-4; Eph. 2:2; 2 Tim. 2:26). Satan also hindered Paul from going to Thessalonica (1 Thess. 2:18). Furthermore, Christians are alerted to Satan's temptations (1 Cor. 7:5; 2 Cor. 2:11; 11:14). It seems that Satan has not been bound since Christ's first advent. Some commentators, realizing that there is Satanic activity in the present age, think that Satan is presently bound by a chain and therefore his power is limited.[63] However, the text speaks of the angel binding Satan, throwing him into the abyss, and shutting and sealing him in it. There is no indication that Satan has freedom to exercise any power during that period of time. This binding of Satan for 1,000 years cannot have reference to the present time but must speak of a future period of time, namely, the Millennium.

---

61. Meredith G. Kline, "The First Resurrection: A Reaffirmation," *Westminster Theological Journal* 39 (Fall 1976):117-19.

62. Cf. Hendriksen, *More Than Conquerors*, pp. 225-29; Hughes, *The Book of the Revelation*, pp. 209-11.

63. Hendriksen, *More Than Conquerors*, pp. 228-29; Oscar Cullmann, *Christ and Time*, trans. Floyd V. Filson (Philadelphia: Westminster, 1964), p. 198.

The third point of emphasis is that after Satan has been bound for 1,000 years, he is released for a short season. If we accept a literal 1,000-year reign of Christ, then it would mean that after that period Satan is for a short time released and deceives the nations as seen in Revelation 20:7-9 and afterward is cast into the lake of fire. But if one thinks that the 1,000-year reign of Christ refers to the present church age and that Satan is bound until Christ's second advent, at which time the new heavens and the new earth are ushered in, when will Satan be released for a short time? Those who hold to a nonliteral 1,000 years tend to be vague on this issue. Some think that Satan will be released sometime just before Christ's second coming,[64] but then Satan is not bound for the entire period between the two advents of Christ. Hughes thinks it occurs just before the renewal of the whole creation,[65] but does he mean before or after Christ's second advent? Krodel thinks that since the resurrected saints would not be affected and the dead are in Hades, this refers to a host of demons who were defeated at the cross,[66] but the passage talks about nations and not demons being deceived and that there is a defeat of an army. Ladd states it well when he says: "These words are difficult to understand if they are applied to our Lord's binding of Satan in his earthly ministry. The victory he won over Satan was won once and for all. Satan will never be loosed from bondage to Christ won by his death and resurrection."[67] Thus, a prior, literal, 1,000-year reign of Christ makes much more sense for interpreting this short season of Satan's release. Revelation 20:1-3 portrays a literal 1,000 years in which Satan will be bound and then released for a short time.

Before discussing the next portion of the text, the view that sees 20:1-3 as a recapitulation of 19:11-21 must be examined. Recently White posed that those who see 20:1-3 as a sequential progression from 19:11-21 fail to see the discrepancy of Satan's being bound thus preventing him from deceiving the very nations which had been destroyed in 19:11-21. In other words, how can nations be deceived that no longer exist?[68]

White thinks the premillennial attempt to resolve this by positing that the nations of 20:3 are survivors of the battle in 19:19-21 is gratuitous, for one cannot assume that the order in which the visions are presented is the order in which they will occur in history. Furthermore, we

64. Hendriksen, *More Than Conquerors*, pp. 233-35.
65. Hughes, *The Book of the Revelation*, pp. 216-17.
66. Gerhard A. Krodel, *Revelation*, Augsburg Commentary on the New Testament (Minneapolis: Augsburg, 1989), p. 337.
67. George Eldon Ladd, *A Commentary on the Revelation of John* (Grand Rapids: Eerdmans, 1972), p. 263.
68. White, "Reexamining the Evidence for Recapitulation in Rev 20:1-10," p. 321.

read in 19:18-21 that all the nations will make war against Christ and all the nations will be defeated.[69] However, the introductory words "and I saw" (*kai eidon*) in 20:1 are also given in 19:11, 17, and 19, which seem to depict a rapid succession not only of visions but also of the unfolding developments in history. Would White see only a sequence in visions but not history with 19:11, 17, 19? There seems to be a progression historically that when Christ comes (19:11) there will be a carnage of the enemies (19:17) and a defeat of kings of the earth as well as the casting of the beast and the false prophet into the lake of fire. Next 20:1 fits into the context to explain the doom of Satan. So it is reasonable in this context to see not only a progression in visions but also in history.

The other problem presented by White is the discrepancy of nations existing when they have been destroyed. However, the destruction in 19:19-21 does not mean that every person of every nation is going to be destroyed. Only the wicked of the nations will be destroyed at the second coming of Christ, not the saints. Certainly 20:4 speaks of the saints who will reign with Christ for 1,000 years and these saints will have come from various nations. It is prophesied in 12:5 and 19:15 that Jesus will rule all the nations with a rod of iron, indicating that there will be nations in the future. Furthermore, even after the 1,000 years there will be nations in the new heaven and new earth (21:24, 26; 22:2). This is consistent with the Old Testament's picture of the messianic kingdom, in which various nations will worship the Lord (Ps. 86:9; Isa. 2:2; 66:19-20; Jer. 3:17; Mic. 4:1-5; Zech. 8:20-23; 14:16-19). Zechariah 14:16 specifically states that those who are left of the nations that went against Jerusalem will go to Jerusalem to worship the Lord. Therefore, Christ will destroy those of the nations who have the mark of the beast when He comes at the second advent. But many will not have the mark of the beast. Some will be martyred (Rev. 7:9, 13-17; 14:12-13); others will survive the Tribulation and will go into the Millennium (20:4; cf. Matt. 24:38-44; Luke 17:22-37). Those in the Millennium will be from among many nations, and there is no reason for the discontinuance of the various nations, including the nation of Israel. Hence there is no discrepancy in the continuance of nations after they have been destroyed.

In conclusion, the best interpretation for this passage is to see that after His second advent Christ will reign for 1,000 years and during that time Satan will be bound in the abyss and afterward will be released for a short time. This interpretation is derived from the plain meaning of the text. It is not fulfilled in the present time but will be in the future.

69. Ibid., pp. 323-24.

The resurrection of the Tribulation martyrs (vv. 4-6)

If we accept the plain teaching of a literal 1,000-year imprisonment of Satan in the abyss and reign of Christ on the earth, then these
verses in their ordinary sense make good sense. John begins with the
familiar introductory words "and I saw" (*kai eidon*), as in verse 1. This
marks progression in the revelation of those who reign with Christ in
the Millennium.

Who are the people sitting on the thrones for the purpose giving
judgment (20:4)? Mounce thinks that since the text is silent regarding
their identity, we can say no more than that they are the heavenly court
depicted in Daniel 7:22, 26.[70] However, Walvoord thinks they are the 24
elders who are to reign on earth (5:10).[71] Ladd and Deere think the
judges are all the saints of all ages.[72] Though it is not critical to the present discussion which of these views is more likely, it seems the last view
is preferable.

The latter part of verse 4 is more specific. The ones judged are
those who were beheaded because of the testimony of Jesus and because of the Word of God, and they had not worshiped the beast or his
image and had not received the mark on their forehead and hand (cf.
Rev. 13:17; 14:9, 11; 16:2; 19:20). They are made alive and reign with
Christ for 1,000 years. The critical problem of this part of the verse is the
meaning of the aorist verb *ezēsan*, rendered "made alive." Does it refer
to physical or spiritual life? As mentioned above, Augustine held that the
first resurrection has reference to the regeneration of the soul in the
present day when one responds to the call of the Son of God.[73] But this is
allegorizing the text. The very fact that they were beheaded because of
the testimony of Jesus and because of the word of God would indicate
that they had been regenerated, and John is stating that death is not the
end but that they will be resurrected. Nothing in this text indicates the
regeneration of the soul, but everything indicates that it refers to resurrection of the body.

More recently Hughes has suggested that the soul is in view rather than the body and proposes that the aorist verb *ezēsan* is not ingressive ("they came to life") but constative ("they lived"). He supports his
view by a three-pronged argument: (1) it would be parallel with the next

70. Robert H. Mounce, *The Book of Revelation*, New International Commentary on the
    New Testament (Grand Rapids: Eerdmans, 1977), pp. 354-55.

71. John F. Walvoord, *The Revelation of Jesus Christ* (Chicago: Moody, 1966), p. 296.

72. Ladd, *A Commentary on the Revelation of John*, p. 263; Deere, "Premillennialism in
    Revelation 20:4-6," pp. 63-64.

73. Augustine *De Civitate Dei* 20. 6.

aorist verb "to reign," which cannot be anything but constative (i.e., "they lived and reigned with Christ"); (2) only twice in the NT does *zaō* ("to live") have an ingressive force (Rev. 2:8; Rom. 14:9); and (3) John is dealing in this verse not with "bodies" but with "souls," which must be disembodied souls, and thus the verb cannot have the ingressive force "come to life" since souls do not die.[74] Deere has given a good point-by-point response to Hughes: (1) grammatically there is no reason that both aorist verbs need to be parallel in every respect, and thus the first verb can be ingressive and the second constative (i.e., "they were made alive and reigned with Christ"); (2) there are more than just two other instances of *zaō* being ingressive in the NT, as well as the Septuagint usage; and (3) one should not make a soul-body dichotomy, since "soul" can refer to a whole person (Acts 2:41, 43; 3:23).[75] Furthermore, this verb is used 12 times in Revelation and its normal usage refers to physical life, whether of Christ (1:18; 2:8; 4:9-10; 10:6) or the beast (13:14; 19:20), and it refers only once to a believer's spiritual life (3:1). Finally, this verb is used again in the next verse where the rest of the dead do not come to life until the 1,000 years are completed. Both uses of the term must be taken in the same way or else, as Alford states, it would bring to "an end all significance in language."[76] Thus, it is best to see this as a literal, physical resurrection of the body.

In verse 5 unbelievers are not resurrected with the saints at the beginning of the Millennium but after it. John states that this is the first resurrection. There has been much discussion on the first resurrection. Shepherd observes that mention is made of the first resurrection but not the second, and so he proposes that one must look outside of Revelation to gain understanding of this passage. From Paul he concludes that there is a twofold resurrection, namely, the believer's resurrection at baptism (Col. 2:12; Rom. 6:4) and the bodily resurrection at the end of the age. He concludes that the span between the first and second resurrection is not the 1,000 years between the literal resurrection of the just and the literal resurrection of the unjust but between the resurrection by baptism and the resurrection of all things at the end of the age.[77] But this does not take the present text seriously. First, Shepherd is making two different kinds of resurrections, which is untenable as discussed above.

---

74. James A. Hughes, "Revelation 20:4-6 and the Question of the Millennium," *Westminster Theological Journal* 35 (Spring 1973):289-98, 300-302.

75. Deere, "Premillennialism in Revelation 20:4-6," pp. 66-67.

76. Henry Alford, *The Greek Testament*, 4 vols., rev. Everett F. Harrison (Chicago: Moody, 1958), 4:732.

77. Norman Shepherd, "The Resurrections of Revelation 20," *Westminster Theological Journal* 37 (Fall 1974):34-43.

Second, he is not accepting the 1,000 years literally, as the text demands. Third, he is importing an explanation from texts that are not discussing physical resurrection, which this text is. Fourth, there is an inconsistency between the two resurrections, for the first resurrection deals only with believers whereas the second resurrection deals with the just and unjust. It seems better to see a parallel of the first resurrection dealing with the bodily resurrection of the believers and the second resurrection dealing with the bodily resurrection of the unbelievers. This is what the context is addressing. In conclusion, it seems that Shepherd has had to read too much into the context to demonstrate his view. The text is able to stand on its own.

Kline observes that there is mention of the first but not the second resurrection and mention of the second but not the first death. He proposes that there is a double binary pattern in which the first resurrection is metaphorical referring to the death of the Christian who is presently reigning with Christ (20:4), the second resurrection is the literal physical resurrection, the first death is physical, and the second is metaphorical, which is the absence of spiritual life.[78] The complexity of this view makes it suspect. Michaels responds by warning against setting up a phantom of a double binary pattern when John does not specifically speak of first death or second resurrection. Michaels correctly observes that one should not think of the second death in a metaphorical or spiritual sense but as a real final physical death in the lake of fire.[79] Kline is attempting to avoid the physical resurrection being designated as the first resurrection. He feels that the first resurrection is to be identified with the living and reigning with Christ for 1,000 years in Revelation 20:4-6 but that the millennium mentioned here is the present age characterized by "the first things," which excludes the premillennial view of the second advent of Christ.[80] Deere rightly observes that Kline builds too much on the use of the adjective "first" from Hebrews 8-10; 1 Corinthians 15; and Romans 5 as referring to the present age when the decisive term is not the adjective but the noun "resurrection."[81] In his response to Michaels, Kline demonstrates a real aversion to a literal millennium because it is incompatible with the Reformed view of the covenant of common grace.[82] But this is arguing deductively from his theology rather than inductively from the text.

78. Meredith G. Kline, "The First Resurrection," *Westminster Theological Journal* 37 (Spring 1975):366-75.
79. J. Ramsey Michaels, "The First Resurrection: A Response," *Westminster Theological Journal* 39 (Fall 1976):100-109.
80. Kline, "The First Resurrection," p. 374.
81. Deere, "Premillennialism in Revelation 20:4-6," p. 72, n. 55.
82. Kline, "The First Resurrection: A Reaffirmation," pp. 110-19.

Philip Hughes thinks that both resurrections are physical, but the first resurrection is Christ's resurrection and the second resurrection is the universal or general resurrection of all men.[83] However, in the present context there is nothing about Christ's resurrection and so the first resurrection cannot refer to that all-important event. Hughes consistently denies a literal 1,000 years and thinks it refers to an undetermined span of time between the first and second advents of Christ.[84]

In conclusion it is best to look at the first resurrection as a physical resurrection of the believers who will be killed in the Tribulation (Rev. 6-18) and who will reign with Christ for 1,000 years in the future.[85] After the Millennium the unbelieving dead will be resurrected and this could be the implied second resurrection. Walvoord states that the first resurrection "is not first in the sense of something that had never occurred before but first in the sense of being before the later resurrection."[86] In verse 6 John states that those who are in the first resurrection will reign with Christ for 1,000 years and will not suffer the second death that the wicked will suffer as described in 20:11-15.

The doom of Satan (vv. 7-10)

Having spoken of the imprisonment of Satan for 1,000 years and his short release (20:1-3), John describes the resurrection of the martyred saints and their reign with Christ for 1,000 years (20:4-6). Next he explains the events that will follow the completion of the 1,000 years (20:7-10). Four things will occur. First, in verse 7 Satan is released from imprisonment as already mentioned in verse 3, which states that it will be for a short time.[87] This does not fit well with an amillennial position because if the present age is the Millennium and Christ comes at the end of it, where does Satan's release fit in? Amillenarian commentators tend to be vague on how this fits. Beckwith feels John is inconsistent.[88] Hughes thinks it is after the 1,000 years and before the renewal of the creation.[89] But

83. Philip Edgcumbe Hughes, "The First Resurrection: Another Interpretation," *Westminster Theological Journal* 39 (Spring 1977):315-18; *The Book of the Revelation*, pp. 213-16; cf. Krodel, *Revelation*, p. 335.

84. Hughes, *Interpreting Prophecy*, pp. 122-26; *The Book of the Revelation*, p. 212.

85. For a discussion of those included in the first resurrection, see Roy L. Aldrich, "Divisions of the First Resurrection," *Bibliotheca Sacra* 128 (April-June 1971):117-19.

86. Walvoord, "The Theological Significance of Revelation 20:1-6," p. 237.

87. Cf. William H. Shea, "The Parallel Literary Structure of Revelation 12 and 20," *Andrews University Seminary Studies* 23 (Spring 1985):42-44.

88. Isbon T. Beckwith, *The Apocalypse of John* (reprint, Grand Rapids: Baker, 1979), p. 745.

89. Philip Hughes, *The Book of the Revelation*, pp. 216-17.

is this not inconsistent? Morris thinks it is a brief reversion to the theme of gathering all the forces of evil against God at the end time.[90]

From a premillennial standpoint it raises no particular problem. John is very clear that Satan's release occurs after the 1,000 years are completed. His use of the temporal particle *hotan* ("when"; 20:7) with the aorist subjunctive *telesthē* ("are completed/finished") indicates that "the action of the subordinate clause precedes that of the main clause."[91] Hence, when the 1,000 years are completed (subordinate clause), Satan will be released (main clause). Though White admits that this is a clear indication that "the events of 20:7-10 are historically subsequent of the events in the visions preceding 20:7," he also thinks "it is equally clear that the phrase does not tell us conclusively whether this historical relationship applies to all the visions preceding 20:7 or to some of them. Only the content of the visions preceding 20:7 can provide conclusive evidence of their historical relationship to 20:7-10."[92] However, this is not a new vision but a continuance of the vision that began in 20:4 or 20:1 or more likely in 19:11. So within the vision there is historical, chronological progression.[93] Therefore, the sequence is that Satan is bound for 1,000 years and then released for a short time and then cast into the lake of fire with the first beast and false prophet. It is not only a chronological progression but also a logical one.

The second thing that will occur is that Satan will be free to deceive the nations and gather a large mass of humanity against the saints and ultimately against God (20:8-9*a*). But why does God allow this? The text does not spell out the reason. It could be that God is going to show man's true condition. In the Tribulation men hate God because the unholy trinity persuades them and because of God's judgment, but in the Millennium it is entirely different. It will start out with only the redeemed. Satan is bound and no temptation will come from him and his realm. The curse will be removed (Isa. 35:9; 65:25), allowing the land to flourish (Isa. 35:1; Rom. 8:19-22), and there will be no sickness (Isa. 33:24; Jer. 30:17; Ezek. 34:16), making for an incredible life-span (Isa. 65:20). There will be the perfect rule of Messiah, with peace (Isa. 2:4; Mic. 4:3) and perfect justice (Isa. 62:2; Jer. 23:5). However, after this period Satan will be released and as many as the sand of the sea will follow

90. Morris, *The Revelation of St. John*, p. 232.
91. Walter Bauer, *A Greek-English Lexicon of the New Testament and Other Early Christian Literature*, trans. William F. Arndt, F. Wilbur Gingrich, and Frederick W. Danker, 2d ed. (Chicago: U. of Chicago, 1979), p. 588.
92. White, "Reexamining the Evidence for Recapitulation in Rev 20:1-10," pp. 325-26.
93. Cf. Richard A. Ostella, "The Significance of Deception in Revelation 20:3," *Westminster Theological Journal* 37 (Spring 1975):238.

him. Who are they and why? These will probably be the descendants of those who originally entered the Millennium after the Tribulation. They will have heard of the Lord and will have experienced the wonderful provisions of the Millennium but will not have personally trusted the Messiah for salvation. When Satan is released, they will believe his lie and go with him. God is going to demonstrate that the reason people reject Him is not because of imperfect circumstances like those of the Tribulation or even the present but because ultimately they hate God. God is also going to demonstrate how utterly wicked Satan is, and this will justify his doom.

The reference to Gog and Magog is reminiscent of Ezekiel 38-39. However, there are at least six differences between the Gog and Magog of Ezekiel and of Revelation 20: (1) in Ezekiel 38:2 Gog and Magog are identified as only a local northern power; in Revelation they refer to all nations; (2) in Ezekiel Gog is a prince; Magog is the land that contains Rosh, Meshech, and Tubal; here Gog and Magog are all nations; (3) in Ezekiel 38:15-16 Gog and Magog go against Israel; here they go against the saints and Jerusalem; (4) in Ezekiel 39:4, 17 the invaders fall upon Israel's mountains; here fire from heaven will devour the invaders (vv. 8-9); (5) in Ezekiel 39:17-20 after the battle, there is a great feast of corpses, which fits well with Revelation 19:17-21 (which is at the end of the Tribulation); in Revelation 20:10 after the battle, Satan is cast into the lake of fire (which is at the end of the Millennium); and (6) in Ezekiel 38-39 the events fit chronologically before the restored millennial Temple; in Revelation 20 the events fit chronologically after the Millennium. Hence, Gog and Magog of Ezekiel 38-39 are different from the Gog and Magog of Revelation 20. Here it portrays the final battle of Satan against the saints and Jerusalem, God's city. It is the ultimate revolt against God.

The third thing that will occur is that fire will come down from heaven to devour those who followed Satan (Rev. 20:9*b*). God is victorious over wicked mankind who believed the lie of Satan.

The final item to be depicted is Satan being cast into the lake of fire, where the beast and the false prophet had been cast (20:10). Satan had been cast out of heaven down to the earth (Rev. 12:7-9) and had worked with the beast and the false prophet (chaps. 12-18). When Christ returns He defeats both the beast and the false prophet, who are then cast into the lake of fire (19:20-21). But Satan was not doomed at that time but imprisoned for 1,000 years while the saints reign with Christ, and after the Millennium Satan is released to deceive the nations. Now climactically Satan is brought to his end.

White thinks that the premillennialist understanding of 20:10 that Satan is finally cast into the lake of fire where the beast and the false prophet were already as the result of Christ's coming in 19:11-21 is not necessarily the only interpretation. He proposes that 20:10 is possibly a recapitulation of 19:11–20:10.[94] White uses four lines of argument to support a recapitulation theory. First, he discusses the use of Ezekiel 38-39 in Revelation 19:17-21 and 20:7-10. He believes the descriptive language and imagery in both 19:17-21 and 20:7-10 come from the one episode in Ezekiel 38-39, and therefore Revelation 19:17-21 and 20:7-10 cannot be two different events but 20:7-10 is a recapitulation of 19:17-21.[95] However, as mentioned above, the Gog and Magog of Revelation 20 are not the same as in Ezekiel 38-39. Furthermore, White uses an outside passage to explain 19:17-21 and 20:7-10. Why not let the text stand on its own? There is a clear and natural chronological progression. Also, normally it is better to understand the later revelation to explain or expand on earlier revelation. Hence, Revelation 19:17-21 and 20:7-10 explain new details not given in Ezekiel 38-39. In addition, if 20:7-10 is a recapitulation of 19:17-21, there is confusion and an inconsistency. In 19:17-21 it is the beast and the false prophet who are cast into the lake of fire, whereas in 20:7-10 it is Satan who is cast into the lake of fire. John never confused the first beast and the false prophet with Satan. They are never one and the same. John is very clear that one event occurred before the Millennium and the other occurred after the Millennium. The plain reading of the text makes good sense. A recapitulation reading only confuses the reader and makes the passage inconsistent.

White's second support for 20:7-10 being the recapitulation of 19:17-21 is that when John refers to the international campaign against Christ and His saints, the noun "war" is always preceded by the article as seen in 16:14; 19:19; 20:8.[96] This is one of White's stronger arguments. However, 12:17 and 13:7 have references to that great war and the noun "war" is anarthrous. Furthermore, the war does not appear as one event. When we examine Revelation 12-18 as well as Ezekiel 38-39, it seems that it is a prolonged war or a series of battles that last for more than three years. Hence, "the war" refers to various facets of the great conflict between Christ with His saints and Satan and his hosts. In Revelation 19-20 this great conflict between Christ and Satan is manifested at the end of the Tribulation and at the end of the Millennium. We should not think that the articular noun always means the same thing in different settings. In 19:17-21 it refers to "the war" between Christ and the beast and the false prophet just before the 1,000 years and in 20:7-10 refers to "the

94. White, "Reexamining the Evidence for Recapitulation in Rev 20:1-10," p. 326.
95. Ibid., pp. 326-28.
96. Ibid., pp. 328-30.

war" between Christ and Satan just after the 1,000 years. The settings of each passage make it clear that they are different times. Though there are parallels, they are not one and the same battle.

The third support White uses to favor a recapitulation of 19:11-21 in 20:7-10 is the reference to the bowl judgments as the end of God's wrath against the unbelievers in 15:1.[97] He attempts to make a case that 15:1 and 16:17-21 coincide with 19:19-21 and 20:7-10 as a recapitulation of that event. However, the bowl judgments are a series of judgments over a period of time. They are God's intervention on the natural world, with sores on men (16:2), the sea turning to blood (16:3), rivers becoming blood (16:4), the sun scorching men (16:8), darkness covering the earth (16:10), the Euphrates drying up (16:12), and lightning, thunder, earthquake, and hail afflicting the earth (16:17-21). These judgments are not the same as Christ's coming depicted in 19:11-21. These judgments seem to precede Christ's second coming because there is, for example, the drying up of the Euphrates River so that the kings of the East can come to battle as well as the rest of the kings of the whole world gathering at Armageddon (16:12-14, 16-17). There is also an interlude where God gives a warning of His coming like a thief and gives a blessing for those who do not follow the unholy triad (16:15), both of which point to the time preceding the second coming of Christ portrayed in 19:11-21. Therefore, to identify the bowl judgments (16:2-21, esp. vv. 17-21) with Christ's second coming is not at all convincing.

The fourth support that White utilizes to substantiate his view that 20:7-10 recapitulates 19:11-21 is the similarity of the accounts of cosmic destruction found in 6:12-17; 16:17-21; 19:11-21; and 20:9-11, recalling OT warfare scenes in which the cosmic shaking is followed by the advent of the Divine-Warrior-Judge.[98] There are some similarities among these visions, but the differences are far greater. In the immediately preceding paragraph differences between 19:11-21 and 20:7-10 are mentioned. In reading Revelation 6-20 we receive the distinct impression that the warfare extends over a period of time—a period of three and one-half years of destructive turmoil. However, when Christ comes back (19:11-21) He will complete the conflict in a short period of time. Hence, the similarities White attempts to find do not indicate identity of the events. There were many similarities between World War I and World War II (e.g., both in Europe, both times Germany fought on two fronts), but they are not the same war and the differences far outweigh the similarities. In the biblical narrative there are many instances of God's wrath

97. Ibid., pp. 330-31.
98. Ibid., pp. 331-36.

on disobedient people or nations, and although there are many similar-ities among instances, nevertheless, they are distinct situations. In Reve-lation 6:12-17 John is talking about the seal judgments, which are distinct from the bowl judgments of 16:2-21. In fact the seventh seal brings forth the seven trumpets and these bring forth the bowl judgments. The seal and bowl judgments are in totally distinct contexts and chronological settings. Another example of differences is seen in the destruction of mankind in 19:21, where they are slain by the sword, whereas in 20:9 they are consumed by fire from heaven.

White makes a final appeal from Hebrews 12:26-27, where the author, quoting from Haggai 2:6, states that there will be "one more" final shaking at the end of the age. Again White uses an outside passage to interpret the present text rather than letting the immediate context help one's interpretation. Two things must be noted. First, Revelation was written later than Hebrews and in the progress of revelation fills in more details. Many OT passages seem to indicate a single event when actually they had reference to both the first and second comings of Christ (cf. Isa. 61:1-2 with Luke 4:17-21). Later revelation gave fuller de-tails. Second, the Hebrews passage is not in all likelihood speaking of the second coming of Christ but of the advent of the new heaven and new earth described in Revelation 21-22 after the Millennium and the great white throne judgment.

Beyond these four arguments, White thinks that the the motif of angelic ascent and descent in Revelation 7:2; 10:1; 18:1; and 20:1 substan-tiate the idea of recapitulation.[99] He observes that with the angelic ascent in 7:2 and the angelic descent in 10:1 the historical sequence is suspend-ed to introduce a retrospective interlude. White thinks that the same thing occurs with the angelic descents in 18:1 and 20:1. However, when one looks at these last two texts there are no interludes but a continua-tion of the narrative. In fact 18:1 has the chronological note "after these things" (*meta tauta*) to indicate a chronological sequence. In 20:1 there is also chronological progression "and I saw" (*kai eidon*) as noted above. Just because there may be an interlude with an angelic ascent and an angelic descent in two texts, it does not follow that this would be true for the other two angelic descents. It simply does not demonstrate that 20:1 introduces an interlude that would support 20:7-10 as a recapitula-tion of 19:11-21.

In conclusion, White's arguments for 20:7-10 as a recapitulation of 19:11-21 are not convincing. A plain reading of the text would ac-knowledge that the events of 20:7-10 are different from those of 19:11-21.

99. Ibid., pp. 336-43.

Conclusion

Only a premillennial view makes sense of the prophetic text of Revelation 20:1-10. It follows well chronologically after the second coming of Christ in chapter 19. In the historical survey it was observed that the reason for giving up a literal 1,000 years was because it was viewed as a time of overindulgence of the flesh. It was not abandoned on the basis of exegesis of the text. The justification for the change was accomplished by allegorizing the text. Once this is done there is no control. The text is at the mercy of the ingenuity of the interpreter.

Every interpreter realizes that the book of Revelation is of a different genre than the rest of the NT. However, we cannot on that basis abandon a literal interpretation. Admittedly, interpretation of this book is difficult at times, but we must be careful to see what the text says. Certainly all interpreters take parts of this book literally. Amillenarians accept a literal return of Christ, great white throne judgment, and the new heaven and new earth, and they do not try to allegorize them. Premillenarians maintain a literal approach for the whole book while recognizing that the genre includes much symbolic imagery and numerous visions. Hence, one should not simply assume that where there is literary succession of events there cannot also be a historical succession of events. One is not exclusive of the other.

With a consistent hermeneutic premillennialists see Revelation 20:1-10 as a crucial text. This passage, however, is not the basis of a premillennial view. The basis of premillennialism goes back to the OT, specifically to the Abrahamic, Davidic, and New Covenants. From these covenants God promised land, seed, and blessings for Israel as well as the whole world. Revelation 20:1-10 only tells the duration of this phase of the messianic kingdom, which will issue into the new heaven and the new earth.

14

PREMILLENNIALISM SUMMARIZED: CONCLUSION

JEFFREY L. TOWNSEND

Pastor
Woodland Park (Colorado) Community Church

The purpose of this final chapter is twofold: (1) to capsulize the exegetical evidence for premillennialism presented in each essay; and (2) to arrange the evidence logically so that a conclusion may be drawn on the millennial issue.

It has been a daunting challenge to summarize the detailed exegetical work of our authors. The following statements are offered as a brief compilation of the exegetical evidence for premillennialism presented in this volume.

THE EVIDENCE FOR PREMILLENNIALISM SUMMARIZED

EVIDENCE FROM HERMENEUTICS:

(1) Biblical interpretation is properly directed by two principles: literal interpretation and the analogy of faith.

(2) Literal interpretation involves a system of limits on the meaning of a text as specified by the textual context. The literal system is necessitated by the nature of Scripture as clear and complete, and by the need of the interpreter for a normative principle of interpretation.

(3) The analogy of faith (Scripture interprets Scripture) is based on the divine authorship of Scripture, which assures the consistency of meanings recorded in the canon over the centuries. The valid use of the analogy of faith recognizes that subsequent statements in the progress of revelation may specify how God will accomplish what He has promised to do. It is a misunderstanding of the analogy of faith to see Scripture as reinterpreting (giving new meaning to) Scripture, for this removes meaning from the original text and destroys any normative governing principle for interpretation.

(4) When applied consistently in the interpretation of prophecy, one predictable result is the doctrine of premillennialism.

EVIDENCE FROM GENESIS:

(1) The personal, national, and universal promises made to Abraham, though conditioned initially on his obedience, were all later ratified by divine oath so that the promises stand certain of fulfillment dependent on God alone.

(2) Subsequent OT passages reflect the unconditionality of the Abrahamic promises, anticipating a day of fulfillment through the nation Israel yet future even to the postexilic writers.

(3) Though the church participates in the spiritual blessings of the Abrahamic promises, Israel still possesses the ancient promises and will have them fulfilled to her at a future time of national salvation, restoration to the ancient land, and rebuilding of Jerusalem. Those future fulfillments correspond to all that other Scriptures teach about premillennialism.

EVIDENCE FROM PSALM 89:

(1) Basing His promise on His loyal love (*ḥesed*), God assured to David an enduring house (line of descent) and throne (right to rule). The resurrected Christ is the one who fulfills the Davidic promises.

(2) That the complete fulfillment of the Davidic promises awaits the second advent of the Messiah is indicated by the argument of Psalm 89. Yahweh's loyal love (*ḥesed*) demands that He be fully faithful to the Davidic promises in spite of Israel's sins. This in turn demands a geopolitical fulfillment to national Israel (which does not equal fulfillment in the church or the eternal state). This geopolitical fulfillment is the heart of premillennialism.

EVIDENCE FROM ISAIAH 2:

(1) Isaiah 2:2-5 envisions a future time when a restored Jerusalem will be the focal point of the worship of God by all the nations.

(2) Isaiah 2:2-5 looks forward to a literal and physical fulfillment because:

(a) When compared with the parallel passage in Micah 4:1-3, the Isaiah text is more narrative than poetic and hence should be understood in a realistic rather than figurative way.

(b) In that context both the destruction and future restoration of Jerusalem are described in a somewhat poetic form. If one (the destruction) is taken literally, so should the other (the future restoration).

(c) Use of poetic form does not preclude reference to historical realities.

(3) Isaiah's language is closely tied to the present earth. Thus the reference is not to the eternal state but to an earthly reign of Christ in Jerusalem prior to the new heavens and new earth. This chronology contributes to the development of premillennialism.

EVIDENCE FROM JEREMIAH:

(1) Jeremiah 3:14-18 presents five promises which must be fulfilled in the historic future in the ancient land of promise; for example, the reuniting of the ten northern tribes and the two southern tribes in "the land that I gave your fathers as an inheritance" (v. 18).

(2) Jeremiah 16:14-18 predicts a restoration of Israelites to the historic land which will surpass the Exodus in fame, preceded by a time of unprecedented trouble for the Jews.

(3) Jeremiah 23:3-8 announces the reign of David's "righteous branch" over Judah and Israel regathered, multiplied, and dwelling securely in the ancient land.

(4) Jeremiah 29:10-14 speaks of Israel's restoration to the land following the Babylonian captivity. However, verse 14 moves on to the distant future and a worldwide regathering of Israel to the ancient land. This must take place on the present earth prior to the eternal state.

(5) Jeremiah 31:35-40, which follows the great New Covenant passage (31:31-34), promises Israel's continuance as a nation and the restoration of Jerusalem on the ancient site with extensions to include areas previously defiled.

(6) Jeremiah 33:6-22 attributes the quality of righteousness to Jerusalem because of the presence of the "righteous branch of David." This fits best with the Messiah's second coming to Jerusalem.

(7) To sum up, the details of Israel's future set forth in Jeremiah cannot be made to fit with any scenario other than an earthly kingdom following the return of the Messiah and prior to the eternal state—the premillennial arrangement.

EVIDENCE FROM EZEKIEL:

(1) Ezekiel 36:16-38 promises a regathering of Israel from all the nations to her own land, a spiritual and numerical transformation of the people, and increased productivity of the land. This restoration will have the purpose of restoring Yahweh's reputation among the nations.

(2) A millennial fulfillment of the promises of Ezekiel 36:16-38 is required because:

(a) The promises were not fulfilled in the postexilic restoration.

(b) The fulfillment is yet future to the NT writers (cf. Rom. 11:26-27).

(c) Fulfillment in the eternal state does not do justice to God's purpose of vindicating Himself among the nations of this earth.

(3) The Temple of Ezekiel 40-48 must be a future millennial Temple because:

(a) The Temples of Solomon, Zerubbabel, and Herod do not meet Ezekiel's specifications.

(b) Symbolic fulfillment in the church begs the correspondence between the intricate detail of Ezekiel's Temple and church-age blessings.

(c) There is no temple in the eternal state (cf. Rev. 21:22).

(4) The sacrifices reinstituted in the millennial Temple are compatible with the once-for-all sacrifice of Christ because:

(a) They are memorials, or

(b) They are for ceremonial forgiveness, or

(c) They are representative of worship in the Millennium using terminology familiar to Ezekiel's readers.

Only premillennialism can accommodate the details of Ezekiel's many prophecies normally interpreted.

EVIDENCE FROM DANIEL:

(1) Daniel consistently uses a word for "kingdom" that allows for an earthly millennial kingdom followed by the eternal state.

(2) According to Daniel 2:31-44, the kingdom established by God will fill the whole (present) earth after destroying all other human kingdoms, and will itself never be destroyed (i.e., it will endure even in the new heavens and new earth).

(3) According to Daniel 7:15-28, dominion over the whole (present) world will be given to the saints of God under the ultimate authority of the Son of Man. As in Daniel 2, the kingdom of the saints/Son of Man begins on this earth and continues into eternity.

(4) The purposes of God's seventy-week program for Israel and Jerusalem in Daniel 9:24 point to a time following the second advent of the Messiah but prior to the eternal state when "everlasting righteousness" will be brought in for Israel and the most holy place of a future Temple will be anointed. This fits well with the premillennial scheme of future events.

EVIDENCE FROM JOEL AND AMOS:

(1) Amos 9:11-15 speaks of a day when Israel will be permanently restored to her ancient land, Davidic rule will be reestablished, and all the Gentile nations will come under the patronage of a spiritually renewed, preeminent Jewish state.

(2) James in Acts 15:15-18 was not claiming the fulfillment of Amos 9:11-12 in the church. Rather he was citing the tenor of OT Scripture to indicate that Gentiles may come into a right relationship with God without losing their identity as Gentiles.

(3) Though one element of what will happen in the future was happening in James's day (the inclusion of Gentiles as God's people), it remains for the prophecies of Amos 9:11-15 to be fulfilled on this earth prior to the eternal state.

(4) Joel 2:26bff speaks of the restoration of Israel in the eschatological Day of the Lord. But Peter in Acts 2 sees a fulfillment of Joel's prophecy in the church.

(5) Fulfillment of Joel 2 both now in the church and later for Israel is possible because the messianic age began with the coming and exaltation of the Messiah. Though Joel 2 explains the events of Pentecost, Pentecost does not exhaust the fulfillment of Joel's prophecies as Acts 3:19-21 indicates. There is yet coming "times of refreshing" (Acts 3:19) and the "period of restoration of all things" (Acts 3:21) when the prophecies of Joel will be fulfilled to physically and spiritually restored Israel. In other words, a partial fulfillment of Joel now in the church does not preclude the full realization of Joel's prophecies to the nation Israel in the eschatological Day of the Lord.

Apostolic use of Amos and Joel passages show the importance of these minor prophets in the construction of premillennial theology.

EVIDENCE FROM MATTHEW:

(1) Matthew presents Israel as rejected by God because of her rejection of the Messiah. But Matthew does not view this state of affairs as the final destiny of the Jews.

(2) The fulfillment texts in Matthew serve to show that though Israel closed her heart to the Messiah, God was nonetheless perfectly fulfilling His ancient plan for the nation.

(3) The promise in Matthew 19:28 that the disciples would, in "the regeneration," sit on twelve thrones judging the twelve tribes of Israel confirms that the OT promises for the nation have not been voided.

(4) A similar expectation of Israel's restoration is found in Matthew 23:39. The quotation from Psalm 118 reinforces the idea that God's chastening of Israel does not preclude the ultimate fulfillment of all His promises to her in a premillennial format.

EVIDENCE FROM ACTS:

(1) Luke-Acts presents the coming of the kingdom in an "already"/"not yet" form. The presence of salvific aspects of the kingdom in the church age does not negate the coming of the fullness of the kingdom (including fulfillment of the national promises to Israel) in the millennial age and beyond.

(2) Two texts in Luke's gospel confirm a future role for Israel:

(a) Luke 22:16 suggests the reinstitution of the fulfilled Passover celebration (with sacrificial elements) in the coming kingdom age.

(b) Luke 22:30 (cf. Matt. 19:28) grants authority to the disciples to judge the nation in the kingdom age.

(3) Acts 1 taken with Acts 3 shows that the restoration of the kingdom to Israel (1:6) will take place at Jesus' return (3:21*a*). This is a restoration featuring the preeminence of Israel and the fulfillment of all her ancient promises (3:21*b*), key elements of premillennialism.

(4) References in Acts 2 and 15 to initial fulfillment of aspects of the kingdom promises in the church age do not negate the ultimate fulfillment of the kingdom promises to Israel in the future.

EVIDENCE FROM ROMANS 9-11:

(1) The term "Israel" in Romans 9-11 always means ethnic, national Israel. The term never includes Gentiles.

(2) Paul's use of Hosea 2:23 and 1:10 in Romans 9:25-26 does not involve a reinterpretation of the OT text, applying Hosea's words to the church instead of Israel. Rather Paul draws an analogy between the manner of the calling of the Gentiles now and the future calling of Israel as being by God's sovereign, electing grace.

(3) The exegetical evidence in Romans 11 leads to the conclusion that at the time of the second advent, all Israel's unconditional covenants (Abrahamic, Davidic, and New) will be fulfilled to her as a nation and she will enjoy a glorious future as a blessing to the Gentiles in the messianic kingdom.

(4) Though not specifically mentioned in the NT, the Abrahamic promises of the land are still valid because the NT authors viewed the Abrahamic Covenant as still in force and there is no indication that the land promises were not included. This guarantees a present-earth fulfillment of the kingdom promises.

Romans is a major link in the chain of biblical evidence for premillennialism.

EVIDENCE FROM 1 CORINTHIANS 15:

(1) First Corinthians 15:24 establishes an interval between the second advent and the consummation during which Christ conquers all enemy powers and finally presents the kingdom to the Father. This interval allows for a millennial reign of Christ, the very kingdom Christ presents to the Father in verse 24.

(2) Paul's argument via the syntax of 1 Corinthians 15:24-25 equates the reign of verse 25 with the conquest of enemies in verse 24. This means that Christ must reign on this earth after the second coming but prior to the eternal state.

(3) Confirmation of this sequence of endtime events is seen in the parallel use of Psalm 110:1 in 1 Corinthians 15:25 and Hebrews 1:13, and Psalm 8:6 in 1 Corinthians 15:27 and Hebrews 2:8. In Hebrews 1-2 as in 1 Corinthians 15, the reign of Christ is located at and after the second coming but before the eternal state, the central distinction of premillennialism.

EVIDENCE FROM REVELATION 20:

(1) For 150 years the church accepted a literal 1,000-year reign of Christ on the earth. Literal interpretation of the thousand years was abandoned not on exegetical grounds but because of the rise of allegorical interpretation and because some taught that the Millennium was a time of sensual indulgence.

(2) Revelation 20:1-10 follows logically and chronologically the events of Revelation 12-19. Revelation 20:7-10 is not a recapitulation of 19:11-21.

(3) The most natural way to take the sixfold use of "a thousand years" in Revelation 20:2-7 is literally.

(4) Thus the passage reveals that after His second advent (19:11-21), Christ will reign with the saints on this earth for 1,000 years (20:4), during which time Satan will be bound in the abyss (20:1-3). Afterward Satan will be released for a short time, provoke a final rebellion, and be cast into the lake of fire (20:7-10).

(5) Just as 20:1-3 cannot be made to fit the church age, neither can 20:4-6. The first resurrection is a literal, bodily resurrection consisting of the Tribulation martyrs who reign with Christ. The first resurrection is separated by 1,000 years from the resurrection of the rest of the dead.

The book of Revelation provides the completion and climax of premillennial teaching in Scripture.

The Doctrine of Premillennialism Summarized

Based on the foregoing evidence, the case for premillennialism may be stated as follows.

DEVELOPED FROM THE OLD TESTAMENT:

The OT covenants with Abraham and David established unconditional promises of an Israelite kingdom in the ancient land ruled by the ultimate Son of David. The OT prophets, from the earliest to the latest, looked forward to the establishment of this kingdom. Its principle features will include: regathering of the Jews from the nations to the ancient land, mass spiritual regeneration of the Jewish people, restoration of Jerusalem as the principal city and her Temple as the spiritual center of the world, the reign of David's ultimate Son over the twelve reunited tribes dwelling securely in the land as the pre-eminent nation of the world. Based on OT Scripture, a this-earthly, spiritual-geopolitical fulfillment of these promises is expected.

DEVELOPED FROM THE NEW TESTAMENT:

The NT writers do not reinterpret the OT kingdom promises and apply them to the church. Instead the church participates now in the universal, spiritual blessings of the Abrahamic, Davidic, and New Covenants without negating the ultimate fulfillment of the covenant promises to Israel. The NT authors affirm rather than deny the ancient kingdom hope of Israel. Matthew, Luke, and Paul all teach a future for national Israel. Specifically, Acts 1 with Acts 3 establishes that the restoration of the kingdom to Israel takes place at the second coming of Jesus Christ. Romans 11 confirms that at the time of the second advent, Israel will have all her unconditional covenants fulfilled to her. First Corinthians 15 speaks of an interim kingdom following Christ's return but prior to the eternal kingdom of God during which Christ will rule and vanquish all His enemies. Finally, Revelation 20 gives the chronology of events and length of Christ's kingdom on this earth prior to the eternal state.

In sum, the case for premillennialism rests on the fact that the OT promises of an earthly kingdom are not denied or redefined but confirmed by the NT. The basis of premillennialism is not the reference to the thousand years in Revelation 20. That is merely a detail, albeit an important one, in the broad pattern of Scripture. The basis of premillennialism is the covenant-keeping nature of our God, affirmed over and over again in the pages of Scripture. God will do what He has said He will do, for His own glory among the nations. And what He has said He will do is fulfill the Abrahamic, Davidic, and New Covenants to a regathered, regenerated, restored nation of Israel at the second coming of Jesus Christ, and for a thousand years thereafter, prior to the eternal kingdom of God.

The authors and editors of this volume believe that premillennialism best explains the details of Scripture concerning the future kingdom of God. Nevertheless, this volume is offered humbly to believers of all millennial persuasions. Our hope is that it will contribute to an enhanced understanding of God's Word and an amiable understanding among believers of differing millennial views.

INDEX OF SUBJECTS

rejected by Israel, 32, 180, 215, 267
reign on earth (millennial), 13, 14,
33, 95, 98, 101, 108, 117, 141,
144, 145, 146, 178-80, 190, 191,
197-98, 200, 234, 236, 240, 241,
243, 244, 247-49, 251-52, 258,
265, 269, 270
resurrection of, 9, 21, 22, 32, 72,
77, 117, 183, 186, 188, 191, 192,
198, 225-29, 234, 251
Savior, 68
second advent/coming/return, 7-9,
13-14, 108, 114-16, 128, 136, 180,
182, 183, 187, 190, 192, 210, 215,
219, 222, 226, 229-32, 234, 235,
236, 240, 243-45, 247, 248, 250-
52, 255, 259-62, 264, 265, 267-70
seed of Abraham, 31-33, 174
seed of the woman, 31-33
Son of David, 31-33, 174, 184, 191,
203
Son of God, 31, 72, 114, 233
Son of Man, 140-43, 146, 155, 266
substitutionary sacrifice, 23. *See
also* Atonement
Church, 8, 9, 60, 79, 81, 82, 87, 98,
100, 101, 107, 115-17, 127,
130, 134, 138, 157, 163, 164,
172, 174, 186, 189, 190, 194,
197, 204, 207, 208, 216, 218,
219, 222, 243, 264, 266, 267,
270
age, 26, 100, 162, 238, 241, 242,
243, 251, 257, 270
mission 165, 176, 180
spiritual/true Israel, 113, 170, 178,
185, 202, 217
spiritual seed of Abraham, 35, 46,
54
Compositional criticism, 93
Covenant premillennialism, 194. *See
also* Premillennialism
Covenant theology, 81, 83, 255
Covenants, biblical, 187, 220, 268,
270. *See also* Abrahamic Cov-

enant; Davidic Covenant; Mo-
saic law; New Covenant
Creation. *See* God, Creator
Cross, 22, 33, 77, 145, 188. *See also*
Christ, death of
Cush, 99
Cyrus, 76, 111

Daniel (prophet), 136, 139, 143
Daniel, book of, 135, 138, 145-46,
266-67
David, 24, 30, 32, 53, 56, 57, 63, 65-
71, 73, 75-77, 104, 106, 115,
116, 130, 157, 174, 192, 198
Davidic Covenant, 24, 41, 56, 58, 61,
63-66, 69, 71-76, 103, 104, 107,
116, 149, 150, 154, 163, 174,
182, 192, 193, 199, 221, 262,
264, 268, 270, 271. *See also*
Davidic king(ship)
fulfillment, 73, 79, 101, 182, 264
key of David, 193
throne of David, 34, 72, 76, 87,
116, 153, 182, 190, 192-94, 198,
264
unconditional, 76, 215
Davidic king(ship)/kingdom, 33, 92,
101, 102, 103, 108, 150, 157,
190, 197, 198, 270. *See also*
Davidic Covenant
restoration of Davidic dynasty,
149, 150, 163, 195, 196, 197, 264,
267
Day of the Lord/Yahweh, 149, 157-60,
162, 191, 192, 267
Death, physical, 226, 227, 231-33,
254, 255
Deity of Christ. *See* Christ, deity of
Dispensationalism, -ist(s), 145, 148,
185, 194
Dragon, 246, 248. *See also* Satan

Edom, 150, 151, 157, 162
Egypt, 99, 100, 133, 137, 174, 175
El Shaddai, 42, 52

binding/release of Satan, 33, 247,
249-52, 256-59, 269
cast out of heaven, 245, 246, 248
doom of Satan, 247, 258, 269
Scripture. *See* Bible
Seal judgments, 261
Second coming. *See* Christ, second
coming
Seed of Abraham. *See* Abrahamic
Covenant, seed/offspring of
Abraham
Seed of the woman, 22, 29-30, 31-33
Seleucids, 137
Sensus literalis, 81, 83
Servant (of Yahweh), 23, 24, 116, 143
Servant songs, 46
Seventy weeks of Daniel, 143, 267
Shem, 103
Sinaitic covenant. *See* Mosaic law
Sodom, 45
Solomon, 56, 107, 115, 129, 130, 193
Spirit. *See* Holy Spirit
Spiritual seed of Abraham. *See* Abra-
ham, spiritual seed
Spiritualization, 16, 25, 81-84, 98,
100, 101, 104, 130, 136, 202,
206, 242. *See also* Allegorical
interpretation
Suzerain-vassal treaty, 69
Syria, 137
Systematic theology, 181, 182

Tabernacle, 27, 115, 129-31, 145
Temple (Jerusalem), 80, 82, 84-89,
95-98, 144, 145, 146, 163, 227,
227, 267, 270
Herod's Temple 169, 172, 266
millennial Temple 128-31, 135,
146, 146, 258, 266

sacrifices reinstituted, 131-34,
185-86, 266
worship, 82, 119, 128-34, 266,
270
Solomon's Temple, 24, 115, 129-
31, 266
Zerubbabel's Temple, 129, 145,
266
Testimonia, 154-55
Theodicy, 175, 199, 202, 203
Thousand years (millennial king-
dom), 14, 83, 84, 105, 185,
234, 235, 239, 241, 249-51,
256, 262, 269. *See also*
Millennium
Throne of David. *See* Davidic Cove-
nant, throne
Tiglath-Pileser III, 150
Times of the Gentiles, 197
Tribulation (period), 108, 112, 143-
45, 160, 245-47, 256, 257, 259
Trinity, 72, 181
Trumpet judgments, 261
Typological interpretation, 80, 82

Unity of meaning(s), 18, 20
Uzziah, 72, 113, 149

Wisdom (literature), 57, 88, 91
Word of God. *See* God, Word of
Worship, 57, 83, 97, 116, 131. *See
also* Temple (Jerusalem), millennial Temple, worship

Yahweh. *See* God

Zacharias, 183, 186, 189, 198, 222
Zechariah (prophet), 127
Zerubbabel, 106, 107, 111

INDEX OF SCRIPTURES

INDEX OF SCRIPTURES

Obadiah

18-20	150

Jonah

1:16	91
3:5ff.	91

Micah

3:12	85, 97
4:1	90, 111
4:1-3	84, 93, 95, 97, 261
4:1-7	221
4:3	92
4:14	107
5:1-9	221
5:2	72
7:11-20	52
7:18-20	221

Zephaniah

1:14-18	162

Haggai

2:6	261
2:9	131

Zechariah

2	113
2:11	107
3:8	109
6:12	109
7:14	53
8:4-8	52
10:10	133
14:10	113
14:16	252

Malachi

1:2-3	204

Matthew

1:1	174, 220
1:21	176
1:22	173
1:23	20, 173
2:1-6	72, 176
2:5-6, 15, 17-18, 23	173
2:15	207
3:9	53
3:15	32
3:16-17	32
4:1-11	31
4:14-16	173
4:18-20	32, 176
4:23	171
5:1-2	32
5:14	176
5:17	176
7:13-27	32
7:29	171
8:17	173, 207
9:35	171
10:5-6	176, 177
10:17	171, 177
10:23	177
12:1-8	167
12:9	171
12:14, 24	32
12:17-21	173
13	19
13:11-17	32
13:19, 25, 28	33
13:23	33
13:35	173
13:54	171
15:24	176
16	138
16:12	166, 167
16:18	172
17:24-27	169
18:17	172
18:19	196

19:28	177-80, 190, 242, 268
20:2, 13	196
21:4-5	173
21:9-10, 23-27, 33-46	32
21:43	171, 174
22:23	166-68
23:34	177
23:38	174
23:39	179, 180, 268
24-25	112
24:15	19
24:38-44	252
26:56	173, 175
27:9-10	173
27:25	176
27:52-53	229
28:15	171
28:18-20	177

Mark

1:11	72
2:23-28	167
4	19
12:18	167

Luke

1-2	184, 189
1:31-33	182, 192, 198, 233
1:46-55, 67-80	222
1:50-55	182, 198
1:68-75	183, 190, 198
4:17-21	261
5:36	196
6:1-5	167
8	19
8:22-25	69
9:10	177
10:9, 18-19	184, 248, 250
11:13	33
11:20-23	184
13:29-30	186

287